Revolution, Yes! Right Liquidationism, No!

Series of Letters Sent to the Headquarters of the Communist Party of Nepal (Maoist)

Yogendra Dhakal

Revolution, Yes! Right Liquidationism, No!
Series of Letters Sent to the Headquarters of the Communist Party of Nepal (Maoist)
Yogendra Dhakal

First English Edition 2016
Reprinted 2017

ISBN : 978-93-5002-417-1 (Pb)

Layout Design
Saman Shrestha

Published by
AAKAR BOOKS
28 E Pkt. IV, Mayur Vihar Phase I, Delhi 110 091
Phone: 011 2279 5505 Telefax: 011 2279 5641
aakarbooks@gmail.com; www.aakarbooks.com

Printed at
Sapra Brothers, Delhi 110 092

Dedicated to
great warriors for their
sacrifice during the
ten-year long glorious
people's war for the
New Democratic Revolution

Contents

Preface to the First English Edition

This book is a collection of the series of letters written between 2008-11 and sent to the party headquarters. The issues addressed here basically relate to the weaknesses and deviations that developed in the Communist Party of Nepal (Maoist) since the Chunbang Meeting. The letters emphasized the need of adhering to the true Marxist-Leninist line to oppose the non-Marxist-Leninist line adopted by the then party leadership. However, the ground reality of that time no more exists now. The political situation of Nepal at that time was quite different, and now the situation has taken a new turn. The bases of people's war revolutionary base area, local people's power, the united front, people's liberation army, and revolutionary communist party have become parts of history. Counter-revolution has been restored. For example, old organs of state machinery (military, police, bureaucracy, and judiciary) have been strengthened and solidified. The so-called Constituent Assembly has fallen into the hands of status quoists and reactionaries. The major fraction of the people's war time party and its leadership has embraced the righteous revisionist line, and the revolutionary communist movement is in a weak condition.

The party took offensive tactics when it was the line of preparation of non-peaceful development of revolution in the past. Accordingly, forms of struggle and organisation were designed. On the one hand tactics of struggle like building revolutionary base areas, local power, guerrilla warfare, attack on security personnel, and military barracks were adopted, and on the other revolutionary strategic organisations matching the methods of struggle were also built. Of them, underground party formation, guerrilla militants group, people's liberation army are may be mentioned. Legal or reformist forms of struggle and organisation could not be compatible to revolution in those conditions.

With the party adopting the line of peaceful development for revolution in the distinct situation to achieve the strategic goal, it was imperative to make a change in the methods of struggle and organisation. Earlier methods of struggle and organisation adopted by the party could not match with the line of peaceful development for revolution. The forms of struggle and organisation to be adopted during the preparation of non-peaceful development of revolution could not go simultaneously with the tactics of peaceful development of revolution adopted by the party. So, it was essential to change the old tactics and adopt methods of struggle and organisation as per the new line.

In the course of addressing the varying phases that occur during the development of the new democratic revolution, various forms of struggle and organisation too have to be practised accordingly. Tactics are a part of the strategy, and they must be subordinated to the tasks and the requirements of the strategy. The task of the party leadership is to master all the forms of struggle and organisation of the proletariat to ensure their proper use and achieve all necessary prerequisites for the preparation of strategic success. The then party leadership failed to take a correct Marxist-Leninist line in handling different types of situations. It did not handle the tactical line of the peaceful development of revolution as a part of the strategic goal of the new democratic revolution by not subordinating it to the tasks and requirements of the strategy considered as the necessary prerequisites for the ultimate success. As a result, the possibility of revolution faded away too. It will be a blunder to explain it just as a mistake of the leadership only in terms of tactics alone as it was related to the strategic plan too. It is how the strategic line of new democratic revolution was replaced by the Loktantrik Ganatantra as proven by its adoption in the form of the strategic plan even after forming the government under its leadership after the election of the constituent assembly and the end of the monarchy.

Suggestions given to the party leadership to adhere to the revolutionary line on the political and military issues as well as other plans and programmes may sound untimely, irrelevant and an adventurism at present. For example, it is not feasible to replace the old state mechanism by a new one, *i.e.* new democracy and capturing central power through armed insurrection. If we evaluate the ground reality, we need to adopt defensive, not offensive tactics. However, defensive tactics should be a part of our strategy of new democratic revolution while preparing the condition for our strategic goal. This is the only way of adhering to the final goal in the present prevailing situation of the country. So, Marxist-Leninists need to push ahead the strategic line of new democratic revolution by changing the forms of struggle and organisation when the revolution faces a setback. However, the counselling given to the party leadership to uphold the revolutionary political and military lines, and the disagreements expressed through a series of letters met with deaf ears, and now they have become the subject of history.

The issues and debates raised in the party over the revolution are of a theoretical nature, not simply related to the tactical alone, but the distinct ones to be raised during the modes of revolution with long-term effects.

Now counter-revolution has emerged victorious, but the law of revolution shows that it does not die forever because of the deception and betrayal of leadership. Revolution does not rise because of desire and bravery of either political party or leadership as it happens only when objective and subjective situations are mature and favourable. In the era of imperialism and proletarian revolution, it emerges out of the fundamental and particular contradictions of imperialism. We can take it for granted that Nepali society will propel new kinds of contradictions due to the strong presence of imperialism, expansionism and comprador, bureaucratic and feudalistic exploitation and oppression. Committed Marxist-Leninists will play their role of midwife for the success of revolution as guided by the law of science of revolution. The ten-year long people's great war will prove to be a rehearsal in the same way as the failure of the 1905 revolution of Russia helped in accelerating the 1917 historic socialist revolution. Lenin also said rightly, "we should dream too much for our movement."

Prachanda and Bhattarai surrendered national and class interests by embracing the rightist revisionism at the cost of revolutionary Marxism. However, they seem naive as they could not show foresight regarding how not to submit to every demand of reactionaries for preserving their own petty interests and using them as bargaining tools in future. History is a witness that revisionists have to take care to protect their interest from the imperialists, otherwise they would have been eliminated by the enemy forces. Imperialism and their domestic agents do not let former communists live with peace even after liquidating the revolutionary communism by chasing them until they do not adopt the capitalistic path openly. Now Prachanda and Bhattarai are just the examples of the tired deer chased by imperialism and their domestic agents, and they will continue to chase with further vigour and tire them out until the former overtly condemn communism, Marxism-Leninism-Mao Tse-tung Thought. Prachanda and Bhattarai cannot return to the earlier place as they have engrossed themselves deeply in the path of revisionism by surrendering national and class interest to an extreme point. If they react to the chasing away from the imperialists by professing their earlier revolutionary line, it will be just like the counter attack of a cat being cornered in a room with no outlet.

Raising the communist movement in Nepal has become a complex subject in the backdrop of the setback faced by the people's war. True revolutionaries have been reduced to a zero condition from the strength of thirty-one thousand people's army, revolutionary base areas, and local powers. The reactionary forces have now strengthened themselves and the powerful communist party and the united front have become severely fragmented. So, it is the historical task for the revolutionary communists of Nepal to galvanize people (the maker of history) for future revolution.

We are in a state of preparing for revolution and the duration of it depends on the national and international situation on the one hand, and on the other the subjective condition of the party. Risk in the communist movement should be identified as the path of preparation for revolution is full of challenges, complexities, and ups and downs. Right liquidationist, bent upon liquidating the revolutionary line, can pose a great danger in the process of preparation for revolution, and the left liquidationist, who portray the challenging, complex and protracted path of revolution with no patience to bear with the hardship of the revolutionary path, can also create obstacles. Both trends are equally harmful and the entire party should remain alert to all such non-Marxist-Leninist thoughts.

In the context of distorted propaganda spearheaded unprecedentedly about Marxism-Leninism-Mao Tse-tung Thought and the history of the communist movement till date, it is our moral responsibility to revive the correct teachings of Marx to Mao Tse-tung regarding the state and revolution, proletarian democracy, proletarian dictatorship, the role of the communist party, the possibility of the peaceful development revolution, Leninist organisational principles, and the question of Stalin. It is for this reason that even long statements from the works of Marx, Engels, Lenin, Stalin and Mao need to be extracted for clarity. I realise the pitfalls of such an exercise as they may make the reading more complex, even inviting a negative impact on the popularity of the book itself. However, it cannot be avoided in order to make the work (book) authentic and reliable. Similarly, I have referred to the long statements made by Prachanda and Bhattari so that readers themselves could grasp the holistic perspective of the proponents of scientific socialism on the one hand, and on the other to counter the false notions advanced by revisionists like Prachanda and Bhattarai with sufficient proof and evidences.

This book has appeared in this form out of my consistent involvement for over three decades in the communist movement as well as my contribution to the political and ideological field. However, it is not the sole result of my effort. My father, the late Bedavraj Dhakal, mothers Lalita Dhakal and Kamala Dhakal, and sisters the late Bidya Dhakal (Jaljala), Kanta Dhakal, Sarala Dhakal, Shanta Dhakal, Sarita Dhakal, and brother Jeetendra Dhakal, have rendered invaluable help in advancing my political work in different ways. Our father inspired and initiated my sister Bidya Dhakal (Jaljala) and other members of the family into the communist movement. He was the first communist teacher of us too. My sister Bidya Dhakal died in the course of party work. The moment of shock hastened my initiation into the communist movement. Accordingly, I dedicated myself to the work of the party and the movement. After my marriage in 1985 to Ajita Dhakal, who hails from a politically active family, I have received full support from her too, and I want to thank her for her cooperation in advancing my political work and writing too. It would have been impossible for me to continue my active political career without the support from my mother Lalita Dhakal and wife Ajita Dhakal. I express my gratitude to them for their sacrifice for my work and solving the family problems on their own without complaints or grudges. I salute them and assure that I will remain committed to fulfil their dreams. I would like to thank my daughters Julie and Shikshya Dhakal for bearing with all difficulties in their childhood during my long absence from home because of my obligation to the party. I appreciate their understanding and never complaining despite having to face hardships in my absence.

I am indebted to the late Comrade Viswanath Pathak who translated this book from Nepali into English; to Comrade Roshan Kissoon and Peter Tobin, who observed the ten-year people's great war and the two-line struggle in the party and the peace process in Nepal, for editing the book. This book is no exception to other books regarding the problems faced in the course of publishing from one language into another language. Moreover, my own long sentence structure as well as definitive words of the Nepali language complicated the process of translation. I appreciate my colleague Prof. Dr. Shreedhar Gautam's contribution in minimising the lapses between the original Nepali text and its English translation in terms of intended meaning of the first text. I thank all critics for sparing their valuable time to read and critique the book. I would like to express my thanks also to India's popular publisher Aakar Books, and K. K. Saxena as well as Pratyush Chandra, associated with the publication, for the opportunity to reach readers through the English language. I have taken every care to avoid some omissions seen in the earlier edition. I am solely responsible for any lapses and omissions despite my care, and assure esteemed readers to fill the gap in the next edition.

Yogendra Dhaka

March 20, 2015
Kathmandu, Nepal

Introduction to the First English Edition

The series of essays in this book furnish detailed political and theoretical opposition to the revisionist trajectory of the UCPN(Maoist) following the 2006 peace agreement that saw the end of people's war. The Maoists then 'came out of the jungle' to enter the multi-party parliamentary politics. Much has been written about the rise of Maoism and the Nepalese revolution by anthropologists, ethnographers, sociologists, and sympathisers, but apart from some translations, it is the first major contribution in English from a party member, providing critical insights into the nature of the Two-Line Struggle within the party over the past nine years. It aims at reasserting the party's revolutionary Marxist-Leninist world-view.

The writer's views on the nature of a Nepalese, post-revolutionary, socialist state are at variance with the majority Maoist long-standing commitment to having a federal thread, woven into the fabric of People's Democracy in future. The majority line was advanced as the Leninist way for the proletarian revolution to redress the historical injustice visited upon the many national minorities (*Janjatis*) by the centralised, 'divine' Hindu kingdom established by Prithivi Narayan Shah and in continuous existence since 1769, albeit under successive polities of the absolute monarchy, Rana despotism, *Panchaayat* monarchy, and the multi-party democracy.

Yogendra Dhakal, on the contrary, advocates a unitary state post-revolution and makes out a strong case for the correct Leninist position. He does so by setting out a Socratic political dialogue, presenting the federal argument accurately and in exacting details from the CPN(Maoist) and *Janjati* sources before refuting it with the reflections on the historic nation state, the theoretical understanding of the process by the Marxists and its application in practice by the communists, following the 1917 revolution in Russia.

Nepalese Maoism is firmly rooted in the terrain of the Asian communist movement that sees, draws upon and, when necessary and contingent, improves proletarian praxis within a continuous history, beginning with Marx and Engels, and continued by Lenin, Stalin and Mao. This may jar with some contemporary Western progressives, whose dismissal of post-1917 socialist states in general is dependent on the rejection of the 'Stalinist' Soviet Union in particular. Convictions shaped by a leftist/Trotskyist discourse that was dominant in the West, even before the collapse of the USSR and Soviet Bloc in 1990, gaining strength and possibility as Western communist parties, demoralised by Khrushchev's 1956 attack on Stalin's record, scuttled away from the proletarian Leninism into petit-bourgeois, peacenik humanism, economism, etc. leaving the field of revolutionary politics and ideology to the ultra-left.

Trotskyites (with some notable exceptions) have little interest or sympathy, with the Third-World struggles, dismissed either as peasant jacqueries that, even when successful, could only produce a mutated 'Stalinist' form of Asiatic despotism. This has produced the contradiction of revolutionaries in the East looking up to the practical achievements of Stalin's Soviet Union and Mao's China, despite their mistakes, whereas the Western left and liberal intelligentsia mostly look down on this historical experience, decrying it as fatally flawed. Some even agree with bourgeois anti-communist ideologues/'historians', that they were, in fact, 'crimes', with a human cost of ever inflating, (and increasingly risible) magnitudes.

This is not the place to detail the sociology between these two world-views, except to point out that one shaped by the levels of absolute immiseration and deprivation produces communist parties valuing practical examples and policies that will tackle these socio-economic iniquities. The Maoists in India and Nepal hold that the real is rational and reject the circle of perfection advocated by the sections of the left intelligentsia in imperial heartlands, who take the line that: 'it might be all very well in practice–but will it work in theory?', as an affectation that arises from relatively pacified conditions of existence.

That Dhakal presents a set of unique and important essays, makes it; therefore, incumbent to understand why Stalin is cited and included among the five giants of proletarian history. On the national question particularly, he cannot be avoided, as he was the leading Bolshevik theoretician, encouraged by Lenin to synthesise contemporary thinking on the subject and who succeeded in fusing it with the proletarian revolution against imperialism. From October 1917, he was part of the leadership that enacted a Leninist political programme putting theory to work; significantly, *inter alia,* framing a federal constitution for the USSR.

Dhakal's critique in subsequent letters, regarding the retreat of UCPN(Maoist) from proletarian revolution in the years following the 2006 peace agreement into revisionist 'parliamentary cretinism', shows him giving a voice, at a high theoretical level, to a critical mass of party cadre. Coalescing around Kiran, they had launched a 'Two-Line Struggle' against the compromising leadership of Prachanda and Bhattarai. In 2012 it produced a split leading to the formation of the CPN-Maoist, aimed at resuming the stalled revolution and overthrowing the oppressive, Brahminical, comprador state by embracing the proletarian politics again.

Two-line struggle defines Maoists rejection of the Soviet party style commandism, so well encapsulated in the old DDR song: "Die Partei Hat Immer Recht" and why, in reaction to this party style an early slogan in GPCR was, 'Bombard the headquarters', signalling assault by Red Guards on a communist party, misled by 'capitalist roaders' and seen as decidedly 'immer unrecht'! It assumes that class-struggle is ubiquitous, even under socialism, even within the party. Therefore, the different tendencies in the communist party are reflections of the classes in that society and expressions of ideological and political lines that rise internally, according to the level of class struggle in specific conjunctures.

Like all Maoists, the Nepalese comrades hold the view that such a situation will remain until class society is abolished. The reflection; therefore, of inherent social conflict in inner-party struggle follows, and any attempt to negate it is unscientific, undermining its centrality to party norms, where unity is relative and struggle absolute. This reading of democratic-centralism is articulated in the line adopted by the Central Committee as:

"Compromise in centralisation and revolution in party democracy."

The series of commentaries is a testimony to the commitment at a high theoretical and political level. Even when their author has a position on the national question that is inimical to party policy, his right of expression is unchallenged. That the party Chairman, Kiran, contributed the foreword is the recognition of unswerving revolutionary commitment, proletarian purpose and erudition. It is clear his contributions are valued, within a normative Maoist style of party work, and especially, as necessary Marxist-Leninist corrective in English to Bhattarai, still trading as Nepal's leading communist revolutionary intellectual and UCPN(Maoist) leader.

These writings exemplify the continuing vigour and vitality of the Maoist movement in Nepal and a valuable contribution to the Marxist-Leninist thought from the inside of the Nepalese revolution and explaining its challenges. In particular it is the first time that such a substantial critique of the UCPN(Maoist)'s descent into revisionism since the 2006 peace agreement has been set before a progressive audience in the English-speaking world.

Also underlined is the need to generalise lessons of the Nepalese revolution if this century is to finally see the chains of imperialism snapped. Its obvious 'weakest links' are similar countries in the Third World, where the objective situation exists for one-two-three-many Nepals.

By serving the Nepalese proletariat with constructive suggestions aimed at advancing their revolution, Dhakal shows himself, in an age of imperialism, as servant to the proletariat everywhere. Concentrating on the role of the vanguard party in this struggle, he stresses the importance of applying a correct line, and that this depends on accurate estimation of balance of all forces in the revolutionary conjuncture. This is a crucial party function that confirms its leadership and offers the masses in struggle the best chance of success against the entrenched forces of reaction.

It is axiomatic for Dhakal and his comrades that the Leninist vanguard party retains its relevance for the struggle of oppressed peoples against imperialism, contrary to the sad sack Western communist parties, who long ago abandoned the Leninist model in the ultimately failed attempt to transform into social-democratic mass electoral organisations. For the communists in the Third World, the flame of revolution burns brighter, calling out for a party equipped with revolutionary theory, united within itself by a combination of democracy and discipline and bound closely to the masses.

Dhakal, in this book, provides the theoretical and political Marxist-Leninist tools to support such a party in Nepal.

February 2015
United Kingdom

Peter Tobin

A Few Words About the Book

The author Yogendra Dhakal, known by his pen name Ajay Sharma, is a veteran of the Nepali Communist Movement. This book is a thorough exposition, analysis, and refutation of the political line that saw the Nepali Maoist party give up the people's war, give up the base areas, give up the People's Liberation Army, and surrender all their revolutionary demands to join the electoral parliamentary system. Nine years since the peace process, the Nepali Maoists have split into two, three and more factions, and are confused and divided amongst themselves.

The Nepali Maoists fought a ten-year people's war, and claimed at one time to control 80 per cent of the territory of Nepal; however, about a decade since the end of the peace process, they have lost all they gained–their movement has liquidated itself. The blame for this cannot ultimately be placed on their enemies, but on the leadership itself and the political line adopted by them.

The disastrous political line was forwarded by Dr. Baburam Bhattarai in his various articles after the *Development of Democracy in the Twenty-First Century*, which was adopted as the official party line at the Chunbang Meeting. Amongst the first to criticise the line was the author of this book through a series of detailed letters to the party headquarters, which make up the contents of this book. It is the most detailed criticism of this line, dealing with the concrete conditions of Nepali politics. The events since the Chunbang Meeting and the peace process have shown clearly the truth of Mao Zedong's famous statement:

> The correctness or otherwise of the ideological and political line decides everything. When the party's line is correct, then everything will come its way. If it has no followers, then it can have followers; if it has no guns, then it can have guns; if it has no political power, then it can have political power. If its line is not correct, even what it has it may lose. The line is a net rope. When it is pulled, the whole net opens out.[1]

To justify their change of line, the Chairman Prachanda and Dr. Bhattarai's leadership introduce a new programme, which claimed to have evaluated all the mistakes of the previous century made by communists. There is nothing wrong with this, in itself. The solutions they offered to

1 Talks with responsible comrades at various places during the provincial tour.

compensate for the supposed mistakes of the International Communist Movement sounded attractive, but in reality they meant nothing more than becoming another electoral 'communist' party, full of empty slogans and promises.

One of the most attractive, and yet completely empty, proposals of this new programme was to suggest that the Paris Commune should be the model of revolution, while negating the Russian and Chinese experiences under the leadership of Lenin, Stalin, and Mao. The new programme also talked about Rosa Luxemburg, and her criticism of the Leninist party. The legacy of Stalin, in particular, was criticised and Bhattarai even praised Trotsky. A new phoney 'sub-stage' was invented, which advocated working with parliamentary parties for a period to develop capitalism. These types of arguments were marshalled, which generally attacked the necessity of the 'Dictatorship of the Proletariat'.

Dhakal meticulously dismantles all these positions in detail and forwards a compelling defence of Marxism-Leninism, upholding the contributions of Stalin without being an apologetic. This is not a popular view, particularly in the Western academia and its offshoots throughout the world. However, the key issue on Stalin is over the attempt to build 'socialism in one country', and the experiences of these attempts. Unfortunately, the term 'Stalinist' is an abuse amongst much of the Western left, and is used effectively to stop any kind of solidarity between Western leftist activists and non-Western communist parties and movements, in effect, to stop Western leftists regarding various Third World Communist struggles as 'their' struggle.

Another extremely important subject is that of the nation, nationalism, and what does and does not constitute a nation. The Nepali Maoists championed the issue of federalism. However, the modality of federalism, the basis on which Nepal be federated–on ethnic or geographic lines–remains a highly contested issue amongst the different political parties. The Maoists stated that there were certain 'nations' in Nepal, and that the 'nations' should have the right of self-determination. Dhakal suggests that there are no nations inside Nepal, but there are pre-capitalist social formations more akin to the tribe, clan, or caste. Dhakal's analysis draws on the work of Friedrich Engels on pre-capitalist society, in particular *The Origin of the Family, Private Property, and the State*, to try and correctly identify the type of social formations in Nepal. The danger of ethnic identity politics is obvious; it has already led to the politics of divide and rule which have proved so divisive and dangerous elsewhere in the world, at worse it could lead to the break up of the Nepali state. The question of how class struggle and ethnic based identity politics intersect is a critical issue, in Nepal and in many other countries around the world.

It is said that 'whoever finishes a revolution only halfway, digs his own grave.'[2] To a close observer of Nepali politics, it must seem as though the Maoists are on the verge of complete defeat. However, the communist movement has deep roots in Nepal, and the betrayal of Prachanda and Bhattarai is only a temporary setback. The struggle continues.

March 2015 Roshan Kissoon
United Kingdom

2 https://plus.google.com/share?url=http://www.poemhunter.com/quotations/famous.asp?people=geor (*Danton's Death*, Georg Buchner).

Foreword to the First Nepali Edition

Comrade Yogendra Dhakal is known by his pen name, Ajay Sharma for long, and I am extremely pleased to express my impression and views on his new book. Comrade Dhakal, recognised for his sharp intellect, has been active in Nepal's communist movement for over three and a half decades. To his credit, he has written many books, concentrating on various issues and problems concerning the revolution in Nepal as well as the struggle in the history of the international communist movement. His writings demonstrate an acute and rigorous theoretical understanding about the struggle for revolution across the world.

This book is a collection of some important letters sent to the Unified Communist Party of Nepal (Maoist) headquarters from Australia, where he served as the Ambassador of Nepal. The issues he addresses basically relate to the weaknesses and deviations that developed in the UCPN(Maoist). We may differ with some of his views in relation to the national question discussed here, but his trenchant defence of Marxism-Leninism and opposition to the right-wing revisionism is correct and apposite.

The UCPN(Maoist) leaders, Prachanda and Bhattarai, have been Janus-faced on the question of Loktantrik Ganatantra (an old-style bourgeois-democratic republic), which was accepted by the Central Committee at the 2005 Chunbang Meeting. They have played a double role by calling it the transitional republic, not a bourgeois parliamentary arrangement, just to deceive the revolutionaries, and at the same time they have defined it as the capitalist republic to keep the reactionaries in good humour. Included here is the strong analysis of the tactics behind the Loktantrik Ganatantra, which accepts the bourgeois parliament in perpetuity, not as a temporary mechanism, to advance the revolution. Comrade Dhakal views the proposal passed at Chunbang, which finds fault with the analysis made by Lenin and Mao in relation to the proletarian strategy and tactics in the imperialist era, 'outdated' and a departure from the Marxist-Leninist line. He refutes all such accusations strongly and defends the Marxist-Leninist line with full conviction, logic and evidences. While acknowledging certain quantitative changes in imperialism, the writer shows that it is still qualitatively the same phenomenon; and the revolutionary strategy and tactics of these past great communist leaders still stand and remain fundamentally correct.

The preface sheds light on the need of adopting strategy and tactics depending upon the objective condition of the concerned country and the world situation for accomplishing revolution and then sustaining it too. Comrade Dhakal believes that the favourable objective conditions pertaining to a specific country and the international situation is necessary for the success of the people's revolution. Reference is made to Lenin's analysis of imperialism and the October Revolution by way of refuting Kautsky's concept of 'ultra-imperialism' and adequate consideration is given to neo-colonialism as referred to by Mao in the course of the Great Debate.

The backdrop given by the writer aims at refuting the analysis on the imperialism made in Chunbang Meeting and the explanation of imperialism advanced by Bhattarai at the Palungtar Meeting. It helps the reader to a great extent to get rid of many confusions created about imperialism. He throws light also on the harmful aspects of the Nepal-India Bilateral Investment Promotion and Protection Agreement (BIPPA) and the need of struggle for national independence, by providing relevant information and materials.

Comrade Dhakal's write-ups are rich in terms of theoretical as well as analytical in-depth. The letters presented here contain theoretical depth and analysis and provide intellectual nutrition for the correct synthesis of the subject matter. At a time when there is a concerted attack on Marxism-Leninism by the right-wing revisionists, such a book is a fitting reply to counter the false propaganda. I congratulate Comrade Dhakal for his political consistency and assiduousness in the pursuit of revolution based on theories propounded by Marx, Engels, Lenin, Stalin and Mao. I wish him all success and hope Dhakal will bring out more such books in future too.

June 9, 2012

Mohan Baidya 'Kiran'
Chairman
Communist Party of Nepal-Maoist

Preface to the First Nepali Edition

Adapting and inscribing strategy and tactics for revolution cannot be detached from the real world. Each is influenced by the general and conjectural world situation, and the objective conditions existing in specific countries. Therefore, they will take into account the level of development of productive forces and the relationship among classes. Wishful thinking cannot alter that objective situation. Starting from this position, it is positive and natural that the critical questions relating to the nature of the objective situation and its unique characteristics gives rise to different opinions and arguments.

In a class-based society, the question of reaching an understanding on the world situation and that of the specific country is not an independent one. It is always related to a class ideology. Today, there are two principal classes, proletariat and capitalist. While the former, through its vanguard is forming its strategy and tactics within a revolutionary paradigm of pursuing proletarian class interests, whereas the capitalist class uses bourgeois political parties and institutions to develop strategy and tactics according to its class interests. Mao writes in this regard:

> The proletariat seeks to transform the world according to its own world outlook, and so does the bourgeoisie. ... It is inevitable that the bourgeoisie and petty-bourgeoisie will give expression to their own ideologies. It is inevitable that they will stubbornly assert themselves on political and ideological questions by every possible means. You cannot expect them to do otherwise.[1]

The task of evolving and determining strategy and tactics is complex and full of contradictions. It is incumbent on the proletariat and its vanguard to expose the unscientific world-view of the bourgeoisie and petty-bourgeoisie; and in the course of struggle against their ideology, they should wage struggle also to prevent an adverse impact on their own class and party, giving rise to the emergence of neo-bourgeois class. So, a constant vigil and struggle against such possibility is equally necessary.

In the history of the world communist movement, the analysing of the current world situation, advancing revolution accordingly, deciding and

1 Mao Tse-tung, "On the Correct Handling of Contradictions Among the People", *Selected Works*, Eng. ed., Foreign Language Press, Peking 1977, Vol. 5, pp. 409, 411.

determining the strategy and tactics, have always generated intense debate. The tremendous struggle in the Second International between the old guard, Bernstein and Kautsky, and the new vanguard, Lenin, Stalin is an early example of this argument. Out of that ideological and political furnace, Leninism and the first socialist state emerged in world history. Central to that struggle was precisely the evaluation of the current world situation, and the right dogmatists of the Second International failed to understand imperialism as a special stage in capitalism. In the changed global phenomenon, as a signal failure, they continued with the same strategy and tactics designed for the struggle in the preceding capitalist stage, whereas under the leadership of Lenin, a revolution succeeded by adapting revolutionary proletarian strategy and tactics in the changed world situation of imperialism, the highest stage of capitalism.

Serious disagreements surfaced even within the world communist movement among those, who recognised the emergence of imperialism as the highest stage of capitalism, in terms of proletarian revolutionary strategy and tactics after the October Revolution of 1917. Trotsky, an influential leader, promoted a distinct strategy and tactics for pursuing worldwide proletarian revolution, emphasising that after seizing power in one country there should not be any building of socialism within that state but instead immediately continue forward to spread the revolution internationally in what he termed a process of 'Permanent Revolution'.

Lenin and Stalin differed fundamentally with that proposition, and emphasised that socialism in one country–the USSR–was the essential part of the world revolution to be followed with the strategy and tactics of proletarian revolution. Kautsky from the right beginning was arguing for backing off from any international revolutionary perspective. By raising the danger of ultra or super-imperialism, he was advocating peaceful democratic strategy and tactics.

After the death of Stalin modern revisionists, citing the danger of World War, advised the proletariat to adopt the strategy of the 'peaceful road to socialism' through participation in the reactionary parliamentary institutions in the First and Second World, and to abandon war for national liberation in the Third World. They declared the end of colonialism and beginning of "new stage".

Under the leadership of Mao, the international revolutionary communist movement refuted this analysis; and defended a Leninist strategy of proletarian revolution and national liberation struggles as still appropriate in an era of continuing and predatory imperialism. Responding to the Letter of March 30, 1963 from the Central Committee of the Communist Party of the Soviet Union, the Communist Party of China clearly states:

> The oppressed nations and people of Asia, Africa and Latin America are faced with the urgent task of fighting imperialism and its lackeys. History has entrusted to the proletarian in these areas the glorious mission of holding high the banner of struggle against imperialism, against old and new colonialism and for national independence and people's democracy, of standing in the forefront of the national democratic revolutionary movement and striving for a socialist future.[2]

Similarly, in an answer to another letter from the Communist Party of the Soviet Union, the Communist Party of China writes:

> An important line of demarcation between the Marxist-Leninists and the modern revisionists is the attitude taken towards this extremely sharp issue of contemporary world politics. The Marxist-Leninists firmly side with the oppressed nations and actively support the national liberation movement. The modern revisionists in fact side with the imperialists and colonialists and repudiate and oppose the national liberation movement in every possible way.[3]

Neo-Trotskyites deviation appeared in the world communist movement regarding the revolution in a particular country for looking at it globally and then totally rejecting the contradiction of internal distinct character, while adopting strategy and tactics of revolution in the aftermath of Mao's death, and revival of capitalism in China. Bob Avakian, Chairman of the Revolutionary Communist Party, USA (RCP, USA) pushed forward this thought as reflected below:

> If we want to look to see what is the underlying and main driving force in terms of the development of revolutionary situations in particular countries at particular times, then too we have to look to the overall development of contradictions on a world scale, flowing out of and ultimately determined by this fundamental contradiction and not mainly to the development of the contradictions within a particular country, because that country and the process there is integrated in an overall way into this larger world process. It's not simply as it was in the feudal era or the beginning of the bourgeois era where you had separate countries more or less separately developing with interpenetration between them; now they've been integrated into this larger process...[4]

Avakian has further criticised Stalin, Mao, and to a certain extent, Lenin, alleging that they paid no attention to the contradictions developed

---

2 "A Proposal Concerning the General Line of the International Communist Movement", *The Great Debate*, Mass Line Publications, Kerala, 1994, p. 11.

3 "Apologists of Neo-Colonialism", *The Great Debate*, Mass Line Publications, Kerala 1994, p. 141.

4 Bob Avakian, "Further Historical Perspectives on the First Advances in Seizing and Exercising Power–Proletarian Dictatorship–and Embarking in the Socialist Road", *Revolution, Special Issue*, RCP Publications, Chicago, USA, 1981, No. 50, pp. 34-35.

worldwide and focused on the contradictions developed within particular countries. Like the Trotskyites, he maintains that Stalin basically deviated from the Marxism-Leninism in this regard. Rejecting these non-Marxist-Leninist thinking, the world communists moved on with non-compromising struggle based on principle. Yet again in our movement, wrong-headed theorising on the nature of modern imperialism has become apparent. Due to the so-called new development of imperialism, our party has declared that Lenin and Mao's analysis and several principles related to proletarian strategy and tactics based on that analysis become redundant. For example, a proposal passed at the Chunbang Meeting of the party in September 2005 states:

> It is necessary for the proletarian revolutionaries of the twenty-first century to pay serious attention regarding how the analysis by Lenin and Mao about imperialism and proletarian strategy taken on that basis have become redundant. Due to the inter-imperialists competition and the nature of war between them for division and redivision of certain territories, Lenin's analysis and the proletarian strategy based on that did not remain relevant after the Second World War. Likewise, Mao's analysis of Three Worlds' situation explained in the form of tactics did not exist in essence after the end of cold war too.
>
> American imperialism, advancing as a globalised state, has left behind Lenin's and Mao's analysis in this regard in the same way as Marx's then analysis and strategy regarding capitalism and had become outdated by the time of Lenin due to the development of imperialism. Therefore, it is incumbent as a matter of urgency for contemporary Marxist-Leninists to develop Marxism-Leninism-Maoism and then decide a new proletarian strategy and tactics that reflect the changed condition in the nature of imperialism. Until serious attention is focused on this issue, challenges for worldwide revolution cannot be faced properly.[5]

Bhattarai illustrates the supposed difference between the imperialism of Lenin's time and that of its contemporary form:

> Firstly, in the period of Lenin, imperialism worked with the mixed capital like finance capital, or industrial capital and banking capital, mainly invested in product areas as germinating capital in the oppressed countries of the third world where cheap labour and raw materials were available. But now globalised imperialism works with mainly financial capital or capital separated from the direct product capital in the form of loans or rentier capital. Being more mobile, it reaches to all corners of the world, but its headquarters are located in the imperialist centres like; New York, London, Tokyo, and Frankfurt. Even at slight danger, it centralises capital at its headquarters. Moreover, this financial capital is mostly multinational capital, made from the capital of many imperialist countries. This affects

5 Prachanda, "Political and Organisational Report", *Selected Works*, Nepalese ed., Janadisha Publications, Nepal, June 2007, Vol. 2, p. 463.

> the strategy and tactics of proletarian revolutionaries because unlike in the past when the country with the imperialist investment government as well as revolutionaries could exert control over the capital, now neither the concerned country nor the revolutionary can put such control because of a hi-tech world of information technology that increases mobility and speed of capital transfers. So, oppressed peoples cannot fight this new form of imperialism directly, and they instead need to concentrate on the internal comprador and bureaucratic classes that serve it.
>
> Secondly, prior to the Second World War, imperialist countries would fight to secure their markets and to ensure the security of their existing colonies while always seeking to establish new ones. That colonial period has ended, and now competition exists for neo-colonial control over specific countries, primarily in the Third World. Therefore, instead of confronting imperialism through direct wars of national liberation, the task for proletarian revolutionaries is to unite proletarian revolutionaries in all countries for a worldwide struggle for carrying the revolution through civil war and armed insurrection.
>
> Furthermore, the change in the nature of imperialism has reduced the possibility of the Third World War and direct inter-imperialist rivalry. Instead what is manifested is the indirect, or proxy wars and a regional tension among the imperialist countries with a view to saving their energy. It is also true that the last few decades have seen the penetration of Finance-Capital in the virgin territories of the Russian Federation, India and Brazil and this has somehow helped in solving the internal conflict in the imperialist countries. This has coincided with the unipolar dominance of America, whose military and economic hegemony have been unchallenged following the dissolution of the Soviet Union. In military terms alone, the USA is more powerful than the next eight states after they are combined and it is responsible for over half the world's expenditure on armaments and weaponry. This has enabled it to establish a strategy based on 'war without end' in defence and extension of its hyper-dominance; therefore, precluding inter-imperialist contradictions exploding into world war.

Prachanda and Bhattarai argue that because imperialism is now a qualitatively different phenomenon than that confronted by Lenin; it is, therefore, necessary to abandon the strategy and tactics defining proletarian opposition to imperialism as it is and substitute it by new ones. In the extract, Bhattarai identifies two new characteristics inherent in the contemporary imperialism that have a direct effect on the strategy and tactics of proletarian revolution. According to him, these "new" characteristics show firstly, revolutions in colonial, semi(neo)-colonial countries cannot take place within a national paradigm as in the era of Lenin, Stalin and Mao, so it must instead be directed into the struggle for democracy only. As he writes:

> Instead of fighting against imperialism, now peoples of oppressed nations, have to directly fight against domestic comprador and bureaucratic capitalist

classes that have grown with the support of imperialism. This means the internal 'democratic' aspect becomes more apparent than the external 'national' aspect.[6]

Secondly, Bhattarai considers that contemporary imperialism has reached a stage of hyper-dominance, and finds its political, economic and military might invincible. His definition implies that instead of confronting it face to face, proletarian revolutionaries should focus on adopting strategy and tactics to the contrary as a defensive measure. Before discussing the "new" strategy and tactics for proletarian revolution as advanced by Prachanda and Bhattarai, it is necessary to examine the "new" analysis of imperialism that informs this approach. The contention, advanced by Prachanda that the "American imperialism, advancing as a globalised state, has left behind Lenin's and Mao's analysis in this regard in the same way as Marx's then analysis and strategy regarding capitalism had become outdated by the time of Lenin due to the development of imperialism", is extremely objectionable. It divides the development of capitalism into three stages; competitive, monopoly and globalised. Establishing this third stage allows him space to change strategy and tactics by comparing with those adopted by Marx and Lenin, resulting from differing objective circumstances. Therefore, Stalin's analysis supported by Mao and the Revolutionary Internationalist Movement (RIM) is a thing of the past and should be regarded accordingly. To the contrary, the nature of imperialism, as identified by Lenin, has only become more pronounced and all the developments in American imperialism in the aftermath of the Second World War, especially around the eighth decade of the 20th century are matters of style, policy, quantitative accretions, and do not represent a qualitatively new phenomena. It can still be understood on the basis of the analyses made by Lenin, Stalin and Mao and the strategy and tactics made by them to resist, terminate and transcend it as a stage still hold true. Actually, Prachanda's definition as an outdated stage for Leninist strategy and tactics on the basis of his "new" analysis is suicidal for the proletarian revolution.

Bhattarai too claims that financial capital or loan capital separated from direct production has become the "latest character or trend" of the world imperialism. He finds it "quite more mobile" that "reaches into all corners of the world" and "even at slight danger centralises capital at its headquarters". He thinks that "this financial capital is mostly multinational capital, made from the capital of many imperialist countries". So, he concludes that it is difficult for revolutionary forces to exert control over such capital because of "a high-tech world of information technology that increases mobility and speed of capital transfers" compared to the earlier period of capitalism. He further asserts that unlike in the time of Lenin,

6 Baburam Bhattarai, "Some Added Explanation to Internal Party Discussion", *Ideological-Political Struggle in the Party*, Jhilko Publications, July 2011, pp. 52-53.

Stalin and Mao, its impact will be felt in the proletarian strategy and tactics. It is not possible to raise the national liberation movement and national war. Hence, his reliance on 'internal democratic struggle' by abandoning frontal assaults on imperialism through the mechanism of people's war and national liberation struggles. He presents his analysis as the "present characteristic and tendencies of imperialism" as the ideological and political reasons to abandon the struggle against imperialism. It is, in fact, a prescription to end revolution in the oppressed countries. This "new" analysis is no more than a stratagem by Prachanda and Bhattarai to cover their support for the continued neo-colonisation of Nepal by imperialism, Indian expansionism and its subservient role within the neo-liberal capitalist global dispensation.

Bhattarai's claim that a distinctive feature of this "new" imperialism is the separation of capital from the application of capital to production is plainly wrong. He and Prachanda submit this as if they had discovered this unique historical feature, which has matured, they assert, since the epoch of Lenin, Stalin and Mao. The separation of capital from production, money capital from industrial capital, rentier capital (which in money capital income-dependent anyway) from the entrepreneur are not new special characteristics as claimed by Bhattarai since they are characteristics of the totality of finance-capital. Certainly, the phenomenon is in flux and this will continue until the objective and subjective situations coincide and resolve the contradiction. However, these "characteristics and trends" that he claims emerged after Lenin, Stalin and Mao were in fact noted by Lenin himself ninety-six years ago:

> It is characteristic of capitalism in general that the ownership of capital is separated from the application of capital to production, that money capital is separated from industrial or productive capital, and that the rentier who lives entirely on income obtained from money capital, is separated from the entrepreneur and from all who are directly concerned in the management of capital. Imperialism, or the domination of finance capital, is that highest stage of capitalism in which this separation reaches vast proportions. The supremacy of finance capital over all other forms of capital means the predominance of the rentier.[7]

Hijacking Lenin's theses and calling it their own as claimed by Bhattarai and Prachanda is deplorable. As Comrade Bhattarai's analysis about the latest character of imperialism and the conclusion drawn from it is wrong, his contention that proletarian revolutionaries should focus their struggle on armed insurrection and civil war in their respective countries as a part of their strategy and tactics for fulfilling revolution, instead of confronting the imperialism directly in the context of its changed character, is equally

7 V. I. Lenin, Imperialism, The Highest Stage of Capitalism, *Collected Works*, Eng. ed., Progress Publishers, Moscow, Third Printing 1977, Vol. 22, p. 238.

condemnable. He has clearly expressed his views in the preamble for not fighting against imperialism. However, he has advanced his argument to continue worldwide movement against imperialism in milder and generalised terms. Likewise, he has defined armed insurrection and civil war purely as an internal matter of a concerned country. Such an analysis of the existing problem does not match with the essence of the present imperialism and proletarian revolutionary era. When Bhattarai says that "oppressed peoples should confront the national democratic struggle against the comprador classes grown up by imperialism instead of challenging imperialism directly", we should note two things; firstly, that he has reached this conclusion without any reference to the specific conditions existing in particular countries, in this case Nepal, but as a general rubric under this newly characterised monolithic imperialism. It implies that imperialism has homogenised the neo-colonies and oppressed peoples, so the task is to devise and implement a long-term strategy of uniting the international proletariat for struggle. To the contrary, no Marxist-Leninist can ignore the national aspect or relegate the necessary tasks of the revolution to a distant future.

Bhattarai's suggestion of concentrating on the fight against the domestic comprador and bureaucratic capitalist class in the era of imperialism and proletarian revolution is not a practical proposition as he acknowledges, that has been created and nurtured by imperialism. So, how can a struggle against it be isolated from the struggle against imperialism? The compradors are the plants that spring from the soil of imperialism, so you can kill a plant or a crop, but if the soil remains fertile others will emerge into the sunlight. The struggle against compradors and quislings cannot be isolated from the struggle against imperialism. Bhattarai contends that the nature of "globalised imperialism" allows revolutionaries room only for concentration on the "internal democratic" aspect and his advice "to follow the strategy and tactics in completing that revolution in specifically similar countries until such time as the long wave of world or regional revolution matures", reveals either his ignorance about proletarian revolution or his motive to end the proletarian strategy and tactics as well as the struggle against the world imperialism. This is essentially a wait and see attitude until the time of synchronised worldwide proletarian revolution erupts. Actually, it urges revolutionaries to abandon anti-imperialist struggles and engage in an unrealistic national, bourgeois 'democratic' diversion. It shows a lamentable grasp of the nature of imperialism and as a consequence it cannot elaborate a realistic strategy and tactics of proletarian resistance.

For a decade or more, there have been intense debates developed within our party regarding the strategy and tactics in forging ahead with the new democratic revolution, leading to a serious ideological-political deviation over the actuality of modern imperialism. The present position of Prachanda and Bhattarai, as described above, should be seen as a logical outcome that provides the parameters around which arguments raged either for forging ahead with the people's war, or for operating within the legal framework of the multi-party system. It means adhering to new democracy as the minimum programme or alternatively accepting a bourgeois capitalist republic either for continuing the struggle against feudals, compradors and bureaucratic capitalists. In other words, it is to engage and ally with them for establishing a revolutionary state against the world imperialism, Indian expansionism and domestic reaction, or instead with some 'progressive nationalist' entity that merges into them for confirming the patriotic policy in the pursuit of national sovereignty or limiting the struggle to 'democracy'; for re-affirming and developing further the leading role of the party, or accepting relegation as one among equals in the multi-party competition.

These problems are dealt with in more detail through the following letters to then party Chairman Prachanda under the title of the book *Revolution, Yes! Right Liquidationism, No!* It is natural that parties make mistakes and they can be corrected. If the leadership is revolutionary and has an underlying proletarian world-view, paralysis in revolution can be avoided. However, this is not the situation in respect of the main leaders of the UCPN(Maoist) as their mistakes and weaknesses are not the result from failure in application, but stem from the degeneration of a proletarian into a bourgeois and petit-bourgeois. Abandoning revolutionary proletarian strategy and tactics and adopting a bourgeois one is not an unnatural precedent. It is, therefore, axiomatic that revolutionary communists in the party and internationally should lead an uncompromising struggle against the wrong thinking, which refutes and sidelines Marxism-Leninism-Mao Tse-tung Thought.

Seven precious years have been wasted pursuing the line of peaceful development of revolution. Yet, in the declaration for the election of the second constituent assembly, Prachanda and Bhattarai confirm that this line will be maintained–for decades and decades if necessary. It is true that in Russia and China, Lenin and Mao used such an opportunity for given periods of months. But, it will vary according to the specific country, period and objective circumstances. It will always be a key period where the line must constantly concentrate on maintaining an unbroken revolutionary force to prevent the enemy from re-grouping and gathering power. Owing to the reformist policies of the Prachanda-Bhattarai clique, over the last seven years in Nepal, the forces established by ten years of people's great war were diminished, fragmented or dissolved while those of reaction flourished and augmented. The trend of our party's leadership to cling to the process of lengthening tactical line of peaceful development and realising the constituent assembly and treading the constitution out of it as the higher democratic practice is absolutely wrong.

Two conditions are essential to be fulfilled for the revolutionary application of the line of peaceful development of revolution. Firstly, the leadership in the party and government should be revolutionary. When the party leadership and the government desert the Marxist-Leninist strategy and tactics and adopt the liquidationist line, the revolutionary application of the tactical line of the peaceful development of revolution is not possible. Even if by electoral hook or crook the present party leadership comes to power, it will not be of the forces of new democracy or patriotism, but that of neo-bourgeois beholden to the world imperialism, Indian expansionism, Chinese state capitalism, domestic comprador, and bureaucratic capitalism.

Secondly, the possibility of the peaceful development of revolution cannot emerge in the era of imperialism by people's peaceful struggle. This is a rare possibility that emerges only after protracted struggle, or war between revolutionary and reactionary forces that brings revolutionary power into existence, creating a dual-power situation. But to think that it could be instantiated in a fast moving revolutionary period is to fail to understand how precisely imperialism and proletarian revolution are juxtaposed. Chasing this illusion, the UCPN(Maoist), under the Prachanda-Bhattarai leadership, produced the opposite, a counter-revolutionary policy, which oversaw the dissolution of the PLA, abandonment of dual-power in the liberated revolutionary base areas, including people's courts, cooperatives, commune, and the village committees that flourished then. All the gains of ten hard years of the people's great war were thus betrayed and frittered away.

The lack of these two conditions will not lead to peaceful development of revolution, but to counter-revolution. Stalin once noted: "A decision which is correct at one particular time may prove to be entirely unsuitable at another." In this light, the commitment to elections, a constituent assembly and constitution writing–correct at one specific conjuncture is now completely devalued and unsuitable too. The line of fulfilling the remaining tasks of the revolution through peaceful means, adopted at the Chunbang Meeting in the context of the distinct situation developed in the national politics, has become redundant now. So, the party should change its present political line of the peaceful development of revolution by firmly grasping the political line of the preparation of the non-peaceful path as in the past. The Prachanda-Bhattarai axis destroyed the PLA, the revolutionary bases, local authority and dual power, leading to the weakening of the subjective aspect (actually later on they were transferred into material bases for future armed insurrection and power) for armed insurrection, during the last seven years. While the success of the line of 'peaceful development of revolution' depends on both these conditions, the line of armed insurrection, however, is also linked to the particular subjective and objective conditions. The necessary revolutionary bases (revolutionary base areas, local government, PLA, *i.e.* the duel power) prepared for the armed insurrection have been completely destroyed by the main leadership of our party during the last seven years of peaceful development of revolution. Such a background does not allow us objectively for armed insurrection immediately. So, we should take the task of building above mentioned prerequisites bases for armed insurrection seriously, though it is a complex and long-term process. Revolutionary phrase mongering and adventurism will be fatal for true revolution. This is what Lenin too says: 'War is a continuation of politics'.

It has been explained in detail that the ideology and politics of Prachanda and Bhattarai regarding proletarian democracy, the role of a revolutionary communist party, state-organisation in the period of democratic or proletarian power, the struggle against bureaucracy, the formation of a strong permanent army and the re-establishment of capitalism are, not a "new synthesis", but a continuation of the revisionist thinking of the K.Venu in the history of the world communist movement. It is merely a continuation of outworn revisionist thinking that has plagued the proletarian struggle since its inception, albeit decked-out in a contemporary garb.

May 21, 2012 Yogendra Dhakal
Kathmandu, Nepal

National Problem in Nepal

First Letter Sent to the Party Headquarters Commenting on the Anti-Leninist View on the National Question

Our party has been vague and confused on the concept of Lenin's right to self-determination of nations since 1994. However, it certainly deserves credit for igniting the movement of various backward and oppressed communities in the country in the last fifteen years. Though it is not the movement, rather the essence of it that is of greater importance. The destination of a movement is not determined by its broadness and strength, but by its essence. Various movements, though broad and powerful at certain times in history, failed or took wrong direction because of their wrong essence.

In the Communist Movement of Nepal, the ten-year long people's great war led by the CPN(Maoist) came as a blow from the blue. However, it has generated a crisis in organisational, political and theoretical issues like state and revolution, proletarian democracy, proletarian dictatorship and the role of the communist party, the possibility of the peaceful development of revolution, Leninist organisational principle as well as the place of Stalin, which have been discussed elsewhere in this book. It has left also an abundance of confusion regarding the racial movement in Nepal as evident from the severe crisis of trust and belief among the friendly forces of revolution.

Till the time Nepal was considered a country of multi-racial/caste/ethnic communities in the communist movement, the racial issue was taken as part of the class struggle as well as the formation of new democratic republic. Different race/caste/ethnic communities, believed in the past that they could change the semi(neo)-colonial and semi-feudal conditions of the country and end the colonial, feudal exploitation and oppression existing in the country, and struggled to fulfil their objective together. Our party encouraged them to live in unity with the other race/caste/ethnic communities for their secure future.

However, situation changed after the imperialism, Indian expansionism, various NGOs/INGO's as well as internal regressive elements penetrated into the movement of the oppressed communities, leading their solidarity under racial umbrella. Our party too itself galvanised them by assuring 'autonomy with the right of self-determination' to draw their support for the people's war. The race based "liberation" struggle of the different communities, instead for an overall change of the semi(neo)-colonial and semi-feudal exploitation and oppression, has been focused on the "liberation" of their race/caste/ethnicity.

The development of capitalism in various ways and the intensification of class struggle over the last few decades has raised the race/caste/ethnic and indigenous movement to a new height in the country. The great people's movement of 1990; the end of the Panchayat System; the great people's war launched under the leadership of the CPN(Maoist); the great people's movement of 2006; the end of the absolute monarchy; the election for the constituent assembly; the end of the 239-year-old system of monarchy; the advancement of the integration of the People's Liberation Army into the Nepal Army by the new republican government as well as the process of writing a constitution are the significant examples of people's awareness for more right.

However, the awareness oriented them to the racial "liberation", rather to the objective of the ten years of people's war, which is not good development. Specifically, since our party joined the exceptional path of the peaceful development of revolution, the poisonous weeds of racism took strong roots for two reasons. The first is the well planned conspiracy by the internal and external reactionary forces to derail the line of 'the peaceful development of revolution'. The other one is our party's emphasis on the momentary benefits and success, neglecting the basic concepts of the class struggle as well as its future consequences. It is the sacrifice of the future for the present. Thus, the non-Marxist-Leninist point of view of our party is instrumental for spoiling the path of revolution and provoking racial demands.

The direction of the race/caste/ethnic people's movement in the country during the last one and a half decades is wrong not only by the norms and values of Leninism but also from the perspective of the general capitalistic norms and values too. Our party has failed to give a correct Leninist solution to this issue. It has neither supported the Second International and the United Nation's view openly, nor has it grasped the Leninist principle strongly. Its policy has turned into an absurd model of eclecticism. So, future generations may curse us for leading the race/caste/ethnic movement to a wrong direction fraught with the harmful consequences (to the extent of the disintegration of the nation).

At present, we are at a difficult turn of history, requiring our party to re-establish the true Marxist-Leninist view to correct its follies immediately and promptly. Only by adopting the true Marxist-Leninist view, can we save the territorial integrity of the country, people and revolution from the rapidly growing racial epidemic. This is what Mao too says, "the correctness or incorrectness of ideological and political line decides everything". Bourgeois parties or the parties that have deviated from scientific socialism cannot solve these problems. Racism can be rendered inactive only with the unity and the indivisibility of class struggle and proletarian internationalism. Our party is the vanguard of the working-class and of all the oppressed communities. So, it is imperative to adopt the correct Marxist-Leninist approach to solve the complicated problem. It should work solidly and firmly against the tide of racism in the country, from whatever corner it may have originated, recalling Mao that "Going against the tide is a Marxist-Leninist principle."

1
Party's View Regarding the Race/Caste/Ethnic Issue in Nepal

The proposal presented by Comrade Sangram at the first National Conference of the party, in 1994, states:

> Our party accepts the right of self-determination of the oppressed nationalities and accordingly justifies the demand of national autonomy. National autonomy right should be given to run national autonomous administration in densely populated regions, districts or localities of different backward races, ethnic people and regional languages.[1]

In an article published in 1995, Comrade Prachanda writes:

> There should be right to self-determination as theoretical foundation to end national oppression and discrimination. People of all nationalities get an opportunity to build their own future by themselves only under the right of

1 *Historical Documents of the Communist Party of Nepal (Maoist)*, Publisher: Central Publication Department, CPN(Maoist), 1998, p. 61.

> self-determination. Right to establish independent national states also comes under the right of self-determination. But, in the present world situation and the situation of the development of Nepalese society, under right of self-determination ... the process of development will be ensured on the basis of language of a particular locality, culture, population density and economic activities.[2]

Likewise, the document passed at the Second Historic National Conference of the CPN(Maoist) organised on February 8-12, 2001 states: "New Democratic Revolution should establish its foundation on the basis of strong national unity based on equality and freedom in line with the principle of national right of self-determination in the present circumstances."[3]

At another place Comrade Prachanda states: "The respect and acceptance of rights of self-determination of oppressed nationalities and the programme of national autonomy reveals the proletarian policy of party regarding this."[4]

In an article published in 2004, Dev Gurung says:

> It is seen that the policy Comrade Lenin followed with reference to the Russian Revolution concords to a great extent to the Democratic Revolution of Nepal as well. The other reality is that the proletarian class opposes all types of oppression by one nation over other nations. The right of self-determination means that it is the fundamental right of the oppressed nation to revolt against oppression as well. With this meaning, the proletarian class has to accept, if according to the right of self-determination any oppressed nation revolts against oppressor nation or state and wants to establish a separate state disintegrating itself. ... Explaining democracy with reference to Nepal, it is seen that the majority of people, in reality, can achieve democratic right only in a democracy with the right of self-determination.
>
> Paying attention to this fact and accepting the right of self-determination of oppressed nations, the CPN(Maoist) is found having forwarded the concept of national and regional autonomous administration for the oppressed nations and regions in its democratic programme ... Accepting Nepal as a multinational country and the reality of oppression based on region, gender, language and religion and so on in practice here, right of self-determination is also accepted for the oppressed nations and regions for their liberation from oppression.
>
> Not taking the question of liberation of oppressed nationalities, which are in vast majority in Nepal as national liberation movement also, is an outcome of

---

2 Prachanda, "Religious and National Problem and its Solution in Nepal: A Comment", *Selected Works*, Janadisha Publications, July 2006, Vol. 1, p. 140.

3 Prachanda, "Great Leap Forward: Inevitable Necessity of History", *Selected Works*, Janadisha Publications, June 2007, Vol. 2, p. 285.

4 Prachanda, "Great Leap Forward: Inevitable Necessity of History", *Selected Works*, Janadisha Publications, June 2007, Vol. 2, p. 332.

the Hilly feudal Brahmin-Chhetri thinking. Because of this, there come two aspects–internal and external when we talk on the question of nationality in Nepal. The internal aspect becomes rather conclusive.[5]

On the occasion of the 10th annual ceremony of people's war, in an interview to weekly *Janadesh*, Comrade Prachanda states:

> The country would not be broken because of the right of self-determination and autonomy; rather a unified and strong Nepal will be formed with new national unity established in the true sense on democratic grounds ... By the virtue of our policy of right of self-determination and autonomy, all oppressed ethnic people, schedule castes, women, and people suffering from regional oppression are experiencing unification in the real sense for the first time. Reactionaries with misleading propaganda are saying that the country can be broken because of the right of self-determination and autonomy. They have the feudal thinking of the same level of those who think all women will divorce their husbands if the right of divorce is given.[6]

In the preface of a book by Comrade Dev Gurung, Comrade Prachanda says: "In the context of the special national situation, the questions related to the right of self-determination, autonomy and federal state have become indispensable questions for the development of strong internal nationality."

Comrade Dev Gurung at one place states:

> The basic difference with present revisionist groups and sub-groups is that they are not yet ready to develop this question in the form of national independence. ... Some explain this question that cannot be taken as a national problem. This understanding does not agree with the historical materialism. ... Some have raised the issue that communities here have not yet developed to the level of nation in the capitalist sense. On that ground, there is a thinking that the question of self-determination adopted by Lenin does not fit here. The question of right that people should be allowed, is related to national oppression. Where there is oppression, the right of self-determination is necessary. The question of that right is not a subject of concern of development or backwardness in the form of nations. It is a question related with oppression. Therefore, this right is not a matter to be allowed to developed capitalist nations, or to the backward tribes under discrimination. If there is oppression, it applies to all stages of development of the community. Even if a community is on a developed stage, if it runs oppression on others, it cannot get the right of self-determination in that situation. Therefore, right of self-determination is a right of revolt for liberation and freedom. This right is needed so long as oppression exists.

---

5 Dev Gurung, *Nationality Question and Federal Restructuring of State in Nepal,* Publisher: Tamu National Liberation Front, Nepal, Central Office, Pokhara, December 2006.

6 Prachanda, "I Want to Give the Message of Liberation (Interview)", *Selected Works*, July 2006, Vol. 1, pp. 490-91.

> Some others have stated that nations and regional communities in Nepal are not at all self-dependent units on economic grounds. So, it is not feasible to allow the right to self-determination in such a condition. If this argument is brought forward, it will be wrong to claim Nepal herself as a separate nation. Nepal is not self-dependent from the industrial capitalist production point of view because of her semi-feudal and semi-colonial production system. But, if seen from the traditional rural agricultural production system, the system of subsistence production is still present there. There is a system of producing everyday necessities in daily life. Life is generally maintained from this perspective. While exploring whether there are bases of self-dependence or not, we find sufficient bases of self-dependence only with reference to Nepal. Not only with reference to the whole nation, economic self-dependency is possible with reference to many regions. But, because of the state policy and the thinking guided by feudal and colonial policy, there is a situation of renouncing self-dependent economy. It is not at all acceptable to deprive people of the right of self-determination.
>
> Therefore, national and regional autonomy with the right of self-determination and one type of federal administration at the centre are necessary for a solution to the national and regional contradictions.[7]

At another place, Comrade Dev Gurung states: "We have to learn lessons and accept the way Lenin ensured the rights of nations during the formation period of the Soviet Union."[8]

He says further:

> The characteristic of present Nepal is multinational, and accepting it at present nullifies the view that Nepal is a unitary nation. In this regard, instead of finding how to solve this contradiction, it is more important to find its theoretical background with reference to Nepal. We have to accept the right of self-determination, as Lenin adopted, in Nepal's case too. It is optional whether it is applied or not, but a communist party, if it is truly communist and truly revolutionary, it shall accept democratic right, democratic right of self-determination. But one who is not a revolutionary communist, will not accept it. That democratic right implies for separation and forming a separate state as well. This is the highest type of democratic right. There must be readiness to grant the right to that extent.[9]

The *Manifesto of the CPN(Maoist) for the election of the Constituent Assembly* includes:

---

7 Dev Gurung, *Nationality Question and Federal Restructuring of State in Nepal*, Publisher: Tamu National Liberation Front, Nepal, Central Office, Pokhara, December 2006, pp. 53-54.

8 Dev Gurung, *Nationality Question and Federal Restructuring of State in Nepal*, Publisher: Tamu National Liberation Front, Nepal, Central Office, Pokhara, December 2006, p. 22.

9 Dev Gurung, *Nationality Question and Federal Restructuring of State in Nepal*, Publisher: Tamu National Liberation Front, Nepal, Central Office, Pokhara, December 2006, pp. 34-35.

> The universal policy of federalism is the right of self-determination of oppressed nations and regions and voluntary unity based on it. We must accept this policy theoretically, if we want democratic restructuring of the state in its true sense. But, keeping in mind the concrete political situation of Nepal, and the different oppressed nationalities and the low level socio-economic development of regions, the programme of national and regional autonomous administration itself is the best available option on the basis of policy of right of self-determination. There can be some difficulties to assimilate this policy and programme in the beginning, when the unitary state is taken for restructuring with no independent states that have joined the federation voluntarily. But all must think that it is only through this way how a new and strong unity can be established on a truly democratic foundation.
>
> The argument that right of self-determination can lead the country to fragmentation is concerned, there has been no country in the world by now split because a voluntary right given to an oppressed nation, or region. Contrary to this, countries have split because they were bound together by force instead of having that kind of right. As all wives do not divorce from their husbands by enjoying the right of divorce.

Further, the *Manifesto of the Communist Party of Nepal (Maoist) for the Election of the Constituent Assembly* discusses the federal structure:

> What can be the main criteria for federal structure in Nepal? In spite of many of the discussions, our conclusion is that it has been the national and regional identity itself that has been relatively more scientific criteria. National here means not ethnicity or race or caste, but it is necessary to understand that people with common language, common geography, common economy and common psychological means a stable group or nationality.

Regarding the movement of oppressed communities, the *Manifesto of the Communist Party of Nepal (Maoist) for the Election of the Constituent Assembly* writes: "In the liberation movement of oppressed nationalities, including Madhesi feudals, landlords, comprador and bureaucratic capitalists are there ... to grab leadership of the national liberation movement from the working-class ..."[10]

Comrade Suresh Ale Magar, in an answer to the question: "Are necessary elements of nation found in race and ethnic groups of Nepal?", replies:

> Certainly, they are found. It may be the Khas caste or Magar or Rai, Limbu, Thakali, Newar or Jirel. Every race/ethnic group has its own common language, common geography, common culture and history, a common way of economic life and its own racial character or psychological structure. ... 'Nation' and 'race/ethnic groups' are the same things. All prerequisites or elements or characteristics of nation are found in these caste/race/ethnic

10 *Manifesto of the CPN(Maoist) for the Election of the Constituent Assembly*, pp. 21-22.

> groups. So, with reference to Nepal, nation and race/ethnic groups are one.[11]

To justify how different caste/race and ethnic groups can make separate countries, he writes:

> If there can be a small country like Mauritius in the world with only eleven hundred thousand population and 2000 square kilometre area that has got membership of the United Nations Organisation as well, what difference will it make if a small country is made in Nepal? There are many castes, ethnic groups with that number of population here. Furthermore, each Tamang race and Magar race are estimated to have thirty hundred thousand populations.
>
> If coexisting or living in unity with other caste/ethnic groups means becoming victims of exploitation, suppression, oppression and crime, there is no meaning and essence of that unity for the oppressed caste/ethnic groups. (For example, if by coexisting or living together with the Khas caste in Nepal, these races get oppressed in all aspects and sectors, what is the justification of such unity for them?) If they become liberated from the exploitation and oppression by splitting, or making a separate state for them, it is not only loving, good and beneficial, but also "indispensable".[12]

Lenin accused the opponents of right of self-determination (Samakovski, Libman and so on) in the then situation of Russia as being opportunists. He said, "to deny applying right of self-determination of nations under socialism is treachery against socialism". Pointing to this thinking of Lenin, Comrade Suresh writes with reference to communists in Nepal:

> It needs to be seen whether communists of our country have faith in socialism, or reserve treachery against it, whether they become socialists or opportunists, become Lenin, or Samakovsky, Libman and Yunkarwich? Including leadership of the communist movement, many activists have come from the oppressor Khas caste, specially Brahmins and Chhetris. They must accept the right of self-determination without hesitation and publicise it as well. Only then, they will be socialists, otherwise national chauvinists.[13]

Our party suffers from confusion regarding the name, policy and programmes and concept about different race/caste/ethnic organisations affiliated to it. The policy and programmes of some of these organisations discussed below further clarify chaos in the party.

Our party categorises minority groups and race/caste/ethnic organisations on racial basis like the Newa National Liberation Front, the

---

11 Suresh Ale Magar, *Marxism and National Question in Nepal*, Nyaik Manch Publications, Pvt. Ltd., pp. 9-10.

12 Suresh Ale Magar, *Marxism and National Question in Nepal, Nyaik*, Manch Publications, Pvt. Ltd., pp. 14-15.

13 Suresh Ale Magar, *Marxism and National Question in Nepal*, Nyaik Manch Publications, Pvt. Ltd., pp. 18-20.

Tamuwan National Liberation Front, the Magar National Liberation Front, the Madhesi National Liberation Front, the Kirat National Liberation Front in an unscientific way because the Rastriya Mukti Morcha (National Liberation Front), for example, cannot be bracketed against every type of injustice or oppression. It is concerned only with the questions of national and colonial issues. It is to be used either against the feudalism or in relation to the formation of a national state, using an organisational frame for the sake of liberation. Colonies of imperialist countries can use the organisational model of the National Liberation Front with reference to political liberation.

Nepal is neither a multinational country nor an imperialist country, and neither are there any foundations for the formation of different national states, nor is there any condition to achieve liberation from an internal colonialism. Rather, Nepal herself has been a semi(neo)-colonial country for centuries. The problems of the different race/caste/ethnic groups mean problems under a single nation. The problems of the different race/caste/ethnic communities are the feudalistic centralisation and semi(neo)-colonialism prevailing in the country as a legacy of history. Undoubtedly, these contradictions are among people, but they are not between enemies and friends, so they should be solved in a friendly way.

The structure of the National Liberation Front can be built only in relation to all of Nepal, and not by each race/caste/ethnic group alone. The problems of the different race/caste/ethnic communities can be solved only after an independent and sovereign Nepal is established after defeating imperialism, colonialism and Indian expansionism. Therefore, the approach of solving them on the basis of race/caste/ethnic organisations is wrong theoretically. The nomination policy and programme should be changed accordingly to meet the socio-economic situation of the country. Parts of the policy and programme of the different race/caste/ethnic organisations affiliated with the party will help us further to understand its view related to the race/caste/ethnic problem in Nepal. As the policy and programme of Newa National Liberation Front states:

> Inside Newa autonomous province, the oppressed Newa nation will take back lost land and power. After having decleared the Kathmandu Valley and surrounding area as the indigenous land of the Newar, a separate autonomous Newa province will be established. To secure rights of other minority nationalities within the Newa autonomous province, they will be represented on the basis of national equality. ... If inequality and oppression persists, the oppressed nation will be allowed to be separate using the right of self-determination.[14]

14 *Constitution and Report of the New National Liberation Front*, Approved by the Second National Conference, March 16-19, 2007.

Likewise, the documents of the Madhesi Liberation Front places on record: "Our political line from now on should be to end the unitary feudal state power and establish a federal republic with the Madhesi autonomy having the right of self-determination."[15]

> The Madhesi National Liberation Front aims at leading the Madhesi national movement in an organised way to defend the survival of the Madhesi nationality of Nepal, mainly to achieve autonomous administration, to reestablish the rights grabbed by the Shah dynasty feudal state power and some Khas, and to solve Madhesi problems permanently, mainly by accepting the right of national self-determination. It is against the parliamentary point of view that leaves the national liberation movement and talks of temporary right.[16] ... Struggle for national liberation, organising all Madhesis compelled to survive in the external and internal colonial situation.[17]

About the location of the so-called Madhesh republic, the document observes:

> The Madhesh republic will be located in the Terai region of Nepal–a semi-feudal and semi-colonial country–to the South from Mahabharat, and Chure Parbat ranges, and to the North from the national boarder "Dasgaza" (10 yard belt) is a plain rectangular land with length longer and breadth shorter and filled with fertile green forest and multiple natural property. It is a region of social diversity community along with Maithili, Bhojpuri, Awadhi, Tharu, Khas Nepali, Urdu, Hindi, Rajbansi, in addition to a dozen languages.[18]

From the authorised programme of the party quoted above, and the policy and programme of the party towards the different race/ethnic organisations affiliated with the party, and the declared policy of those organisations, a full picture of our party stance can be grasped. Even from a cursory glance of the picture, we can conclude that our party's line, regarding the race/caste/ethnic issues of Nepal is not in line with either Marxism-Leninism or with the bourgeois view too. Its position is like a crow lost in the mist. A proper and correct Marxist-Leninist analysis will help comprehend the comparison correctly and explicitly.

---

15 *Political Report and Constitution of Madhesi National Liberation Front*, Approved by Second National Conference, October 9-12, 2007, p. 23.

16 *Political Report and Constitution of Madhesi National Liberation Front*, Approved by Second National Conference, October 9-12, 2007, p. 27.

17 *Political Report and Constitution of Madhesi National Liberation Front*, Approved by Second National Conference, October 9-12, 2007, p. 29.

18 *Political Report and Constitution of Madhesi National Liberation Front*, Approved by Second National Conference, October 9-12, 2007, p. 9.

2
Development Process of Human Community

Marxism-Leninism states that the development of human communities goes through different stages. The most developed and stable community of people, *i.e.* the nation at present, is the result of the development of human society for thousands of years. This special and higher form of human society has reached the present stage by passing through different stages.

The clan, a group of people bound in one society through blood relations, is the oldest form of human society. It means the members of the clan share a common language, a common way of life, a tradition, marriage within the clan, common ownership, and a common economic system based on common distribution, considered as the major characteristics of a clan.

Social and economic needs give birth to the development of human communities. The clan form could not fulfil the advanced socio-economic needs of human development, necessitating new aspects to the form. The advance of human society would be blocked in the absence of the new aspects. So, the tribal stage of human society and the tribal form of community was formed on the basis of one language and a specific territory. Kinsmen, out of blood relations, living together, sharing a common language and a common territory are the characteristics of homogeneous clans living in one place.

The abolition of feudalism and the process of development of capitalism (business, communication and the development of bigger towns), hastened the scattering of races and tribes. Members of different races, tribes or castes, moved away from their ancestral places, from the boundaries of blood relations, language, territory, culture and went to different places in the search of livelihood, study, teaching, and so on. After dispersing into different places, they met people with whom they neither had blood relations nor a shared language, culture, or similarity of thinking. Later, some of the dispersed race and tribe people settled permanently in the new places. Due to socio-economic and political development, class struggle also emerged, and created the condition of the development of a mixed type of community. National relations or nationality developed as the natural consequence of the advancing inter-caste or ethnic mutual relationship after breaking away with racial and indigenous boundary.

The relationship emerging out of this process was not based on special caste and ethnic consideration. According to the historical materialist point of view, a mixed community is a higher form of society than the race, and tribal forms. This process did not advance throughout the world uniformly, and in some countries it gave birth to many nationalities and nations; many nation-states were formed, whereas in other places nations developed within the state boundary. Some nationalities were not strong enough economically due to the interference by the rulers of powerful nations who used the state mechanisms from the very beginning to keep emerging nationalities and nations within the old boundaries by force.

After the international unity of capital in economic, political and cultural spheres, the emerging situation did not allow capitalism to survive just by keeping different nationalities and nations within a state boundary by force. The extension of the state appeared indispensable for capitalism in the latter days, so their states through colonial victories became a basic characteristic of modern capitalism, making an important addition to the national issue. Lenin and Stalin analysed the world situation for a correct solution to the national problem and gave a suitable proletarian view. Not taking the national issue as an internal problem of any particular country, Leninism established it as an international problem to liberate the oppressed people of dependent countries and colonies from the grip of imperialism.

To find the solution of the race/caste/ethnic problems in Nepal, the Marxist-Leninist analysis of the development of human society is useful. Although the English word 'nation' is translated in both Hindi and Nepali as "Jati" or "Rastra", they are not essentially the same in the context of our country. The Nation (Rastra) is a historical category of a certain epoch, of the abolition of feudalism and of the emerging capitalist epoch, which did not exist before capitalism. "Jati" is a broad term, and it means not only nation, the higher form of human society with reference to a country like Nepal, and this term can also be used to mean race/caste/ethnicity.

The major question is not whether the term 'nation' is used to mean race/caste/ethnicity, rather whether in our country human communities have developed into the form of nations, or whether they are race/caste/ethnic communities. The main question is this–do the different race/caste/ethnic communities form a 'nation' on the basis of a common language, territory, economic life and common culture? If the answer is yes, then these communities are nations and there is no difference to use either the term "Rastra" or "Jati". If the answer is negative, then these communities are essentially historical categories of a pre-capitalist epoch, and it is incorrect to use the term 'nation'. According to Marxist-Leninist principles and socialist norms and values established by now, more than a hundred communities of our country cannot be considered nations:

> A nation is not merely a historical category but a historical category belonging to a definite epoch, the epoch of rising capitalism. The process of elimination of feudalism and development of capitalism is at the same time a process of the constitution of people into nations. Such, for instance, was the case in Western Europe. The British, French, Germans, Italians and others were formed into nations at the time of the victorious advance of capitalism and its triumph over feudal disunity.[19]

According to Stalin: *"A nation is a historically constituted, stable community of people, formed on the basis of a common language, territory, economic life, and psychological make-up manifested in a common culture."*

The absence of a single of any of the above four characteristics in any community means the community cannot be a nation. Stalin puts it:

> It must be emphasised that none of the above characteristics taken separately is sufficient to define a nation. More than that, it is sufficient for a single one of these characteristics to be lacking and the nation ceases to be a nation. It is possible to conceive of people possessing a common "national character" who, nevertheless, cannot be said to constitute a single nation if they are economically disunited, inhabit different territories, speak different languages, and so forth ... It is possible to conceive of people with a common territory and economic life who nevertheless would not constitute a single nation because they have no common language and no common "national character." ... Finally, the Norwegians and the Danes speak one language, but they do not constitute a single nation owing to the absence of the other characteristics. ... *It is only when all these characteristics are present together that we have a nation.*[20]

By the Marxist-Leninist standard, our party's definition of Nepal as a multi-nation state, and the various race/caste/ethnic communities as separate nations, is completely a faulty concept. Current data show more than a hundred race/caste/ethnic communities in Nepal. Synthetically, this social composition of the country can best be termed multi-caste, multi-racial rather than multi-nation. Treating various race/caste/ethnic communities as nations and then to struggle for the national liberation movements by our party is diametrically opposed to the Marxist-Leninist view. It negates the basic differences between different stages of the development process of human communities. Furthermore, the development of capitalism and intensification of the class struggle is furthering the process of scattering the different race/caste/ethnic communities. So, different race/caste/ethnic

19 *The Essential Stalin, Major Theoretical Writings 1905-52*, "Marxism and the National Question", Edited and with an introduction by Bruce Franklin, First Indian Edition, January 2010, Rahul Foundation, p. 78.

20 *The Essential Stalin, Major Theoretical Writings 1905-52*, "Marxism and the National Question", Edited and with an introduction by Bruce Franklin, First Indian Edition, January 2010, Rahul Foundation, p. 74.

communities go in the search of livelihood, business, study, teaching and so on to the different parts of the country, where they meet people with whom they neither share blood nor any language or culture closeness. Some of these groups have settled permanently in the new place, strengthening the inter-relationship between the different race/caste/ethnic communities, leading to the creation of a mixed type of settlement. By breaking the race/caste/ethnic boundaries, the development of mixed relationships has developed in the country, forming a single nationality from the different race/caste/ethnic forms of society.

Nepali society is not based on a particular race/caste/ethnic group society, rather it is a mixed relationship made up of the different groups which together comprise the Nepal nation. It represents the highest stage of development in accordance with the historical materialistic world view. This Nepali nationality is advancing to the direction of building Nepal as a mature nation. Having completely neglected the historical materialistic point of view regarding the development process of Nepali nationality and Nepal nation, our party has been trying to establish anarchic thinking such as different race/caste/ethnic communities "to develop in the form of national independence", by treating the different race/caste/ethnic communities as different nations, suggesting that nation and ethnicity are the same in Nepal.

The development of capitalism in the country for several decades has enhanced the economic condition of some race/caste/ethnic communities. It would be wrong to define some of them living in primitive/backward/underdeveloped states. The Newar and Muslim communities have developed into minority group from their previous position, but not into separate nations, just a minority group. Some other indigenous groups (for example the Thakali, Gurung and so on) are also developing in the form of minority group. However, this also does not mean that all the race/caste/ethnic communities necessarily deserve to be separate nations. Some race/caste/ethnic communities develop into nations and out of them, some create their separate nation states, whereas, others remain within the boundary of several nation states. Some other race/caste/ethnic communities either scatter as a result of the development of capitalism and the acuteness of the class struggle and get unified into another nation, or they are extinct in the long run because of the extreme suppression of the ruling class as determined by the historical situations developing in a particular place.

Some scholars wrongly define the Janajati (ethnic communities) as nationalities. Such thinking is unscientific. Nationality is the pre-form of a nation. The nation comes into existence only after the scattering and mixing of different races, castes and indigenous people as a result of the development of capitalism and the acuteness of class struggle. The meaning of nationality comes into existence as the scattering of communities with one common ancestor, blood relation, language, culture, territory, psychological relation so on and the development of mixed relationship between different race/caste/ethnic communities, leading to the creation of a nation. The racial form of human community and nationality have a fundamental difference. Janajatis are characterised by the characteristics of having one ancestor, blood relation, language, culture, geographical region, psychological relation and so on. Nepal's Janajati's are races or tribes, not nations because a nationality comes into existence only after the characteristic features of a race or tribe are scattered.

Our party should correct its view to solve the race/caste/ethnic problem in Nepal. A nation can be defined as "Jati" or "Rastra", but with reference to Nepal, race/caste/ethnic communities are not nations. Likewise, in the context of Nepal use of the term 'indigenous' and 'ethnic' seems to have an ulterior motive. If the ethnic people are automatically indigenous as defined, the two terms can be used as synonymous. By international and national maxims, some castes and ethnic communities may be indigenous, while others may not be. So, the use of indigenous, as 'indigenous ethnic' together should be discarded forthwith.

3
Metaphysical View on the Right of the Self-determination of Nations

Our party defines the right of self-determination proposed by Lenin and Stalin in an absolutist sense as revealed by the documents of the party and the comments from the senior leaders. On the one hand, it has presented itself as the only true follower of Lenin's principle of the right to self-determination of nations, on the other it rejects the essence of Leninism in this regard. Such a non-Leninist position might benefit temporarily the party's organisational aspect and gain cheap popularity, but in the long-term, it will prove to be suicidal. It shows how the view, policy and programme of our party differs with the thought of Lenin and Stalin as discussed below.

The right of self-determination of nations put forward by Lenin and Stalin is not a theory of revolt against a general form of oppression as Comrade Dev Gurung says. Its concern is not with a general form of oppression, rather with a special form of oppression, especially when a nation comes into existence under a certain epoch, the emerging capitalist epoch. Leninism says that only human communities that have developed fully to the level of nation can use the right of self-determination, but no every race/caste/ethnic community is authorised to use this right. It is not named just the right of self-determination, but it is explicitly called the right of the self-determination of nations. Nepal is a multi racial/caste/ethnic country, not an aggregate of multi-nations. Nepal is a single nation, so to talk of the right of self-determination of nations is no more than an infantile "leftist" notion.

A major mistake of our party lies in trying to establish the right of self-determination based on the misunderstanding of the basic difference between other forms of human community and the nation. With reference to Nepal, it is misleading and unscientific to take race/caste/ethnic group and nation as being the same thing, so the issue of self-determination of nations in Nepal is redundant.

Our party accepts the right of self-determination of the oppressed nations with phrases such as; "people of all nationalities get opportunity to build their own future by themselves only under the right of self-determination", "the way Lenin ensured the rights of nations during the formation period of the Soviet Union, learning the same lesson, we have to accept the right of self-determination that Lenin adopted and it should be adoptable to us with reference to Nepal", and "if any oppressed nation revolts against the oppressor nation or state and wants to establish a separate state disintegrating itself, the proletarian must accept it". On the other, the party believes that in the present world situation as well as in the current development of Nepalese society, the national unity and development of Nepal will be achieved by guaranteeing national freedom on the basis of language, culture, population density and economic activities with the right of self-determination, in the form of national and regional autonomy. Under such a situation, it is impossible for our party to give correct leadership to the complex race/caste/ethnic problem, without studying Lenin and Stalin honestly. In some situations, contradiction can arise between the right of self-determination of nations and party's programme is understood by the Marxist-Leninists. What has been accepted theoretically may not enter into the programme of the party. The party can support some particular rights of people, but in its programme it may not be included, or should be included only to a certain limit. So, even after the right of self-determination of nations is accepted, it will not be wrong to propose national, regional autonomous administration for the territorial integrity of the country. Even after the contradiction between the rights of people and the party's programme is solved, it will not resolve the contradictory position of our party related to the right of self-determination of nations.

It seems that the party has understood the contradictory position between this right and the particularity of Nepal. Taking this right in the programme, either the danger of orienting the country towards a disintegration is understood or the right of self-determination is understood only in the form of autonomous regional administration. On the other, the party says, "We have to accept the right of self-determination that Lenin adopted with reference to Nepal. That democratic right means right to be separated, *i.e.* right of making a separate state. This is the highest type of democratic right, so there should be readiness to grant the right to that extent." It seems that the party has grasped the definition of the right of self-determination as given by Lenin and Stalin theoretically. Does the party take the right of self-determination with reference to Nepal in the form of a theoretical right only? Does it regard it as impossible to put into practice? Or is this limitation only a present hurdle, and the various "nationalities" will get that right after socio-economic development, or after the proletariat capture the power? Or is the party trying to strengthen its organisation by stirring up sentiment? So, either the party has to state whether the theory of the right of the self-determination of nations as adopted in Russia (which was a multinational country with colonies and dependent countries) does not apply at all in a multi race/caste/ethnic group country like Nepal under semi(neo)-colonial conditions; or the party should support this right to the extent of political separation. The party, which has been caught midway, must clarify its position.

The position of the party on the right of self-determination of nations is a sign of anarchic deviation, not a creative development of Leninism in the 21st century. Nepal is a single nation and never had been colony, rather it has been a semi-colony for about two hundred years continuously. So, to give full democratic rights under the unitary structure of Nepal to different race/caste/ethnic communities would be the creative application of the Leninist principle of the right of self-determination of nations.

For about one hundred year ago, the right of the self-determination of nations has been defined in two ways. The leaders of the Second International defined the right of the self-determination of nations as the right of cultural, social or economic autonomous administration. Leninism exposed this confusion and extended it to the political arena in the form of the right of nations to establish independent existence. For example, clarifying the basic difference between the leaders of the Second International and Lenin in relation to the right of self-determination of nations, Stalin writes:

> Formerly, the principle of self-determination of nations was usually misinterpreted, and not infrequently it was narrowed down to the idea of the right of nations to autonomy. Certain leaders of the Second International

> even went so far as to turn the right to self-determination into the right to cultural autonomy, *i.e* the right of oppressed nations to have their own cultural institutions, leaving all political power in the hands of the ruling nation. As a consequence, the idea of self-determination stood in danger of being transformed from an instrument for combating annexations into an instrument for justifying them. Now we can say that this confusion has been cleared up. Leninism broadened the conception of self-determination, interpreting it as the right of the oppressed peoples of the dependent countries and colonies to complete secession, as the right of nations to independent existence as state.[21]

Lenin stated: "The right of nations to self-determination implies exclusively the right to independence in the political sense, the right to free political separation from the oppressor nation."[22]

The United Nations Organisation also emphasises the right of self-determination of indigenous people, which is closer to the Second International's view. However, the definition of the United Nations Organisation is fundamentally based on the concept of human rights and the fundamental rights of citizens. It does not encourage the separation of race/caste/ethnic communities internally except those of dependant and oppressed nations under imperialist rule. For example, the declaration of the United Nations Organisation states:

> Indigenous peoples have the right of self-determination. By virtue of that right they freely determine their political status and freely pursue their economic, social and cultural development. ... Indigenous peoples, in exercising their right to self-determination, have the right to autonomy or self-government in matters relating to their internal and local affairs, as well as ways and means for financing their autonomous functions.

Some indigenous organisations are asserting their demand for self-determination under the banner of the United Nations. However, they have not limited themselves to the declaration of the United Nations as revealed by their demand for an independent state. The demand for an independent state by some indigenous organisations under the banner of the United Nations related to the right of the self-determination of nations is a serious matter. These positions orient the country towards a fragmentation, so the demand cannot be supported by imagining that it is a demand under the provision of human rights or for the right of economic, social and cultural development by the indigenous community. Our party needs to clarify its vague position immediately in relation to the right of the

---

21 J. V. Stalin, "Foundation of Leninism", *Problems of Leninism,* Eng. ed., Foreign Language Press, Peking, 1976, p. 68.

22 V. I. Lenin, "Socialist Revolution and Self-determination", *Collected Works*, Eng. ed., Progress Publishers, Moscow, Third Printing, 1977, Vol. 22, p. 146.

self-determination of nations. The party still seems in confusion regarding its wider implication. What is the point of view of it in this regard to the Second International and to the United Nations?

4

National Problem: Problem of Imperialism and Proletarian Revolution

Our party has rejected the essence of principle of the right of the self-determination of nations defined by Lenin and has understood it only as a principle that aids mainly internally oppressed communities. Such an understanding of the right of self-determination of nations is mistaken and incomplete in the epoch of imperialism and proletarian revolution. The problem of creating nation states is the problem of the emerging capitalist epoch. In the course of abolishing feudalism and the development of capitalism, nations came into existence and national struggle for liberation began, and it is the characteristic of the first stage of the development of capitalism. Now, we are not in the first stage of capitalism, but in its mature stage, *i.e.* under imperialism. So, to understand Leninism narrowly only as the principle of the first stage of the national problem is wrong. With the principle of the right of self-determination of nations, Leninism has given a complete solution to the national problem in the developed capitalist era under imperialism. This principle of Lenin has "linked the national question with the question of the colonies." As Stalin says: "The national question was thereby transformed from a particular and internal state problem into a general and international problem, into a world problem of the liberation of the oppressed peoples in the dependent countries and colonies from the yoke of imperialism"[23]

By defining the right of self-determination of nations only as the principle of the internal problem, our party has separated the head from the body. Lenin's exposition of this principle and his latter thinking expressed during the practice of it in Russia after the socialist revolution illustrates that the right of self-determination of nations is the right of dependent countries and the oppressed peoples of colonies to become independent states from imperialism. In the Fourth International Conference held in London by the Second International in 1896, for the first time, the decision was taken in favour of the liberation of the oppressed peoples in the

23 J. V. Stalin, "Foundation of Leninism", *Problems of Leninism*, Eng. ed., Foreign Language Press, Peking, 1976, p. 68.

dependent countries and colonies from the yoke of imperialism. Regarding the right of self-determination of nations, Lenin discussed three types of countries. The first is "the advanced capitalist countries of Western Europe and the United States ... "great" nations oppresses other nations both in the colonies and at home."

The second, with reference to Eastern Europe, Austria, the Balkans and particularly Russia, Lenin says:

> The tasks of the proletariat in these countries, both in completing their bourgeois-democratic reforms, and rendering assistance to the socialist revolution in other countries, cannot be carried out without championing the right of nations to self-determination. The most difficult and most important task in this is to unite the class struggle of the workers of the oppressor nations with that of the workers of the oppressed nations. The third, regarding the colonial countries like China, France, Turkey, and India, he says: Socialists must not only demand the unconditional and immediate liberation of the colonies without compensation–and this demand in its political expression signifies nothing else than the recognition of the right to self-determination.[24]

The essence of the way Lenin has categorised countries with reference to the right of self-determination is nothing more than a declaration for the complete independence of dependent and colonial countries from imperialism. At another place, Lenin discusses the right of self-determination of nations:

> The socialists must explain to the masses that British socialists who do not demand freedom to separate for the colonies and Ireland, German socialists who do not demand freedom to separate for the colonies, the Alsatians, Danes and Poles, and who do not extend their revolutionary propaganda and revolutionary mass activity directly to the sphere of struggle against national oppression, or who do not make use of such incidents as that at Zabern for the broadest illegal propaganda among the proletariat of the oppressor nation, for street demonstrations and revolutionary mass action–Russian socialists who do not demand freedom to separate for Finland, Poland, the Ukraine, etc., etc.–that such socialists act as chauvinists and lackeys of bloodstained and filthy imperialist monarchies and the imperialist bourgeoisie.[25]

About the liberation of colonies, Lenin repeatedly states: "The demand for the liberation of the colonies is nothing more than the recognition of the right of nations to self-determination."[26]

---

24 V. I. Lenin, "Socialist Revolution and Self-determination", *Collected Works*, Eng. ed., Progress Publishers, Moscow, Third Printing, 1977, Vol. 22, pp. 150-51.

25 V. I. Lenin, "Socialist Revolution and Self-determination", *Collected Works*, Eng. ed., Progress Publishers, Moscow, Third Printing, 1977, Vol. 22, pp. 153-54.

26 V. I. Lenin, "The Discussion on Self-determination Summed Up.", *Collected Works*, Eng. ed., Progress Publishers, Moscow, Third Printing, 1977, Vol. 22, p. 337.

Lenin states further:

> The proletariat of the oppressor nations must not confine themselves to general, stereotyped phrases against annexation and in favour of the equality of nations in general, such as any pacifist bourgeois will repeat. The proletariat cannot remain silent on the question of the *frontiers* of a state founded on national oppression, a question so "unpleasant" for the imperialist bourgeoisie. The proletariat must struggle against the enforced retention of oppressed nations within the bounds of the given state, which means that they must fight for the right to self-determination. The proletariat must demand freedom of political separation for the colonies and nations oppressed by "their own" nation.[27]

Lenin spoke on the separation of Norway from Sweden in August 1905 with reference to the right of self-determination. Rosa Luxemburg argued that the separation was wrong, whereas Lenin argued how the way of the separation of Norway was justified. The following facts brought forward by Lenin explain what type of separation of nations Lenin was arguing for:

> To analyse this example in Marxist fashion, we must deal, not with the vices of the awfully terrible "Fracy", but, first, with the concrete historical features of the secession of Norway from Sweden, and secondly, with the tasks which confronted the *proletariat* of both countries in connection with this secession.
>
> The geographic, economic and language ties between Norway and Sweden are as intimate as those between the Great Russians and many other Slav nations. But the union between Norway and Sweden was not a voluntary one, and in dragging in the question of "federation" Rosa Luxemburg was talking at random, simply because she did not know what to say. Norway was *ceded* to Sweden by the monarchs during the Napoleonic wars, against the will of the Norwegians; and the Swedes had to bring troops into Norway to subdue her. ... This example shows us on what grounds cases of the secession of nations are practicable, and actually occur, under modern economic and political relationships, and the *form* secession sometimes assumes under conditions of political freedom and democracy. ... In the question of the self-determination of nations, as in every other question, we are interested, first and foremost, in the self-determination of the proletariat within a given nation.[28]

Lenin explained two aspects as well as two historical tendencies of the national question under imperialism:

> Developing capitalism knows two historical tendencies in the national question. The first is the awakening of national life and national movements, the struggle against all national oppression, and the creation of national

27 V. I. Lenin, "Socialist Revolution and Self-determination", *Collected Works*, Eng. ed., Progress Publishers, Moscow, Third Printing, 1977, Vol. 22, pp. 147-48.

28 V. I. Lenin, "The Right of Nations to Self-determination", *Collected Works*, Eng. ed., Progress Publishers, Moscow, Third Printing, 1977, Vol. 20, pp. 426-28.

states. The second is the development and growing frequency of international intercourse in every form, the break-down of national barriers, the creation of the international unity of capital, of economic life in general, of politics, science, etc. Both tendencies are a universal law of capitalism. The former predominates in the beginning of its development, the latter characterises a mature capitalism that is moving towards its transformation into socialist society.[29]

In reality:

For imperialism these two tendencies represent irreconcilable contradictions; because imperialism cannot exist without exploiting colonies and forcibly retaining them within the framework of the "integral whole"; because imperialism can bring nations together only by means of annexations and colonial conquest, without which imperialism is, generally speaking, inconceivable.[30]

At another place Stalin summarises Lenin on the solution of the national problem:

a) The world is divided into two camps: the camp of a handful of civilised nations, which possesses finance capital and exploit the vast majority of the population of the globe; and the camp of the oppressed and exploited peoples in the colonies and dependent countries, which constitute that majority.

b) The colonies and dependent countries, oppressed and exploited by finance capital, constitute a vast reserve and a very important source of strength for imperialism.

c) The revolutionary struggle of the oppressed peoples in the dependent and colonial countries against imperialism is the only road that leads to their emancipation from oppression and exploitation.

d) The most important colonial and dependent countries have already taken the path of the national liberation movement, which cannot but lead to the crisis of world capitalism.

e) The interests of the proletarian movement in the developed countries and of the national liberation movement in the colonies call for the union of these two forms of the revolutionary movement into a common front against the common enemy, against imperialism.

f) The victory of the working-class in the developed countries and the liberation of the oppressed peoples from the yoke of imperialism are impossible without the formation and consolidation of a common revolutionary front.

---

29 V. I. Lenin, "Critical Remarks on the National Question", *Collected Works*, Eng. ed., Progress Publishers, Moscow, Third Printing, 1977, Vol. 20, p. 27.

30 J. V. Stalin, "Foundation of Leninism", *Problems of Leninism*, Eng. ed., Foreign Language Press, Peking, 1976, p. 75.

g) The formation of a common revolutionary front is impossible unless the proletariat of the oppressor nations renders direct and determined support to the liberation movement of the oppressed peoples against the imperialism of its "own country", for "no nation can be free if it oppresses other nations". (Engels)

h) This support implies the upholding, defence and implementation of the slogan of the right of nations to secession, to independent existence as states.

i) Unless this slogan is implemented, the union and collaboration of nations with a single world economic system, which is the material basis for the victory of world socialism, cannot be brought about.

j) This union can only be voluntary, arising on the basis of mutual confidence and fraternal relations among peoples.[31]

In the era of imperialism and proletarian revolution, Leninism links the national problem to the problem of colonies and proletarian revolution together.

We have almost completed one hundred years from the era of developing capitalism and have come far from a national life and the awakening of a national movement in the struggle against oppression and the main task of the creation of national states. At present, we are not in the era of the development of capital within state boundaries, but in the era of international unity of capital, *i.e.* the era of finance capital. The main perspective of this new situation is not to create a separate state within an existing state boundary of nations, but to make a complete separation of dependent countries, and oppressed peoples from imperialism in the form of an independent state. Still in some parts of the world, there are national problems within state boundaries and their revolutionary solution is necessary.

A favourable situation for the development of race and tribal forms of human community into nationalities and nations prevailed during the emergence of capitalism. Therefore, many nationalities, nations and national movements developed and many national states came into existence. However, when capitalism grew mature; when capitalism developed into an international phenomena; when industrial capital developed in the form of finance capital; when competitive capitalism developed into monopoly capitalism; when capitalism developed as the highest stage of imperialism, the development of human communities was affected. In the period of developing capitalism, the formation of nation states was a progressive and democratic process. In the present epoch of imperialism and proletarian revolution, the free development of nationality and nation states within existing state boundaries is not possible. It has to either develop as an

31 J. V. Stalin, "Foundation of Leninism", *Problems of Leninism*, Eng. ed., Foreign Language Press, Peking, 1976, pp. 73-74.

integral part of the world imperialism or it has to develop as an integral part of the world proletarian revolution. No way in between these two is possible because of a further reason: Nationalities, nations and national movements cannot come into existence independently which are not free from imperialism and Indian expansionism.

The development of nationality, nation and national movements within state boundaries means the abolition of feudalism and the development of capitalism within that boundary. Is the development of capitalism possible independently in a country under imperialism? Not at all. Whatever state boundary within we are talking about, the free development of that state is already dependent, or a neo-colony of imperialism. How can we imagine a nationality, nation and a free national movement within a country that is already dependent, or a neo-colony of imperialism? Consider the case of Nepal: Nepal has been a semi-colony for about two hundred years, first of British-India and then of India after 1947. With this historical background, how can our party conclude that there are dozens of nationalities and nations within Nepal and argue for the right of self-determination with a supposed Leninist meaning? No race/caste/ethnic group has developed into a nation in Nepal, which has been a racial, tribal, minority and caste community. It is ridiculous that our party has given the right to different communities which Lenin gave only to the oppressed people of colonies, dependent countries and nations to be separated as independent states only after becoming free from imperialism.

In reality, the right of self-determination is needed not for the race/caste/ethnic communities of Nepal, but to the Nepal nation itself. Our country is under semi(neo)-colonial domination for about two hundred years, and must be in a position to liberate itself completely from imperialism and Indian expansionism and to have an independent existence, which is the crux of the national problem of Nepal. Only in this sense can we take the national problem of our country, which will be the correct use of the right of self-determination of the nation with reference to Nepal.

5

Federalism with Self-determination: Copying Russia Unscientific

After having put forward how Lenin and Stalin established a federal system with the right of self-determination in the post revolution Russia in 1917, our party has presented the race/caste/ethnic question completely in a distorted way. The main question is not how this issue was addressed in Russia, or how it was addressed in China. Some of us may adopt the Russian solution absolutely and others may adopt the Chinese one. Stalin says the concrete historical condition has to be the "starting point" and the dialectical presentation is "the only correct way" to present the issue as a "key" to the solution of the national question. Criticising those who copied the example of Austria with reference to the national problem, he says:

> And so we have different presentations of the question, different prospects and methods of struggle, different immediate tasks. Is it not clear that, such being the state of affairs, only pedants who "solve" the national question without reference to space and time can think of adopting examples from Austria and of borrowing a programme? ... To repeat: the concrete historical conditions as the starting point, and the dialectical presentation of the question as the only correct way of presenting it–such is the key to solving the national question.[32]

This is perfectly true regarding the race/caste/ethnic problem in our country. Should Nepal adopt the one adopted by Russia or by China or seek a different type of solution to this problem? The answer to this question depends on the concrete national and international historical conditions. Without adopting the Russian or Chinese model, the solution to the national problem should be sought on the basis of historical conditions developing in our country as well as the world. Different economic, political and cultural situations, specifically of different race/caste/ethnic communities in Nepal, different from Russia or China, can be the base for solution of national problems. If dialectical outlook is needed on the question of Nepal's revolution, probably it is more essential regarding race/caste/ethnic problem. As with other issues, while settling the policy and programme in relation to the national or race/caste/ethnic people's issues, Lenin considered an analysis of the concrete conditions to be the soul of Marxism. He writes:

> The categorical requirement of Marxist theory in investigating any social question is that it be examined within *definite* historical limits, and, if it refers to a particular country (*e.g.* the national programme for a given country), that account be taken of the specific features distinguishing that country from others in the same historical epoch.

What type of concrete analysis of concrete situation is needed in relation to national, or the race/caste/ethnic people's problem? A long quote of Lenin gives a satisfactory answer to this question:

> First of all, it implies that a clear distinction must be drawn between the two periods of capitalism, which differ radically from each other as far as the

32 *The Essential Stalin, Major Theoretical Writings 1905-52*, "Marxism and the National Question", Edited and with an introduction by Bruce Franklin, First Indian Edition, January 2010, Rahul Foundation, p. 90.

> national movement is concerned. On the one hand, there is the period of the collapse of feudalism and absolutism, the period of the formation of the bourgeois-democratic society and state, when the national movements for the first time become mass movements and in one way or another draw *all* classes of the population into politics through the press, participation in representative institutions, etc. On the other hand, there is the period of fully formed capitalist states with a long-established constitutional regime and a highly developed antagonism between the proletariat and the bourgeoisie–a period that may be called the eve of capitalism's downfall.
>
> The typical features of the first period are: the awakening of national movements and the drawing of the peasants, the most numerous and the most sluggish section of the population, into these movements, in connection with the struggle for political liberty in general, and for the rights of the nation in particular. Typical features of the second period are: the absence of mass bourgeois-democratic movements and the fact that developed capitalism, in bringing closer together nations that have already been fully drawn into commercial intercourse, and causing them to intermingle to an increasing degree, brings the antagonism between internationally united capital and the international working-class movement into the forefront.
>
> Of course, the two periods are not walled off from each other; they are connected by numerous transitional links, the various countries differing from each other in the rapidity of their national development, in the national make-up and distribution of their population, and so on. There can be no question of the Marxists of any country drawing up their national programme without talking into account all these general historical and concrete state conditions.[33]

Lenin's quote suggests that communist revolutionaries of every country should prepare a programme related to national problem, distinct from Russia or China, as the case may be, due to the specific characteristics of a particular nation, race, caste or ethnic group as well as the concrete and the general historical situation of the country. Our programme regarding the problem of race/caste/ethnicity should not be prepared just by copying the programme of communist revolutionaries in Russia or China; and not ignoring the characteristics of the national issue as well as the concrete and historical conditions. The first measure relating to our race/caste/ethnic question is to search for shoes that fit one's own feet, whereas the second measure is to cut the feet to fit the shoe size. Our party argues that "The way Lenin ensured the rights of nations during the formation period of the Soviet Union, learning the same lesson, we have to accept the right of self-determination that Lenin adopted should be adoptable to us with

33 V. I. Lenin, "The Right of Nations to Self-determination", *Collected Works*, Eng. ed., Progress Publishers, Moscow, Third Printing, 1977, Vol. 20, pp. 400-401.

reference to Nepal" is the same as cutting one's own feet so as to fit the shoe size.

Nepal is neither a country with a multinational structure, nor is it an imperialist country. Lenin and Stalin adopted a policy to solve the national and colonial problem after the socialist revolution in Russia. However, ours is a multi-caste, multi-religious and multi-cultural country under a unitary administration for centuries. No race/caste/ethnic group is in the majority and a mixed settlement of society is developing fast. So, to accept the right of self-determination that Lenin adopted in Russia, with reference to a national and dependent position under semi(neo)-colonial domination, in a country such as ours does not correspond to the objective reality. After differentiating Nepal from China on the question of race/caste/ethnic communities, and observing the total phenomenon, it is not correct to adopt the way used in China to solve Nepal's problems.

Considering the specific social structure, the need for our race/caste/ethnic issue is not a federation with the right of self-determination. Providing local autonomy under the unitary structure is the need of the hour. Nepal has its own order of historical development of race/caste/ethnic communities. To copy the policy and programme adopted in relation to countries colonised by the Russian imperialism under the leadership of the communist party, in the period of the proletarian dictatorship after the socialist revolution, it is wrong to adopt so in the semi-feudal and semi(neo)-colonial condition of Nepal.

The right of self-determination, federation, and regional autonomy are not good or bad in themselves as their character as good or bad is not an absolute, but a relative one. In respect of their relation with the concrete condition, two things must always be kept in mind in this regard. Firstly, we are talking in relation to a solution in a semi(neo)-colonial country, and not in an imperialist country. Our country is neither a summation of multi-nations, nor have we made countries dependent or colonies. Rather, we ourselves have been a semi-colony for centuries. Our social structure is a summation of multi-racial/caste/ethnic groups, languages, religions and cultures. Secondly, we are not seeking a solution to this problem after the success of a socialist revolution in an imperialist country like Russia, or after the success of the new democratic revolution in a colonial, semi-colonial country under the leadership of communist party with a overwhelming majority (96%) of one race (Han), as in China. Rather we are seeking the solution to the problem in the context of an alliance with the comprador-bureaucratic political parties such as the Nepali Congress, the neo-bourgeois Communist Party of Nepal(UML), along with other parliamentary forces after the election of the constituent assembly and the elimination of the 239 -year-old monarchy.

The changes that we have recently achieved have a great political importance, and it can be the opportunity for the formation of a free, sovereign and developed Nepal. However, in spite of these achievements and opportunities, no change has been marked in the socio-economic system of our country. The neo-colonial domination also still exists in our country. Internally, feudal production is as it was in the past. On the basis of some changes merely in the superstructure, the hope of changing both aspects–base and superstructure–under the same old socio-economic base will prove to be a mistake. So, copying the solution adopted by Russia for our national problem is wrong.

6
Lenin and Stalin's View on Federation with Self-determination Provision: A Product of Historical Situation

After preparing the model of the restructuring of Nepal, our party has advocated for the federation with the right of self-determination to nations as put forward by Lenin, whose policy of federation with the right of the self-determination of nations was a natural product of the historical situation of Russia at that time. Lenin is consistent in his dialectical view in relation to a federation. Whether the federation or the federation with the right of self-determination, he supports or opposes them depending on the analysis of the concrete condition. The absolute view is contrary to Leninism.

Before the October Revolution, Lenin was not mainly in favour of a federation of state for Russia. At that time, he looked at the problem with the prospect of a bourgeois-democratic revolution. He maintained that the federation of bourgeois republics could not solve the national problem, and his policy of not supporting the idea of a federation was based on the whole class analysis of Russia. At that time, in many nations and dependent countries, and especially in rural and distant regions, the number of proletarians was quite low and the struggle for the proletarian class could not take a clear shape. As Russia was an imperialist country as well, the proletarian struggle was urban centred. The proletariat had not conducted and extended the class struggle in rural areas as was the case in China. In that situation, to support a federation meant to support the formation of the bourgeois-nation state, weakening the unified revolutionary movement of all working-classes in the country. So, Lenin emphasised on leading the movement with the unified revolutionary initiative of the working-class people basing on the democratic norms and values within the unitary system.

In spite of such thinking about federation for Russia at that time, he supported federation for some other countries, and gave consent to the federation between England and Ireland as forwarded by Marx. Likewise, in 1912, Lenin observed that the slogan of a Balkan Federal Republic demanded by workers of Balkan to be a consistent with "democratic solution of the national problems in the Balkans."[34] Lenin further refined and sharpened his thinking in relation to the colonial and national issue from the lessons of the First World War, in an imperialist country that had made other countries its colonies and where revolution was building up. However, it was only after the October Socialist Revolution that Lenin brought forward clearly the path to a federation with the right of self-determination in relation to finding a solution to national and colonial problems in Russia. Stalin expresses rightly: "Conditions, like everything else, change, and a decision which is correct at one particular time may prove to be entirely unsuitable at another."[35]

Lenin put forward the proposal of a federal system with the right of self-determination of nations in Russia in a new and completely changed situation after the First World War, the Great Socialist Revolution and the dictatorship of the proletariat. In January 1918, he says: "The new system of the socialist Soviet Republic, as a federation of free republics of the different nations inhabiting Russia, has been finally accepted in this country in the sphere of domestic politics."[36] Russia at that time, was a capitalist country with strong feudal characteristics, but backward compared to Western Europe, despite being an imperialist country with colonies. At that time, Russia had to solve national as well as colonial problems. After the socialist revolution took place in an imperialist country, the new government, in addition to the question of nationality, also had to face the problem of countries made dependent by it in the past.

The communist party faced danger from national and international capitalists as well as all regressive elements thrown up by the revolution to excite different nationalities and colonies captured in the Czarist period against the Soviet power. In that situation, to find a correct solution to the national and colonial problem was a great task because even a slight mistake by the party could spoil the attempts to create a new social order. Turning

34 V. I. Lenin "A New Chapter of World History" *Collected Works*, Eng. ed., Progress Publishers, Moscow, Fifth Printing, 1978, Vol. 18, p. 368.

35 *The Essential Stalin, Major Theoretical Writings 1905-52*, "Marxism and the National Question", Edited and with an introduction by Bruce Franklin, First Indian Edition, January 2010, Rahul Foundation, p. 85.

36 V. I. Lenin, "Third All-Russia Congress of Soviets", *Collected Works*, Eng. ed., Progress Publishers, Moscow, Third Printing, 1977, Vol. 26, p. 479.

that challenge into an opportunity, the communist party under the leadership of Lenin and Stalin adopted a strategy of making all nations and colonies true partners of the proletarian struggle for strengthening the advancement of socialism by way of giving the right to self-determination with a real meaning. Not just talking of handing over of power, Lenin declared the right of settling the form of state management voluntarily by themselves for all the nations and colonies under the former Russian empire.

The case of equal right of all nations is only a show for the bourgeoisie, just like the showing of teeth by the elephant. Only a mentally imbalanced person can seriously think of the liberation of colonies possible under the leadership of capitalist ruling class. The right of self-determination was allowed after the revolution, and the colonies could participate in the Soviet Union voluntarily as a different state from it or be a free country as before. It was only by making this type of the highest democratic right available to nations within Russia and countries that were made colonies by the Russian empire, it became possible to found the first proletarian state power and get it strengthened even with the imperialist enclosure in the situation of civil war instigated by the domestic reactionaries and imperialists. Stalin states:

> The revolution would not have been victorious in Russia, and Kolchak and Denikin would not have been crushed, had not the Russian proletariat enjoyed the sympathy and support of the oppressed peoples of the former Russian Empire. But to win the sympathy and support of these peoples it had first of all to break the fetters of Russian imperialism and free these peoples from the yoke of national oppression.
>
> Without this, it would have been impossible to consolidate Soviet power, to implant real internationalism and to create that remarkable organisation for the collaboration of peoples which is called the Union of Soviet Socialist Republics.[37]

In January 1918, the declaration of the federation of liberated republics of different nations into the socialist Soviet Republic by Lenin was the first and the most significant step of the great campaign to shatter the chains of imperialism. At that time, the stability of the socialist state and the strengthening of it was directly linked with the victory over the nations and countries made dependent beforehand. In the situation of the revolutionary Russian proletarian, being a part of former oppressor Russia, the strengthening of socialism among the workers and peasants of all the nations and countries made colonies beforehand was not possible without creating a new faith and new base in the workers of different nationalities towards the representatives of the ruling nation. It was necessary to deal with the national attitude of all nations and colonies

37 J. V. Stalin, "Foundation of Leninism", *Problems of Leninism*, Eng. ed., Foreign Language Press, Peking, 1976, p. 76.

within Russian boundaries very carefully. To solve this problem, Lenin adopted the policy of a federation with the right of self-determination, and it became possible to answer the joint intervention of imperialists and the civil war imposed by internal reactionary elements through a united Soviet force after the revolution.

After the October Socialist Revolution, reactionaries of the world had nursed a strategy to excite the internal capitalist class and the nations of imperialist Russia and dependent countries against socialism with the demand for a separate state. Soon after the revolution, Lenin repeatedly warned that there was a serious danger that the capitalist class and imperialism could lead a federation with the right of separation to reunite with capitalism in one way or another. Immediately after the revolution, internal and external reactionary elements, attempting to cause a split in the people and finish off Soviet power could be defeated only through a joint action of the working people of all the nations and dependent countries. With a correct national and colonial policy of the Bolshevik Communist Party under the leadership of Lenin and Stalin, the capitalist "national" movements' efforts to separate from the Soviet Union were foiled effectively.

Lenin enacted the policy of a federation with the right of self-determination to solve the national and colonial problem of Russia. Either Lenin had to give an opportunity in relation to the nations that were made colonies in the past and those living within Russia to choose their future independently; or continue the colonial policy of the Czar. He chose the first by giving the nations the right of self-determination and earned the infinite admiration, faith and support from the nationalities and the previous colonies for the Russian proletarian and the October Socialist Revolution. Lenin says himself:

> The revolution has won, and those who have won are allied with us in a mighty revolutionary federation. We do not rule by dividing, as ancient Rome's harsh maxim required, but by uniting all the working people with the unbreakable bonds of living interests and a sense of class. This our union, our new state is sounder than power based on violence which keeps artificial state entities hammered together with lies and bayonets in the way the imperialists want them. ... There is the basis of our federation and I am profoundly convinced that more and more diverse federations of free nations will group themselves around revolutionary Russia. This federation is invincible and will grow quite freely, without the help of lies or bayonets. The laws and the state system which we are creating over here are the best convinced of its invincibility.[38]

38 V. I. Lenin, "Third All-Russia Congress of Soviets", *Collected Works*, Eng. ed., Progress Publishers, Moscow, Third Printing, 1977, Vol. 26, pp. 480-81.

This step established that pre-revolutionary Russian imperialism was committing injustice to the oppressed nations and colonies and that the national and colonial policy of the Bolshevik Communist Party was correct. As a result, they joined the Soviet Union, reaching the conclusion that unless they united with the Russian proletarian class and with the Soviet power, it would not be possible to attain a genuine freedom. Had Lenin not adopted this type of policy on the national and colonial problem, there could not have been the formation of the vast Socialist Soviet Union. World imperialism and the internal capitalist class were plotting to separate nation states by stirring up the oppressed nations under the yoke of Russian imperialism. These types of states were going to be parts of imperialism, not of socialism. As that type of regressive outcome was certain, adopting a federal system with the right of self-determination by Lenin was far sighted and a true Marxist political line as verified by the given examples.

The communists of Turkmenistan, Estonia, Latvia, Azerbaijan and Tatar did not formulate the slogan of establishing a sovereign national republic. As the question of autonomy was not raised in the Third Congress of Turkmenistan Soviet in 1917 by the Turkmenistani Bolsheviks, the bourgeois-nationalist elements established a counter-revolutionary government. However, later, in 1918, the Bolsheviks rectified their mistakes and declared the autonomy of Turkmenistan. The attempt to retain an anti-revolutionary government by bourgeois nationalist elements failed thereby too.

Lenin gave great emphasis on the right of self-determination in relation to the nations of Central Asia. The main course of this was the colonial policy of the Czarist government in those nations. With reference to the policy of the Czarist government, because of the declaration of Lenin on giving the right of self-determination to those nations, the communists gained great support and it weakened the influence of the local bourgeois capitalists, reactionary Islamic mullahs and the bourgeois intellectuals who were against the new socialist state. Soon after the revolution, the imperialists helped anti-revolutionary forces in Don, Cuban and around the Terek River and in the regions of Astrakhan, the Urals and Northern Caucasia. Likewise, internal and external regressive forces tried to create bourgeois-nationalist governments in Crimea, Bessarabidha and Ukraine. American, British, French and German imperialists helped the counter-revolutionary bourgeois class to stay in power in regions around the Caucasus where proletarian power was not established during the period of revolution. The comment of Lenin is important in relation to this: "Independence of Georgia has become a sheer fraud. In actual fact it amounts to the occupation and complete seizure of Georgia by the

German imperialists, an alliance of German bayonets with the Menshevik government against the Bolshevik workers and peasants."[39]

During the First World War, the bourgeois revolution of February and after up to the October Socialist Revolution, the different nationalities and colonies had been separated from one another. In that situation, although the proletarian class had captured power there with the people's armed insurrection, its power in some nations was quite weak. Contact between the proletarian centre and the outer rural areas was broken. The proletarian class concentrated on capturing the central power. In the regions where the proletarian class was not powerful, reactionary elements in the country and international imperialism were active. It was activating its activities in the centre itself and in the outskirts to destroy the new socialist power. In that situation, it was necessary to adopt the measures that could link the separated nationalities and former colonies with one thread. In reality, the policy of the Bolshevik Communist Party of the federation of Soviet Republics with the right to self-determination played a historical role in unifying the nations and former colonies from the bottom up.

With the October Revolution, the national movement developed in Russia and the Czarist government became quite weak during the First World War. The position of the Czarist government weakened considerably. So, the hold of the central government loosened over the colonies seized in the past and the nationalities within Russia itself. In that situation, the pre-revolutionary and pre-First World War policy of Lenin to give autonomy under the structure of a whole state would not be practical for socialism. Having understood this special situation of Russia, Lenin opted for the federal system. In fact, having brought forward the federation with the right of self-determination, in relation to nations and dependent and colonies under Russia, the Bolshevik Communist Party verified practically that the proletarians of Russia and Soviet power would not tolerate any type of oppression on the oppressed nations and former colonies. Had it not been done, so confusion would have lingered whether the new power meant to eliminate oppression or impose colonialism in new form; and then the bourgeois-nationalists in cooperation with international imperialism would take the leadership of the "national liberation movement" developed on the basis of that confusion.

The view of the previously oppressed nationalities and colonies towards the proletarian class of the previous ruling nation would be of great importance to strengthen socialism. As Russia was a ruling and oppressor nation, even after the revolution, other nationalities and colonies looked at

39 V. I. Lenin, "Session of All-Russia C.E.C., July 29, 1918", *Collected Works*, Eng. ed., Progress Publishers, Moscow, Third Printing, 1981, Vol. 28, p. 22.

it and understood the Russian nation in the form of an oppressor, although within the Russian nation, there was a class in existence whose only aim was to end exploitation and oppression of man by man and nation by nation. That class is the revolutionary proletarian class, the product of modern capitalism. Keeping the target in sight, this class led the October Socialist Revolution to success. It was necessary for the Russian proletarian class of the previous ruling nation to make clear to other nationalities its intention. This could not be fulfilled by ordinances from above. The National and Colonial policy of the Bolshevik Communist Party, under the leadership of Lenin, fulfilled that historical responsibility.

7
Republican Unitary State: A Necessity of Historical Development

Let us discuss the federation with the right of self-determination that our party has brought forward in Nepal. Our party's main condition is "to end unitary structure of the state and restructure it into federal structure."[40] Equally, it claims that the thinking of "national (actually racial –Yogendra) and regional identity" is "more scientific and practical" for this. On this very "scientific and practical" "foundation" the party has proposed Seti-Mahakali and Mechi-Karnali federal states on regional grounds, and Magarat, Tharuwan, Tamuwan, Newa, Tamsaling, Kirat, Limbuwan, Kochila and Madhes federal states on "national" (actually racial–Yogendra) grounds. In Madhes, Mithila, Bhojpura and Awadh sub-states are proposed on the basis of language. The *Manifesto of the Communist Party of Nepal (Maoist) for the Election of the Constituent Assembly*, says "having changed the unitary structure of the state, to restructure into federal model" should be taken as "the most important condition". Such a statement is unscientific and objectionable too. Nepal is a semi(neo)-colonial and semi-feudal country for centuries. Because of centralised feudal rule, working people and different race/caste/ethnic communities have been victimised, whereas the world imperialism and Indian expansionism have inflicted injustice and suppression upon the whole nation. The different race/caste/ethnic communities of our country have been establishing closer contact in their struggle against feudalism and world imperialism of then British-India and at present Indian expansionism. We found the highest development of this struggle during the people's great war, run for ten years under the leadership of our party. In that period, all race/caste/ethnic communities participated actively in a unified way with an

40 *Manifesto of the Communist Party of Nepal (Maoist) for the Election of the Constituent Assembly*, p. 20.

encouraging presence of women and men in the People's Liberation Army. The higher presence of men and women of different race/caste/ethnic communities, not only in the People's Liberation Army, but in the legislative parliament and in the present constituent assembly shows the affinity among the different race/caste/ethnic communities. The special characteristic of our historical development has created a situation for cooperation between different race/caste/ethnic communities, so the federal system with the right of self-determination will create conflict between race/caste/ethnic group generating a favourable soil to the world imperialism and the Indian expansionism.

With reference to the specific historical development, the new Nepal should not be a union of various entities, rather it should be a democratic unitary state. It would be suicidal to seek a solution to this problem in any other way. The view that the country should be divided into federal states has come like a tidal wave. Our party, as well as other big political parties, state leaders, and most of the intellectuals, have not spoken against the powerful wave. If somebody speaks against the federal system, he/she is projected as reactionary or monarchist by the enthusiasts of a federation. Whether the federal or unitary systems are applicable is decided by the special condition of the concerned country. Not all the countries with a federal system are better, and not all countries with a unitary system are worse.

Out of 192 member nations of the United Nations Organisation, 28 countries have a federal system. They are: Argentina, Australia, Austria, Belau, Belgium, Bosnia-Herzegovina, Canada, Comoros, Democratic Republic Congo, Ethiopia, Germany, India, Iraq, Malaysia, Mexico, Micronesia, Nigeria, Pakistan, Russia, Saint Kitts, South Africa, Spain, Sudan, Switzerland, United Arab Emirates, USA and Venezuela. By studying these countries listed as federal, we know that all those countries are not adhering to the norms and values of democracy. "Some unitary countries are more decentralised in practice than some federations." "In fact, some unitary countries have developed more substantial powers to their constituent units than have some federations:"[41] The provision of emergency and no provision for the autonomy of states in countries like India, Pakistan, Nigeria, Argentina, Russia are examples of this. In the USA, Mexico, Brazil, Nigeria and Spain, the right to self-determination, *i.e.* to be separated and make national states is not allowed constitutionally.

Contrary to this, in some unitary countries, different nationalities and race/caste/ethnic communities and regions enjoy more democratic rights than in federal ones. Some countries with the federal system are functioning well, whereas some are facing crisis. Likewise, in some countries with a

41 George Anderson, *Federation: An Introduction*, Oxford University Press, 2008, pp. 5-6.

unitary system, different race/caste/ethnic communities have got more democracy in practice. The economic development of some race/cast and regions is found balanced one whereas some are in a critical position and are facing huge problems. So, both types of systems are not of absolute nature, but just relative. Those countries with the unitary or federal system matching the concrete condition of their respective historical development are in good condition. Those countries not matching the concrete conditions of their respective historical development, and the countries which have copied others' system under pressure, are facing vicious crisis too.

Historical facts reveal that federal state is possible only in special historical conditions, and this is not a simple device of either formation or dissolution of nation in the present context. In future, when world imperialism gets weaker and the socialist camp gets stronger, a voluntary federal system will prove to be a strong medium for the dissolution of the state. Now, to think like this is not to understand the ABC of Marxism about the state. Let us see a related record presented by history.

Firstly, the movement for the formation of a federal state is launched if free states are voluntarily involved in the federation. Some states try to make the association and go for a bigger unity for collective defence and welfare, to be safe from the intervention of some other powerful nations. When some countries feel the danger of imperialist intervention on them, they join a federation. Marxism supports such a demand firmly. Lenin's view, in the pre-First World War situation, in relation to the demand of Balkan states is worth mentioning. To stop the advance of European imperialism and Russian world power, Lenin emphasised on the federation of Balkan states (including Turkey) to be an adequate solution to the immediate problems. Secondly, oppressed nationalities and colonies, with the hope of the new social system to be established after revolution opt for a federal system with the right of self-determination. The only example of this is the Soviet Republic at the time of Lenin and Stalin. Thirdly, countries with the unitary system where the federal system is to be established while restructuring the state. The countries adopting the federal system of that type had a unitary system, but they did not have a strong centre.

Let us take the example of India. During the British-India period, India had a unitary state, with many oppressed nations and colonies. First, they had their separate policies and rules and an undeclared unity and struggle between them. Second, from a geographical point of view, the unified India was vast. Third, it had a long and painful history of racial and linguistic duel. It was necessary to stop a split in a unified country by restructuring the country into separate federal states on the basis of language/race/caste/ethnicity and region. In that situation, the country under the unitary state system itself could be a hindrance for retaining the previous position, so a federal system was a necessity there.

None of the characteristics instrumental in establishing a federal system in other countries exist in Nepal. There is no history of free countries inside Nepal, with a unitary state for centuries. The vision of a federal Nepal that our party has brought forward can neither be a federal state formed voluntarily by free states nor can it be a federal state with the right of self-determination of oppressed nations and colonies. It is neither a country without a single centre nor is it a vast area that creates difficulties to pay attention directly to all parts of the country. It does not have a history of caste or linguistic rivalry either. It is also not a country where a situation is now required to move into a federal system as the final measure to save the country from a split, not being able to solve problems under a unitary system.

If our party's line regarding the race/caste/ethnic problem in Nepal remains the same and the penetration of world imperialism and Indian expansionism and I/NGO continues for some more years, a situation may arise in our country forcing us to choose the federal system as the only option to save country's territorial integration. But, this dreadful situation does not exist now. Nepal is a medium size country, surviving continuously as a semi(neo)-colonial, semi-feudal country under a feudal unitary monarchy for centuries. From the point of view of the base of development, it is weak and whatever base of development exists is centred in the capital and in some towns. We have a history of a strong hold of a strong centre and a single Nepali nationality with multi-racial communities living in harmony. Equally, the development of national capitalism is at a low level and the country is under the yoke of comprador and bureaucratic capitalism. If we seriously considered these fundamental characteristics of Nepal, the federal state system is not viable from any angle.

Regarding this matter, the *Manifesto of the Communist Party of Nepal (Maoist) for the Election of the Constituent Assembly* accepts the question of re-structuring the federal state system as a "difficulty". For example, it says: "As with us, free states have not been involved into the federation voluntarily, a unitary state is being restructured into federal states, and there can be some difficulty to digest this policy and programme to begin with."

The question of "difficulty" that the *Manifesto of the Communist Party of Nepal (Maoist) for the Election of the Constituent Assembly* discusses is limited to the subjective aspect, whereas the main base and aspect of the "difficulty" is the objective aspect, *i.e.* the special socio-economic condition of Nepal. If the special condition of the country would match the restructure to a federal state system, victory over the problem of the question of understanding would be easy. Restructuring the state into a federation system is not a practical and wise step in view of the present socio-economic condition of Nepal which has been a unitary state for centuries. The policy and programme of our party to restructure the country into a federal state will be unproductive for national independence, sovereignty and territorial integrity. So, our party must instantly scrap the present line, and it should follow the policy and programme in a true democratic manner, *i.e.* being based on the principle of democratic norms and values. The state should be restructured under a unitary state system alone as demanded by the objective condition.

The main thing required for different race/caste/ethnic communities and different linguistic groups is not a federal state. It is not the unitary state system that has irritated different race/caste/ethnic communities. It is not an artificial federation, rather a full democratic right they need. In fact, as Stalin says: "*Equal rights of nations in all forms (language, schools, etc.) is an essential element* in the solution of the national question."[42]

Two main things are mainly responsible for the oppression of different race/caste/ethnic communities: The first is a feudal-centred bureaucratic system that has existed in the country for long. Such a structure has affected the use of their mother tongue, getting education in the mother tongue, freedoms of migration and so on. As a result, the survival of some race/caste/ethnic communities' culture seems in crisis as some of their languages and cultures have vanished. For centuries, they have been the victims of discrimination of the ruling class and their representatives. The second is that the country has been a semi-colony for two hundred years. Nepal has been under the torture of colonial slavery of British-India after the Sugauli Treaty of 1816 and India after 1947. The country is a ground downed by neo-colonial exploitation and oppression of world imperialism and its international agencies such as the World Bank, International Monetary Fund, World Trade Organisation and Asian Development Bank. In this background, overall change and the formation of a sovereign Nepal is the basic solution to the racial/ethnic/indigenous problem of the country.

The matter is presented as if the above problem will have to be solved by restructuring the unitary state into a federal state, which cannot guarantee automatic democratisation of the country. Full democratisation of the country can be either within the unitary or federal state system. It depends on some other factors and the form of relations of production, form of ownership over the instruments and the means of production and essence of state power. Basic changes such as full democratisation mean the end of feudal production-relations and establishment of a new type

42 *The Essential Stalin, Major Theoretical Writings 1905-52*, "Marxism and the National Question", Edited and with an introduction by Bruce Franklin, First Indian Edition, January 2010, Rahul Foundation, p. 93.

of socialism-oriented capitalist production relation; end of the private ownership system on the instruments and the means of production; establishment of collective and state ownership system oriented to public ownership system; and state power under the leadership of the proletariat based on cooperation of the peasant and all patriotic elements.

The Nepalese people have gained significant success over the years from the political point of view. Yet, there has been no change in the basic characteristics of the country as the feudal production relation is intact. No change has taken place in the previous ownership system over the instruments and the means of production. Although the government has been formed under the leadership of the CPN(Maoist), it consists of political representatives of feudal, comprador and bureaucratic capitalism as well. The structure of army, police, judiciary and bureaucracy remains almost unchanged. In this light, a unitary state converting into a federal state does not mean the oppressed and exploited as well as the backward race/caste/ethnic communities will enjoy democratic rights in real terms.

Our achievements over the years have been insufficient to bring even slight changes in the external factors. The people's movement of 2006 against the despotic step of the king; the election of the constituent assembly; the end of the monarchy and establishment of the republic were not organs of a national liberation movement of Nepal. The people's movement of 2005/06 sidelined Nepal's liberation from imperialism and the Indian expansionism, a basic weakness of the movement. It was launched internally, with the aid of the comprador capitalist class and its political representatives like the Nepali Congress, and the neo-bourgeois class and its political representative the CPN(UML) and with the external mediation of the ruling circle from a country that has been colonising Nepal for centuries, so it was just natural for such a movement to completely ignore the question of liberating the country from the world imperialism and the Indian expansionism. Was it just a coincidence or is there more to the fact that movements for the end of the Rana regime and the monarchy were both mediated by the Indian rulers? Completely ignoring this reality, the solution of the national problem of Nepal is not possible. Without seeking independence from imperialism and Indian expansionism, our party has presented "restructuring of the unitary state into a federal state" as a magic wand that will solve all problems.

Until the modernisation of agriculture, which forms the backbone of the Nepalese economy, the solution of the present problem of race/caste/ethnic people is not possible. The backward condition of agriculture affects the largely backward race/caste/ethnic communities. It is equally applicable to industry, mechanisation of agricultural and trade. As a result of the strong hold of comprador and bureaucratic capitalism in the Nepalese economy, national industry, mechanisation of agricultural and trade have not developed. To sum up, the formation of our own independent national economy is the most vital and important thing for Nepal. The most negative effect of this condition and situation of the economy is felt, especially by backward race/caste/ethnic communities. Feudal ownership, production and distribution along with colonial relations existing in the country for centuries are equally responsible for the backward condition of different race/caste/ethnic communities.

It is wrong to present the question in the form that the racial, ethnic and indigenous problem will automatically be solved after introducing a federal state. If the federal restructuring of the state is carried out under colonial relations, the supposed solution of these problems of the country will be a far cry. Rather, it will strengthen colonial domination hugely. The ability of all race/caste/ethnic communities to enjoy democracy is linked with an independent character of the country as only the people of a sovereign country enjoy available democratic rights. A semi(neo)-colonial country cannot provide full democratic rights to its citizens. For any government that seeks to give its citizens democratic rights through its own ideals, norms and values, the neo-colonial form of colonialism stands as an obstacle. As long as Nepal is dependent on world imperialism and Indian expansionism, the people cannot enjoy their rights in whatever state system-unitary or federal. So, the unitary state system with the local autonomous administration, after ending the feudal-centralised and bureaucratic unitary state structure of Nepal, is the most appropriate system, and not the federal state system. At least, democratic unitary state structure does not hasten the process of disintegration of a country in the liberation struggle against world imperialism and Indian expansionism, and it makes different race/caste/ethnic communities aware of their common responsibility and fate too.

8
Going Against the Tide of Racism: Marxist-Leninist Principle

At present, a race/caste/ethnic epidemic is on the rise in the county and the thinking of federalism has become a powerful tide. Our party leaders and most of intellectuals have failed to go against the tide, but any slackness in this regard can endanger the communist movement and future of the country too. True Marxist-Leninists need to launch an uncompromising struggle against such an epidemic. Going against this tide is the duty of Marxist-Leninists as exemplified by history.

Continuing the unitary structure of the state on a democratic basis and restructuring the state on a federal structure are two different models. Our model of state restructuring should be guided by the need of forging unity of the working-class from different race/caste/ethnic groups for the class struggle that pushes the new democratic revolution towards socialism. At present, having abandoned the line of armed struggle, in the specific political condition of the country, our party is heading to the peaceful development of revolution. The meaning and aim of advancing along the line of 'peaceful development of revolution' is to move towards completing the remaining tasks of revolution. Adopting a peaceful line of revolution and using reactionary organisations and their representation are two different things. They are the products of two different circumstances. In the first, we are moving towards accomplishing the revolution, whereas in the second we are preparing the base for revolution with full realisation of the unfavourable situation at present. Under these two political lines, forms of tactics and struggle will also be different.

Our party's proposal is not a proletarian, rather it is bourgeois tactics as it neglects the task of completing the revolution and strengthening the new proletarian state. It feeds the poisonous weeds of racism with manure and creates the conditions for aborting the revolution. Our party's proposed "solution" to the race/caste/ethnic problem at a time when revolution was about to be completed under its own leadership to the extent of weakening the future proletarian power is like smashing one's own's leg with an axe. It is an irony that our party has forwarded a proposal that our internal and external enemies would like to propose either to obstruct the completion of revolution or to prevent it from getting stronger and sustainable.

The development of capitalism, the people's movement of decades and the ten-year long people's great war have intensified and broadened the class struggle in the country, bringing it to the surface. In the case of the higher class struggle, the federal restructuring of the state on a race/caste/ethnic basis weakens the broad and unified class struggle, and opens the gate for the formation of race/caste/ethnic identity based organisations. The responsibility for communists of Nepal is to organise the working-class of Nepal in one organisation, *i.e.* to form and strengthen one communist party at a national level. With the policy and programme of our party for the federal restructuring of the state on the basis of race/caste/ethnicity, the proletarian responsibility has become 'outdated' and the party has opened the gate for race/ caste based organisations. In the future, it would be no surprise if not only worker and peasant organisations, but also communist parties start organising in every state on the basis of a particular race/caste/ethnic community. The restructuring of the federal model on a race/caste/ethnic basis prepares the ground for the division of the different race/

caste/ethnic communities, creating a rift in the unified communist party and then leading into separate race/caste-state communist parties fragmented. As a result, the worker and peasant movements will also get fragmented. Furthermore, the strong communist movement at present nationally, and the strong unified class movement that exists now will get divided into diverse race/cast/ethnic identity based movements. The advancement of our party in this direction, *i.e.* towards a federal restructuring of the state on the race/caste/ethnic basis means giving up the proletarian stand on race/caste/ethnicity and the advancement towards socialism. This is how the party has distorted Marxism-Leninism-Mao Tse-tung Thought to suit the racial agenda.

The demarcation of state boundaries according to race/caste identity will promote the formation of organisations based on race/caste/ethnic identity, which will divide the total population on a race/caste/ethnic basis, including working-class people belonging to different race/caste/ethnic communities. As a result, all-Nepal level organisations of workers, peasants, intellectuals, students and women will start forming on the basis of race/caste/ethnic identity in the future.

Such a development is completely opposed to the Marxist-Leninist proletarian class responsibility to unify the working people and oppressed classes of all race/caste/ethnic communities into a single collective body within a single and unified communist party. Advocates of the federal system think that the Marxist-Leninist type of (central party structure of working-class) party organisation negates the broad autonomy of different race/caste/ ethnic groups. They should not feel worried that such a situation will arise in the context of the end of the feudal-centralised and bureaucratic unitary system when the party structure based is found on democratic norms and values. The central party structure of labouring (toiling) masses will be in favour of them, and it will seek a Marxist-Leninist solution to racial issues too. Illuminating the importance and role of this type of organisation of workers formed on the basis of internationalism, Stalin writes:

> The type of organisation influences not only practical work. It stamps an indelible impress on the whole mental life of the worker. The worker lives the life of his organisation, which stimulates his intellectual growth and educates him. And thus, acting within his organisation and continually meeting there comrades from other nationalities, and side by side with them waging a common struggle under the leadership of a common collective body, he becomes deeply imbued with the idea that workers are *primarily* members of one class family, members of the united army of socialism. And this cannot but have a tremendous educational value for large sections of the working-class. Therefore, the international type of organisation serves as a school of fraternal sentiments and is a tremendous agitational factor on behalf of

internationalism. But this is not the case with an organisation on the basis of nationalities. When the workers are organised according to nationality they isolate themselves within their national shells, fenced off from each other by organisational barriers. The stress is laid not on what is *common* to the workers but on what distinguishes them from each other. In this type of organisation the worker is *primarily* a member of his nation: a Jew, a Pole, and so on. It is not surprising that *national* federalism in organisation inculcates in the workers a spirit of national seclusion. Therefore, the national type of organisation is a school of national narrow-mindedness and stagnation. Thus we are confronted by two *fundamentally* different types of organisation: the type based on international solidarity and the type based on the organisational "demarcation" of the workers according to nationalities.[43]

Our party has pleaded for such a solution to the race/caste/ ethnic problem under the banner of a Marxist-Leninist principle. Had the "solution" brought forward by our party in Nepal appeared in the form of an open bourgeois solution, it would have been easily identified and contested sharply. But, the proposal brought under the camouflage of Marxism-Leninism, becomes difficult to identify, and then the wage struggle against our party's view about the race/caste/ethnic problem. Comment by Stalin on the national movement of Austria is apt in regard to our party's policy:

True, such nationalism is not so transparent, for it is 'skilfully masked by socialist phrases', but it is all the more harmful to the proletariat for that reason. We can always cope with open nationalism, for it can easily be discerned. It is much more difficult to combat nationalism when it is masked and unrecognizable beneath its mask 'protected by the armour of socialism', it is less vulnerable and more tenacious. Implanted among the workers, it poisons the atmosphere and spreads noxious ideas of mutual distrust and segregation among the workers of the different nationalities.[44]

Federal restructuring of the state, on the basis of race/caste/ ethnicity and language in Nepal is in contradiction to the development of modern human society. Differences and malice between the different race/caste/ ethnic communities are gradually lessening because of the development of capitalism and the intensity and broadness of class struggle in the country.

The *Communist Manifesto* states:

National differences and antagonisms between peoples are increasingly vanishing, owing to the development of the bourgeoisie, to freedom of commerce, to the world market, to uniformity in the mode of production

43 *The Essential Stalin, Major Theoretical Writings 1905-52*, "Marxism and the National Question", Edited and with an introduction by Bruce Franklin, First Indian Edition, January 2010, Rahul Foundation, pp. 94-95.

44 J. V. Stalin, *Marxism and National Question*, Eng. ed., Books and Periodicals, Calcutta, p. 46.

and in the conditions of life corresponding thereto. The supremacy of the proletariat will cause them to vanish still faster."[45]

The programme of restructuring of the state on the basis of race/caste/ethnicity itself gives continuity and legality to the present system of exploitation within castes and ethnic communities. Lenin has said: "There are two nations in every modern nation."[46] The meaning of Lenin is that in modern society, *i.e.* in every nation under capitalism, has a minority oppressor class and a majority oppressed class. Therefore, there is not a single interest of any nation in an absolute term. This statement of Lenin applies to a certain extent to the majority of human communities like tribal and race, not yet developed as a nation, though with a variance in form and broadness, even in the era of imperialism and proletarian revolution. In so many race/caste/ethnic communities of Nepal, the development of capitalist production and intervention of an enlightened group has brought class struggle into existence. In this context, to restructure the state into a federal structure in regard to race/caste/ethnic communities means to be in the wilderness as slaves and creating a safe fort for keeping the majority of working people by a handful of cunning exploiters. This proposal puts race/caste/ethnic communities under an identity label, rendering a low level of economic development, and rejecting the beneficial aspect of the unitary state. So, we should rescind the policy and programme of restructuring the state on the basis of race/caste/identity, and lead the different race/caste/ethnic communities back into the common flock of Nepal for a progressive solution to race/caste/ethnic problem in conformity with the Marxism-Leninism-Mao Tse-tung Thought.

Restructuring of the state on a race/caste/ethnic basis means addressing the demand of various ethnic communities depending on their wishes, which will bring the situation to a dangerous mode. But our party that led the ten-year people's great war does not address the interests of working people as with different race/caste/ethnic communities as per the Marxist-Leninist line. Restructuring of state on a race/caste/ethnic and language basis in Nepal can create an environment of an infinite federationism that can develop into separatism. The proposal of our party for the federal state system with the right of self-determination has opened the gates to this possibility. At present, our party has proposed nine states on the basis of race/caste/ethnic and language. After a few race/caste/ethnic communities get this right, the remaining communities can demand that right in future. In a neo-colonial country like Nepal, world imperialism and

45 Karl Marx and Frederick Engels, "Manifesto of the Community Party", *Selected Works*, Progress Publishers, Moscow, Fourth Printing, 1977, Vol. 1, pp. 124-25.

46 V. I. Lenin, "Critical Remarks on the National Question", *Collected Works*, Eng. ed., Progress Publishers, Moscow, Third Printing, 1977, Vol. 20, p. 32.

specifically, Indian expansionism will increase its colonial influence further and penetrate further into the different race/caste/ethnic movements, and mobilise them to demand new federal states or even demand a separation.

Our party's restructuring plan evades the issue of liberation from neo-colonialism because under the present epoch of imperialism and proletarian revolution, the problem of caste/ethnic people is not a purely internal problem. It is a problem of making the country independent from semi(neo)-colonial exploitation and oppression of world imperialism and Indian expansionism, but our party's restructuring plan on the basis of race leaves the socio-economic structure in the hands of world imperialism and Indian expansionism, which is like turning over the power to world imperialism, and specifically Indian expansionism. If we move ahead according to the policy and programme of our party, we will not achieve the goal of independence. Realising this reality and freeing themselves from the racial obsession for state restructuring, the working-class of all the different race/ethnic and caste communities should move towards changing the feudal-centralised bureaucratic and semi(neo)-colonial state into a full democratic and sovereign unitary state. They should break relations with feudal and neo-colonial forces to end the grip of foreign powers on Nepal.

The problem of different race/caste/ethnic communities of Nepal is not an independent question; it must be seen as a whole. If the programme to the race/caste/ethnic problem runs contrary to the whole, Marxist-Leninists should not support that type of demand or programme. We should evaluate the race/caste/ethnic demands or programme not from an absolute point of view, rather from the point of view of the new democratic revolution and the world socialist revolution. For example, Lenin says: "The several demands of democracy, including self-determination, are not an absolute, but only a *small part* of the general-democratic (now: general-socialist) *world* movement. In individual concrete cases, the part may contradict the whole; if so, it must be rejected."[47] Stalin, in this regard, further states: "The national question is a part of the general question of the proletarian revolution, a part of the question of the dictatorship of the proletariat."

Further he writes:

> The question is as follows: *Are* the revolutionary potentialities latent in the revolutionary liberation movement of the oppressed countries *already exhausted*, or not; and if not, is there any hope, any basis, for utilising these potentialities for the proletarian revolution, for transforming the dependent and colonial countries from a reserve of the imperialist bourgeoisie into a reserve of the revolutionary proletariat, into an ally of the latter?

47 V. I. Lenin, "The Discussion on Self-determination Summed Up, *Collected Works*, Eng. ed., Progress Publishers, Moscow, Third Printing, 1977, Vol. 22, p. 341.

> Leninism replies to this question in the affirmative. This does not mean, of course, that the proletariat must support *every* national movement, everywhere and always, in every individual concrete case. It means that support must be given to such national movements as tend to weaken, to overthrow imperialism, and not to strengthen and preserve it. Cases occur when the national movements in certain oppressed countries come into conflict with the interests of the development of the proletarian movement. In such cases support is, of course, entirely out of the question. The question of the rights of nations is not an isolated, self-sufficient question; it is a part of the general problem of the proletarian revolution, subordinate to the whole, and must be considered from the point of view of the whole.
>
> This is the position in regard to the question of particular national movements, of the possible reactionary character of these movements–if, of course, they are appraised not from the formal point of view, not from the point of view of abstract rights, but concretely, from the point of view of the interests of the revolutionary movement.
>
> The same must be said of the revolutionary character of national movements in general. The unquestionably revolutionary character of the vast majority of national movements is as relative and peculiar as is the possible reactionary character of certain particular national movements.
>
> Lenin was right in saying that the national movement of the oppressed countries should be appraised not from the point of view of formal democracy, but from the point of view of the actual results, as shown by the general balance sheet of the struggle against imperialism.[48]

The above statements related to the national movement help us understand the caste/race/ethnic problem in Nepal, a semi-colony for centuries, and discern the way to solve the problem. The world imperialism and Indian expansionism have perpetuated colonial exploitation in a new form, so the duty of true Marxist-Leninists should be to finding a solution to the problem of different race/caste/ethnic communities, and only after freeing the country from world imperialism and Indian expansionism, we can turn Nepal into an independent and sovereign country. It is impossible to educate the working-class of the various race/caste/ethnic communities with true internationalism and prepare for the new democratic revolution and advancement towards socialism by restructuring the country on a race/caste/ethnic basis. Their issues can be addressed only when the semi(neo)-colonial domination of world imperialism and Indian expansionism, existing in Nepal for centuries, are broken. This is the true Marxist-Leninist procedure to train the different race/caste/ethnic communities, especially the working-classes of those communities to prepare for new democratic revolution and move to socialism.

48 J. V. Stalin, "Foundation of Leninism", *Problems of Leninism*, Eng. ed., Foreign Language Press, Peking, 1976, pp. 70-73.

9
Restructuring of the State and Addressing the Scheduled Caste Problem

The problem of the scheduled caste (Dalit) in Nepal holds a unique dimension and its solution cannot follow the measures adopted in Russia and China. Ignoring this particularity of the problem, our party has brought a policy and programme for restructuring the state on the basis of race/caste/ethnic identity. With the exception of raising the issue in some of our authorised publications, the party does not have a concrete programme for its solution, which means the party has taken the Dalit problem under the same banner as the other race/caste/ethnic communities with no distinct vision. It simply says "country will be declared a free region of untouchability", the "state will manage special rights until there is equality in all fields", [49] etc., which means after the other problems are solved, the Dalit problem will automatically be solved too.

Speciality of feudalism in Nepal needs to be taken seriously while restructuring Nepal and framing a new constitution with a view to solving the problems, left over by history as a legacy and common responsibility of all. In the past, the Hindu religion had a great influence on state power in Nepal and it affected the feudal production system, directly and indirectly. Almost all the rulers, after the (feudalist) unification of Nepal by Prithvi Narayan Shah, established themselves as Hindu feudal rulers as reflected in the feudal character of the state power. They perpetuated the untouchability as part of the religious, cultural-social system of the Nepal state which has no scientific basis. To a certain extent, indigenous communities were influenced by the Hindu politics in different ways. Feudalism is mainly responsible for the present condition of Dalits. So, breaking the central place of Hinduism by waging a struggle against the feudalism in the state is vital to solve the Dalit problem in Nepal. So, the method of struggle adopted in Europe or other countries against feudalism is not sufficient to wage a struggle for the emancipation of the Dalits of Nepal. We need to adopt distinct measures, not blindly copying other countries, to solve the problem created by the mingling of the Hindu religion and feudalism.

Our party's approach for restructuring the state by ending the unitary system of the state leaves many questions unanswered. The problem of Dalits are deeply rooted in the economic, political, administrative and socio-cultural fields and they are different compared to other race/caste/ethnic communities. Unlike the problem of other race/ethnic communities,

49 *Manifesto of the CPN(Maoist) for the Election of the Constituent Assembly*, p. 33

the Dalits' problems are tied to the specific economic issues because of fusion of the Hindu religion and feudalism. Through landlessness, unemployment and the extreme feudal exploitation system of the country, they have been oppressed for centuries. Twenty-three percent of them in the Hills and 46% in Terai are landless. Dalits with less than two Ropani land 77% are in the Hills, and 95% in the Terai. The number of Dalits with less land compared to other races is 90% in the Hills. The main cause of the bonded land tiller (Haliya) system is the stigma of landlessness itself, by compelling a citizen born free to live a life of bondage. Along with the development of capitalism, the system of payment for harvest for agricultural tools and materials along with traditional works such as plough making, ironing tools and pot making, tailoring, shoe making, etc., carried out by Dalits have gradually declined. At present, less than 60% of Dalits are engaged in their traditional professions in rural areas, creating an unemployment problem. Because of the stigma of untouchability, unemployed Dalits feel constrained even to enter any kind of profession.

The history of Nepal shows the place of Dalits in executive, judicial, legislative and administration posts is negligible. Although a few reached high positions in the past, it was due to the kindness of the ruling class to save their own class interest, not to solve the Dalit problem. After the multi-party system was restored, only one candidate was elected on behalf of Dalits in the general election of 205 members to represent more than 2.5 million Dalits. In 1995 and 1999, the representation of Dalit was nil. In the national assembly of 60 members, two members in 1991, two in 1993, three in 1995, three in 1997, and four in 1999 were nominated. In the cabinet, the presence of Dalits was modest in 2001 and 2005. No Dalit has ever occupied the post of secretary in the history of the administration of Nepal. Likewise, the judiciary too has almost no representation of Dalits.

Under the social-cultural-structure of the country now, the lack of justice and access to education is pathetic for the Dalits. The social-cultural structure, guided by the Hindu religion deprives Dalits of humanitarian treatment, and they face problems in choosing their profession. They are conditioned by their caste and low economic status and get no justice and education too. If we compare the position of Dalits in the economic, political, administrative and social-cultural situations with other race/caste/ethnic communities considered oppressed, the position of the other groups is far better. So, by bringing forward a programme of restructuring the state on a race/caste/ethnic and language basis with no concrete plan and programme, we cannot solve the Dalit problem. Problems of Dalits in the economic, political, administrative and social-cultural areas, like landlessness, unemployment and feudal exploitation, lack of the Dalits' place in the executive, legislature and judiciary, the lack of justice, and lack of possibilities in education for the Dalits need a special plan and programme. The movements of Dalits are against the Hindu feudal-centralised and bureaucratic state system, instrumental for their exploitation. The unitary administrative system based on democracy would not be instrumental for their exploitation. The demand of the Dalit movement cannot be solved by a federal system any more. It can be solved in the real sense only with the establishment of the unitary administration system based on democratic, progressive social structures, participatory and local autonomous administration, by ending the Hindu feudal-centralised social structure.

Establishment of the federal system based on racial identity is not an end of the Hindu feudalistic system. Instead of solving the problem of Dalits, such a state structure will weaken their national level place, energy and movement by way of splitting them on narrow consideration. Their unified movement to reach their goal will be more difficult in the federal system than in the unitary system. Some people are of the view that the unitary system, by virtue of being a centralised system, cannot solve their problem properly. So, they prefer the federal system to the unitary system. However, such a concern does not seen reasonable and objective in a situation of centralised system based on democracy.

Dalits are the most oppressed people of all the oppressed race/caste/ ethnic communities. The policy, programme, and planning of this problem must be directly under the centre. They can get their emancipation only under the direct leadership of the centre. So, the solution to their problems in the federal system is not feasible as it creates practical problem for them. Nothing is explained in the proposal of our party to restructure the unitary state into the federal outline structure on the race/caste basis, and about how to address the Dalit problem and how it can be better addressed than under the unitary system. The party has proposed the federal system with the provision of separation, if the race/caste/ethnic communities are unwilling to remain under the existing federation. If it is implemented, what would be the condition of Dalits in that state? Is it compulsory for Dalits to separate themselves because the race/caste/ethnic base community is separated from the existing federation? It is not practical not to be separated in the federal system proposed by the party. Economic, political, administrative, cultural, including the relation with land, will also create a division in the federal state. Will it be wise for the Dalits to support such a demand or proposal for the federal state with the right to get separated? The party is completely silent about these questions.

The federal restructuring of the state on the basis of race/caste/ ethnicity weakens the intermingling of Dalits with different race/caste/ ethnic communities. It is easier and more practical for intermingling between different race/caste/ethnic communities under a unitary state system. It would be a mistake to understand the restructuring of the state on a race/caste/ethnic basis only to mean the formation of territorial units. It is the restructuring of political, economic, administrative, social, and cultural areas, which is possible only under a unitary administration system based on democratic norms and values, not under a federal outline of the state on the race/caste/ ethnic basis.

The basic difference lies between the Dalit problem and the problem of other races and indigenous people. The other races and indigenous problems are related to territory, language, affection for descendants, pride and preservation of cultural heritage. These especial features separate races and indigenous people from one another and they strive for their preservation and protection. The nature of the solution to the problems of the human community of this type are usually similar. However, the Dalit problem is different from that of other races and indigenous people. It does not have the protection of territory, language, affection for descendants, pride and cultural heritage; rather it is a problem produced by the feudalistic structure and of the worst conditions existing for long. The Dalit problem demands a policy, programme and planning for a special solution, not a usual policy, programme and plan. Restructuring the state into a federal system cannot solve that problem necessarily. Providing local autonomy based on full democratic right is the answer to the Dalit problem under the unitary structure.

10
Unique Social-Economic Condition and the Natural Structure of Nepal

Nepal is a land-locked country in South Asia. It occupies 0.03% and 3% of land area of the world and Asia respectively. It is an almost rectangular size, approximately 885 kilometres length from East to West, and 145-241 km. breadth from North to South. Its total area is 147181 sq.km. Nepal shares a border with India, with the states of Uttar Pradesh, Bihar, Sikkim and West Bengal to the South, East and West respectively and the Chinese autonomous region of Tibet lies to its North. The Himalaya Region occupies 15% of the whole land (22077.151 sq.km.), the Hilly region occupies 68% (100083.08 sq.km.) and the Terai Region occupies 17% (25020.77 sq.km.) of the land of Nepal. Nepal is a multi-caste, multi-religious, multi-lingual and multi-cultural country. There are more than one hundred race/caste/ethnic communities, more than ninety linguistic communities and more than ten religious communities. Although some race/caste/ethnic communities are in a large number in their primitive homelands, no race/caste/ethnicity is in majority in Nepal.

According to the census of 2001 the Kusundas have a 150-164 population, then the 3.5 million Chhetris happen to be the second most populous community. Although, Brahmins and Chhetris have a large population, in percentage they are respectively 15.80% and 12.74%. Among other castes, Magars are 7.14%, Tharus are 6.75%, Tamangs are 5.64%, Newars are 5.48%, Muslims are 4.27%, Kamis are 3.94%, Yadavs are 3.94%, Rais are 2.79%, Gurungs are 2.39%, Damains and Dholis are 1.72%, Limbus are 1.58%, Thakuris are 1.47%, Sarkis are 1.40%, Telis are 1.34%, Chamars and Harijans are 1.19%, and Koiris are 1.11%. All the other castes/ethnic communities are less than 1%. Out of these, there are communities such as the Punjabi and Sikh, Kisan, Raji, Byangsi, Hayu, Koche, Dhunia, Walung in 0.01% altogether Jaine, Munda, Raute, Yehlmo, Patharkata/Kusuwadia, and Kusunda cannot be taken in percentage.

The position of languages is almost the same, except the Nepali Bhasa (language). Out of ninety-two languages recorded in the census of 2001, the largest percentage (48.61%) of people speak Nepali. Out of the recorded ninety-two languages, twenty are foreign languages (English, Chinese, Naga and so on). In other languages, Maithili is spoken by 12.30%, Bhojpuri by 7.53%, Tharu by 5.86%, Tamang by 5.19%, Newar by 3.63%, Magar by 3.39%, Awadhi by 2.47%, Bantawa by 1.63%, Gurung by 1.49%, Limbu by 1.47% and Bajjika by 1.05%, and the other languages spoken are less than 1% of the people. Out of these, languages spoken by less than 0.01% are Dura, Meche, Pahari, Lepcha, Bote, Bahing, Koi, Raji, Hayu, Byangshi, Yamphu, Ghale, Khariya, Chhiling, Lohorung and Punjabi. There are also thirty other languages spoken, but it is not possible to get a percentage. Among these, Sadhani is spoken only by two, Assamise by three, Lhomi by four, Nagamise by six, Mizo by eight, Chhintang by eight, Kuki by nine, Dzonkha by nine, and Kagate by ten.

The religious structure is different. According to the census of 2001, Hindus are 80.62%, Buddhists are 10.74%, Muslims are 4.20%, Kirats are 3.60%, Christians are 0.45%, Sikhs are 0.03%, Jains are 0.02%, Garautes are 0.01%, Tajpurias are 0.01%, Bahais are 0.01%, and 0.35% belong to other religions.

Not only from the perspective of caste, language, religion, culture and the natural diversity, a great variation lies in Nepal regarding climate, vegetation, temperature, soil, rivers, lakes, land surface, population, crops, minerals, and rocks. Various types of soil, namely, Alluvial, Glacial, Silty, Rocky, Orange coloured-Alluvial and Lacustrine soil are found in Nepal. Soil is found in layers in the stretch of East to West. These are not all equally fertile in terms of crop production. Alluvial is found in the Terai from the East to the West (except Dang Valley). This soil, not found in the higher up land surface, is fertile for paddy, wheat, sugar cane, oil seeds, potato, and green vegetables.

The Terai is the storehouse of food grains and vegetables, and it supplies these products for the capital and other big towns, without which the whole country would not survive even for a month. In the Dang area, Chitwan and Nawal Parasi, orange coloured-alluvial types of soil are found. These areas in Terai make good contributions to the country in terms of production. The area of silty soil stretches from East to West. It has a quite insignificant contribution in the national food supply. The third area is rocky which is comparatively broader and stretches from East to West. At some points, this type of soil surfaces reaches the northern border, which is favourable for production of maize, coffee, and some fruits. The role of the glacial area is insignificant in terms of production.

Nepal is diverse in terms of vegetation and climate. Tundra, Alpine, coniferous, deciduous and subtropical forests are in Nepal. In the northern area from East to West, there is a snow fall area in broken stretches. In other words, particular types of vegetations and climate are found in different climatic zones.

Nepal possesses potential in terms of rivers, basins and glaciers. A unique feature of Nepal is the unavailability of water reservoirs, glaciers and snow-pools in all parts of the country. Glaciers and snow-pools are not found in the Terai and its upper part.

Diversity is also an important characteristic of Nepal regarding types of cliff and rocks. Towards the Northern part of Nepal lies the world's highest peak. In the South belt, the land surface is only sixty metre heights from the sea level. In such a narrow breadth, a great difference in height is a serious problem in itself.

Because of this situation, the long-term soil deposits in the Terai are in danger of getting water logged a great challenge to us. The danger is further terrifying as the Terai might be turned into a dirt-fill due to deforestation.

Nepal is full of diversity with mineral deposits scattered across the country. Although from the study of minerals as studied thus far, the position of the Terai is relatively poor for minerals. Study and investigations show that metallic and energy deposits such as copper, gold, iron, lead, zinc, magnesium, coal, gas and oil, etc., and non-metallic minerals such as graphite, limestone, magnetite, marble pyrite (combined mineral of iron and copper), salt, silica sand, etc., are found in Nepal.

Naturally, custom posts are situated at borders. It depends on the different factors regarding which of the borders should have more custom posts, when border meets the border of more than one countries. Out of twenty-seven custom posts in Nepal, nineteen are in the East, West and Southern border, *i.e.* at the border with India and the remaining eight posts are in the North, *i.e.* at the border of the Chinese autonomous region of Tibet. Out of all seventeen business centres in the country, eleven are in the Terai and the other six are in other parts of the country, which is not absolute and final as such posts and centres can increase or decrease as per the demand of the particular situation.

Furthermore, in terms of irrigation facility, the Terai belt has more possibilities. Because of the uniqueness of Nepal, a network of transport and irrigation cannot be developed in Hilly and Himali regions as easily as in the Terai.

With 885 km. length and 193 km. breadth, from sixty metres above sea level to 8848 metres Mount Everest (Sagarmatha), the world's highest peak, eight out of the world's top twenty highest peaks, more than one hundred race/caste/ethnic communities, more than ninety languages spoken are special features of Nepal. Likewise, more than ten religions, and about one dozen world heritage sites, 848 varieties of birds, 4% mammals, eleven out of fifteen butterflies on earth, 600 classes of natural vegetation, 319 types of orchids and the rare one horned rhino, infinite water resources and infinite hydroelectricity generation capacity too differentiate Nepal from other countries in the world.

While writing the constitution, restructuring of the state and preparing a blueprint of economic development, the given peculiarities of the country should be studied, not out of subjective desire or under external pressure that may create castles out of air, and push the country backward. Our party policy for new constitution writing, restructuring of state and economic development has not addressed the above peculiarities of the country. The restructuring of the unitary system of the state into a federal model is defective and it cannot address the problems of the country. The restructuring of the state on a (mainly) race and language basis into a federal outline separates one part of Terai from the other part of Tarai itself, especially the Terai from the Hilly and the Himali region. Our party's plan of restructuring the state on the basis of race and language not only divides the territory, it divides the paddy, wheat, sugarcane, cotton, tobacco, oil seeds, not grown in the Hilly and Himali area, as the products from the states and sub-states of the Terai belt. Likewise, food grains and fruits are not considered the produce of the people of the Terai, rather the products of Hilly regions. Terai is almost mineral deprived, lacking deciduous, coniferous and Alpine forest, lacking glaciers and snow pools, lacking the highest peak identified in the world, whereas the Hilly and Himali areas do not have tropical forests and alluvial.

If the state becomes federal on the basis of race and language, will Nepal remain one country? Our party honestly does not want to see Nepal divided, but honesty is not everything and it is not a test of correctness or incorrectness. Lenin has explained this repeatedly that whether any plan of action is right or wrong is determined by the consequence. After restructuring the state into the federal model on race and language base, we may have to face many problems from the Southern state and sub-states for several reasons.

Our party is not proposing a federal state without the provision of the right of separation, as in India, America, Australia and Canada, but with the right of self-determination, as in the Soviet Republic under Lenin and Stalin. It is known to all that Indian penetration and influence is deep and widespread, with a grand design in the Terai region for long, and it has captured about sixty thousand hectares of Nepalese land. Furthermore, Indian citizens are settling in the Terai in a systematic way and Indian rulers are pressurising to change the Nepalese Citizenship Act in different ways to make Nepalese citizenship easily available to Indian citizens settled there. India is an influential factor in Nepal's citizenship policy as evidenced by the event of 1979 and the manipulation by the Indian government during the interim government of Nepal before holding the first constituent assembly.

The nature and demands of some organisations in the Terai show that they want to separate the flat land and join with India or form a separate country. The restructuring of the state into a federal model will weaken the control of the centre on the states, creating a favourable opportunity for internal and external forces to instigate a separatist movement covertly or overtly. If those states put the demand for separation from Nepal on the basis of the present promise of our party for a federation with the right to self-determination, then a demand for split in the Terai cannot be ruled out. If this demand is forwarded in the most democratic (in formal sense) manner, *i.e.* through a referendum, will our party's "honesty" become an armour to defend the territorial integrity of Nepal?

Even if the danger does not go up to the extent of separation from Nepal, in the special location of the Terai belt, in future when any disagreement between states and sub-states of that belt erupts, even over petty affairs, serious problems may arise in business, leading to supply of food grains and vegetables being blocked, including international trade with India or any third country via India. While restructuring the Nepal state, politics, economy, society, culture, balanced economic development, national independence, sovereignty and territorial integrity of the country, need to be taken into consideration in a country like Nepal which has been a semi-colony for long. The proposal of our party for restructuring of the state completely neglects these important factors. If a federal system of the state on the basis of race/caste/ethnic or linguistic basis restructuring is carried out, the door opens for the fragmentation of Nepal as a country. In future, race/caste/ethnic communities not yet eligible for state/sub-state, may demand a separate state too when the present states demand separation.

Regarding the unique and special social, economic and natural structures mentioned above, the nation should be divided by mixing different types of territorial regions, race/caste/ethnic communities, languages and cultures, providing local autonomy based on full democratic right under the unitary structure. In the uniqueness of Nepal, the North-South vertical territorial and administrative division is balanced from the point of view of national independence, sovereignty and territorial integrity, economic development and unity among race/caste/ethnic communities that have existed for centuries. Such a division will end the discrimination regarding the caste, race, language and region. Not only alluvial, paddy, wheat, green vegetables, cotton, tobacco, tropical forests and summer warmth, but also the world top peaks, minerals, glaciers and snow pools will belong to the Terai people. Likewise, people of Hills and Himalayan range will have not only deciduous, coniferous and Alpine forests, but also will have subtropical forests, and a large food grain store. So, only the territorial and administrative North-South vertical based restructure under the unitary structure can give the right direction for the country.

May-December, 2008
Canberra, Australia

Liquidationist View on the State and Revolution

Second Letter Sent to the Party Headquarters Regarding the Anti-Marxist-Leninist View on the State and Revolution

1
Party's View on the State and Revolution

Our party, after forwarding the new democracy as the minimum programme, chose the violent revolution as a universal path, which like in our country is the path of protracted people's war for achieving the goal, later embraced the "transitional" state system of 'Loktantrik Gantantra' (old type of democratic republic), especially since 2001. Though the "transitional" line was raised informally now and then, it was established as an authentic line of the party since the Chunbang Meeting (October, 2003), abandoning the new democracy as the minimum programme of the party. Since the Chunbang Meeting, the party is principally focusing on the "transitional" Loktantrik Gantantra and strengthening it too. By discarding the minimum programme of new democracy, why did the party hasten to materialise the "transitional" state system of Loktantrik Gantantra?

The party documents and quotations from the leadership will clarify the issue. 'The Political and the Organisational Report', approved by the Chunbang Meeting states:

> Remaining constant on the objective for tactics to serve the strategy, the party takes Loktantrik Gantantra neither as bourgeois parliamentary democracy, nor as direct new democratic republic. This republic will play the role of transitional multi-party republic to deal with the broad issue of state restructuring and to solve the problems of caste, region and gender existing in the country.
>
> After the end of the domination of monarchy in the old state power, this slogan will lead to peaceful solution to the civil war. Capable of opening the door to peaceful solution to civil war, this slogan will rightly address the aspiration of people for transformation and peace, and indirectly will play the positive role for preparation of general insurrection. Therefore, at present, the party should take active initiation to lead this process to a logical end with a solid unity.[1]

Occasional statements made by Chairman Prachanda further clarify the line of our party. In response to the question from the *Kantipur Daily* "What is your maximum goal?", Prachanda says:

> Being a communist party, our goal is socialism, communism... But, the circumstances of international power balance and economic, political and social conditions of the country do not allow us to realise that goal instantly. We must realise this ground reality. Thinking that, we must be flexible in accordance with the power balance between classes and the international condition, we have raised the voice for Loktantrik Gantantra and the constituent assembly. This is the policy, not a tactics."[2]

In response to another question, "Is the proposal of building... a common army a trick to lead parties towards the people's war?", he says:

> How could such a proposal be a trick to bring parties to the people's war? Rather we have entered into the politics of parties. We have preferred the constituent assembly and Loktantrik Gantantra. We have gone to bourgeois democracy.[3]

In response to yet other question from *Kantipur*, he says:

> We are analysing to scrutinise what mistake our class made in twentieth century. We summed up the process to know why the state machinery after the death of Lenin could not be democratic any more, and it became

1 Prachanda, "Political and Organisational Report", *Selected Works*, Janadisha Publications, Nepal, July 2007, Vol. 2, pp. 467-68.

2 Prachanda, "We Want to Stop Bloodshed (Interview)", *Selected Works*, Janadisha Publications, Nepal, February 2007, Vol. 1, p. 407.

3 Prachanda, "We Want to Stop Bloodshed (Interview)", *Selected Works*, Janadisha Publications, Nepal, February 2007, Vol. 1, p. 409.

mechanical; and why the masses became slowly engrossed with monotomy. Life should be as fresh and vibrant as the floating water. Three years ago, we concluded in our Central Committee that there has been a mistake in that aspect. We passed the resolution of the twenty-first century democracy. We raised the slogan of Loktantrik Gantantra with full reflection and retrospection. We have reviewed the twentieth century.[4]

Responding to a question, "Political parties are agreed on the issue of the constituent assembly, have you abandoned the demand of republic or has it been postponed?" from *The Hindu*, published in India:

Prachanda says:

We have not abandoned the demand of Loktantrik Gantantra. We have not given up the slogan of Loktantrik Gantantra that we used to raise before. Considering the power balance and having evaluated the all round situation, we realised the responsibility to adopt a peaceful way with a view to avoiding bloodshed.[5]

On another occasion, in response to a question posed by the BBC World Service, he says: "We have said that there should be Loktantrik Gantantra in Nepal. Our struggle is for Loktantrik Gantantra. We believe that Loktantrik Gantantra will be established in Nepal through the constituent assembly, and it will solve problems and lead the country ahead to the direction of progress."[6]

On the occasion of the 10th anniversary of the people's war, in an interview to the weekly *Janadesh*, Comrade Prachanda states:

It will be appropriate to understand the relationship among the New Democracy, Constituent Assembly and Loktantrik Gantantra as inter-relationship between strategic firmness and tactical flexibility in reality.

The slogan of Loktantrik Gantantra that our party has raised means a transitional revolutionary slogan that helps lead the class struggle in the specific conditions of power balance.

The 12-point agreement has been termed as the first milestone in the process to reach complete democracy (Loktantrik Gantantra that we mean) through the election of the constituent assembly.[7]

---

4 Prachanda, "We Want to Stop Bloodshed (Interview)", *Selected Works*, Janadisha Publications, Nepal, February 2007, Vol. 1, p. 413.

5 Prachanda, "Realisation of the Responsibility to Adopt a Peaceful Way (Interview)", *Selected Works*, Janadisha Publications, Nepal, February 2007, Vol. 1, p. 426.

6 Prachanda, "We Believe in People's True Democracy (Interview)", *Selected Works*, Janadisha Publications, Nepal, February 2007, Vol. 1, pp. 440-41.

7 Prachanda, "I Want to Give New Message of Liberation (Interview)", *Selected Works*, Janadisha Publications, Nepal, February 2007, Vol. 1, pp. 471-72.

The party has presented Loktantrik Gantantra as a "transitional" state power of pre-new democratic state power. For example, Comrade Baburam Bhattarai writes:

> With reference to Peace Talks on April 27, 2003 in the 'An Executive Summary of the Proposal Put Forward by CPN(Maoist)' for the Negotiations, an outline of transitional state power is presented for the pre-new democracy/ pre-people's democracy. In the given circumstances of present Nepal, our party believes that the vision of a transitional state power is progressive rather than parliamentarianism. Though it has not reached the level of new democracy, it is appropriate, theoretically and practically.

Comrade Bhattarai further writes:

> After the end of absolute monarchy, when bourgeois democracy is not established fully, it is necessary to realise the possibility of adopting different mixed and transitional democratic forms in the process of reaching up to proletarian democracy through dictatorial monarchy to bourgeois democracy.

Bhattarai suggests this line to be "the essence of the decision made with reference to development of democracy under the leadership of Comrade Prachanda."[8] On another occasion, he states:

> Keeping in mind the backward standard of the country, fear and suspicion about revolutionary changes in one group of urban middle class, and specific geopolitical situation of the country altogether, the policy of our party is not to exert emphasis on any immediate revolutionary option, so long as the optional path to progressive reform is available.

There are not only two revolutionary and regressive options for Comrade Bhattarai. He sees a more objective third option:

> Besides counter-revolutionary and revolutionary options, the immediate possibility of the middle way found is the path of progressive reform with common consensus of all political forces to give completion to the bourgeois republic. We think that a round table conference, interim government and the election of constituent assembly could be the minimum epoch of parliamentary and non-parliamentary political forces for acquiescence. There has been constant controversy over the issue who the sovereign power of the nation should be. The issue of the constituent assembly, capable to make the final decision about it, has always been postponed. It is why even the capitalist democracy has not materialised fully. There is no reason for anybody, who takes himself to be a democrat, to get frightened to finalise the debate on present power allocation through the constituent assembly as this is the supreme form of democracy. In this situation, this is self-evident that the constituent assembly can be the instant minimum common path of agreement for all the three political forces, *i.e.* monarchists,

8 Baburam Bhattarai, "Question of Building a New State Power", *People's Council*, The Organ of the Joint Revolutionary People's Council, Nepal, July 2004, No. 1, pp. 10, 13.

> parliamentarians and new democracy supporters. In spite of tremendous sacrifice and dedication of people, inspired by the spirit of responsibility, to avoid a situation for the foreign forces role in increasing dangerous civil war, our party became flexible to seek a solution to the problem by adopting the programmes of new democracy in a peaceful way. In the context of Nepal, the king and the royalists too should not feel reluctant to deal with the question of constituent assembly election as it was for the first time promised by the late king Tribhuvan in 2007. In such a situation, it is evident that the constituent assembly could be the minimum common point of agreement among the parliamentarians, royalists and the supporters of new democracy. It is our considered view that in the present specific condition of Nepal, only through this process, can we give completion to the bourgeois democracy, which will ultimately lead us to the path of new democracy and then to socialism.

In reply to "What result will come out if parliamentarian and monarchist forces are not prepared to choose this reformist path, between the counter-revolutionary and revolutionary paths?" Comrade Bhattarai writes:

> If there is no serious effort for finding this third progressive reformist option specifically on the part of parliamentarian political forces, the conclusive combat between the counter-revolutionary and revolutionary path will break out. To whatever extent painful it may be, it will be appropriate for all to understand that, revolution defeats counter-revolution conclusively as shown by the law of history.[9]

Explaining the party's analysis related to Loktantrik Gantantra explicitly, Comrade Bhattarai writes:

> In general, from the period of preparation and beginning of people's war and concretely since the period of June 1, 2001 of the infamous Narayanhiti massacre, the party has been forwarding Loktantrik Ganatantra as the main immediate tactical slogan. After the complete and naked restoration of the dictatorial monarchy on February 1, 2005, the slogan of Loktantrik Ganatantra has become a common slogan of other parliamentary forces and the common public too. It is necessary for revolutionaries to understand rightly and adopt the fact that the party of the proletariat has accepted the slogan of the bourgeois multi-party Loktantrik Gantantra as the immediate minimum tactics. For the party that has accepted the line of capturing local power and building base areas, it is also necessary to grasp well the justification of raising the slogan of interim central power.
>
> As Engels says, "In reality, however, the state is nothing but a machine for the oppression of one class by another, and indeed in the democratic republic of less than in the monarchy." (Introduction by Engels for the third German

9 Baburam Bhattarai, "The Crisis Invited by War and the Basic Question of Immediate Political Exit", *War and Talk*, Jana Dhwoni Publications, Kathmandu, May 2009, pp. 21-22.

> edition of Marx's, *The Civil War in France*, published in 1891). Communist revolutionaries should not be confused that in that sense, the thing called Loktantrik Gantantra itself is the highest form of bourgeois dictatorship, and it is not a proletarian class state. However, as Engels explains in another reference, "The highest form of the state, the democratic republic, which under our modern conditions of society is increasingly becoming inevitable, and this is the form of state in which alone the last decisive struggle between proletariat and bourgeoisie can be fought out. (*Origin of the Family, Private Property and State*, March-May 1884). In this situation, if this thing is true for all historically, the only dictatorial monarchy (with exception of a short interval of a few years) of state power of about two hundred and fifty years onwards since the central government is formed in Nepal, to establish Loktantrik Gantantra after ending that, it will certainly be a helpful and necessary step. Standing on the same theoretical-ideological ground and paying attention to the present national and international class and political force balance, the Nepalese proletariat's party has forwarded the tactics of Loktantrik Gantantra.
>
> This is necessary to be understood by all revolutionary democratic forces that the slogan of Loktantrik Gantantra forwarded in the context of the present semi-feudal and semi-colonial Nepal where capitalist objective ground is not yet prepared fully, is not a parliamentary republic of classic meaning, but a 'transitional multi-party republic', simply one step ahead of that but has not reached the level of new democracy.

Comrade Bhattarai further states regarding the theme of Loktantrik Ganatantra:

> Firstly, after the monarchy is abolished, the sovereignty and the state power will be handed over to the people to be guaranteed by the new constitution framed by the elected members of the constituent assembly, which adequately represents all classes, castes, regions, women, Dalits, minorities, and oppressed communities. Secondly, a new national army will be established dissolving the present Royal Army, and that army will be under the elected representatives of the constituent assembly. Thirdly, elected assembly of people's representatives with adequate representation of different classes, castes, regions, women, Dalits, linguistic and religious groups and persons will be supreme body of the country and other organs of the state will be accountable to it. Fourthly, democratic and civil rights such as multi-party competition, adult voting right, rule of law, speech and press freedom and so on will be fully guaranteed. Fifthly, national and regional autonomy with the right of self-determination will be fully guaranteed to all oppressed nationalities, Madhesies and oppressed regions. Sixthly, the state will be fully indifferent or neutral to religion. Seventhly, education, health and employment will be maintained as fundamental rights and free basic education and health services will be made available to all people by the state. Eighthly, feudal land relations will be ended, and under the principle of 'land to the tiller' revolutionary land reform will be applied, and the policy

> of self-dependent national industrialisation will be followed with protection to national capital and national property. Ninthly, the Nepal-India Treaty of 1950, including all discriminatory (unequal) treaties will be scrapped and independent foreign policy based on Panchsheel will be followed. ... In that Loktantrik Gantantra of anti-feudal and anti-imperialist character, the proletarian party will try to transform into the direction of socialism by moving to the new democracy with continuous intervention in state power through political competitions agreeable to law. ... The party has followed this tactics with the faith that local power and base areas can be protected only through continuous political interventions at the centre and then the people's war can be pushed forward to its aimed destination.[10]

With reference to this, some parts of the *Manifesto of the CPN(Maoist) for the Constituent Assembly Election* further clarifies:

> It has been proved by the historical facts that the ten-year long people's great war is the highest peak of revolutionary movement to fulfil the political tasks that have remained incomplete in repeated armed struggle since 1951. Nobody can even imagine the present political change without the contribution of the Maoist people's war. The main credit of awakening as seen in class, caste, religion, gender and Dalit struggle in the country and the declaration of a federal Loktantrik Ganatantra by the Interim Constitution goes to the ten-year long people's war. Had there not been a people's war, the monarchy would not have knelt down so easily; it would be unimaginable.
>
> Revolutionary communists hold their strong determination and accreditation that in a country like Nepal with semi-feudal and semi-colonial, foundation stone of socialism can be laid only after ending all forms of feudalism and monarchy after the completion of the bourgeois-democratic revolution. Standing congruous to that, the main current of revolutionary communists, CPN(Maoist) has been reiterating that the constituent assembly is the highest form of capitalist democracy.
>
> Along with the development of people's war, the process of raising the slogan of the constituent assembly and enriching it began. First of all, the Second Party Conference held in 2000, codified the then tactics in 'round table conference, interim government, election of constituent assembly'. Based on this demand, election for the constituent assembly was presented as the central political demand during the first Peace Talk of 2000.[11]

The party's stand on the Loktantrik Gantantra is explicit from the above extracts. Historical materialism teaches that policy, programme or slogan could be right or wrong depending upon the concrete situations. Based on this Marxist-Leninist principle, the Loktantrik Gantantra

10 Baburam Bhattarai, "Ten Years of People's War–Development of New People's Power and the Question of Democracy", *Ten Years of People's War*, Jana Dhwoni Publications, Kathmandu, June 2006, pp. 57-60.

11 *Manifesto of the CPN(Maoist) for the Election of the Constituent Assembly*, pp. 6, 10.

forwarded by the party should be evaluated. So, accepting the Loktantrik Gantantra as the immediate minimum programme (actually not immediate but minimum programme of the Nepalese revolution) is quite wrong for our party, after initiating the protracted people's war with the explicit goal of the new democratic republic as its minimum programme, which means the party has deviated from the fundamental Marxist-Leninist principle in relation to the state and revolution by taking the direction of liquidation.

How is the line of the Loktantrik Gantantra non-revolutionary?

The answer to this question will be given by the detailed comments and the arguments forwarded by the party leadership to justify the bourgeois-democratic republic (that is Loktantrik Ganatantra). The pillars on which the old type of bourgeois republic is proposed by our party further reveals how far the party has deviated from the Marxist-Leninist line.

2
Present World Situation and Democratic Revolution

After ditching the New Democratic Revolution for an old type of democratic republic (that is Loktantrik Gantantra), our party leadership justifies it as the "ground reality" of the "present national and international class and political balance of power". Is it not possible to pursue the goal of the new democratic republic in the present world situation as our party leadership argues? Is the Loktantrik Gantantra really the "ground reality", as the Chairman Prachanda says? Has "our party forwarded the tactics of the Loktantrik Gantantra with a consideration over the present national and international class and political balance of power" as claimed by Comrade Bhattarai?

The correct answer to these questions is given by a historical materialist analysis of the present world situation, which means the 'present world situation' does not mean just the last couple of decades. It relates to the stage of the development of capitalism. Marxism-Leninism understands the whole period of development up to the present by dividing it into two parts. The first is the competitive stage. With the characteristic of free competition among capitalists, and the possibility of the development of capitalism in individual nations considered as the independent units. The main form of capital was industrial capital and the production of commodities and their export were the bases of economic life at that stage. Commercial activities were an integral organ of this stage with the extension of commodity production, and increasing demand of raw material, cheap labour and a secure market for commodity encouraged capitalist colonisation unlimitedly.

The basic character of the development of capitalism reached its highest stage by the end of the 19th century and the early years of the twentieth century, which Marxism-Leninism understands as the new stage for the worldwide monopoly stage of finance capital, or imperialism. As a result, the concentration of production and monopolies came into existence. Now we see the monopoly of a handful of capitalists not of a state of competition, mainly in the areas of production, distribution and price determination. As Lenin says, this situation has become "a general and fundamental law of the present stage of development of capitalism."[12] Industries that do not obey the monopolists and do not want to come under their influence, are harmed and controlled by the monopolists through various means. The organising exchange holders, who understand the relation between industry and the banks, remain at the centre of economic activities, whereas the first stage of economic activities of experienced commercial traders are centred in identifying the needs of buyers. The foundation of commodity production is getting weaker now, and a large share of profit is centralised in the hands of exchange holders.

Although the form of production now is getting socialised everyday, it is not the producer but the financial exchange holders who enjoy its fruit. The role of banks has undergone a sea change from the early capitalism (from the point of view of quantity as well as quality). At present, the bank occupies the position of monopolist of countless industries and businesses from the position of mediator. In this process, big banks have pushed out smaller banks. An excessive percent of total capital in the world is centralised in a handful of big banks. The importance and role of the banks has changed fundamentally due to the centralisation of capital and the banks' extended activities. The control of big banks over capitalists and their organisations has gradually increased. In essence, contrary to the epoch of industrial capitalism, control of the banks dominates industrial capital in this epoch. Industrial capitalists are dependent on big banks. The world economy has shifted into the hands of the big banks due to the centralisation of banks and banking capital. In relation to building capital, unlike in the past, a fundamental characteristic of monopoly capitalism, is the unholy link between the industry and business, and then with government. Owing to this development, the governments of all countries are a parasitical body to the world capital. Likewise, the mixing of banking with industry developed the finance capital, and the power of ordinary capital came under the power of finance capital.

---

12 V. I. Lenin, "Imperialism, the Highest Stage of Capitalism", *Collected Works*, Eng. ed., Progress Publishers, Moscow, Third Printing, 1977, Vol. 22, p. 200.

In modern capitalism, as Lenin says:

> The ownership of capital is separated from the application of capital to production, that money capital is separated from industrial or productive capital, and that the rentier who lives entirely on income obtained from money capital, is separated from the entrepreneur and from all who are directly concerned in the management of capital.[13]

In the present epoch of capitalism, the separation of money capital from industrial or productive capital has already taken a broad shape. The separation between a handful of interest seekers (moneylenders) and entrepreneurs who live on the income from money capital itself, and the numerous people with direct involvement in the management of capital, has become wider and deep. In this epoch, the development of capitalism, industrial capital and finance capital, the two in combination, earn immense profit from the investment in the land property, transport, education, health and communication, and not just from moneylending. The present world is an international net of finance capital. At this stage of the development of capitalism, worldwide export of capital has transformed a great number of nations into integral parts of world-finance capital by destroying their national borders. Previously, the development of capitalism in countries was comparatively healthy. However, the development of imperialism, capitalism develops according to the "holy" will of exported capital in the undeveloped, backward, or colonial countries. As Lenin says, "The export of capital influences greatly accelerates the development of capitalism in those countries to which it is exported." Lenin brings forward other overlooked and serious questions of importance. For example, "The capital-exporting countries are nearly always able to obtain certain "advantages", the character of which throws light on the peculiarity of the epoch of finance capital and monopoly".

In reality, under the present world system, every constituent of the money market sanctions loan-capital with different interests. In that reference, the main purpose of capital export is to strengthen neo-colonialism in the capital-exporting countries, and encourage commodity and service export. Lenin says further:

> Finance capital has created the epoch of monopolies, and monopolies introduce everywhere monopolist principles: the utilisation of "connections" for profitable transactions takes the place of competition on the open market. The most usual thing is to stipulate that part of the loan granted shall be spent on purchases in the creditor country, particularly on orders

13 V. I. Lenin, "Imperialism, the Highest Stage of Capitalism", *Collected Works*, Eng. ed., Progress Publishers, Moscow, Third Printing, 1977, Vol. 22, p. 238.

> for war materials, or for ships, etc. ... The export of capital thus becomes a means of encouraging the export of commodities.[14]

As the world market is a product of modern capitalism, monopolist associations, cartels, syndicates and trusts capture industries of their countries and the world market as well. Lenin states:

> As the export of capital increased, and as the foreign and colonial connections and "spheres of influence" of the big monopolist associations expanded in all ways, things "naturally" gravitated towards an international agreement among these associations, and towards the formation of international cartels.[15]

After the death of Lenin, specifically in the aftermath of the Second World War, the direction of organising international cartels was generally completed. The World Bank, International Monetary Fund, World Trade Organisation (previously GATT), Asian Development Bank, inter-government world and regional institutions and huge multinational companies divided the world on a mutual understanding, and ended the situation of competition for dominance, at least temporarily. However, this situation is not absolute because the basic character of capitalism is one of uneven development, which creates the necessity for redivision, during intervals of decades or several decades. Lenin has expressed repeatedly that objective bases are continuously active.

> The capitalists divide the world, not out of any particular malice, but because the degree of concentration which has been reached forces them to adopt this method in order to obtain profits. And they divide it "in proportion to capital", "in proportion to strength", because there cannot be any other method of division under commodity production and capitalism. But strength varies with the degree of economic and political development.
>
> The epoch of the latest stage of capitalism shows us that certain relations between capitalist associations grow up, *based* on the economic division of the world; while parallel to and in connection with it, certain relations grow up between political alliances, between states, on the basis of the territorial division of the world, of the struggle for colonies, of the "struggle for spheres of influence".

The division of the world, "in proportion to capital", "in proportion to strength", etc., carried out after the First World War, proved to be "unjust" at the beginning of the fourth decade. The result was the Second World War, which created new divisions of the world on a new proportion of capital and strength. Later, some relations developed amongst the capitalist powers

14 V. I. Lenin, "Imperialism, the Highest Stage of Capitalism", *Collected Works*, Eng. ed., Progress Publishers, Moscow, Third Printing, 1977, Vol. 22, pp. 243-44.

15 V. I. Lenin, "Imperialism, the Highest Stage of Capitalism", *Collected Works*, Eng. ed., Progress Publishers, Moscow, Third Printing, 1977, Vol. 22, p. 246.

different from the time of the previous redivision. Likewise, during this period new relations between political organisations have cropped up which are different from the past regional division of the world as a struggle for economic regions. Such a development is the result of the redivision of the world in accordance with new proportion and balance of power and capital.

Lenin has correctly defined the present world as "a peculiar epoch of world colonial policy." He has concluded that the present epoch has a close relationship with a new stage of the development of capitalism. The question arises what the term "epoch" means. This latest stage is nothing more than the stage of finance capital. In the present era, the colonial policy of imperialism is different from the earlier commercial and industrial policy of capitalism as Lenin states: "In the first place, two questions of fact arise here: is an intensification of colonial policy, a sharpening of the struggle for colonies, observed precisely in the epoch of finance capital? And how, in this respect, is the world divided at the present time?"[16]

The question raised by Lenin is more relevant and important even after about one hundred years because only by getting the correct answer of the question can we understand issues like state power, system of governance, class struggle, enabling us to adopt a true Marxist-Leninist policy.

In the previous world situation, in the epoch of competitive capitalism, commercial and industrial capital had an interest in raw materials discovered already, whereas the finance capital is interested in new possible sources in addition to those already discovered. At present, due to the remarkable development of science and technology, more return is possible. In the context of natural resources almost over, it will enable the owners of finance capital to earn excessive profit. It is vital to secure a safe position in the developing countries for finance capital in the present background where division of the world has already been completed and only redivision is possible. In this epoch of capitalism, the superstructure stands on the base of finance capital, which applies not only in relation to the countries where finance capital has developed and is mature, but also to the developing countries as well. Although some feudal elements and relations still exist in the economic base and superstructure of all developing countries, their foreign policy, defence, etc., are framed so as to be favourable to the finance capital. It appears that the colonial system does not exist, at least on the surface, at present.

However, the developing countries remain as parts of the cogwheels of the world finance capital as the development of capitalism within a national boundary is impossible unless it is an integral part of the former at this stage

16 V. I. Lenin, "Imperialism, the Highest Stage of Capitalism", *Collected Works*, Eng. ed., Progress Publishers, Moscow, Third Printing, 1977, Vol. 22, pp. 254-55.

of the capitalistic monopoly. Finance capital and foreign policy based on world finance capital create countless transitional forms of dependence of the state. If looked at deeply, those different forms of dependence of states are nothing more than financial and diplomatic dependence.

The following statement of Lenin clarifies this:

> The interests pursued in exporting capital also give an impetus to the conquest of colonies, for in the colonial market it is easier to employ monopoly methods (and sometimes they are the only methods that can be employed) to eliminate competition, to ensure supplies, to secure the necessary "connections", etc. The non-economic superstructure which grows on the basis of finance capital, its politics and its ideology, stimulates the striving for colonial conquest.

Hilferding correctly observes that "Finance capital does not want liberty, it wants domination." At present, unlike in the past, capital cannot establish a direct colony as that would not be profitable for its long-term interest. To achieve its long-term interest, the finance capital has established indirect measures. Financial and diplomatic dependence of weaker countries are indirect measures as viewed by Lenin:

> Finance capital and its foreign policy, which is the struggle of the great powers for the economic and political division of the world, give rise to a number of *transitional* forms of state dependence. Not only are the two main groups of countries, those owing colonies, and the colonies themselves, but also the diverse forms of dependent countries which, politically, are formally independent, but in fact, are enmeshed in the net of financial and diplomatic dependence.[17]

Dozens of countries in the world are dependent financially on imperialism just as financial colonies. Finance capital, invested in the important sector on a big scale for controlling the economic and political life of the concerned dependent countries, functions as a loyal diplomacy. Those bigger firms, industries and international non-government organisations (INGOs), connected to the big banks and imperialists for loan and help possess such objectives and achieve too. There are numerous examples of loan lender countries and organisations pressurizing the loan taking countries. The World Bank, International Monetary Fund and Asian Development Bank are the specific examples of them. At present, along with political freedom, financial and diplomatic dependence also exist. The particularity of the past relationship between bigger and smaller countries has become a general process at present, a strong link in the chain of international finance capital.

In the history of capitalism, as Lenin and Stalin say, the above mentioned situation is the development of contradiction of capitalism

17 V. I. Lenin, "Imperialism, the Highest Stage of Capitalism", *Collected Works*, Eng. ed., Progress Publishers, Moscow, Third Printing, 1977, Vol. 22, pp. 262-63.

to the ultimate extent, and after crossing it to the extent of eruption of revolution. Stalin talks of three contradictions as the basic outcome of the developed substantial contradictions under the new situation of monopoly capitalism:

> The *first contradiction* is the contradiction between labour and capital. Imperialism is the omnipotence of the monopolist trusts and syndicates, of the banks and the financial oligarchy, in the industrial countries. In the fight against this omnipotence, the customary methods of the working-class–trade unions and cooperatives, parliamentary parties and the parliamentary struggle–have proved to be totally inadequate. Either place yourself at the mercy of capital, eke out a wretched existence as of old and sink lower and lower, or adopt a new weapon–this is the alternative imperialism puts before the vast masses of the proletariat. Imperialism brings the working-class to revolution.

> The *second contradiction* is the contradiction among the various financial groups and imperialist powers in their struggle for sources of raw materials, for foreign territory. Imperialism is the export of capital to the sources of raw materials, the frenzied struggle for monopolist possession of these sources, the struggle for a redivision of the already divided world, a struggle waged with particular fury by new financial groups and powers seeking a "place in the sun" against the old groups and powers, which cling tenaciously to what they have seized. This frenzied struggle among the various groups of capitalists is notable in that it includes as an inevitable element imperialist wars, wars for the annexation of foreign territories. This circumstance, in its turn, is notable in that it leads to the mutual weakening of the imperialists, to the weakening of the position of capitalism in general, to the acceleration of the advent of the proletarian revolution and to the practical necessity of this revolution.

> The *third contradiction* is the contradiction between the handful of ruling, "civilised" nations and the hundreds of millions of the colonial and dependent peoples of the world. Imperialism is the most barefaced exploitation and the most inhuman oppression of hundreds of millions of people inhabiting vast colonies and dependent countries. The purpose of this exploitation and of this oppression is to squeeze out super-profits. But in exploiting these countries imperialism is compelled to build there railways, factories and mills, industrial and commercial centres. The appearance of a class of proletarians, the emergence of a native intelligentsia, the awakening of national consciousness, the growth of the liberation movement–such are the inevitable results of this "policy." The growth of the revolutionary movement in all colonies and dependent countries without exception clearly testifies to this fact. This circumstance is of importance for the proletariat inasmuch as it saps radically the position of capitalism by converting the colonies and dependent countries from reserves of imperialism into reserves of the proletarian revolution.

In this regard, Stalin concludes further: "Such, in general, are the principal contradictions of imperialism which have converted the old, "flourishing" capitalism into moribund capitalism."[18]

After we define the world situation of the present like this, as in the socialist revolution, in a semi-feudal, semi(neo)-colonial country like Nepal, the form and breadth, depth, and thinking related to the plan of revolution should be made. Had Lenin, Stalin and Mao not prepared the plan for the proletarian revolution according to the changed world situation, the revolutions of Russia and China would not have succeeded. The Second International failed because of a misunderstanding of the new stage that had developed in the history of capitalism. In the new situation as well, they came with a plan of revolution suitable for the first stage. What kind of plan should be prepared for a semi-feudal and semi(neo)-colonial country like Nepal, in the imperialist era?

This question figured since the First World War, specifically after the First Great Socialist Revolution of October 1917. By developing Lenin's thinking, Stalin suggested that under imperialism, the proletarian class should take the leadership of the democratic revolution, uniting the anti-imperialist forces with the cooperation from the peasantry; whereas the previous thinking suggested that the capitalist class should be given leadership until the capitalist revolution reached its full development, and then the proletarian class should struggle for the socialist revolution.

While leading the revolution in semi-feudal, colonial and semi-colonial China, Mao Tse-tung raised the thought of Lenin and Stalin to a new height and gave the world communist movement a complete theory, strategy and tactics regarding the democratic revolution in the present epoch of imperialism and proletarian revolution. The theory of democratic revolution forwarded by Mao in semi-feudal, colonial and semi-colonial China was not correct only for the then situation of China. It is correct in other semi-feudal and neo-colonial countries too. We are at present in the epoch of imperialism, which may continue for several decades. So, the theory, strategy and tactics of the new democratic revolution propounded by Mao Tse-tung is basically correct for a country like Nepal, and no new theory for revolution needs to be invented.

The analysis by Mao, in relation to the historical character of the Chinese revolution illuminates basic aspects of the minimum programme of the new democratic revolution. For example, Mao says: "The historical characteristic of the Chinese revolution lies in its divisions into the two stages, democracy and socialism". He signifies "the first being no longer

18 J. V. Stalin, "Foundation of Leninism", *Problems of Leninism*, Eng. ed., Foreign Language Press, Peking, 1976, pp. 4-6.

democracy in general, but democracy of the Chinese type, a new and special type, namely, New Democracy."

How did this historical characteristic emerge? Mao says:

> A brief study of the historical development of China and of the world shows that this characteristic did not emerge immediately after the Opium War, but took shape later, after the first imperialist world war and the October Revolution in Russia. Let us now examine the process of its formation.
>
> Clearly, it follows from the colonial, semi-colonial and semi-feudal character of present-day Chinese society that the Chinese revolution must be divided into two stages. The first step is to change the colonial, semi-colonial and semi-feudal form of society into an independent, democratic society. The second is to carry the revolution forward and build a socialist society. At present the Chinese revolution is taking the first step.
>
> The preparatory period for the first step began with the Opium War in 1840, *i.e.* when China's feudal society started changing into a semi-colonial and semi-feudal one. Then came the Movement of the Taiping Heavenly Kingdom, the Sino-French War, the Sino-Japanese War, the Reform Movement of 1898, the Revolution of 1911, the fourth May Movement, the Northern Expedition, the War of the Agrarian Revolution and the present War of Resistance Against Japan. Together these have taken up a whole century and in a sense they represent that first step, being struggles waged by the Chinese people, on different occasions and in varying degrees, against imperialism and the feudal forces in order to build up an independent, democratic society and complete the first revolution. The Revolution of 1911 was in a fuller sense the beginning of that revolution. In its social character, this revolution is a bourgeois-democratic and not a proletarian-socialist revolution. It is still unfinished and still demands great efforts, because to this day its enemies are still very strong. When Dr. Sun Yat-sen said, "The revolution is not yet completed, all my comrades must struggle on", he was referring to the bourgeois-democratic revolution. A change, however, occurred in China's bourgeois-democratic revolution after the outbreak of the first imperialist world war in 1914 and the founding of a socialist state on one-sixth of the globe as a result of the Russian October Revolution of 1917. Before these events, the Chinese bourgeois-democratic revolution came within the old category of the bourgeois-democratic world revolution, of which it was a part. Since these events, the Chinese bourgeois-democratic revolution has changed, it has come within the new category of bourgeois-democratic revolutions and, as far as the alignment of revolutionary forces is concerned, forms part of the proletarian-socialist world revolution. Because the first imperialist world war and the first victorious socialist revolution, the October Revolution, have changed the whole course of world history and ushered in a new era.
>
> It is an era in which the world capitalist front has collapsed in one part of the globe (one-sixth of the world) and has fully revealed its decadence

> everywhere else, in which the remaining capitalist parts cannot survive without relying more than ever on the colonies and semi-colonies, in which a socialist state has been established and has proclaimed its readiness to give active support to the liberation movement of all colonies and semi-colonies, and in which the proletariat of the capitalist countries is steadily freeing itself from the social-imperialist influence of the social-democratic parties and has proclaimed its support for the liberation movement in the colonies and semi-colonies. In this era, any revolution in a colony or semi-colony that is directed against imperialism, *i.e.* against the international bourgeoisie or international capitalism, no longer comes within the old category of the bourgeois-democratic world revolution, but within the new category. It is no longer part of the old bourgeois, or capitalist, world revolution, but is part of the new world revolution, the proletarian-socialist world revolution. Such revolutionary colonies and semi-colonies can no longer be regarded as allies of the counter-revolutionary front of world capitalism; they have become allies of the revolutionary front of world socialism.
>
> Such a revolution in a colonial and semi-colonial country is still fundamentally bourgeois-democratic in its social character during its first stage or first step, and although its objective mission is to clear the path for the development of capitalism, it is no longer a revolution of the old type led by the bourgeoisie with the aim of establishing a capitalist society and a state under bourgeois dictatorship. It belongs to the new type of revolution led by the proletariat with the aim, in the first stage, of establishing a new-democratic society and a state under the joint dictatorship of all the revolutionary classes. Thus this revolution actually serves the purpose of clearing a still wider path for the development of socialism. In the course of its progress, there may be a number of further sub-stages, because of changes on the enemy's side and within the ranks of our allies, but the fundamental character of the revolution remains unchanged.
>
> Such a revolution attacks imperialism at its very roots, and is therefore not tolerated but opposed by imperialism. However, it is favoured by socialism and supported by the land of socialism and the socialist international proletariat. Therefore, such a revolution inevitably becomes part of the proletarian-socialist world revolution.

To emphasise his thesis of China being "a part of world revolution", he writes:

> The "World Revolution" no longer refers to the old world revolution, for the old bourgeois world revolution has long been a thing of the past; it refers to the new world revolution, the socialist world revolution. Similarly, to form "part of" means to form part not of the old bourgeois, but of the new socialist revolution. This is a tremendous change unparalleled in the history of China and of the world.[19]

19 Mao Tse-tung, "On New Democracy", *Selected Works*, Eng. ed., Foreign Language Press, Peaking, 1965, Vol. 2, pp. 342-45.

Taking this theory, strategy and tactics of Mao related to the state and revolution, as the guiding principle, communist parties and organisations under the umbrella of the Revolutionary Internationalist Movement (RIM) or out of the RIM are drafting a plan of revolution in their countries. The declaration of the RIM states:

> The point of reference for elaborating revolutionary strategy and tactics in the colonial, semi (or neo) colonial countries remains the theory developed by Mao Tse-tung in the long years of revolutionary warfare in China. ... The target of the revolution in countries of this kind is foreign imperialism and the comprador-bureaucrat bourgeoisie and feudals, which are classes closely linked to and dependent on imperialism.[20]

In the present era of imperialism and proletarian revolution, the theory of democratic revolution, as advanced by Lenin and Stalin, and then developed by Mao, is suitable for a semi(neo)-colonial country like Nepal. By throwing this theory, strategy and tactics into the dustbin, our party has accepted a neo-bourgeois theory, strategy and tactics. Further analysis will clarify more.

3
Is Loktantrik Ganatantra a Transitional System?

In the proposal of 'Loktantrik Ganatantra' as the immediate (actually not immediate, but minimum programme) minimum programme, our party has forwarded the argument like the "peculiarity" of international and national situations as expressed in the statements of party leaders. Comrade Prachanda asserts that "the republic, after the broad restructuring in state power, will help solve the problems of class, nation, gender, and region present in the country, and it will play the role of transitional multi-party people's republic." Our party's slogan says Loktantrik Gantantra represents a transitional revolutionary wave to lead the class struggle in the specific situation of power balance. Comrade Bhattarai says, "in the present specific situation of Nepal, the transitional state power above the bourgeois parliamentary system, but not reached the level of new democracy, will be appropriate theoretically and practically, in the present semi-feudal and semi-colonial Nepal where the capitalistic objective ground is not yet prepared fully." He further says, "it is not a parliamentary capitalist republic of classic meaning, but transitional 'multi-party republic', one step ahead of that. So, only through continuous political interventions in the centre, the people's war can be pushed to its aimed destination". All these remarks clarify the leaders' deviation from the Marxist-Leninist line.

20 *Declaration of the Revolutionary Internationalist Movement (RIM)*, p. 31.

The party's claim that due to the domestic and international situation new democracy cannot be achieved by pursuing the revolutionary line, so the minimum programme (new democracy) should be substituted for the programme of Loktantrik Gantantra is wrong on ideological and political grounds. With the argument, the party neglects the "Promise" that the Meeting of Central Committee made in July 1995:

> (a) Our plan will be based on the lesson of Marxism-Leninism-Maoism in regard to revolutionary violence. Once again, our party promises to remain firm to the theory of people's war in the form of universal and invincible Marxist military theory of proletarian class developed by Mao, with reference to initiation of planning of this process to go ahead in the form of protracted people's war based on the strategy of surrounding city from countryside according to the specific characteristic of our country.
>
> (b) Our starting of the people's war will be based on accreditation that "all except state power is illusion." The major objective of armed struggle is to capture political power for people. Our party expresses its firm pledge to struggle continuously against all types of deviationist thinking and tendencies, including economism, reformism and anarchism.
>
> (c) Our plan will be based on the objective of achieving communism, the golden future of the human race, by destroying feudalism and imperialism to complete the new democratic revolution, and in continuation to move to the socialist revolution, and the theory to continue revolution under the proletarian dictatorship by launching cultural revolutions. We are committed and clear that arms once raised to end without fulfilling its objective is a crime to the proletarian class and people. This struggle will not be allowed to be a tool to end with partial reform in the condition of people, or with compromise by exerting pressure on reactionaries. Through this process only, our armed struggle will be free of all types of petty-bourgeois, sectarian, nationalistic, religious, communal, and caste illusions"[21]

A full surgical assessment of the "transitional" state system of Lokantrik Ganatantra, shows how much the party has deviated from the "Promise", which the full sitting of the Central Committee made in the course of initiation of the People's War.

'The Evaluation of the Domestic Situation and the Tactics of the Party' by the much discussed Chunbang Meeting that passed the programme for a "safe landing" (*i.e.* to liquidate revolution) of the people's war:

> (a) The people's war, started under the leadership of our party to solve the contradictions of the Nepalese people with the state power of feudal, bureaucratic and comprador capitalist class-based on union with feudalism and imperialism with the minimum programme of New Democratic Revolution

21 Prachanda, "First Plan of Historical People's War", *Selected Works*, Janadisha Publications, Nepal, July 2007, Vol. 2, p. 46.

and strategy, has brought a vast change in the power balance in national politics in ten years. Old state power is crushed in rural areas of the country. Though in its preliminary stage, people's national, regional and autonomous republican and local powers have come into existence, people's power is advancing towards achieving a central government of federal people's republic with Nepalese characteristic. Having passed the stage of strategic defence and balance against the enemy's military power, and entering into the offensive stage, the People's Liberation Army has implemented its first plan, which is a major characteristic of the present domestic situation."[22]

The reasons given by the party to justify the proposal of Loktantrik Gantantra do not comply with the 'The Evaluation of Domestic Situations and the Tactics of the Party'. How can the evaluation of the same thing on the same sitting be different? Both analyses cannot be correct. The party needs to explain its position regarding the difference between those two analyses.

Certainly, a basic difference lies between them. The first analysis brings forward the proposal that the "Promise" or "Pledge" made in June 1995 cannot be fulfilled by pursuing the protracted people's war and the bourgeois Loktantrik Ganatantra should be accepted as the immediate minimum programme. The second analysis advocates that the "Promise" that the party made during the people's war can be fulfilled if the party adheres to the clear objective of the new democratic republic.

From other examples as well, the eclecticism of the Chunbang Meeting is seen clearly. In the document passed by that sitting under 'The Programme of Counter-Offence in Relation to Future Work and Programme' the slogan is:

Organise extensive front in favour of Loktantrik Gantantra!
Raise political and military counter-offence to a new height!

Here, the matter of achieving Loktantrik Gantantra and achieving a new democratic republic are amalgamated. Under the counter-offensive plan, taking Loktantrik Ganatantra as the front slogan and also in the first place, is wrong. The counter-offensive is a higher step during the protracted people's war that gives a feeling of new democracy to be realised in future. However, here, the plan of the political and military counter-offensive of the party is presented just for achieving the bourgeois Loktantrik Ganatantra, which is contrary to sub-point (c) of the "Promise" made in the course of initiation of the people's war.

Comrade Prachanda says: "Our struggle is for Loktantrik Gantantra... Loktantrik Gantantra will be established in Nepal through the constituent

22 Prachanda, "Political and Organisational Report", *Selected Works*, Janadisha Publications, Nepal, July 2007, Vol. 2, p. 465.

assembly. This will solve the problem; will lead the country further towards the progressive direction." And, Comrade Bhattarai too says: "In general, the party has been bringing forward the slogan of Loktantrik Gantantra as the tactical slogan since the preparation and start of the people's war..." Both statements do not comply with "Promise" the party made in the course of its preparation and during the ten-year long people's great war. Had the party brought forward the slogan of Loktantrik Ganatantra as the aim and goal of the great people's war? Was the people's war and sacrifice of tens of thousands of brave warriors for the Loktantrik Ganatantra, not for the new democratic revolution? Nursing in general the objective of achieving Loktantrik Ganantantra ever since the preparation period and beginning of people's war by the paıty is tactics or strategy? Tactics are taken in the light of a specific situation, whereas strategy is the long-term plan. The contradiction between the monarchy and parliamentary parties increased remarkably during 2005/06, and the demand to end the monarchy and establish a republic can be seen as a tactical question. In that situation too the tactics should be under strategy, *i.e.* with reference to the aim of establishing a new democratic republic, which will be discussed under a separate sub-topic.

After forming the local power and the base areas, reaching the stage of political and military counter-offensive with a minimum programme of new democratic revolution; having a clear objective for a new democratic republic, having followed the path of protracted people's war; in the light of internal reactionaries suffering from contradictions and the difficulty in continuing the old system; it is sad for a communist party and its leaders to fight for Loktantrik Ganatantra as their final goal. If the party had put a proposal of election of the constituent assembly with the objective of Loktantrik Gantantra and its attainment under the system of dictatorial monarchy, without ever having started the people's war, it would have certainly been a progressive demand.

The party raised the bourgeois demand of constituent assembly and old type of bourgeois Loktantrik Ganatantra in the background of political events developed in the country, *i.e.* the Royal Palace massacre, the dictatorial step of the then king Gyanendra and its increasing contradictions with the parliamentary forces like the NC and the CPN(UML). The tactics were right to the extent of isolating the monarchy from the parliamentarian forces and ending the 239-year-old monarchy. However, the party totally failed to understand the characteristic of the epoch, to get closer to the aim of revolution by adopting the correct Marxist-Leninist practice under the specific situation. Rather, the party kept undoing one by one the achievements of the ten-year long people's great war.

The view of Comrade Prachanda that: "Complete democracy can be achieved through election of the constituent assembly" and treating the Loktantrik Gantantra to be "complete democracy" are totally wrong ideologically. It does not have anything in common with the Marxism-Leninism-Mao Tse-tung Thought as it accepts bourgeois, formal democracy as a pivot, as discussed in the *Third Letter.*

Comrade Bhattarai's "Justification of the party for having accepted the line of going ahead by capturing the local power and making base areas by giving the slogan of interim central power as well", and another statement, "local state power, and base areas can be defended and strengthened and people's war can be led to the destination only by intervening continuously centrally", need serious inspection. On that basis, he justifies the tactics (in actuality strategy) of Loktantrik Gantantra, without understanding that by doing so, he himself is entrapped irreversibly.

In the first phase of the people's war, our party approved the line of making base areas and capturing local power. Seizure of central power is its natural step further. The history of the world communist movement has proved time and again that the central power can be captured only by armed insurrection under the leadership of the party, which comrade Bhattarai cannot deny directly at present too. Therefore, by avoiding the fact of the interim central state power (in fact it is to capture the present government leadership), he has tried to justify the line of Loktantrik Gantantra. He has given the interim central state power the same rank as the local power to be captured by the forces of the people's war and with the revolutionary base areas. He has created great confusion by defining the capturing of the present government leadership as the interim central power and giving it the same rank as the local power to be captured by the forces of people's war with the revolutionary base areas. Loktantrik Gantantra is, by essence, a bourgeois republic of the old type, which is achieved by the joint effort of Nepali Congress, CPN(UML), Madhesi-based Parties and the CPN(Maoist). Even we reach time and again to power under this republic, it is wrong to think its peaceful transition ahead of the new democratic state. The interim state power of this nature (Loktantrik Ganatantra) has not any relation with the revolutionary base area and local power achieved by the people's war. Comrade Bhattarai's saying that "it is possible to reach the destination of people's war by continuously intervening in the interim state power" (Loktantrik Ganatantra), is nothing else than the rotten logic of the Second International and modern revisionists.

To justify Loktantrik Gantantra, Chairman Prachanda and Bhattarai advance another argument of the transitional state. Comrade Prachanda explains Loktantrik Ganatantra as the "transitional multi-party republic with broad restructuring in state power", whereas Comrade Bhattarai says, "transitional multi-party republic not of a classical parliamentary capitalist republic type, but a step ahead, but not developed to the level of the new democratic republic." How do communists take the transitional state in this light? Do communists approve of this type of transitional state?

In the present era of imperialism and proletarian revolution, the only transitional state power is the new democratic state power, in relation to semi(neo)-colonial and semi-feudal countries. We are passing through the same stage, and our party is presenting Loktantrik Gantantra between monarchy and new democratic state power as a transitional state power, which is a non-Marxist-Leninist line.

Mao has put political power in three basic groups based on the class character in the present epoch of imperialism and proletarian revolution. He says: "(1) republics under bourgeois dictatorship; (2) republics under the dictatorship of the proletariat; and (3) republics under the joint dictatorship of several revolutionary classes."

Analysing it further, he says:

> For a certain historical period, this form (Soviet type of form -Yogendra) is not suitable for the revolutions in the colonial and semi-colonial countries. During this period, therefore, a third form of state must be adopted in the revolutions of all colonial and semi-colonial countries, namely, the new democratic republic. This form suits a certain historical period and is therefore transitional; nevertheless, it is a form which is necessary and cannot be dispensed with.

Mao has explained that the third type of state system can have specific characteristics, but basically and in essence it is the same. He says:

> The third kind is the transitional form of state to be adopted in the revolutions of the colonial and semi-colonial countries. Each of these revolutions will necessarily have specific characteristics of its own, but these will be minor variations on a general theme. So long as they are revolutions in colonial or semi-colonial countries, their state and governmental structure will of necessity be basically the same, *i.e.* a new-democratic state under the joint dictatorship of several anti-imperialist classes.[23]

The view that Mao expresses in relation to the Chinese revolution also helps us understand Marxist-Leninist thinking related to a transitional state in relation to semi(neo)-colonial and semi-feudal countries like ours. He says:

> The Chinese revolution in this first stage (with its many sub-stages) is a new type of bourgeois-democratic revolution and is not yet itself a proletarian-

23 Mao Tse-tung, "On New Democracy", *Selected Works*, Eng. ed., Foreign Language Press, Peking, 1965, Vol. 2, pp. 350-51.

> socialist revolution in its social character, it has long become a part of the proletarian-socialist world revolution and is now even a very important part and a great ally of this world revolution. The first step or stage in our revolution is definitely not, and cannot be, the establishment of a capitalist society under the dictatorship of the Chinese bourgeoisie, but will result in the establishment of a new-democratic society under the joint dictatorship of all the revolutionary classes of China headed by the Chinese proletariat. The revolution will then be carried forward to the second stage, in which a socialist society will be established in China.[24]

First Mao says the question of leadership in a state power. The new democratic state power to be established in semi(neo)-colonial countries is an integral part of world proletarian revolution, a transitional form of state that leads to the second stage, *i.e.* socialism. The transition does not become complete by itself and to realise it the leadership of the new democratic state power is essential to be in the hands of the proletarian class. The history of two-line struggle–the life and death struggle between moving towards socialism under the leadership of Mao and the plan of consolidation of capitalism under the leadership of Liu Shu-chi and company even after the proletarian leadership at the helms of state power in China–should be taken seriously. In the above statements of Mao's words "headed by the Chinese proletariat", are explicit in meaning. By neglecting such an explicit explanation, the analysis and guidance of our party states that "In the Loktantrik Ganatantra, continuously intervening in state power through legal political competition, the party of proletariat is to transform towards the direction of socialism going through new democracy."

If it were possible in the Loktantrik Gantantra, as viewed by our party, "for the party of the proletarian class to intervene continuously in state power through legal political competition", and onward for the transition into socialism through new democracy, the comments of Comrade Bhattarai expressed at another place: "Loktantrik Gantantra is the highest form of bourgeois dictatorship and there should not remain confusion in revolutionary communists", should be taken seriously. If the two expressions are put together, the conclusion is that nothing else but transition from capitalism into socialism can be realised through the path of bourgeois democracy or formal democracy in a peaceful way without the revolutionary violence.

The other is the question of the bourgeois world revolution. The Marxist-Leninists the world over have held the view for long that after the First World War, specifically the October Socialist Revolution of 1917, the era of bourgeois world revolution was replaced by the epoch of world proletarian socialist revolution. In the epoch of monopoly capitalism, in

24 Mao Tse-tung, "On New Democracy", *Selected Works*, Eng. ed., Foreign Language Press, Peking, 1965, Vol. 2, p. 347.

a semi(neo)-colonial, semi-feudal country like Nepal, it is not possible to develop national capitalism, but the development of world-finance capitalism is possible through the old type of bourgeois revolution. As Mao says:

> It is all the more dependent on colonies and semi-colonies for survival and will certainly not allow any colony or semi-colony to establish anything like a capitalist society under the dictatorship of its own bourgeoisie. Just because Japanese imperialism is bogged down in serious economic and political crises, just because it is dying, it must invade China and reduce her to a colony, thereby blocking the road to bourgeois dictatorship and national capitalism in China.[25]

Neglecting the direction of Mao Tse-tung Thought, Comrade Bhattarai considers the Loktantrik Gantantra to be "the highest form of bourgeois dictatorship" and terms it an "anti-feudalist and anti-imperialist character" that "ends with feudalist land relation". Under the Loktantrik Ganatantra, he also suggests that "the party of proletariat needs to transform the state power in the direction of socialism through new democracy by continuously intervening, through legal political competition in the state power." This is nothing more than making Nepal like Turkey under the Kemalist dictatorship. Given the ten-year long people's great war, the sacrifice of thousands of martyrs, the presence of a strong People's Liberation Army and the specific background of revolutionary experience, it will be an ideological and political blunder to recreate the Kemalist Turkey in Nepal too.

Comrade Bhattarai says: "The Slogan of Loktantrik Gantantra, the highest form of bourgeois dictatorship, became necessary as the capitalist objective base is not completely ready in the semi-feudal and semi-colonial condition of Nepal." In other words, in a semi-feudal, semi(neo)-colonial country like Nepal, the objective base for proletarian revolution, new democratic revolution, is not possible, so the party has to abandon the minimum programme of the new democratic revolution and opt for the Loktantrik Gantantra which, in Comrade Bhattarai's own words, is "the highest form of bourgeois dictatorship". These are similar to his other statements quoted above, which make things clearer: "In a semi-feudal, semi-colonial country like Nepal, the base for socialism can be prepared only after the capitalist democratic revolution is completed by way of eliminating the forms of feudalism and monarchy." This, he says, to be "determination and faith of revolutionary communists from the very beginning". Bhattarai views like "preparing base for socialism", "bourgeois-democratic revolution", "highest form of bourgeois dictatorship", are nothing, but Loktantrik Ganatantra. The statement that follows immediately also makes it quite clear. "According to that very recognition, CPN(Maoist), the mainstream of communists, taking

25 Mao Tse-tung, "On New Democracy", *Selected Works*, Eng. ed., Foreign Language Press, Peking, 1965, Vol. 2, pp. 354-55.

the constituent assembly as the highest form of capitalist democracy, has been expressing its strong loyalty to it." The naked opportunism of Comrade Bhattarai can be seen when he says, "It is our opinion that only after giving perfection to bourgeois democracy, can we go ahead along the path of new democracy and socialism." This is completely a wrong view in the epoch of imperialism and proletarian revolution, especially in regard to revolution in a semi-feudal and semi(neo)-colonial country. It divides the bourgeois-democratic revolution into two stages–the stage of Loktantrik Gantantra, and new democracy. To say that without perfecting bourgeois democracy, *i.e.* Loktantrik Ganatantra, a new democratic revolution cannot be completed in a country, such as ours, is a false notion.

Comrade Bhattarai quotes a sentence from Engels and uses it as a strong weapon to justify the line of Loktantrik Ganatantra:

> The highest form of the state, the democratic republic, which under our modern conditions of society is more and more becoming an inevitable necessity, and is the form of state in which alone the last decisive struggle between the proletariat and bourgeoisie can be fought out. *(Origin of the Family, Private Property and State, March-May 1884).*

Comrade Bhattarai tries to show that it is right to accept the minimum programme of the bourgeois Loktantrik Ganatantra for our party. Engels' book was written about three and a half decades before the First World War and the Great Socialist Revolution of Russia in October 1917, when capitalism had hardly completed its competitive stage as it had not yet developed into imperialism. This statement is applicable only to a previous stage of bourgeois world revolution. Since then, there has been a drastic change in the world situation, so no one can oversight the changes from the bourgeois revolution as part of the bourgeois world revolution has been converted into a part of socialist world revolution too, as seen from the First World War and the Great October Socialist Revolution of Russia. So, Bhattarai's argument that in semi-feudal and semi(neo)-colonial countries, advance towards the new democracy and socialism can be possible only after the establishment of the old type of democratic republic is ridiculous. Contrary to the clear direction provided by Lenin, Stalin and Mao in relation to the bourgeois-democratic revolution under imperialism, in the new epoch of imperialism and proletarian revolution, Bhattarai quotes a part of a book written by Engels in the epoch of the bourgeois world revolution with great emphasis, without mentioning the period and the country and actual historical conditions of the time. He does not follow the most basic rule of dialectics and neglects the fact that, "a decision which is correct at one particular time may prove to be entirely unsuitable at another."[26]

26 *The Essential Stalin, Major Theoretical Writings, 1905-52*, Edited and with an introduction by Bruce Franklin, Published by Rahul Foundation, First ed., January 2010, p. 85.

4
Constituent Assembly Issue

Our party's policy in relation to the constituent assembly is not a true Marxist-Leninist one. A statement of the party quoted above clarifies further:

> Along with development of the people's war, the slogan of the constituent assembly was raised and made stronger. The Second Party Conference, held in 2000, codified the then tactics as round table conference, interim government and election of constituent assembly, first of all, and on the basis of that at the first peace talk in 2001, demand of election of constituent assembly was presented as central political demand.

Bhattarai's mistaken thinking is reflected in another statement quoted above:

> It is self-evident that the constituent assembly can be the then minimum outlet for all the three, monarchy, parliamentarians and new democrats. Being inspired with the reasonable spirit that civil war will intensify in the country, let it not be the situation of the fraud of a foreign power, and let the appropriate political outlet come about peacefully, in spite of sacrifice and martyrdom of a great scale, in order to find a solution through talk and discussion and postponing the programme of the new democratic revolution, the party has shown readiness to come down to the bourgeois programme of the constituent assembly for that.

This is a formal, legal and typical bourgeois view. By absolutely neglecting the complex class struggle and its extreme form, and the great people's war existing in Nepal, our party's view does not comply with the proletarian class, which is a betrayal of the proletariat. Lenin says:

> Every direct or indirect attempt to consider the question of the Constituent Assembly from a formal, legal point of view, within the framework of ordinary bourgeois democracy and disregarding the class struggle and civil war, would be a betrayal of the proletariat's cause, and the adoption of the bourgeois standpoint.[27]

It is disgusting for our party and the world proletariat for its claim to raise the slogan for the constituent assembly and strengthening it while waging a protracted people's war and capturing local power and making a revolutionary base to achieve a new democratic republic. It raises the question whether the party leadership fought the people's war for the constituent assembly and bourgeois democracy, not for the new democratic revolution. The party of the proletariat with the goal of the new democratic republic is

27 V. I. Lenin, "Theses on the Constituent Assembly", *Collected Works*, Eng. ed., Progress Publishers, Moscow, Third Printing, 1977, Vol. 26, p. 382.

not expected to raise and enrich in an epoch making way the slogan of the constituent assembly, but it should have gone for class-struggle, local power and extension of the base areas, proletarianisation of the party, proletarian internationalism for capturing the central power through violent revolution. However, the revolutionary communists do not deny the possibility of adopting a constituent assembly as an immediate slogan in the people's war when the contradiction between enemy forces takes a specific shape. Here the question arises–why did it become necessary to voice the slogan of the constituent assembly during the period of the people's war? It was to intensify the process in order to establish a new democratic republic. To our great surprise, our party postponed the programme of the new democratic revolution, and gave the slogan for the Loktantrik Ganatantra, which, as Lenin has explained in the following sentence, "In a bourgeois republic the Constituent Assembly represents the highest form of democracy."[28]

Comrade Prachanda and Bhattarai have defined the constituent assembly in different ways to convey its importance. Comrade Prachanda asserted from the field of people's war: "Complete democracy (in our sense Loktantrik Ganatantra) can be achieved through the constituent assembly." Comrade Bhattarai has argued in favour of a capitalist programme of the constituent assembly to stop civil war and possible foreign interference because of the war, and find an appropriate political outlet. He declares that the Loktantrik Ganatantra is the "base" for new democracy and then to move towards socialism, and it is possible only by agreeing to a bourgeois programme of the constituent assembly, which is a great climb down.

The *Manifesto of the CPN(Maoist) for the Election of the Constituent Assembly* highlights the importance of the constituent assembly:

> Our dream of almost sixty years is going to be realised for a new history. Old history of Nepal of thousands of years is changing sides with the end of the black epoch of feudalism and monarchy. We are entering a new epoch of bourgeois democracy and republic, and going to election of the constituent assembly to prepare the written form of this epoch change soon. With the highest practice of sovereign and state power entrusted to the Nepalese people, we are going to draw our fate-line and write our constitution for the first time in Nepalese history, for which the election of the constituent assembly is on the threshold.
>
> On behalf of the Communist Party of Nepal (Maoist), we want to make public some of our important promises to carry on a leading role in the great campaign of making new Nepal at the historical opportunity to institutionalise the change through the constituent assembly election. Being a political force and having played a leading role for the constituent assembly

28 V. I. Lenin, "Theses on the Constituent Assembly", *Collected Works*, Eng. ed., Progress Publishers, Moscow, Third Printing, 1977, Vol. 26, p. 379.

> with the greatest sacrifice, we realise our additional responsibility to present our work plan to build a new democratic and prosperous Nepal through the constituent assembly election. We would like to introduce a new leadership with new ideas to our respectable voters for the sake of the new Nepal.

The party says that the constituent assembly will institutionalise revolutionary change with different trends. It says, "We are in the process of institutionalizing revolutionary changes now with different trends for defending the achievements of the people's war. The forthcoming election of the constituent assembly at hand is a link of the same."[29] For the party of the proletariat that has adopted the path of the protracted people's war and reached the counter-offensive stage, making revolutionary base areas and capturing local power–to present the constituent assembly as the wand that will solve all problems is to insult the ten-year old people's war and thousands of martyrs who sacrificed themselves to achieve a new democratic republic of Nepal.

Regarding the constituent assembly our party views: "Our dream of almost sixty years"–is going to be realised and "we are going to make new history". This is a wrong presentation of the subject matter. With some turns in the history of Nepal over the last sixty years, revolutionary communists have also supported the slogan of the constituent assembly, but they never made it their minimum programme. The attainment of a new democratic republic is their minimum programme, but our party presents the communist movement as if it has been struggling for the constituent assembly, as a bourgeois movement, not fighting for a new democratic republic. Revolutionaries dream higher than the constituent assembly as they have moved ahead already to shake the earth and reach the sky. The dream of revolutionaries during the Jhapa Movement to build a new Nepal with the republic of people's democracy in the 1970s and the dream of the Nepali people, along with the oppressed people worldwide galvanised under our party's flag in 1996 in their fight against feudalism, imperialism and Indian expansionism are the most remarkable examples. No words will be sufficient to condemn our party's policy to divert or imprison anti-expansionist and imperialist public opinion into a sixty-year-old reformist demand at a time when the Nepali proletariat had reached the stage of building local power with a rapid expansion of revolutionary base areas by developing the counter-offensive stage politically and militarily with a view to realising this dream. To completely neglect the present, qualitatively different from the past, and to start talking about "making new history" by fulfilling a bourgeois demand is ridiculous. Such a view totally ignores the distinct characteristics of the present imperialism and proletarian era.

29 *Manifesto of the CPN(Maoist) for the Election of the Constituent Assembly*, pp. 2, 7.

The question to our party leadership is: "In what way does the new epoch of bourgeois democracy and republic" that our party honours with the title of "epoch change" differ from the semi(neo)-colonial and semi-feudal state power in the present epoch of world finance capitalism? According to the class character of the political state power, on what basis can we speak of an "epoch change" at all? Nepal has been a semi(neo)-colonial state for more than two hundred years, which means Nepal has been a part of imperial power. Accepting this truth, only liberation from semi(neo)-colonialism can be considered an "epoch change". The monarchy was in collusion with imperialism to fulfil its interest in Nepal. Political parties such as the Nepali Congress, CPN(UML), National Democratic Party and so on also helped imperialism and Indian expansionism to fulfil their interest in Nepal. Even after the end of monarchy in the country, no change has occurred in the semi(neo)-colonial conditions. Feudal relations of production are the same as they were in the past. The only thing that is different is that one imperialist agent (monarchy) is no longer in the picture. How can our party seriously define it as an "epoch change?" To make people of their country sovereign and capable of exercising state power revolutionary communists should not forget the first and basic condition of making Nepal an independent country by taking it out of the wheel of world finance capitalism. The country should be liberated from the semi(neo)-colonialism, but our party has climbed down from the minimum programme of the new democratic republic and protracted people's war after capturing local power and making a revolutionary base areas to free Nepal from the cogwheel of world-finance capitalism and Indian expansionism and to liberate it from the semi(neo)-colonial condition existing for centuries. It has adopted the bourgeois line to perfect the old type of bourgeois republic through a common consensus with all the political parties (Nepali Congress, CPN(UML), as well as feudal, comprador and bureaucratic capitalist political forces). Ironically, it states the bourgeois point of view to be in harmony with "new developed chain of thought of the Prachanda Path". For example, the *Manifesto of the Communist Party of Nepal (Maoist) for the Election of the Constituent Assembly* states:

> It is appropriate to mention here that CPN(Maoist) has raised the question of the constituent assembly not in the old classical meaning, but with the new meaning of democracy that developed as a chain of thought of the "Prachanda Path". Proposal related to the *Development of Democracy in the Twenty-First Century* by Chairman Prachanda and approved by the party in 2003, is in harmony not only, at present, in the stage of bourgeois revolution, but also tomorrow, in the socialist stage as well. The procedure of constitution writing, or constituent assembly by elected representatives of people in multi-party competition is in agreement to our developed chain of thought.[30]

30 *Manifesto of the CPN(Maoist) for the Election of the Constituent Assembly*, p. 11.

It is disgusting that our party has eulogised the procedure of constitution making through the constituent assembly that allows uninterrupted right of competition to framers of the anti-terrorist law that termed the people's war as terrorism and those, who put a price on the heads of our party leadership, the representatives of imperialism, Indian expansionism, feudal, comprador and bureaucratic capitalism, and their political vanguards the Nepali Congress, CPN(UML), NDPs, and Madhesi-based parties.

5
Restructuring of the State

Nepal has been under the feudal centralised system for centuries, first as a semi-colony of British-India and then of India. So, restructuring Nepal state is a vital issue. There have been several people's movements, armed conflicts and people's war for decades against such a state. The Jhapa armed uprising in the 1970s, the people's movement of 1990 and 2006 and the people's war launched under the leadership of CPN (Maoist) since February 13, 1996 are significant ones. Though they have not brought drastic political change in the country, they have been instrumental in bringing substantial changes in the socio-economic and political spheres. As a result of the ten-year people's war and developing contradictions among reactionary and status quoist forces in the country, the end of the monarchy, and the establishment of the republic have been realised. Restructuring the past structure of the army, police, bureaucracy, judiciary, and national defence policy and the past structure for governance is the necessity of the hour to make the people feel the pulse of change. In accordance with these political changes state restructuring should take place in order to safeguard them.

In relation to the restructuring of all the sectors, three things must be kept in mind:

Firstly, strengthening national independence, sovereignty, territorial integrity and unity among castes, races and regions; secondly, the end of the semi(neo)-colonial condition that has existed for about two hundred years and establishment of an independent sovereign Nepal; and thirdly, the end of feudal relations and solution to land problems, and development of national industry, and trade for building a national economy to promote socialism. All classes and their political parties may not have the same view regarding restructuring the state. The henchmen of imperialism and Indian expansionism, comprador and bureaucratic capitalist classes and their political parties will try to restructure the state according to their long-term class interests. Contrary to this, Marxist-Leninists emphasise restructuring of all the aspects of the state as per the objective of completing the remaining tasks of revolution, which is the characteristic of class struggle of the present Nepalese society. Our party's proposal about the restructuring of the state does not agree with the special conditions of class struggle at present, rather it agrees with the interests of henchmen of imperialism, Indian expansionism, comprador and bureaucratic capitalist classes and their political representatives. The restructuring of territory and the administrative unit on a racial and language basis and the complete negligence of the three important things mentioned above in the course of restructuring are some examples.

Our party had the objective of establishing a new democratic republic as the minimum programme to end the present semi(neo)-colonial and semi-feudal condition of Nepal, including state machinery (army, police, bureaucracy and judiciary) that has existed for centuries, with revolutionary violence, and to build a state machinery of revolutionary classes under the leadership of the proletariat. Now why it has accepted the plan of restructuring within the circumference laid out by the bourgeoisie is questionable. Why has our party after having built revolutionary base areas and local power, and entering the stage of political and military counter-offensive, instead of completing the remaining tasks of revolution, supported the bourgeois restructures? It means it wants just restructuring the old structure, without destroying it. Does this strategy synchronise with Marxism-Leninism-Mao Tse-tung Thought?

Our party's line of a new Nepal that "it is possible to go ahead along the path of new democracy and socialism" without destroying semi(neo)-colonial and semi-feudal state machinery does not match with the Marxism-Leninism-Mao Tse-tung Thought. The root of this opinion in our party is linked with the wrong view regarding the revolution in semi(neo)-colonial and semi-feudal countries in the era of imperialism and proletarian revolution. Our party has accepted the bourgeois multi-party republic as a minimum programme by dropping the line of the new democratic republic at a time when it was advancing towards the path of people's war, and creating a local power as well as revolutionary base areas and developing political and military counter-offensive. It no more considers the need of destroying the old state machinery and creating a state machinery that will be in line with the joint dictatorship of all revolutionary classes under the leadership of the proletarian class. It has forwarded a plan of restructuring the state in line with a bourgeois-democratic republic, which will not lead to new democracy and socialism.

Regarding the state and revolution, our party seems to have nursed the belief that winning an election with majority means capturing the state power. It is for this reason that our party has promised the strategy of moving to people's democracy and socialism after gaining the majority of seats in the constituent assembly. However, this is a very complex issue, not an easy question as viewed by our party. As Lenin said, it is a question of "the relation of the revolution to the state".

Our party has made a statement about capturing state power in its meetings and in the articles of leading comrades, but it has neglected the universal law of proletarian revolution with violence, for revolution in our country to destroy the old state machinery of feudal, comprador and bureaucratic capitalist classes, as a preliminary condition, which is also an universal law of the revolution of all semi(neo)-colonial countries of the world. The given emphasis has no meaning as it has abandoned the responsibility of proletarian revolution, forgetting Marx, who has taught us that "the proletariat cannot simply win state power in the sense that the old state apparatus passes into new hands, but must smash this apparatus, must break it and replace it by a new one."[31] Under the old type of democratic republic, no party of the proletariat can end the state machinery of imperialism, expansionism and feudal, comprador and bureaucratic capitalist through legal and political competition in a peaceful way. The birth of a new state machinery is possible only after the destruction of the semi(neo)-colonial and semi-feudal state machinery–army, bureaucracy judiciary and police. The following statements from Marx and Engels help us understand further to a great extent: "The working-class cannot simply lay hold of the ready-made state machinery, and wield it for its own purposes."[32] At another place, he says, "No longer attempt to transfer the bureaucratic-military apparatus from one hand to another, but to *smash* it."[33]

In the present era of imperialism and proletarian revolution, in a semi(neo)-colonial and semi-feudal country such as Nepal, the state machinery is either an organ of imperialism/world finance capitalism or an organ of the world proletarian revolution, which either strengthens bourgeois relations in the country–that is financial capitalist relations; or the world proletarian relations, *i.e.* world socialism, with no middle way. The Loktantrik Gantantra is a bourgeois state power, an organ of world

31 V. I. Lenin, "The State and Revolution", *Collected Works*, Progress Publishers, Moscow, Fourth Printing, 1980, Vol. 25, pp. 480, 489.

32 Karl Marx and Frederick Engels, "The Civil War in France", *Selected Works*, Progress Publishers, Moscow, Fourth Printing, 1977, Vol. 2, p. 217.

33 Marx to Kugelmam, "Karl Marx and Frederick Engels", *Selected Correspondence*, Eng. ed., Progress Publishers, Moscow, Third Revised Edition 1975, p. 247.

imperialism. So, our party's proposal of reforming the state machinery actually strengthens bourgeois relations in the country.

The above given facts clarify that our party leadership is oriented towards opportunism in relation to the new democratic revolution and the state. It has not only forgotten the experiences of the world socialist revolution, especially the experiences of China during the new democratic revolution; it has added "new" dimensions in Marxism, by creating a favourable situation for the bourgeois class, with a realisation that any attempt to destroy the old state mechanism (army, police, bureaucracy and judiciary) will bring trouble to it. Contrary to the correct Marxist line for revolution, not reform, in a semi(neo)-colonial and semi-feudal state mechanism, our party's line favours imperialists, Indian expansionist, feudal and comprador-bureaucratic capitalist elements to help further strengthen their control over Nepal.

6
War and Peace

Regarding the relation of the proletarian revolution to the violent path too, our party has deviated from Marxism-Leninism-Mao Tse-tung Thought and moved closer to the Second International and modern revisionism. The statement of Chairman Prachanda about the Loktantrik Ganatantra helps us understand the situation: "The slogan of the Loktantrik Ganatantra opens the gate for a peaceful solution of civil war as well, so it addresses the desire of people for change and peace and in another way plays a positive role in preparation of general insurrection." Likewise, Bhattarai too says: "After having evaluated the whole situation in terms of balance of power and desire of people and to stop bloodshed, we too have realised a sense of responsibility to adopt the peaceful way." This statement of Comrade Bhattarai further clarifies our party's view on the revolutionary violence:

> Being inspired by responsible thinking that the civil war may intensify the situation for foreign intervention, and that a solution could be found in a peaceful way, in spite of the sacrifice and martyrdom of a great many, we go for postponing the programme of the new democratic republic, and show readiness to come down to the bourgeois programme of the constituent assembly.

The relationship between proletarian revolution and revolutionary violence is discussed in the article 'War, Science and an Art', written with reference to the twelfth annual celebration of people's war in May/June 2007. So, the focus is now on how our party's leadership justifies the old type of democratic republic.

Having entered the stage of counter-offensive politically and militarily with its people's liberation army, revolutionary base areas and local power; the party now proposes an old democratic republic "to open the gate for a peaceful solution of civil war" on the pretext of not to let "bloodshed" and not to let the "situation out of control for foreign intervention", by "intensifying civil war". It has abandoned even an iota of Marxism in relation to proletarian revolutionary violence. It analyses civil war, peace and bloodshed in an abstract manner and denies the class and national character of war and bloodshed. Putting peace above class, the party presents it as a perfect thing in itself. How can our party take such a line in the name of Marxism that concedes Marxism-Leninism-Maoism as the guiding principle?

What is the real meaning of civil war? What is bloodshed and is it absolutely negative? Will the danger of intervention from a foreign country increase, if a revolutionary civil war intensifies? Our party has used words and phrases like "civil war", "peace", "bloodshed", "so far foreigners to play" with reference to the special condition of our country, *i.e.* waging the protracted people's war for a new democratic revolution as the minimum programme and having the People's Liberation Army along with the revolutionary base areas and local power as signs of reaching the stage of counter-offensive politically and militarily. Marxist-Leninists neither oppose civil war absolutely nor support peace absolutely as they are revolutionary, reactionary, just, and unjust depending upon their nature. So long as classes are in existence in society, the conditions of exploitation, suppression and oppression will survive, and the exploiter class inflicts oppression to such a degree that at a stage it gives birth to protest. In relation to the colonial and semi(neo)-colonial countries, imperialist countries perpetuate exploitation and oppression to the extent of extremity, forcing national liberation to resist the oppression. Politics becomes dominant for a certain duration in relation to the protest against class and national oppression making other means of war inevitable. When the problem cannot be handled or led by politics, war becomes inevitable. Or, to say: "War is a continuation of politics."[34] Lenin presents it in another place:

> War is a continuation of policy by other means. All wars are inseparable from the political systems that engender them. The policy which a given state, a given class within that state, pursued for a long time before the war is inevitably continued by that same class during the war, the form of action alone being changed.[35]

Emphasising the same insights of Lenin more forcefully, Mao says: "When politics develops to a certain stage beyond which it cannot proceed

34 V. I. Lenin, "Eighth All-Russia Conference of R.C.P. (B.)", *Collected Works*, Eng. ed., Progress Publishers, Moscow, Third Printing, 1977, Vol. 30, p. 179.

35 V. I. Lenin, "War and Revolution", *Collected Works*, Eng. ed., Progress Publishers, Moscow, Fourth Printing, 1980, Vol. 24, p. 400.

by the usual means, war breaks out to sweep the obstacles from the way."[36] For Marxism-Leninism-Mao Tse-tung Thought, both class war and a war for national liberation are the highest forms of politics. This means that it supports revolutionary national war and revolutionary class war and directs them believing that the achievement of real peace is possible only through such a war as suggested by Mao:

> War, this monster of mutual slaughter among men, will be finally eliminated by the progress of human society, and in the not too distant future too. But there is only one way to eliminate it and that is to oppose war with war, to oppose counter-revolutionary war with revolutionary war, to oppose national counter-revolutionary war with national revolutionary war, and to oppose counter-revolutionary class war with revolutionary class war. History knows only two kinds of war, just and unjust. We support just wars and oppose unjust wars. All counter-revolutionary wars are unjust, all revolutionary wars are just. Mankind's era of wars will be brought to an end by our own efforts, and beyond doubt the war we wage is part of the final battle.[37]

Our party neglects the Marxist-Leninist theory and experience of centuries related to war and peace by seeking a "peaceful solution of civil war", without "bloodshed". The people's war did not start and spread in Nepal just haphazardly; it was the highest stage of the development of class and national struggle for decades. It is related with the political system of the country and the world existing for centuries. As a result of the development of the continuation of politics, *i.e.* the struggle between proletariat, democratic and patriotic forces on the one hand, and on the other perpetuating the status quo of Nepal as a neo-colony for imperialist, Indian expansionist, internal feudal, comprador, and bureaucratic capitalist forces propelled people's war into existence at a certain stage. As long as the situation of exploitation, suppression or oppression of one class over another exists in society, the exploiter class oppresses others to the extent that creates resistance as its repercussion.

Our party understood the specific stage of development of those policies (*i.e.* politics) in the past, and led the people's war against those obstacles, but now it is "dedicated" to stop "bloodshed" and seek a "peaceful solution of civil war." Generally, this higher stage of political development will be stopped after the end of the obstacle, *i.e.* the attainment of the political goal. War will continue until the goal is attained. Mao says:

> When the obstacle is removed, our political aim will be attained and the war concluded. But if the obstacle is not completely swept away, the war will

36 Mao Tse-tung, "On Protracted War", *Selected Military Writings*, Foreign Language Press, Peking, 1967, p. 227.

37 Mao Tse-tung, "Strategy in China's Revolutionary War", *Selected Military Writings*, Foreign Language Press, Peking, 1967, pp. 80-81.

> have to continue till the aim is fully accomplished... It can therefore be said that politics is war without bloodshed while war is politics with bloodshed.[38]

Let us put more questions to our party leadership. Had the ten-year of people's war solved the contradictions of Nepalese society? Did the ten-year people's war attain our minimum programme of a new democratic republic? Certainly, our leadership cannot answer these questions in the positive. Therefore, why did the party declare an end to the people's war, dissolving revolutionary base areas and local power for a "peaceful solution"? Our descendants will be asking these questions in future.

The proposal of a "peaceful solution of civil war" and stopping "bloodshed", from our party leadership forgets the essence of the ten-year people's war, forming revolutionary base areas and local power and reaching the counter-offensive stage politically and militarily. It neglects the resistance against the reactionary class war through a revolutionary class war, national reactionary war through national revolutionary war and an unjust war versus a just war. It is incomprehensible that by strangling ie revolutionary protest, our party leadership has sought to establish peace in the country. Will "peace" be established in the country after revolutionaries quit the path of the people's war and "bloodshed"? The history of revolt from the slave revolt to proletarian class revolt gives a negative answer. The reality is that basic changes are not possible in semi(neo)-colonial and semi-feudal nations such as Nepal without civil war and national war. The "solution of civil war" proposed by our party leadership cannot give that result at all. Lenin says:

> Civil war is just as much a war as any other. He who accepts the class struggle cannot fail to accept civil wars, which in every class of society are the natural, and under certain conditions inevitable, continuation, development and intensification of the class struggle. That has been confirmed by every great revolution. To repudiate civil war, or to forget about it, is to fall into extreme opportunism and renounce the socialist revolution.[39]

Marxism-Leninism does not support unnecessary sacrifice. The party must lead the masses of people and party to avoid unnecessary sacrifices by adopting a correct strategy and working policy. However, Marxism-Leninism, in the journey of revolution endorses necessary sacrifice. The main issue is whether the ideological-political line is right or wrong. If the ideological-political line is wrong, the revolution cannot be completed even with whatever sacrifice and bloodshed. On the contrary, if the ideological-political line is correct, we can avoid unnecessary sacrifice or bloodshed.

38 Mao Tse-tung, "On Protracted War", *Selected Military Writings*, Foreign Language Press, Peking, 1967, p. 227.

39 V. I. Lenin, "The Military Programme of the Proletarian Revolution", *Collected Works*, Eng ed., Progress Publishers, Moscow, Fifth Printing 1981, Vol. 23, pp. 78-79.

The claim of our party to come down to the old type of democratic republic by dropping the new democratic revolution as the minimum programme, and ending the protracted people's war to escape bloodshed is absolutely wrong. The Communist Party of China, under the leadership of Mao, states in 1963: "To abandon revolution on the pretext of avoiding sacrifices is in reality to demand that the people should forever remain slaves and endure infinite pain and sacrifice."[40]

Is the party orienting Nepal into the direction of being slaves forever under infinite sufferings and terrible sacrifices by fabricating the fear of 'bloodshed'? Has the party not given up the issues of liberation from neo-colonial and feudal, comprador and bureaucratic capitalist slavery? Is the party leading the country and the people to the direction of vicious suffering and terrifying sacrifices? Abundant reasons exist to raise these questions. In the epoch of world finance capitalism, *i.e.* imperialism, exploitation, oppression and bloodshed that the present system imposes on masses of working people is greater than the pain of revolution. Even if revolutionaries accept the path of peace, by turning away from the revolutionary war fearing the sacrifice, bloodshed will not be stopped because imperialism, expansionism and their domestic agents do not allow working-class people to live in peace. To dream of permanent peace is a one-sided view as there is no reduction in sacrifice and bloodshed as proven by the usual incidents in the country. Lenin says rightly that "even with the most peaceful course of events, the present system always and inevitably exacts countless sacrifices from the working-class."[41]

Comrade Bhattarai says, "The civil war may intensify the situation for foreign intervention, and that a solution could be found in a peaceful way." Comrade Bhattarai's argument reminds us of Nikita Khrushchev. Is it a repetition of history? The views by Khrushchev in relation to national and class war and those of Comrade Bhattarai's about the people's war in Nepal are the same. At that time, Khrushchev said, "A small spark can be a cause of fierce fire to change the world into ash", "local wars are dangerous", "We must work hard to stop sparks arousing wars" and so on. Here the symbolic words that Khrushchev used, such as "small sparks", "local wars", "spark rousing wars", etc., meant national liberation struggles in different countries of Asia, Africa and Latin America against imperialism and domestic reactionaries as well as class struggles in the developed countries. Then too the modern revisionists suggested not to launch revolutionary

40 "A Proposal Concerning the General line of the International Communist Movement", *The Great Debate*, The Polemic of the General Line of the International Communist Movement, Mass Line Publications, 1994, p. 16.

41 V. I. Lenin, "Another Massacre", *Collected Works*, Eng. ed., Progress Publishers, Moscow, Fifth Printing, 1977, Vol. 5, p. 25.

struggles because of the fear of another world war and claimed it was their responsibility to stop revolutionary struggles, whereas revolutionary Marxist-Leninists worldwide launched a historical struggle under the leadership of Mao against the servants of imperialism.

Almost after about a half century, Comrade Bhattarai counsels the proletariat and the patriots of Nepal that the people's war should not be intensified to stop the foreign powers from intervening in Nepal. He means it must be stopped instantly and an appropriate outlet should be found. But, he neglects the basic issue that the Communist Party of China raised regarding Khrushchev's mistake. He (Bhattarai) "makes no distinction between just and unjust wars and betrays the communist stand of supporting just wars."[42]

Comrade Bhattarai expresses a non-Marxist-Leninist view in relation to the (people's) war, by proposing to give completion to the bourgeois republic with common consensus of all parliamentary and non-parliamentary political forces for the round-table conference, interim government and election of constituent assembly as a formula to solve the problem in a peaceful way. He suggests that proletarian and all patriotic forces of Nepal live in peaceful "coexistence", after having forsaken the ten-year people's war against imperialism, Indian expansionism, and feudal, comprador and bureaucratic capitalism.

Professing their desire for peace, Marxist-Leninists prefer the revolution, whether it is a national liberation or socialist revolution, should be a peaceful one if possible. However, the result is not determined by a person's or party's desire. The situation determines the way to achieve the goal. Neglecting this fact, modern revisionists put forward the line of "peaceful transition" from capitalism to communism and "peaceful coexistence" among colonies and imperialists, between the proletarian class and the capitalist class. Certainly, Marx and Lenin too raised the possibility of peaceful development of revolution in some specific situations. Marx expressed the possibility of the development of revolution in a peaceful way in countries such as Britain, America, and Holland where monopoly capitalism was not mature then and militarism and bureaucracy had not developed to such a high level. Lenin emphasised that when imperialism develops, peaceful development of revolution is not possible. However, Lenin put forward the view after the full development of imperialism, in the last period of the First World War. But he said that peaceful development of revolution is an opportunity, "very seldom to be met with in the history of revolution". The *Sixth letter* will clarify Lenin's view on this question at length.

42 Apologists if Neo-Colonialism, *The Great Debate*, The Polemic of the General Line of the International Communist Movement, Mass Line Publications, 1994, p. 149.

7
Loktantrik Ganatantra: Tactics or Strategy?

Our party has termed the slogan of Loktantrik Ganantra (old type of bourgeois republic) as the tactics for the strategic goal. Comrade Prachanda states, "we should understand the inter-relationship between new democracy, constituent assembly and Loktantrik Gantantra as an inter-relationship between strategic determination and tactical flexibility." For him, it is a "transitional revolutionary slogan, helpful to lead the class struggle ahead in a specific situation of power balance." Likewise, Comrade Bhattarai says: "Party of Nepalese proletarian forwarded the tactical slogan of Loktantrik Gantantra after analysing the present national and international class and political power balance." Is the slogan of 'Loktantrik Gantantra' just a tactical slogan as our party leadership claims? An analysis of the Marxist-Leninist point of view in relation to strategy and tactics will answer these questions. Stalin has rightly said: "The strategy and tactics of Leninism constitute the science of leadership in the revolutionary struggle of the proletariat." The strategy and tactics of Leninism is the science of leadership for revolutionary communists all over the world, throughout the whole epoch of imperialism and proletarian revolution. The "tactics" of Loktantrik Ganatantra that our party advanced on the touchstone of Leninist strategy and tactics will be analysed later. Stalin says:

> Strategy is the determination of the direction of the main blow of the proletariat at a given stage of the revolution, the elaboration of a corresponding plan for the disposition of the revolutionary forces (main and secondary reserves), the fight to carry out this plan throughout the given stage of the revolution.

He further says: "Strategy deals with the main forces of the revolution and their reserves. It changes with the passing of the revolution from one stage to another, but remains basically unchanged throughout a given time."

Stalin too expresses the Marxist-Leninist point of view on tactics like this:

> Tactics are the determination of the line of conduct of the proletariat in the comparatively short period of the flow or ebb of the movement, of the rise or decline of the revolution, the fight to carry out this line by means of replacing old forms of struggle and organisation by new ones, old slogans by new ones, by combining these forms. Tactics pursue less important objects; for their aim is not the winning of the war as a whole, but the winning of some particular engagements or some particular battles, the successful carrying through of some particular campaigns or actions corresponding to the concrete circumstances in the given period of rise or decline of the revolution. Tactics are a part of strategy, subordinate to it and serving it.

> Tactics change according to flow and ebb. ... Tactics deal with the forms of struggle and the forms of organisation of the proletariat, with their changes and combinations. During a given stage of the revolution tactics may change several times, depending on the flow or ebb, the rise or decline, of the revolution.[43]

The overall analysis of our party's view about Loktantrik Ganatantra exposes that it is not mere tactics as claimed by the party leadership. The old type of bourgeois republic is not a tactics adopted in a particular situation, *i.e.* "fall" in the people's war, nor is it a tactics adopted in the specific situation of the "rise" of people's war. It is also not a short period policy forwarded "to complete any particular campaign or action successfully" that our party adopted in a certain situation of a particular period of rise or fall during the ten-year people's war. It has presented Loktantrik Ganatantra as a "transitional" state power that can advance towards new democracy and socialism.

However, it is wrong to understand limiting it as a "tactical deal with the proletarian forms of struggle and organisation and the consequent changes and coincidence that follow". How can the programme of "transitional state power, higher than the bourgeois parliament, but not yet reached the level of new democracy", forwarded to give perfection to the capitalist republic with common consensus of political forces, be tactics? How can a "transitional" state system which tries to perfect the old type of bourgeois democracy by postponing (actually abandoning) the programme of the new democratic revolution be tactics?

The old type of bourgeois republic is an issue related to the dictatorship with a state power having a certain political class character. In the context of Nepal, it is a republic under the feudal comprador and bureaucratic dictatorship. Our party leadership says, the "Loktantrik Ganatantra is the highest form of bourgeois dictatorship". So, ditching the new democratic programme, the strategy of a certain political class, just by replacing the bourgeois programme with its own distinct character to gain power cannot be mere tactics.

Tactics that comes by displacing a strategy is a strategy in itself. The Loktantrik Ganatantra is neither an organ of new democracy nor is it subordinate to it, which is an opposed form of people's dictatorship. Therefore, the claim of our party forwarding tactics of Loktantrik Ganatantra to fulfil remaining tasks of revolution is totally wrong. Our party leadership has ditched the people's democratic republic for a bourgeois-democratic republic.

---

43 J. V. Stalin, "Foundation of Leninism", *Problems of Leninism*, Eng. ed., Foreign Language Press, Peking, 1976, pp. 80, 82-84.

The Second National Conference of 2000 codified a "round table conference, interim government and election of the constituent assembly" as "immediate tactics". In the 2001, first peace talk, the election of a constituent assembly was presented as the central political demand. The meeting of the central committee of the party, held in October 2005, led the journey of tactics to its destination, forsaking the protracted people's war of ten years and accepting the old type of bourgeois-democratic republic. So, the Chunbang Meeting has a specific importance in the history of the party.

The round table conference, interim government and constituent assembly are not bad as tactics. A party involved in people's war and waging a protracted people's war can adopt such tactics for assisting the minimum programme of the party as per the changes in the external and internal situations. To deny this is not Marxism-Leninism, but anarchism. The Communist Party of China raised the same type of demand by forwarding a specific programme in 1945 for a democratic coalition government, with the representation of all anti-Japan parties and people, even not affiliated to any party for a national government with nationwide support after dissolving the dictatorial Kuomintang rule. The main issue is whether there are really burning demands in the situation or whether the demands are for a "safe landing" (*i.e.* to liquidate revolution) of the leadership. It is to be seen whether demands are subordinate to new democracy of the party.

The history of the world communist movement shows that tactics is double edged sword as numerous communist parties got lost themselves in a Right-wing or Left-wing marsh after having adopted the policy to participate or boycott the parliamentary process tactically. However, the party of Lenin, having adopted the same tactics, remained revolutionary, and later on, adopted a revolutionary line in the First World War, and completed the Great Socialist Revolution. This is true for our party as well which has adopted tactics of using parliamentary elections in the past and established itself in the position as the third political power in the parliament. Several political parties of Nepal, participated in parliament tactically, and abandoned their Marxist-Leninist character under the guise of utilisation and changed into a bourgeois party in the past. Our party utilised parliamentary election as tactics and adhered to the goal of a new democratic republic, as proven by the protracted people's war in 1996, which reveals that tactics in itself is neither good nor bad. The main thing is which ideological-political line is leading it.

Having accepted the line of peaceful development of revolution, numerous communist parties of the world sank into the rightist opportunism. However, the Communist Party of Russia, under the leadership of Lenin, having adopted the same line, after the February revolution, successfully led the Great Socialist Revolution in October 1917. Regarding the two basically different results of the same tactics, it is found that communist parties that adopted this line for furthering the revolutionary line ultimately succeeded in their goal as they never allowed the tactics to override the strategy, whereas the communist parties which failed do so, ended with their degeneration into the revisionist party. The greatest weakness of our party is that it has presented the old type of democratic republic of a strategic character under the pretext of tactics. It will displace the party strategy, which means degeneration of the proletarian party into a bourgeois party. If we adopt the new democracy and take revolutionary violence as a universal path of revolution in the epoch of imperialism, we must instantly change the line of the old type of democratic republic to avoid an reverse effect.

The future of our party depends much on this. Our party leadership, instead of correcting this serious mistake justified it with the expressions from Marx, Engels, Lenin, Stalin and Mao given at different times. The statement of Engels has been made a strong base to justify the present line by the party leadership. This is Engels' statement: "The highest form of the state, the democratic republic, which under our modern conditions of society is more and more becoming an inevitable necessity, and is the form of state in which alone the last decisive struggle, between the proletariat and bourgeoisie can be fought out."[44]

Taking support from the above statement, Comrade Bhattarai states:

> This will be a helpful and necessary step for the progressive run of society to establish a democratic republic by ending monarchy, in the situation where it has been the only state system continuously (except a few short periods) as dictatorial monarchy almost in two hundred and fifty years' period since the central state system has been formed in Nepal. Based on this political and theoretical ground and paying attention to present national and international class and political balance, the party of the Nepalese proletarian class has brought forward tactical slogan of Loktantrik Ganatantra.

Though Lenin's view was not treated as the view of Engels as the basis in a written form, the party leadership has brought forward the 'tactics' of the old type of democratic republic as per its understanding of Lenin's view, regarding democratic revolution. In that context, Lenin's view by quoting here is appropriate: "A revolution incapable of *directly* overstepping the bounds of a mere democratic revolution."[45]

> Marxism teaches the proletarian not to keep aloof from the bourgeois revolution, not to be indifferent to it, not to allow the leadership of the

44 Frederick Engels, "Origin of the Family, Private Property and State", Marx and Engels, *Selected Works*, Progress Publishers, Moscow, Fourth Printing, 1977, Vol. 3, p. 329.

45 V. I. Lenin, "Two Tactics of Social-Democracy in the Democratic Revolution", *Collected Works*, Eng. ed., Progress Publishers, Moscow, Fourth Printing, 1977, Vol. 9, p. 87.

> revolution to be assumed by the bourgeoisie but, on the contrary, to take a most energetic part in it, to fight most resolutely for consistent proletarian democractism, for the revolution to be carried to its conclusion.[46]

On another occasion, he says: "We must not forget that there is not, nor can there be at the present time, any other means of bringing socialism nearer, than complete political liberty, than a democratic republic."[47]

Some aspects of the above quoted statements of Engels and Lenin are necessary to discuss. Engels' view was expressed during the epoch of the bourgeois world revolution. In the present epoch of imperialism and proletarian revolution, accepting the "tactics" of the bourgeois-democratic republic, as Comrade Bhattarai suggests, is a serious mistake. Certainly, communists in a semi(neo)-colonial and semi-feudal country such as ours should fight for a democratic republic, but it should be an organ, not of bourgeois world revolution, but of a world socialist revolution, *i.e.* an integral organ of world proletarian revolution. This is the new democratic republic, not the old type of democratic republic that our party has proposed.

Lenin's statements were related to revolution before the First World War, specifically before the Great Socialist Revolution, *i.e.* at the beginning of the era of imperialism and proletarian revolution cannot prove the validity of the "tactical" (actually strategical) slogan of our party. But, Lenin's view below shows the embryo of a new type of bourgeois-democratic revolution:

> At the head of the whole people, and particularly of the peasantry–for complete freedom, for a consistent democratic revolution, for a republic! At the head of all the toilers and the exploited–for socialism! Such in practice must be the policy of the revolutionary proletariat, such is the class slogan which must permeate and determine the solution of every tactical problem, every practical step of the workers' party during the revolution.[48]

On another occasion, he states his further mature thinking in relation to the bourgeois-democratic revolution:

> From the democratic revolution we shall at once, and precisely in accordance with the measure of our strength, the strength of the class-conscious and organised proletariat, begin to pass to the socialist revolution. We stand for uninterrupted revolution. We shall not stop half-way.[49]

---

46 V. I. Lenin, "Two Tactics of Social-Democracy in the Democratic Revolution", *Collected Works*, Eng. ed., Progress Publishers, Moscow, Fourth Printing, 1977, Vol. 9, p. 52.

47 V. I. Lenin, "Two Tactics of Social-Democracy in the Democratic Revolution", *Collected Works*, Eng. ed., Progress Publishers, Moscow, Fourth Printing, 1977, Vol. 9, p. 112.

48 V. I. Lenin, "Two Tactics of Social-Democracy in the Democratic Revolution", *Collected Works*, Eng. ed., Progress Publishers, Moscow, Fourth Printing, 1977, Vol. 9, p. 114.

49 V. I. Lenin, "Social Democracy's Attitude Towards the Peasant", *Collected Works*, Eng. ed., Progress Publishers, Moscow, Fourth Printing, 1977, Vol. 9, p. 237.

Referring to the above statement, Stalin correctly says:

> This was a new line in the question of the relation between the bourgeois revolution and the socialist revolution, a new theory of a regrouping of forces around the proletariat, towards the end of the bourgeois revolution, for a direct transition to the socialist revolution–the theory of the bourgeois-democratic revolution *passing into* the socialist revolution.[50]

Lenin's emphasis on the establishment of a democratic republic to end Czarist dictatorship also cannot prove the "tactics" of the old type of democratic republic of our party correct. For Lenin and the Communist Party of Russia, establishment of the democratic republic was not tactics, but a strategy. That was the minimum programme of the party and the period stretched from 1903 to February 1917, when there was no change in the strategic plan but tactics changed many times. Stalin writes about changes in the tactics during that period:

> In the period from 1903 to 1905 the party pursued offensive tactics, for the tide of the revolution was rising, the movement was on the upgrade, and tactics had to proceed from this fact. Accordingly, the forms of struggle were revolutionary, corresponding to the requirements of the rising tide of the revolution. Local political strikes, political demonstrations, the general political strike, boycott of the Duma, uprising, revolutionary fighting slogans–such were the forms of struggle that replaced each other during that period. These changes in the forms of struggle were accompanied by corresponding changes in the forms of organisation. Factory committees, revolutionary peasant committees, strike committees, Soviets of workers' deputies, a workers' party operating more or less openly–such were the forms of organisation during that period.
>
> In the period from 1907 to 1912 the party was compelled to resort to tactics of retreat; for we then experienced a decline in the revolutionary movement, the ebb of the revolution, and tactics necessarily had to take this fact into consideration. The forms of struggle, as well as the forms of organisation, changed accordingly: instead of the boycott of the Duma–participation in the Duma; instead of open revolutionary actions outside the Duma–actions and work in the Duma; instead of general political strikes–partial economic strikes, or simply a lull in activities. Of course, the party had to go underground during that period, while the revolutionary mass organisations were replaced by cultural, educational, cooperative, insurance and other legal organisations.[51]

To summarise Stalin, the relation of tactics is with the forms of struggle, an organisation of the proletariat and the consequent changes and

---

50 J. V. Stalin, *History of the Communist Party of the Soviet Union (Bolsheviks)*, Short Course, Kamgar Prakashan, Delhi, October 1985, p. 75.

51 J. V. Stalin, "Foundation of Leninism", *Problems of Leninism*, Eng. ed., Foreign Language Press, Peking, 1976, p. 83.

coincidence that occur. This talk on tactics by Stalin, under the minimum programme in the period of the Russian Revolution, *i.e.* establishment of democratic republic (from 1903-February 1917) after the end of Czarist dictatorship is a grand practical form of Leninism. This is the correct use of tactics, and it gives a good lesson regarding what tactics are and how they should be used.

The round table conference and the election for a constituent assembly can be ways of struggle, and it was right to be accepted in the context of political change (the situation of contradictions intensified between the monarchy and other parliamentary political forces). Making use of the contradiction amongst enemies was correct to the extent for strategic success. However, for a communist party, which led a protracted people's war for ten years, and accepted the minimum programme of new democratic revolution, proposing a minimum programme of bourgeois revolution under the name of tactics, is an extreme distortion of the Leninist tactics.

Some comrades have compared the programme of Loktantrik Gantantra to the coalition government proposed by the Communist Party of China under the leadership of Mao with other democratic parties, including the Kuomintang in April 1945. If Mao was right in putting forward that type of demand, why is it not correct to put forward the demand for a Loktantrik Ganatantra? With this claim, they have made a futile attempt to prove the bourgeois political line correct. Comparative study of the 'Political Report' presented by Mao passed at the Seventh National Congress of the Communist Party of China, known as 'On Coalition Government' and other materials 'On Peace Negotiations with the Kuomintang–Circular of the Central Committee of the Communist Party of China', and 'On the Chungking Negotiations', and the works of our party leaders regarding the tactics for Loktantrik Ganatantra, will clarify the subject matter appropriately.

Opportunists everywhere, especially rightist opportunists within the party who want to abandon the revolutionary line and seek an excuse for that, find the opinions of Marx and Engels related to the democratic republic, opinions of Lenin and Stalin related to the possibility of peaceful transition from capitalism to socialism after the bourgeois revolution of February 1917, and the proposal of Mao of April 1945 related to formation of coalition government with parties, including the Kuomintang and Chungking Agreement and so on for the "safe landing" (*i.e.* to liquidate revolution) as irrefutable weapons. The Communist Party of China, under the leadership of Mao, stressed in the Seventh Congress, with emphasis, that socialism cannot be attained without crossing the stage of republic (supremacy of people) and without completing the bourgeois-democratic revolution. This example cannot prove the validity of the Loktantrik Ganatantra as a tactical slogan.

Our party leadership has compared the old type of democratic republic to the coalition government demanded under the general programme of the new democratic republic by the Communist Party of China. But there is no similarity between Loktantrik Ganatantra of our party and the demand for joint government of the Communist Party of China at that time. It is clear that the demand for a 'Coalition Government' and the 'Chungking Negotiations' were completely under Leninist tactics. While presenting those demands, the Communist Party of China was accelerating the new democratic revolution and bringing its success closer. Whereas the "tactics" of the Loktantrik Gantantra of our party has dissolved the ten-year people's war, the People's Liberation Army formed on the blood and sweat of the people, giving up revolutionary base areas and local power one by one and consolidating bourgeois relations in the country. A comparative study of the Communist Party of China which brought forward a specific programme, *i.e.* Coalition Government at that time and the "tactics" of Loktantrik Gantantra brought forward by our party will make it clearer.

The Communist Party of China forwarded the proposal of a specific programme based on the development level of the minimum programme as well as the analysis of objective and subjective situation. The party sees the possibility that if a specific programme is separated from its general programme, political and ideological question may arise about the line of the party, and opportunists can use the specific programme accordingly. The specific programme is adopted by the Communist Party of China in accordance with the historical materialism in essence. The Communist Party of China, before entering the specific programme writes:

> First, China should not have a feudal, fascist and anti-popular state system under the dictatorship of the big landlords and big bourgeoisie, because eighteen years of government by the chief ruling clique of the Kuomintang have already proved its complete bankruptcy. Second, China cannot possibly establish the old type of democratic dictatorship–a purely national-bourgeois state–and therefore, should not attempt to do so, because on the one hand the Chinese national bourgeoisie has proved itself very flabby economically and politically, and on the other, for a long time now a new factor has been present, namely, the awakened Chinese proletariat with its leader, the Chinese Communist Party, which has demonstrated great capacity in the political arena and assumed leadership of the peasant masses, the urban petty-bourgeoisie, the intelligentsia and other democratic forces. Third, it is likewise impossible for the Chinese people to institute a socialist state system at the present stage when it is still their task to fight foreign and feudal oppression and the necessary social and economic conditions for a socialist state are still lacking.

> What then do we propose? We propose the establishment, after the thorough defeat of the Japanese aggressors, of a state system which we call New Democracy, namely a united-front democratic alliance based on the overwhelming majority of the people, under the leadership of the working-class.

Further, Mao says:

> The politics of New Democracy which we advocate consists in the overthrow of external oppression and of internal feudal and fascist oppression, and then the setting up not of the old type of democracy but of a political system which is a united front of all the democratic classes.
>
> If any Communist or Communist sympathiser talks about socialism and communism but fails to fight for this objective, if he belittles this bourgeois-democratic revolution, relaxes or slows down ever so slightly and shows the least disloyalty and coolness or is reluctant to shed his blood or give his life for it, then wittingly or unwittingly, such a person is betraying socialism and communism to a greater or lesser extent and is certainly not a politically conscious and staunch fighter for communism. It is a law of Marxism that socialism can be attained only via the stage of democracy. And in China the fight for democracy is a protracted one. It would be a sheer illusion to try to build a socialist society on the ruins of the colonial, semi-colonial and semi-feudal order without a united new-democratic state, without the development of the state sector of the new-democratic economy, of the private capitalist and the cooperative sectors, and of a national, scientific and mass culture, *i.e.* a new-democratic culture, and without the liberation and the development of the individuality of hundreds of millions of people–in short, without a thoroughgoing bourgeois-democratic revolution of a new type led by the communist party.

Mao writes in relation to the specific programme of the party presented in April 1945:

> Our party must also have a specific programme for each period based on this general programme. Our general programme of New Democracy will remain unchanged throughout the stage of the bourgeois-democratic revolution, that is, for several decades. But from phase to phase during this stage, conditions have changed or are changing and it is only natural that we have to change our specific programme accordingly. For example, our general programme of New Democracy has remained the same throughout the periods of the Northern Expedition, the Agrarian Revolutionary War and the War of Resistance Against Japan, but there have been changes in our specific programme, because our friends and enemies have not remained the same in the three periods.[52]

52 Mao Tse-tung, "On Coalition Government", *Selected Works*, Eng. ed., Foreign Language Press, Peking, Second ed., 1967, Vol. 3, pp. 229-30, 232-33, 235.

Our party leadership also accepts the need for a bourgeois-democratic revolution and its importance, in relation to our country, as done in China by Mao. In that sense, our party leadership is loyal to the socialism and communism, and it has followed Marxist theory that socialism can be attained only after crossing the stage of democracy. But this was true in the past, not in the present as clarified from its "tactics" of the old type of democratic republic. Our party adopted the theory of Mao in relation to the bourgeois-democratic revolution honestly and strictly when it was committed to the new democratic revolution as the minimum programme, and entered the stage of counter-offensive, through the strategic balance of protracted people's war by forming revolutionary base areas and local power. However, since the Chunbang Meeting, it brought forward the "tactics" of the old type of democratic republic, by forsaking the theory and strategy of new democratic revolution as revealed from the statements of Comrade Bhattarai who emphasises the establishment of a "transitional state power before new democracy/people's democracy", "giving perfection to bourgeois republic with common consensus of all political forces (feudal, comprador and bureaucratic capitalist forces-Yogendra) in the country." Celebrating the slogan of the old type of democratic republic, the slogan of other parliamentary forces, Bhattarai further says: "The party of proletarian class, with continuous intervention through legal political competition under the old type of democratic republic, passing through new democracy, will transform it into socialism".

In the general programme of the party and the specific programme presented in 1945, Mao has nowhere stated that the third type of state system between colonial, semi-colonial and semi-feudal state power and new democratic state power is essential. Nowhere has he said that "advance along the path of new democracy and socialism" is not possible without "giving perfection to bourgeois democracy". He has never said that a party of proletariat "should show" readiness to come down to the bourgeois programme of the constituent assembly by postponing (actually abandoning) the programme of the new democratic revolution. Let's leave the general programme, this type of view is found nowhere even in a specific programme. Rather, he emphasised the general programme of the party, based on that programme; "the party should have a specific programme for every period" and "the general programme of new democracy remains unchanged during the whole capitalist democratic stage." Contrary to that, our party has decided to "postpone" (actually to abandon) the minimum programme of the party to serve the old type of democratic republic. According to Lenin, Stalin and Mao, a specific programme, *i.e.* tactics should serve the general programme, *i.e.* the minimum programme. However, our party leadership puts the minimum programme of revolution in the service of the tactics, which means it is not the dog wagging its tail but the tail wagging the dog. This stand of the party leadership is a serious deviation from the Marxism-Leninism-Mao Tse-tung Thought.

The basic ten points of the specific programme were discussed in the Seventh National Congress of the Communist Party of China. We can take them as the main subject matter of specific programme. No independent existence of the essence of those programme is created. Every point is linked with the party strategy of a new type of democratic revolution to be completed as an integral part of world proletarian revolution. These points clear that their only mission is to support completing the general programme, *i.e.* new democratic revolution. Our party has also presented the "tactics" of the old type of democratic republic, enriched with nine internal subject matters. So, these two presentations appear similar.

However, from the point of view of essence, there is no similarity between them. They represent two separate epochs–the demand for a coalition government proposed in the Seventh National Congress of the Communist Party of China under the leadership of Mao, was a specific programme of democratic revolution to occur in the era of imperialism and proletarian revolution, whereas, "tactics" of the old type of democratic republic, proposed by our party, represents a minimum programme of the old type of world bourgeois revolution, in a country like ours in the epoch of imperialism and proletarian revolution.

Two questions should be addressed which will fundamentally address other questions too.

The essence of the specific programme of the Communist Party of China, under the leadership of Mao, is national liberation and democracy. Mao explained that the liberation of China from Japanese aggressor must be immediately attained which was possible only through the formation of a democratic joint government after ending the single party dictatorship of the Kuomintang. The "tactics" of the old type of democratic republic proposed by our party is silent on the liberation of Nepal from the semi(neo)-colonial situation. Our party's stance also on democracy is faulty. The end of the monarchy and the establishment of the republic is not a people's democracy, but a bourgeois formal democracy. What is necessary for Nepal, and for Nepalese people, is people's democracy, not bourgeois democracy, or formal democracy. National liberation can be attained only by making real democracy available to the people and unifying them under that flag. National liberation and people's democracy, the heart of the specific programme of the proposal of the Communist Party of China, is missing in the "Loktantrik Ganatantra" proposed by our party.

In the context of Nepal, to speak of the democracy of the people is to speak of democracy for workers and peasants. The character of revolution in our country, with a large percentage of peasants, is agricultural revolution. Peasants are the source of industrial workers of Nepal and the main political force to fight for democracy. Peasants are the most oppressed class for centuries, from imperialism and expansionism, who are oppressed by the monarchy, feudal and rich peasants, and the comprador and bureaucratic capitalist class. Therefore, without solving the problems of peasants, the democracy means exchanging of individuals to government or a change of people in the government. However, our party has stated the aim of "end of feudal land relation" and "protecting national capital and property, following the policy of self-dependent national industrialisation" as "tactics" of the Loktantrik Ganatantra.

It is good to know why the Communist Party of China, demanded a coalition government. At that time, coalition government was required because the old government, the single party dictatorship of the Kuomintang could not solve the burning issues of the country. This means to solve certain problems, a certain type of government is necessary.

The Communist Party of China, while demanding a coalition government, had also outlined the constituent parts of that type of government for clarity. The constituents of such government were nationalist-democratic forces. Our party has established a so-called Loktantrik Ganatantra in coordination with the world imperialism, Indian expansionism and their Nepalese agents (feudal, comprador and bureaucratic capitalist class). From a government constituted in harmony with such political forces, even if our party leads the government, can it address the problems related to democracy and people's livelihood, and national independence, sovereignty and territorial integrity? Certainly not.

Let's discuss feudal land relations. At present, there is joint government under our party leadership. Is it possible, under the present structure of government and constituent assembly to carry out revolutionary land reform or scientific land reforms as mentioned in the Interim Constitution, 2007? It is disgusting that our party is giving false promises to peasants to implement revolutionary land reform under this very government and constituent assembly, but in reality it is doing the reverse. During the people's war, the party somehow solved the problems of feudal relations and the issue of land ownership in a revolutionary way, despite having some weaknesses. Implementing land reform is quite distant under the present government and constituent assembly, and a marked danger of peasants being deprived of the achievements of the ten-year people's war. This is true in relation to "national capital and property protection" and "national industrialisation." To say that a policy of "national capital and property protection" and "national industrialisation" under the present structure of government and constituent assembly is possible means to deceive the people and the country.

The policy of the Communist Party of China, the tactics adopted in the course of the 'Coalition Government' and the 'Chungking Negotiations' to handle the People's Liberation Army, revolutionary base areas and local power, will be discussed in the following chapters. In the proposal for a Coalition Government, the Communist Party of China gave much importance to the people's army. It stated that the Chinese people could not attain freedom and unification without a people's army. It stated to the extent that it was not possible to defeat the Japanese aggressors and establishment of the proposed Coalition Government without the people's army. For example, the Political Report passed in the Seventh Congress states:

> Without an army standing on the people's side, it is impossible for the Chinese people to win freedom and unification, establish a coalition government, thoroughly defeat the Japanese aggressors and build a new China. At present the only armed forces that stand wholly on the people's side are the Liberated Areas' Eighth Route and New Fourth Armies, which are not very large; they are far from sufficient. Yet the Kuomintang group which opposes the people is ceaselessly intriguing to undermine and destroy the armies of the Liberated Areas. In 1944 the Kuomintang government presented a so-called memorandum demanding that the Communist Party should "disband, within a definite time limit", four-fifths of the armed forces of the Liberated Areas. In 1945, during the most recent negotiations, it has further demanded the handing over of all the armed forces of the Liberated Areas by the Communist Party, after which it would grant the Communist Party "legal status". ... These people tell the Communists, "Hand over your troops and we will grant you freedom." According to their theory, a political party that does not have any army should enjoy freedom."

Further it states: "It is the duty of the whole nation to struggle for the creation of the army of the Chinese people. Without a people's army the people have nothing. On this question there must be no empty theorizing whatsoever."[53]

Let us see the above statements from our perspective. Do not those views appear as pertinent in our own context? Certainly. Whatever Mao said about the people's army was based on the living experience of revolution from the time of the Paris Commune to China. As proven in China during Mao's time, we could neither continue the people's war of ten years nor form revolutionary local power and revolutionary base areas without the existence of a people's army, standing in favour of the people. Likewise, we

53 Mao Tse-tung, "On Coalition Government", *Selected Works*, Eng. ed., Foreign Language Press, Peking, Second ed., 1967, Vol. 3, pp. 245-47.

could not have weakened the feudal relations in rural areas, addressed the land problem and eliminate the monarchical system of 239 years without the presence of the people's army. Why couldn't a communist party achieve these things four and a half decades earlier? The straight answer is that the Communist Party of Nepal did not have the people's army at that period. This was why it could not make these achievements earlier for the Nepalese people. Our party could not put forward a correct Marxist-Leninist line on the most important issue of the People's Liberation Army to the opposition parties while signing the 12-point Agreement, Comprehensive Peace Accord and Interim Constitution, 2007. The behaviour of the reactionary ruling clique towards the People's Liberation Army that Mao talked about was based on the living experience of revolution from the time of the Paris Commune to China. A people's army itself is always a strong obstacle in the path of a counter-revolutionary conspiracy of the ruling clique. Reactionary rulers have used the reactionary army to oppress the people for decades. They form an armed force, in the form of the main mechanism of state, to make their reactionary rule stronger and longer; the more they centralise and strengthen the army, the more forcefully people raise their voice against injustice, oppression and national surrender of ruling class or activities of foreign intervention. When people are unable to retaliate to injustice, tyranny, suppression and oppression by other means, they form people's army. This is the most bitter situation for reactionaries who oppose it from the very beginning. They demand the instant dismemberment of the people's army as revealed from the one and a half month long negotiations between the Communist Party of China and the Kuomintang in October 1945.

By agreeing with the fundamental policy of peaceful national renovation, presented by the communist party in the discussions with the representatives of the Communist Party of China, the Kuomintang accepted "long-term cooperation, to stop civil war and to build a free, prosperous and strong China." It accepted the democratisation of political life, nationalisation of the army and the equality and legality of political parties as necessary measures for national renovation. They agreed on ending the patronisation of the Kuomintang as soon as possible by organising a conference of political advisers to guarantee the freedom that people in all democratic countries enjoy, for example faith, speech and press related freedom and freedom of assembly and organisation, and those related to nullifying ordinance and stopping to arrest people by judiciary and police, filing cases against them, releasing political prisoners, and implementation of local autonomous administration actively. Certainly, this agreement between the Kuomintang and the Communist Party of China is important in the history of China. In the above agreement, the Kuomintang did not accept two demands of the Communist Party of China, namely, the unifying a military chain of command, and that the government reorganising the armed forces of the country, preparing a programme to implement this stage by stage, fix military areas with new patterns and settling a compulsory employment and remuneration system. The other was that the government should give legal recognition to the elected governments in all liberated areas. The first proposal was related to give legal recognition to the people's army and the other was related to give legal recognition to the people's power of the liberated areas. Why did the Chiang Kai-shek government reject these two demands?

The Chiang Kai-shek government knew that the other proposals of the Communist Party of China could be fulfilled within the limitations of formal bourgeois democracy. After the end of the Second World War, it was necessary to create an environment for every nation to return to its general condition. There was no specific problem for the Kuomintang to accept the other demands of the Communist Party of China. Therefore, with focus on the national and international situation, the Chiang Kai-shek government approved of those demands. But, it rejected the issue of the people's army and revolutionary local government, directly related to revolution. When Chiang Kai-shek government was not ready to accept these two demands, the Communist Party of China put these questions at the centre of demands at the Chungking negotiations; as a result, there could be no agreement.

Beginning from the 12-point agreement to the Interim Constitution, 2007, the dialogue held between the CPN(Maoist) and Nepali Congress, CPN(UML) and then later between the CPN(Maoist) and the government have been fruitful. The other party accepted many demands of our party, though they have not been implemented, and still limited to paper. As Mao said, "Words written on paper are not real. It is not possible without making great efforts before getting them implemented." In our context as well, the issue of the people's army, revolutionary base areas and local power have been the most unsolvable issues of peace-talks. The ruling clique and state machinery, specifically the Nepal army, have a strategy to dissolve the People's Liberation Army and confiscate its weapons. According to their perception, as the CPN(Maoist) has people's army, so it cannot be a national party. To get legal recognition as a national party, it must hand over its people's army and weapons to the old state power. However, it is vital to understand Mao's statements such as "without a people's army, the people have nothing" and "a party with army along can enjoy freedom" and accept that in a real sense. If the party leadership accepts the demands of reactionaries, in the name of flexibility, regarding the issue of a people's army, it will be suicidal to the nation, people and the party itself.

The Communist Party of China, under the leadership of Mao, said if the Kuomintang would cut down its armed force, it would also do so. The Communist Party of China brought forward the proposal of reducing its armed force to 48 divisions if the Kuomintang was ready to reduce its army. The Communist Party of China was ready to reduce in proportion to 43 divisions, 24 divisions and 20 divisions respectively. Although, the Communist Party of China was prepared to reduce its armed force with the Kuomintang on a reciprocal basis, it was fully against dissolving the people's army and handing over its weapons. There was no agreement at the Chungking talks and a statement of Mao makes his view clearer. He says: "The arms of the people, every gun and every bullet, must all be kept, must not be handed over."[54]

The Nepali Congress, the CPN(UML), Madhesi-based parties, the National Democratic Parties and others are demanding that the CPN(Maoist) should hand over the People's Liberation Army instantly on the ground that the army must be under the control of the state. The watchmen of the old power, the feudal, comprador and bureaucratic political parties are not demanding any new thing. Chiang Kai-shek made a similar demand to the Communist Party of China in 1945. Why have the reactionaries of Nepal put the same type of demand to the CPN(Maoist) after so many decades? Because the reactionaries of Nepal and the Kuomintang have the same class character, so they are insisting on handing over the people's army to the state. The answer to that problem was given by Mao to the Kuomintang in relation to that demand:

> 'The army belongs to the state'–that is perfectly true, and there is not an army in the world that does not belong to a state. But what kind of state? A state under the feudal and fascist dictatorship of the big landlords, big bankers and big comprador, or a new-democratic state of the broad masses of the people? The only kind of state for China to establish is a new-democratic state and, on this basis, she should establish a new-democratic coalition government; all the armed forces of China must belong to such a government of such a state so that they may safeguard the people's freedom and effectively fight foreign aggressors. The moment a new-democratic coalition government comes into being in China, the Liberated Areas of China will hand their armed forces over to it. But all the Kuomintang armed forces will have to be handed over to it at the same time.[55]

Our party leadership should make Mao's remark their guiding principle in discussions with the government and other political parties in relation to the People's Liberation Army and its weapons.

54 Mao Tse-tung, "On Chungking Negotiations", *Selected Works*, Eng. ed., Foreign Language Press, Peking, First ed., 1961, Vol. 4, p. 57.

55 Mao Tse-tung, "On Coalition Government", *Selected Works*, Eng. ed., Foreign Language Press, Peking, Second ed., 1967, Vol. 3, p. 246.

On the question of revolutionary base areas and local power, the Communist Party of China, under the leadership of Mao, insisted with the Kuomintang an almost equal status with the people's army and as a result, no agreement was made. However, regarding the revolutionary base areas and local power, our party has already adopted the path of liquidation. Our revolutionary base areas and local power are subjects of history. At present, the counter-revolution has been completed and again, comprador, feudal and police rule has been revived. Party leadership does not appear conscious of having lost any important thing. They seem "confident" that revolutionary base areas and local power were formed when there was nothing. If needed, the same can be done again. Does Marxism define the relationship between revolution and the revolutionary local power and the base area in the same way? Doubt arises if this point of view of the party leadership becomes dominant over the questions of the People's Liberation Army and its weapons. Will the party dissolve the people's army and hand over its weapons to the present government in the name of flexibility?

May-December, 2008
Canberra, Australia

Development of Democracy in the Twenty-First Century

Third Letter Sent to the Party Headquarters Regarding the Anti-Leninist View on Democracy and Dictatorship

The Marxist fundamental principle has been attacked or distorted ever since the inception of the world communist movement, in general democracy and dictatorship, particularly the proletarian democracy and dictatorship. Such a situation has to be understood basically as a struggle between classes in society and its impact on the communist movement. In the present imperialist era, the form of struggle to be launched by the Marxist-Leninists against the attack and distortion on proletarian democracy and dictatorship from the imperialists and within the movement should be understood in the light of the present exploitative system, an outgrowth of the origin of state and individual property that has led to the exploitation of man by man, and the exploitation of nation by nation, is rather protected, complex and painful too.

During Marx and Engels' time proletarian democracy and dictatorship was attacked or distorted by the right and "left" which had an influence within the communist movement. Marx and Engles launched an uncompromising struggle against the bourgeois or petty-bourgeois attacks or distortions from inside or outside the movement. The experience of the Paris Commune of 1871 solidified Marx and Engels' views about democracy and dictatorship.

After the development of capitalism into imperialism, the issue of democracy and dictatorship have become more complex. Attacks or distortions from inside and outside the communist movement have multiplied. As further specific characteristics of this new era of capitalism, hostile elements within the communist movement itself, *i.e.* bourgeois "communists", took direct or indirect initiative to attack or distort the Marxist principle of democracy and dictatorship. The Second International, and its main leaders like Bernstein and Karl Kautsky served the interests of imperialism by turning away from the proletarian revolution at a time when the inter-imperialist contradictions were on the peak, leading to the First World War.

Marxism-Leninism advocates for a special type of state system to be established after the proletarian revolution. Lenin defended and developed the fundamental principle of Marxism in relation to proletarian democracy and dictatorship under the imperialistic era, especially during the First World War and completing the Great Socialist Revolution. Under the leadership of Lenin, the Great October Socialist Revolution was a grand example of the defeat of opportunists of the Second International and the victory of the fundamental principle in relation to democracy and dictatorship as defined by Marxism.

Bernstein advocated peaceful transformation from capitalism into socialism, and Karl Kautsky opposed Lenin's theory, strategy and tactics of proletarian revolution. The modern revisionists distorted the concept of Lenin's theory of proletarian democracy and dictatorship, with the advocacy of peaceful transformation from capitalism to communism, "party of whole people, " and "state of whole people". Likewise, immediately after the Second World War and in the following decades, Marshall Tito and the "Communists" of France, Italy and Spain revised the fundamental principle of Marxism-Leninism, mainly the proletarian democracy and dictatorship to make it acceptable to imperialists and their agents. Marx, Engels, Lenin, Stalin and Mao defended the principles by launching a complex, painful, uncompromising and protracted struggle against the revisionism.

The dissolution of the Soviet Union and the Eastern European revisionist states impacted seriously, increasing the danger of East European deviation in the world communist movement. The Revolutionary Internationalist Movement (RIM) stated that the open declaration of capitalism from inside the revisionist states, discarding their earlier covert capitalism, exposed the degeneration of revisionism, and justified the struggle of Marxist-Leninists all over the world under the leadership of Mao. Despite the correct stand and analysis by the RIM, the main leadership of the CRC, CPI(ML), which played a significant role in its formation, became the victim of revisionism. While analysing the failure of socialism, it blamed the communist party for its wrong direction and role during the proletarian democracy and dictatorship, practices of class struggle, democratic-centralism, and ultimately it took a nihilistic approach over the period spanning from the 1917 socialist revolution to 1976.

After nearly one and a half decades, from within the RIM, our own party, the Communist Party of Nepal (Maoist) that struggled with the explicit objective of the new democratic revolution during the people's great war of ten years, and formed revolutionary base areas and local power, is now pursuing the liquidationist view. Our party's concept presented in the *Development of Democracy in the Twenty-First Century* is a continuation of the view of the CRC document *On Proletarian Democracy.*

The questions raised in the *Development of Democracy in the Twenty-First Century* regarding proletarian democracy and dictatorship are quite serious. Marxist-Leninists should launch a non-compromising struggle against the anti-Marxist-Leninist proposal.

1
Development of Democracy in the Twenty-First Century

Our party has raised the question of development of democracy with great importance, terming the subjective understanding in the exercise of democracy to be the main cause of counter-revolution in the socialist states. It claims that socialist state power can be safeguarded from the danger of counter-revolution in future by developing democracy in the twenty-first century.

In the *Development of Democracy in the Twenty-First Century*, the party states:

> The experience of the twentieth century makes it clear that question of moving towards withering away of the state with continuous democratisation of state power is a thousand times more complicated and difficult than capturing state power. The reality of not remaining even a single socialist state power in the world after the success of great revolutions in countries, including Russia and China and the development of a strong world socialist camp within the single century, and the massive events of counter-revolution shows the importance and seriousness of the subject matter.
>
> In spite of many historical and theoretical reasons for the success of capitalist imperialism to confuse the world opinion about military fascist essence with the mask of so-called democracy and proletarian class and its

> democratic essence, it has failed to strengthen its hold. The problem of the development of democracy is as acute as a burning issue, and it needs to be settled for a proper balance between the need of dictatorship against the defeated enemy and the need of exercise of people's democracy.
>
> Why did people's democracy or proletarian democracy become formal, mechanical and sectarian under people's democratic dictatorship or the dictatorship of the proletariat? ... After all, a true democratic dictatorship, or proletarian dictatorship can be strong in the process of broad and live democratisation of state power, with no exception to this scientific principle of democratic-centralism. Why did parties successful earlier in capturing state power with correct exercise of democratic-centralism come to be the prey of formal democracy and bureaucratic centralism afterwards? The argument that it is because of the revisionism dominated the party, is not sufficient to address this problem."[1]

Likewise, on the question of the development of democracy, in the editorial of *Jan Parishad* (People's Council), the organ of the Joint Revolutionary Council (Issue 1, June, 2004), it states:

> It is necessary to take discussion in relation to the development of democracy in two stages and meanings. One is in the meaning of bourgeois democracy and the other is in the meaning of proletarian democracy.
>
> First, we have to take seriously the one which means immediate or bourgeois democracy in a country like ours with semi-feudal and semi-colonial structure and long tradition of absolute monarchical system, progressive transformation and the fast development of society is not possible without uprooting all forms of feudal absolutism and exercising development of bourgeois democracy to a certain extent. On the one hand, it is necessary to develop the industrial capitalist production system on a large-scale to build minimum prerequisites on economic account for socialism, on the other to build a socialist system, its practice and culture is not possible without the minimum development of a competitive capitalist system and its practice by ending feudal tyranny, craze and conservatism on political, social and cultural account as well. Again in a country like ours feudalism is also not fully developed historically, and sufficient tribal remains and class along with national, regional, gender exploitation and oppression born on a limited island of dependent bureaucratic capitalism because of imperialist manipulation, still exist. But, the blind imitation of the Westminster model of bourgeois parliamentary democracy so far adopted has not succeeded to represent class, national, regional, and gender properly and to achieve expected industrial capitalism. In the present era of imperialism, on the one hand, development of capitalism is not possible and bourgeois democracy on the other cannot be sustainable in a country like ours. So, other successful models in practice, as in Switzerland and the Scandinavian countries,

1 Prachanda, "Development of Democracy in the Twenty-First Century", *Selected Works*, Janadisha Publications, Nepal, July 2007, Vol. 2, pp. 413-14

> should also be considered as other models possible. Thinking on this line, the CPN(Maoist) has been bringing forward a new model of bourgeois democracy with reference to our specific context, which in the continuously changing international and national situations, should be taken sincerely by all concerned.

The editorial further writes in relation to the second stage of the development of democracy:

> The other long lasting and further important question related to the development of democracy is the development of proletarian democracy. Proletarian state power is an interim state power that reaches stateless and classless communism by ending all types of powers and in that sense as Marx says it is not traditional state power at all. It is like the proletarian democracy finally that reaches a totally new type of democracy to be dissolved into 'administration of things' by ending state and democracy in the form of 'government of persons'. The main characteristic of the historical Paris Commune and proletarian democracy seen in Russian Soviets in the beginning is an exercise of direct democracy of working-class and general masses, and it should be expressed in the form of direct participation, supervision and interference of all organs of state power.
>
> Taking lessons from the serious events that took place in the past in all proletarian state powers, including Russia and China immediately after the revolution such as development of bureaucracy, the development of the new bureaucratic capitalist class inside themselves, who undertook the responsibility of state power mobilisation, but understood state power as a monopoly of party and individuals instead of proletarian class, and the counter-revolution from within the proletarian state power itself, we must take courage to develop proletarian democracy in a new way. The Proletarian Cultural Revolution under the leadership of Mao established the right to revolt for the proletariat and masses theoretically, but in that short and specific duration, an agreeable system of continuous revolutionisation of state power and the institutionalisation of the right to revolt could not be developed. The experience of counter-revolutions by now is that those who played an important role during the revolution and who reached the high leadership of party and state power themselves led the counter-revolution after the revolution, and the majority of cadres and masses could not revolt against them. Therefore, instead of taking any chain of events to be mistaken for any person or group, it should be accepted as a mistake in the exercise of proletarian state power or system of democracy.
>
> The role of complexity created by external imperialist intervention and attack and historical specificity as well cannot be denied. But, the main reason of development or destruction of being an internal aspect itself, according to the law of revolutionary dialectics, we must accept weakness in the exercise of proletarian democracy itself and take courage to correct it and develop it. So, all revolutionaries must take the 'Question of the

Development of Democracy in the Twenty-First Century' brought forward by the CPN(Maoist) very seriously, not confining to oral support.[2]

Likewise, Comrade Bhattarai says in relation to the development of democracy:

> Although, the concept of the new democratic state power, developed by Mao in general is correct and reasonable, the party has been thinking of some additional development in the concept of democracy with a consideration to the experience of counter-revolutions of the past and continuously changing world and national periphery.[3]

Raising the question on the development of democracy is not wrong in itself as Marxism-Leninism does not take it as a rigid and unchanging concept. Democracy itself is always in motion; it is always moving from today to tomorrow. It moves ahead unless environment is not ready to wither away. It is in motion not only in different social systems, but also in the proletarian state. The Marxist-Leninist believes that people's democracy can be developed only through class struggle under the dictatorship of the proletariat. Truly, democracy gets an appropriate environment to bloom, expand and finally to wither away only in the state power under the leadership of the proletariat through its vanguard. Our party's proposal the *Development of Democracy in the Twenty-First Century* does not propose the development of proletarian democracy (under both a democratic and socialist state system) practised in the past under the leaderships of Lenin, Stalin and Mao, but it suggests to build a "new" type of democracy by destroying what was practised in the past, which is nothing else but going back to bourgeois democracy.

In the present era of imperialism and proletarian revolution, Marxism-Leninism-Mao Tse-tung Thought divides democracy into two stages. The first stage is a new type of democracy to be established in semi(neo)-colonial and semi-feudal countries. The social form of the first stage of democracy is basically bourgeois democracy, not a socialist. The specific objective is to develop bourgeois democracy and not go for establishment of the socialist type. In spite of this, its objective is not to establish bourgeois democracy under a bourgeois dictatorship, rather a new democracy as a prelude to proletarian democracy. The movement to establish this type of democracy, which is anti-imperialist, anti-feudal, anti-comprador and anti-bureaucratic capitalist class under the leadership of the proletariat with the active participation of all revolutionary classes, is a transitional democracy, which makes the development of proletarian democracy easier

2 "Question of the Development of Democracy (Editorial)", *People's Council*, The Organ of the Joint Revolutionary People's Council, Nepal, July 2004, No. 1, pp. 2, 5.

3 Baburam Bhattarai, "Question of Building of a New Type of State Power", *People's Council*, The Organ of the Joint Revolutionary People's Council, Nepal, July 2004, No. 1, p. 10.

and faster. If democracy cannot be changed into proletarian democracy, it remains a bourgeois or formal democracy.

Our party's view regarding the development of democracy in the era of imperialism and proletarian revolution is incompatible with the fundamental principle of Marxism-Leninism-Mao Tse-tung Thought. Instead of understanding the new type of democracy as an integral part of the proletarian world revolution at the first stage in the semi(neo)-colonial and semi-feudal countries, our party states it is necessary to have discussions related to the development of democracy, at the first stage "with the meaning of bourgeois democracy", and at the second stage "with the meaning of proletarian democracy". This view states the impossibility of the progressive transformation and rapid development of society "in a country like ours with semi(neo)-colonial and semi-feudal structure and a long tradition of monarchic dictatorship", "without developing bourgeois democracy to a certain extent", to uproot all forms of feudal oppression in the country. Our party has not expressed such views in a normal sense in a country like ours having a long history of absolute monarchy. These views were expressed while leading a discussion about the development of democracy just before its first stage, *i.e.* proletarian democracy (the party considers it the second stage of the development of democracy), as proved by the above quoted statement which states that the socialist system and culture cannot be developed without first eradicating on the one hand the political, cultural and feudal absolutism along with capitalist system, and on the other, without developing large-scale industrial production system as a yardstick for minimum infrastructure for socialism from the economic perspective.

An understanding and analysis of imperialism is missing here. The principle of the new democratic revolution of Mao has not been even remembered. According to our party, the country's present context offers only the options of dictatorial monarchy or bourgeois democracy. In the era of imperialism and proletarian revolution, in a semi(neo)-colonial and semi-feudal country, forgetting the new democratic revolution and the demand of elimination of the monarchy and a bourgeois democracy can only knowingly or unknowingly serve the world imperialism and Indian expansionism.

Certainly, Marxism-Leninism believes that building socialism is not possible in a backward economic, political, social and cultural condition, so it is necessary to develop a large-scale industrial production system. Furthermore, without a minimum development of productive forces a socialist system, tradition and culture cannot be built. In discussing the general principle of Marxism-Leninism-Mao Tse-tung Thought in relation to socialism, our party has completely ignored some fundamental principles, specially four issues. The first is that in the present era of imperialism and proletarian revolution, the enemy of the revolution in semi(neo)-colonial and semi-feudal countries is imperialism, and in our context, Indian expansionism too. Having completely neglected this fact, it states that it is possible to have a large-scale capitalist production system from the bourgeois democracy perspective to develop a competitive production system for the sake of socialism. Is the formation of national capitalism, politics and culture possible without liberation from imperialist exploitation and oppression? Is the establishment of socialism possible without the formation of national capitalism, politics and culture?

The second is that in the era of imperialism and proletarian revolution, democracy in semi(neo)-colonial and semi-feudal countries should not be an integral part of the old type of bourgeois world democracy. Rather, it should be an integral part of world proletarian democracy. In this era, we need the embryo of proletarian democracy, not the old type of bourgeois democracy. Having neglected, the question of building the new type of democracy, our party has made a serious mistake of emphasising building and strengthening the old type of bourgeois democracy.

The third is that our party has expressed concerns over preparing the requirements to build socialism. The meaning of readiness towards socialist revolution from a democratic revolution in semi(neo)-colonial and semi-feudal countries in the present era is to adopt the principle of uninterrupted revolution of Marxism. For that, it is necessary to put forward political programmes as the separate link of a chain. For example, in Russia and China, two stages of revolution at its minimum and maximum stages were agreed upon. Taking revolution on the whole, and dividing it into stages means that the minimum programme should always be in accordance with the maximum programme, and it should be changeable into the maximum programme legibly and directly. To settle the minimum programme with negative effect that harms or paralyses the maximum programme is deviation from the principle of uninterrupted revolution of Marxism. By neglecting the issue of struggling against imperialism and Indian expansionism, as well as the issue of liberating the country, the present line of our party has developed and strengthened bourgeois democracy, derailing the path to socialism, which can be achieved only by creating a new type of democracy, not by building and strengthening the old type of democracy.

The fourth is that the Marxism-Leninsm-Mao Tse-tung Thought suggests an undivided leading role of the proletarian class through its vanguard communist party in the struggle for democracy. In countries under semi(neo)-colonial and semi-feudal oppression, the social form of democracy at the first stage is bourgeois democracy. Although its objective is to open the path to development of capitalism, it is not an old type of bourgeois revolution led by the capitalist class to establish capitalist society and state under bourgeois dictatorship. It is a new type of democratic revolution, led by the proletarian class to establish a new type of democratic society and state under a joint dictatorship of all revolutionary classes against imperialism, comprador-bureaucratic capitalism and feudalism from the very first stage. Completely neglecting this issue, our party has proposed a multi-party competitive "democratic" republic in the name of the development of democracy in the twenty-first century. It has been discussed in detail in the *Second Letter* regarding what our party has brought forward in relation to the development of democracy, which is a restatement of the argument that revisionists within communist movement have been putting forward for over a century.

Our party's document the *Development of Democracy in the Twenty-First Century* clarifies many things. For examples, Comrade Bhattarai's statements, "We should keep in mind that apart from the British parliamentary model of bourgeois democracy, there are other models in practice in Switzerland and Scandinavian countries and so on", and "Revolutionary democrats must launch a huge struggle against rightist conservative thinking who seek to stick with the same worn out Westminster Parliamentary model of bourgeois democracy", makes it further clear. The mixed form of the same worn out Westminster parliamentary model of bourgeois democracy, and the bourgeois models in the Scandinavian countries and Switzerland, is the form of Loktantrik Gantantra "developed" (actually followed) by our party. As claimed by our party, it is not an additional development to the principle of new democracy of Mao. Such a view amends the basic thinking of Mao's cooperative concept between the communist party and other democratic parties.

Our party's view about the development of proletarian democracy, like the view about the new democracy, fundamentally against Marxism-Leninism-Mao Tse-tung Thought. The party's statements such as "after the revolution, the development of bureaucracy led to a new bureaucratic capitalist class, who undertook responsibility of state power mobilisation, understanding state power as a monopoly of party and individuals instead of that of proletarian class, and then the counter-revolution from within the proletarian state itself", is completely against the general principle of class struggle during the socialist period. Our party has minimised the importance and role of the Great Proletarian Cultural Revolution, the highest form of class struggle in the socialist transformation, by stating that it failed to "organise the right of revolt" and "develop proper procedure by continuously revolutionising the state power."

What is democracy? Lenin says:

> Democracy is *not* identical with the subordination of the minority to the majority. Democracy is a *state* which recognises the subordination of the minority to the majority, *i.e.* an organisation for the systematic use of *force* by one class against another, by one section of the population against another.[4]

Lenin's short statement captures the essence of Marxism in relation to democracy. The word, organisation referred to by Lenin, is not the form of governance, but the form of state. Now, the question arises, which class represents the majority of society and which class is kept in subordination? This is determined according to the essence of the state power. Our party has raised the question of development of democracy, *i.e.* democracy for the oppressed under the previous capitalist state and dictatorship over exploiters in a proletarian state. Comrade Bhattarai says:

> It is necessary to lead the exercise of proletarian democracy from the very beginning in a new way, realising that the main subjective reasons of counter-revolution in socialist and people's democratic state power of the past are inadequate to establish dictatorship against the enemy, not mobilising or being unable to mobilise broad masses of people continuously to implement democratic-centralism among people, and not organising in a way to be able to apply the right of revolt when necessary.[5]

After the proletarian class has taken the state power under its leadership (in both socialist and new democratic state power), it should mobilise the broad masses to establish all round dictatorship against the enemy and implement it. Its higher application was the Great Proletarian Cultural Revolution. Lenin, Stalin and Mao developed and protected proletarian state power by adopting this kind of procedure. Despite unfavourable international and national situation–the existence of bourgeois rights and small-scale production; inequality between mental and physical labour and between town and countryside; capitalist roaders in the party and government; as well as external intervention–Russia and China succeeded in building socialism. With the revival of capitalism in the Soviet Union and in China, after the death of Stalin and Mao, our party has concluded that all previous proletarian state power failed due to the lack of correct exercise of democracy. Marxist-Leninists all over the world have been quite serious while analysing the problem for several decades, especially since capitalism was revived in the Soviet Union. Under the leadership of Mao, they reached the conclusion that the main reason for the revival of capitalism is objective,

4 V. I. Lenin, "The State and Revolution", *Collected Works*, Eng. ed., Progress Publishers, Moscow, Fourth Printing, 1980, Vol. 25, p. 461.

5 Baburam Bhattarai, "Question of Building of a New Type of State Power", *People's Council*, The Organ of the Joint Revolutionary People's Council, Nepal, July 2004, No. 1, pp. 12-13.

and the event should be taken as a form of the outcome of general law of class struggle under socialism. They stated the subjective aspect to be secondary. Under the leadership of Mao, revolutionaries took the important step to neutralise the reasons for the capitalist revival by trying to correct the subjective weaknesses–the Great Proletarian Cultural Revolution was the higher form of this attempt. However, capitalism was revived in China after the death of Mao.

The restoration of capitalism in China shocked the Marxist-Leninists all over the world. To struggle against that restoration and give continuity to the socialist system and advancing communism for the future, they organised the First International Conference in 1980. After four years, they organised the Second International Conference and formed the RIM in 1984. The RIM, the communist parties and the organisations affiliated with it, precipitated the revival of capitalism in China in the light of Mao Tse-tung Thought. Therefore, they stressed the study and investigation of weaknesses of the subjective aspects, which were secondary to that event, so as not to let them occur again in the future. The RIM and the Communist Parties and Organisations were generally honest followers of Mao in relation to the revival of capitalism in a socialist state. RIM's declaration clarifies:

> Today, the Revolutionary Internationalist Movement, together with other Maoist forces, are the inheritors of Marx, Engels, Lenin, Stalin and Mao, and they must firmly base themselves on this heritage. But they must also, on the basis of this heritage, dare to criticise its shortcomings. There are experiences which people should praise and there are experiences which should make people grieve. Communists and revolutionaries in all countries should ponder and seriously study these experiences of success and failure so as to draw correct conclusions and useful lessons from them.
>
> The summation of our heritage is a collective responsibility which must be carried out by the entire international communist movement. Such a summation must be done in a ruthlessly scientific manner, basing itself on Marxist-Leninist principles and fully taking into account the concrete historical conditions which existed then and the limits they placed on the proletarian vanguard and above all in the spirit of making the past serve the present, in order to avoid metaphysical errors of measuring the past with today's yardstick, disregarding historical conditions.
>
> The summation of historical experience has, itself, always been a sharp arena of class struggle. Ever since the defeat of the Paris Commune, opportunists and revisionists have seized upon the defeats and shortcomings of the proletariat to reverse right and wrong, confound the secondary with the principal, and thus conclude that the proletariat "should not have taken to arms." The emergence of new conditions has often been used as an excuse to negate fundamental principles of Marxism under the signboard of its "creative development."

> In fact, history has shown that the real creative development of Marxism (and not phoney revisionist distortions) has always been inseparably linked with a fierce struggle to defend and uphold basic principles of Marxism-Leninism. Lenin's two-fold struggle against the open revisionists and against those, like Kautsky, who opposed revolution under the guise of "Marxist orthodoxy" and Mao Tse-tung's great battle to oppose the modern revisionists and their negation of the experience of building socialism in the USSR under Lenin and Stalin while carrying out a thorough and scientific criticism of the roots of revisionism are evidence of this. Today a similar approach is necessary to the thorny questions and problems of the history of the international communist movement.[6]

Such a view agrees with the Marxism-Leninism-Mao Tse-tung Thought in relation to the experience of the world communist movement. Our party has deviated from the RIM's view on evaluating the proletarian democracy, and it has said forcefully that "the experience of counter-revolutions by now is that those who played an important role during the revolution and who reached the high leadership of party and state power themselves led the counter-revolution after the revolution, and the majority of cadres and masses could not revolt against them ... should be accepted as a mistake in the exercise of proletarian state power or system of democracy." Such a thinking from our party neglects the law of Marxist dialectics, namely, "one divides into two" and also the changes occurring in the position and character of contradictory elements in the course of development.

During the revolution, changes occur with the shift in the character of contradictory forces, change in the national and international situation, and either the fulfilment or failure of certain programmes of revolution. For example, let us consider the roles of different persons involved at different stages in the Russian Revolution. Let us talk about the minimum programme of the Bolshevik Communist Party, a bourgeois-democratic programme. Therefore, the elements, who wanted to establish a capitalist production system and capitalist production relations abolishing autocratic monarchy and feudalism in the country, supported the programme of revolution of the Bolshevik Communist Party. The bourgeois-democratic revolution was over in February 1917. For the Bolsheviks, a bourgeois-democratic revolution and a socialist revolution were two links of the same chain as incessant flows of the whole Russian Revolution. However, it was not correct in the case of bourgeois elements, who participated in the revolution, supporting the programme of the bourgeois-democratic revolution forwarded by the Bolshevik Communist Party.

After the completion of the bourgeois-democratic revolution, the Bolshevik Communist Party adopted a strategy to free the country from

6 *Declaration of the Revolutionary Internationalist Movement (RIM)*, pp. 12-13.

the imperialist war and overthrow the imperialist power, till the October 1917 socialist revolution with the support of people. The revolution unfolded fundamental differences amongst supporters of the Bolsheviks. For communists, the fulfilment of this strategy was to establish a proletarian dictatorship, but for those who supported and participated in the anti-war slogan of the Bolshevik Communist Party, the goal was to end the war, not for strengthening the proletarian democracy. Despite having the same major force in the Russian Revolution, the reserve force and the direction of strike were different. The reserve force of one stage can be the main target of attack at the other stage of revolution.

The same thing is true in relation to the New Democratic Revolution in China, despite major forces at different stages being the same, differences are found over the main target of strike and reserve forces. Naturally, this situation commits a change in the position and form of contradiction. So, it is no need to wonder that the counter-revolution was led by some of those who "fulfilled important roles and reached high leadership of the party and state power" at a previous stage of revolution. It is the same regarding the "counter-revolution within a proletarian state power itself, " which goes through different stages of development. Just as in relation to the different stages of revolution, there occur changes at the target of attack at different stages of development of a proletarian state power. A short talk on the deep and extended two-line struggle seen within the Communist Party of China, immediately after the nationwide success of the new democratic revolution, answers correctly the problem seen in our party. In the Second Plenary Session of the Seventh Central Committee of the party, organised before the revolution (March, 1949), Mao had emphasised that after the completion of revolution a major internal contradiction in China would remain "between the working-class and the bourgeoisie." This was Mao's dialectical analysis of the future character of Chinese society. Immediately after the revolution, Liu Shao-chi and his group emphasised strengthening new democracy in the country, whereas revolutionaries under the leadership of Mao emphasised moving ahead towards socialism.

In November 1951, Liu Shao-chi said, "Firmly establish the new democratic social order". He emphasised establishing "cooperation in five regions" to strengthen the new democratic system and forwarded the slogan of "sustain private property". Mao Tse-tung refuted calling it a "right deviationist view that departs from the general line", and called for it to be refuted nationwide. In 1951, the capitalist roaders opposed the party policy to form mutual cooperation teams of poor and petty, medium peasants at the agriculture cooperative level at Shansi and other places, and declared this policy to be an "erroneous, dangerous and utopian notion of agrarian socialism".

The point here is not to talk on the life and death struggle that went on in the government and party between the capitalist roaders and the revolutionaries in China. Rather it is to present a glimpse of how a previous unity breaks between co-travellers after a certain stage of revolution, and how a struggle erupts in a new form. According to dialectics unity among contradictory elements gets broken after reaching a certain point and then the struggle compulsorily starts among them in a new form. During the period of the bourgeois-democratic revolution in China, although contradictions were present there, unity between (national) capitalist and the working-class was necessary. The two contradictory forces fought against imperialism and feudalism together for an independent China. Some of these elements got involved in the revolution and to some extent in the party under the influence of the programme of a bourgeois-democratic revolution, *i.e.* the minimum programme of the Communist Party of China, but it was not possible to continue along the road of uninterrupted revolution for them. So, it was natural for the capitalist roaders to take a counter-revolution. Our party has presented such a general law of class struggle under a socialist period in an exacerbating way, and argues that the main cause of the counter-revolution was the inherent fault with the socialist states in the practice of proletarian democracy itself.

2
Question of Democracy and Multi-Parties

The essence of the *Development of Democracy in the Twenty-First Century* presented by our party seeks to establish a multi-party competition system, in both a new democratic and socialist state, as a safeguard against the danger of counter-revolution. It states that a multi-party competitive state system is an adequate procedure and an institutionalised process to stop the danger of counter-revolution. As the *Development of Democracy in the Twenty-First Century* says:

> A Party that had been revolutionary and democratic or socialist state power in a certain country, period or situation, might be changed into a counter-revolutionary one in another time, place or environment. In that situation the masses and revolutionaries should revolt justifying the synthesis of the Great Proletarian Cultural Revolution. By thinking that once democratic or socialistic state power is established under the leadership of a communist party, one may think it remains proletarian forever, and this may pose restrictions for politically free democratic or socialist competition against it by the masses. On the one hand, no compulsion of competition gradually changes situation into a mechanical, bureaucratic state under the power

> of its leadership, and on the other the danger of formal democracy, will obstruct the creative and dynamic fertility of people as marked in history. According to the principle of uninterrupted revolution, emphasis should be placed on the need of a lively and scientific organisation of process of control, supervision and obstruction of people for a proper solution to the problem.
>
> For this, a situation should be created for continuous proletarianization and revolutionization of the communist party by organising political competition within the constitutional limitation of democratic state power against imperialism and feudalism. Counter-revolution cannot be stopped effectively if the party does not revolutionise itself continuously by ensuring the right of the masses institutionalised to allow another revolutionary party or leadership to take state power. Emphasis should be laid on mechanical relation of cooperation among different anti-feudalist and anti-imperialist political parties and institutions that accept the constitutional system of democratic state power, and the communist party, and on a democratic political competition for dialectical relation to serve people well.
>
> Once state power is captured, from the very beginning emphasis should be given to create a situation in the party and to prove the status of the right stand of its leadership, to earn people's faith with sacrifice, devotion and loyalty to people. A situation should be created where the self-decision of the masses are not curtailed because of created centralisation of thinking and leadership in the state power.[7]

Likewise, the weekly *Janadesh* asked Comrade Prachanda: "The much talked about proposal of the party related to the *Development of Democracy in the Twenty-First Century* has brought forward the idea of multi-party competition in a socialist society as well. What is the essence and justification of that? Is it possible to achieve a communist goal such as the withering away of all classes, party and state?"

Comrade Prachanda replies:

> The proposal of development of democracy is a proposal brought forward by the party, mainly on the basis of the study of positive and negative experiences of dictatorship and democracy in the twentieth century. According to that proposal, the party believes that only by organising party competition within the limitation of the constitutional structure in socialist society, proletarian dictatorship can be strengthened and the power of counter-revolution can be prevented from raising its head and also by making control, supervision and interference of masses in people's lives. Only the dictatorship strengthened on the basis of the development of democracy in this way, finally, can prepare the necessary prerequisite for withering away of class, party and state. Through multi-party competition in

7 Prachanda, "Development of Democracy in the Twenty-First Century", *Selected Works*, Janadisha Publications, Nepal, July 2007, Vol. 2, pp. 414-16.

form, this process, capable of leading continuous improvement of political awareness, will make the socialist competition lively in its essence as Lenin, the Great, says. The more extensively and lively socialist competition is organised, the more extensive and fast the base will go on being prepared for withering away of the state. Making proletarian democracy lively by saving this itself from being mechanised and formal is the underlying truth related to the development of democracy.[8]

In answer to a question posed in the monthly *Sansleshan*, Comrade Prachanda says: "By going one step forward, democracy of the twenty-first century is a system to organise political competition, under the dictatorship of the proletariat in socialism as well. We have defined it as the democracy of the twenty-first century with political competition under the dictatorship of the proletariat."[9]

Regarding the party's position of new democracy and multi-party competition in socialism, it is essential to understand Bhattarai's views to grasp the concept of multi-party competition during the proletarian democracy.

Erasing the gap between the communist party and state power, a mistake committed in the past, in all socialist countries, must be rectified by the revolutionaries of this epoch. On the basis of the bitter experience of deletion of the gap between the party and institutions of people's representatives, leading the party to bureaucratic and capitalistic, and then taking the power and leadership as the monopoly, we have to explore a new and correct way to establish class dictatorship for perpetuating and proletarian leadership. We must have a clear understanding that the concept of dictatorship is not of party or individual, but of class and proletarian leadership, not to be imposed as a monopoly, but to be earned by the revolutionary behaviour to implement it democratically. We should end the irony of bourgeois dictatorship succeeding to confuse people with its counter-revolutionary essence and attractive outer appearance, whereas the new democratic or proletarian dictatorship receiving condemnation from the masses, despite its revolutionary essence, because of its distorted outer face. For this, first of all the communist party must establish in practice that state power leadership is earned not as monopoly, but because of the proletarian revolutionary character by institutionalising the system to enable the class and masses to disown and condemn the party that has lost its proletarian character. Likewise, the proletarian dictatorship is not the dictatorship of party, or its leadership, rather it is the dictatorship to be implemented through elected representative institutions (Soviet or people's council) of class and masses. We should strongly grasp the

8 Prachanda, "I Want to Give a New Message of Liberation" (Interview), *Selected Works*, Janadisha Publications, Nepal, February 2007, Vol. 1, p. 480.

9 Prachanda, "Revolt is Inevitable if Consensus Breaks" (Interview), *Selected Works*, Janadisha Publications, Nepal, February 2007, Vol. 1, p. 506.

dialectical law that even if the essence of proletarian dictatorship being the principal factor, it will harm the cause of revolution if its outer form is not implemented correctly.[10]

However, Comrade Bhattarai has not explicitly mentioned that, in the new democratic and socialist system, even the opponents of socialist transformation should be allowed to organise competitively in multi-party system. The following statement expresses his hidden intention.

> Taking a lesson from the bitter experience of the masses' inability to wage an organised revolt against the counter-revolution in the past, we must guarantee the system of founding political party with the framework of certain progressive and revolutionary vision for 'cooperative', as well as 'competitive' activities in relation to the communist party in power. After the source of political and economic monopoly of the feudal and bourgeoisie, respectively on land, capital and the military monopoly over hired occupational army are crushed, there remains no factual or logical argument to hesitate for a communist party that claims the majority of proletarian and oppressed class representation to allow political competition within a certain constitutional process. We should grasp this, not as bourgeois pluralism, rather the MLM that follows the scientific method to solve contradictions among people as long as society is divided into classes.[11]

Whatever the party may say, the abstract is nothing than the conclusion that there should be full freedom for existing different classes to form political organisations, representing their class interests to launch activities, to wage an electoral competition with the communist party, even to push it into being an opposition party. Such a demand rejects the fundamental principles of Marxism-Leninism-Mao Tse-tung Thought on the leadership in the new democratic or socialist state power, class-struggle, the social bases for capitalistic restoration, and single party or multi-party. It shows how the party has adopted the petty-bourgeois view on these questions.

Whether multi-party or single party is the system of government, it is not the state power. The system of government is the appearance aspect and the state power is the essence. So, the system of government is determined by its essence aspect, *i.e.* the type of state power. In a sense, the system of government is an organ of state power and it must be always subordinated to the state power and serve it too. Certainly, Marxism-Leninism-Mao Tse-tung Thought recognises separate forms of system of government according

10 Baburam Bhattarai, "Question of Building of a New Type of State Power", *People's Council*, The Organ of the Joint Revolutionary People's Council, Nepal, July 2004, No. 1, p. 12.

11 Baburam Bhattarai, "Question of Building of a New Type of State Power", *People's Council*, The Organ of the Joint Revolutionary People's Council, Nepal, July 2004, No. 1, p. 13.

to the specificity of different countries, but they should serve to the state power in their different ways while remaining subordinate to it. This is true about bourgeois as well as proletarian state systems. When any form of system of government is out of track, it must be immediately changed and a system of government that suits the state power should be established. If it is not done in time, it can change the essence of state power. Such is the dialectics of relation between state power and the system of government as explained by Marxism.

The concept of multi-party political competition propounded by our party as a development, or as a "new" dimension to the fundamental principle of Marxism-Leninism-Mao Tse-tung Thought in relation to democracy is not a peculiarity only in the case of Nepal, but has come as an essential contribution to the historical and class concept of state power to establish in the form of a general question, with the amendments of the Marxism-Leninism-Mao Tse-tung Thought that considers the multi-party system and the right to vote as a special issue of revolution. However, we should not forget that the general and particular character and place of revolution are the objective ones and our subjective attempts cannot change that. Lenin stated that depriving the exploiter class of the voting right was purely a special case of Russia. He warned the communists not to take that question as a general question of proletarian dictatorship. Lenin states:

> It should be observed that the question of depriving the exploiters of the franchise is a *purely Russian* question, and not a question of the dictatorship of the proletariat in general. ... For theory, *i.e.* the reasoning about the general (and not the nationally specific) class foundations of democracy and dictatorship, ought to deal not with a special question, such as the franchise, but with the general question of whether democracy can be *preserved for the rich, for the exploiters* in the historical period of the overthrow of the exploiters and the replacement of their state by the state of the exploited.

Further he says:

> The question of restricting the franchise is a nationally specific and not a general question of the dictatorship ... it is *not absolutely necessary* for the exercise of the dictatorship, it is not an *indispensable* characteristic of the logical concept "dictatorship", it does not enter as an *indispensable* condition in the historical and class concept "dictatorship". "The indispensable characteristic, the necessary condition of dictatorship is the *forcible* suppression of the exploiters as a *class*, and, consequently, the *infringement* of "pure democracy", *i.e.* of equality and freedom, *in regard* to that *class*.
>
> In which countries, and given what national features of capitalism, democracy for the exploiters will be in one or another form restricted (wholly or in part), infringed upon, is a question of the specific national

> features of this or that capitalism, of this or that revolution. The theoretical question is different: is the dictatorship of the proletariat possible *without infringing democracy* in relation to the *exploiting* class? ... The fact that the proletariat cannot achieve victory *without breaking the resistance* of the bourgeoisie, *without forcibly suppressing its adversaries*, and that, where there is "forcible suppression", where there is no "freedom", *there is, of course, no democracy.*[12]

Lenin has said much about whether voting rights should be granted to class enemies after the socialist revolution. However, our party is proposing to institutionalise the right for the supporters of revolution, not to the enemy forces, to be affiliated to a political party and compete in elections with the communist party in the new democratic and socialist state. A cursory look suggests similarity between the opinion expressed by Lenin about voting rights after the revolution and the proposal of our party to institutionalise the multi-party system under a new democracy and socialist system. This is true superficially, not in substances. The main question, as Lenin says, is the question of how to implement dictatorship. After coming to power, our party embraced only the class thrown out as an enemy force by the revolution. From the point of view of our party, the result is that "after having destroyed economic monopoly over land and capital, *i.e.* sources of political monopoly of feudal and bourgeois and military monopoly over hired occupational army", "there can be no reason at all for hesitation to allow political party for competition, not just for cooperation with the communist party". In fact the question of "destroying economic monopoly over land and capital, *i.e.* source of political monopoly of feudal and bourgeois and military monopoly over hired occupational army", is related to immediately after capturing state power.

By basing on the task that can be done by the proletarian class immediate the seizure of power, to say that "there can be no reason at all for hesitation to opening political party for 'competition' and not for 'cooperation' with the communist party" is totally against the fundamental principles of Marxism-Leninism as it totally neglects how a captured state power is retained, consolidated and made invincible. The party has taken lightly the counter-revolutionary activities of the neo-bourgeoisie who engenders continuously basing on national and international social ground.

The history of approximately one hundred years of building of socialism teaches us that it is not sufficient for the proletarian class to capture state power through new democratic or socialist revolution. As Stalin says: "The seizure of power is only the beginning. For many

12 V. I. Lenin, "Proletarian Revolution and Renegade Kautsky", *Collected Works*, Eng. ed., Progress Publishers, Moscow, Third Printing, 1981, Vol. 28, pp. 255-57.

reasons, the bourgeoisie that is overthrown in one country remains for a long time stronger than the proletariat which has overthrown it. Therefore, the whole point is to retain power, to consolidate it, to make it invincible."[13]

The question of retaining and strengthening proletarian state power is a very complicated and of a protracted nature. The danger of losing state power captured by the proletarian class looms large as long as imperialism is not eliminated worldwide.

Lenin says:

> The transition from capitalism to communism takes an entire historical epoch. Until this epoch is over, the exploiters inevitably cherish the hope of restoration, and this *hope* turns into *attempts* at restoration. After their first serious defeat, the overthrown exploiters–who had not expected their overthrow, never believed it possible, never conceded the thought of it–throw themselves with energy grown tenfold, with furious passion and hatred grown a hundredfold, into the battle for the recovery of the "paradise", of which they were deprived, on behalf of their families, who had been leading such a sweet and easy life and whom now the "common herd" is condemning to ruin and destitution (or to "common" labour...). In the train of the capitalist exploiters follow the wide sections of the petty-bourgeoisie, with regard to whom decades of historical experience of all countries testify that they vacillate and hesitate, one day marching behind the proletariat and the next day taking fright at the difficulties of the revolution; that they become panic-stricken at the first defeat or semi-defeat of the workers, grow nervous, run about aimlessly, snivel, and rush from one camp into the other–just like our Mensheviks and Socialist-Revolutionaries.[14]

Leninism illustrates that the restoration of a defeated capitalist class is not baseless, *i.e.* there exists a strong social ground behind that.

> In the strength of international capital, the strength and durability of their international connections.[15] ... For a long time after the revolution the exploiters inevitably continue to retain a number of great practical advantages: they still have money (since it is impossible to abolish money all at once); some movable property–often fairly considerable; they still have various connections, habits of organisation and management; knowledge of all the "secrets" (customs, methods, means and possibilities) of management; superior education; close connections with the higher technical personnel

13 J. V. Stalin, "Foundation of Leninism", *Problems of Leninism*, Eng. ed., Foreign Language Press, Peking, 1976, p. 39.

14 V. I. Lenin, "Proletarian Revolution and Renegade Kautsky", *Collected Works*, Eng. ed., Progress Publishers, Moscow, Third Printing, 1981, Vol. 28, p. 254.

15 V. I. Lenin, " 'Left-Wing' Communism: An Infantile Disorder", *Collected Works*, Eng. ed., Progress Publishers, Moscow, Third Printing, 1977, Vol. 31, p. 24.

(who live and think like the bourgeoisie); incomparably greater experience in the art of war (this is very important), and so on and so forth.[16]

In the *force of habit*, in the strength of *small-scale production*. Unfortunately, small-scale production is still widespread in the world, and small-scale production *engenders* capitalism and the bourgeoisie continuously, daily hourly, spontaneously, and on a mass scale. Because, the abolition of classes means, not merely ousting the landowners and the capitalists–that is something we accomplished with comparative ease; it also means *abolishing the small commodity producers*, and they *cannot be ousted*, or crushed; *we must learn to live* with them. They can (and must) be transformed and re-educated only by means of very prolonged, slow, and cautious organisational work.[17]

Understanding the reality of this situation, Stalin says: "To attain this it is necessary to carry out at least three main tasks". They are as follows:

a) To break the resistance of the landlords and capitalists who have been overthrown and expropriated by the revolution, to liquidate every attempt on their part to restore the power of capital;

b) To organise construction in such a way as to rally all the working people around the proletariat, and to carry on this work along the lines of preparing for the elimination, the abolition of classes;

c) To arm the revolution, to organise the army of the revolution for the struggle against foreign enemies, for the struggle against imperialism.[18]

Marxism-Leninism-Mao Tse-tung Thought declares that proletarian dictatorship is necessary to implement and fulfil the above responsibilities. For example, Karl Marx says: "Between capitalist and communist society lies the period of the revolutionary transformation of the one into the other. Corresponding to this is also a political transition period in which the state can be nothing but *the revolutionary dictatorship of the proletariat*."[19]

According to Lenin, "The fundamental question of every revolution is the question of power." Stalin further elaborates Lenin's statement: "The seizure of power is only the beginning. For many reasons, the bourgeoisie that is overthrown in one country remains for long stronger than the proletariat. Therefore, the whole point is to retain power, to consolidate it, to make it invincible."

---

16 V. I. Lenin, "Proletarian Revolution and Renegade Kautsky", *Collected Works*, Eng. ed., Progress Publishers, Moscow, Third Printing, 1981, Vol. 28, p. 253.

17 V. I. Lenin, " 'Left-Wing' Communism: An Infantile Disorder", *Collected Works*, Eng. ed., Progress Publishers, Moscow, Third Printing, 1977, Vol. 31, pp. 24, 44.

18 J. V. Stalin, "Foundation of Leninism", *Problems of Leninism*, Eng. ed., Foreign Language Press, Peking, 1976, p. 39.

19 Karl Marx and Frederick Engels, "Critique of Gotha Programme", *Selected Works*, Progress Publishers, Moscow, Fourth Printing, 1977, Vol. 3, p. 26.

Stalin further says about what is necessary to fulfil that task:

> The revolution can defeat the bourgeoisie, can overthrow its power, even without the dictatorship of the proletariat. But the revolution will be unable to crush the resistance of the bourgeoisie, to maintain its victory and to push forward to the final victory of socialism unless, at a certain stage in its development, it creates a special organ in the form of the dictatorship of the proletariat as its principal mainstay.[20]

Marxism-Leninism says that above mentioned responsibilities cannot be fulfilled over a short time, so a full historical era is required. For example, Karl Marx says: "We say to workers, you will have to go through 15, 20, 50 years of civil wars and international wars, not only in order to change existing conditions but also in order to change yourselves and fit yourselves for the exercise of political power."[21]

Marx says in another place:

> This socialism is the *declaration of the permanence of the revolution,* the *class dictatorship* of the proletariat as the necessary transit point to the *abolition of class distinctions generally*, to the abolition of all the relations of production on which they rest, to the abolition of all the social relations that correspond to these relations of production, to the revolutionising of all the ideas that result from these social relations.[22]

Broadening and developing this thinking of Marx, Lenin says: "Under the proletarian dictatorship, millions of peasants and small proprietors, hundreds of thousands of office employees, officials and bourgeois intellectuals, of subordinating them all to the proletarian state and to proletarian leadership, of eradicating their bourgeois habits and traditions".

Lenin says about how we can do that:

> In a protracted struggle waged on the basis of the dictatorship of the proletariat–re-educate the proletarians themselves, who do not abandon their petty-bourgeois prejudices at one stroke, by a miracle, at the behest of the Virgin Mary, at the behest of a slogan, resolution or decree, but only in the course of a long and difficult mass struggle against mass petty-bourgeois influences.[23]

---

20 J. V. Stalin, "Foundation of Leninism", *Problems of Leninism*, Eng. ed., Foreign Language Press, Peking, 1976, pp. 38-39.

21 Karl Marx, "Revelations About the Cologne Communist Trial, October-December, 1852", Karl Marx and Frederick Engels, *Collected Works*, New York : International Publications, 1979, Vol. 11, p. 403.

22 Karl Marx and Frederick Engels, "The Class Struggle in France", *Selected Works*, Progress Publishers, Moscow, Fourth Printing, 1977, Vol. 1, p. 282.

23 V. I. Lenin, " 'Left-Wing' Communism: An Infantile Disorder", *Collected Works*, Eng. ed., Progress Publishers, Moscow, Third Printing, 1977, Vol. 31, pp. 115-16.

Stalin puts the lessons from Marx and Lenin in simple, clear and strong words:

> There is not the slightest possibility of carrying out these tasks in a short period, of accomplishing all this in a few years. Therefore, the dictatorship of the proletariat, the transition from capitalism to communism, must not be regarded as a fleeting period, of "super-revolutionary" acts and decrees, but as an entire historical era, replete with civil wars and external conflicts, with persistent organisational work and economic construction, with advances and retreats, victories and defeats. This historical era is needed not only to create the economic and cultural prerequisites for the complete victory of socialism, but also to enable the proletariat, firstly, to educate itself and become steeled as a force capable of governing the country, and, secondly, to re-educate and remould the petty-bourgeois strata along such lines as will assure the organisation of socialist production.[24]

We should be guided from the basic principle of Marxism-Leninism regarding capturing and retaining state power and making it invincible. By ignoring over a hundred year of experience of the formation of socialism and revival of capitalism has shown that building socialism is a complicated process, our party's advocacy of the multi-party system as a magic rod to solve such serious problems is ridiculous. What form of state organisation should be adopted after the proletariat captures the state power depends on the situation of socio-economic development in the country, the role of parties in revolution, *i.e.* the national and international conditions–not on the wish of the party. Certainly, the active role of the party and leadership can affect to a great extent, but never to the extent of changing the objective situation. For example, the above analysis shows that capitalism exists in the country in different forms for long even after a socialist revolution. Although the capitalist class is overthrown forcefully by revolution, it settles in different areas on economic ground and superstructure in such a way that it cannot be ousted away instantly as it requires a long historical period to cross. Bourgeois right, small-scale production, differences between town and countryside, and physical and mental labour and so on are the birth marks of capitalism, which cannot be wiped out within a short period. Marx has named the duration as the first phase of communism.

> What we have to deal with here is a communist society, not as it has *developed* on its own foundations, but, on the contrary, just as it *emerges* from capitalist society; which is thus in every respect, economically, morally and intellectually, still stamped with the birth marks of the old society from whose womb it emerges.

24 J. V. Stalin, "Foundation of Leninism", *Problems of Leninism*, Eng. ed., Foreign Language Press, Peking, 1976, pp. 41-42.

Let us examine bourgeois rights. In the first phase of communist society, every member consumes from a public store according to one's labour, which seems like the right of equality. In fact, this is an unequal situation, as all people are not equal physically. Some are physically healthy and can work longer and some cannot; some have a large family and others small. Certainly, the situation of getting things on the basis of the quantity of labour from a public store is a situation of formal equality of capitalism that is called bourgeois right. As Marx says that under this type of equal distribution of right in socialism "one will in fact receive more than another, one will be richer than another." The existence of bourgeois rights in a proletarian state is a serious defect, but coexistence with bourgeois rights is essential to a certain extent in the first phase of communist society. Furthermore Marx says: "These defects are inevitable in the first phase of communist society as it is when it has just emerged after prolonged birth pangs from capitalist society. Right can never be higher than the economic structure of society and its cultural development conditioned thereby."[25] In this very context, Lenin says: "There are no other rules than those of "bourgeois law". To this extent, therefore, there still remains the need for a state, which, while safeguarding the common ownership of the instruments and the means of production, would safeguard equality in labour and in the distribution of products."

Having experienced the end of exploitation of man by man, the end of private property ownership over factories, machines, land and so forth, in the first phase of communist society, some still do not accept the existing bourgeois right and do not understand the need and importance of a high level of alertness and awareness by the proletariat and its vanguard party. The history of socialism shows that the bourgeois right will be over after the public ownership system is established and the private ownership system over the instruments and the means of production is ended. But in the distribution of products and allotment of labour between the members of the society, the bourgeois rights still remains active. Lenin clarifies:

> In the first phase of communist society (usual called socialism)"bourgeois law" is *not* abolished in its entirety, but only in part, only in proportion to the economic revolution so far attained, *i.e.* only in respect of the means of production. "Bourgeois law" recognises them as the private property of individuals. Socialism converts them into *common* property. To *that extent*–and to that extent alone–"bourgeois law" disappears.
>
> However, it persists as far as its other part is concerned; it persists in the capacity of regulator (determining factor) in the distribution of products and the allotment of labour among the members of society. The socialist

25 Karl Marx and Frederick Engels, "Critique of Gotha Programme", *Selected Works*, Progress Publishers, Moscow, Fourth Printing, 1977, Vol. 3, pp. 17, 19.

> principle, "He who does not work shall not eat", is *already* realised; the other socialist principle, "An equal amount of products for an equal amount of labour", is also *already* realised. But this is not yet communism, and it does not yet abolish "bourgeois law", which gives unequal individuals, in return for unequal (really unequal) amounts of labour, equal amounts of products.[26]

In the first phase of communist society, when a system of exploitation of man by man and private ownership over the instruments and the means of production like factory, machinery, land come to an end, and the previous exploiters disappear as a class, as the result; remnants of exploiters, mainly capitalists and the factors, like small-scale production, law of value, and the differences between town and countryside, and physical and mental labour responsible for bringing capitalist exploitation into existence exist, though in the process of decline. Under socialism, *i.e.* throughout the whole period of first phase of communist society, the main contradiction lies between the working-class and the capitalist class. The first phase of communist society does not differ from the capitalist society fundamentally in this sense. In capitalism, the capitalist class is the ruling class while the proletarian class is the ruled one, and the contradiction between them is the main contradiction. However, in a socialist society, the proletarian class is the ruling class and the capitalist class is under proletarian rule. The contradiction between them is the main contradiction of that society, though other contradictions exist in society. In spite of the change in the position of classes, *i.e.* proletarian class and capitalist class, both in capitalism and socialism, the contradiction between the working-class and capitalist class is the main contradiction. This is the basic principle of Marxism-Leninism-Mao Tse-tung Thought in relation to class struggle in the capitalist and socialist society.

Our party says:

> After the source of political and economic monopoly of feudal and bourgeoisie, respectively on land, capital and the military monopoly over hired occupational army are crushed, there remains no factual or logical argument to hesitate for a communist party that claims the majority of proletarian and oppressed class representation to allow political competition within a certain constitutional process.

The statement suggests that after having lost the instruments and the means of production, there is no need to be afraid of the exploiter class. Such a view exposes the concept of the *Development of Democracy in the Twenty-First Century*. The document is concerned with the democratic bourgeois tasks and it has centralised and focused on fulfilling them. It does

---

26 V. I. Lenin, "The State and Revolution", *Collected Works*, Eng. ed., Progress Publishers, Moscow, Fourth Printing, 1980, Vol. 25, p. 472.

not care about the proletarian task as marked clearly in every word, every sentence and every page of the document. The negligence shown by our party to classes and struggle between them needs to be studied in this light.

Contrary to our party's view, the old exploiters exist for long in society, even after they are deprived of the ownership over the instruments and the means of production. Similarly, they exist because of the presence of small-scale production, inequality between countryside and town, and mental and physical labour. In this situation, the capitalist class remains always active for its revival. Lenin and Mao have emphasised the importance of understanding classes and class struggle under socialism seriously, by shedding light on the remains of the capitalist class and the struggle against them, and the discussing in detail the social foundations that generate new capitalist elements under socialism. The *Development of Democracy in the Twenty-First Century* of our party has no Marxist-Leninist plan of elimination of classes.

If I have understood correctly the above statement of our party, after capturing state power, establishing socialist ownership over the instruments and the means of production by the proletariat, the existence of hostile classes will end, except the friendly contradictions among the different strata of people. Such a thinking is completely against Leninism as discussed on different occasions by Lenin himself:

> Clearly, in order to abolish classes completely, it is not enough to overthrow the exploiters, the landowners and capitalists, not enough to abolish *their* rights of ownership; it is also to abolish *all* private ownership of the means of production, it is necessary to abolish the distinction between town and country, as well as the distinction between manual workers and brain workers. This requires a very long period of time. In order to achieve this an enormous step forward must be taken in developing the productive forces; it is necessary to overcome the resistance (frequently passive, which is particularly stubborn and particularly difficult to overcome) of the numerous survivals of small-scale production; it is necessary to overcome the enormous force of habit and conservatism which are connected with these survivals.[27]

The role of undivided leadership of a communist party is explained in the *Fourth Letter.* Regarding this, Lenin too says: "Only the proletariat is in a position to unite and lead the scattered and backward sections of working and exploited population."[28] By amending the fundamental principle of Marxism-Leninism-Mao Tse-tung Thought in relation to the undivided

27 V. I. Lenin, "A Great Beginning", *Collected Works*, Eng. ed., Progress Publishers, Moscow, Third Printing, 1977, Vol. 29, p. 421.

28 V. I. Lenin, "First Congress of Communist International", *Collected Works*, Eng. ed., Progress Publishers, Moscow, Third Printing, 1981, Vol. 28, p. 466.

leadership of proletariat, *i.e.* the leading role in the first phase of communist society, our party has forwarded a discourse that in the name of development of democracy in the twenty-first century, any petty-bourgeois party could do that work. It says the proletariat need not send its vanguard compulsorily for that and advocacy for the multi-party competition as a transition phase to enter into the second stage of communist society, which is completely against the Marxist-Leninist principle.

The proletarian state power is a state power under the undivided leadership of the proletarian class. Without continuing leadership of the proletariat, the great campaign for class elimination cannot yield the required result. Out of the oppressed classes and working people, the proletarian class alone is a class that can take the great journey of elimination of classes successfully.

Lenin states:

> Throughout the whole of this transition period, resistance to the revolution will be offered both by the capitalists and by their numerous myrmidons among the bourgeois intellectuals, who will resist consciously, and by the vast mass of the working people, including the peasants, who are shackled very much by petty-bourgeois habits and traditions, and who all too often will resist unconsciously. Vacillations among these groups are inevitable. As a working man the peasant gravitates towards socialism, and prefers the dictatorship of the workers to the dictatorship of the bourgeoisie. As a seller of grain, the peasant gravitates towards the bourgeoisie, towards freedom of trade, *i.e.* back to the "habitual", old "time-hallowed" capitalism.

How can the goal of elimination of classes be achieved in this situation? Lenin says:

> What is needed to enable the proletariat *to lead* the peasants and the petty-bourgeois groups in general is the dictatorship of the proletariat, the rule of one class, its strength of organisation and discipline, its centralised power based on all the achievements of the culture, science and technology of capitalism, its proletarian affinity to the mentality of every working man, its prestige with the disunited, less developed working people in the countryside or in petty industry, who are less firm in politics.
>
> The abolition of classes requires a long, difficult and stubborn *class struggle*, which, *after* the overthrow of capitalist rule, *after* the destruction of the bourgeois state, *after* the establishment of the dictatorship of the proletariat, *does not disappear* (as the vulgar representatives of the old socialism and the old Social-Democracy imagine), but merely changes its forms and in many respects becomes fiercer.
>
> The proletariat, by means of a class struggle against the resistance of the bourgeoisie, against the conservatism, routine, irresolution and vacillation of the petty-bourgeoisie, must uphold its power, strengthen its organising

> influence, "neutralise" those groups which fear to leave the bourgeoisie and which follow the proletariat too hesitantly, and consolidate the new discipline, the comradely discipline of the working people, their firm bond with the proletariat, their unity with the proletariat–that new discipline, that new basis of social ties in place of the serf discipline of the Middle Ages and the discipline of starvation, the discipline of "free" wages-slavery under capitalism.
>
> In order to abolish classes a period of the dictatorship of one class is needed, the dictatorship of precisely that oppressed class which is capable not only of overthrowing the exploiters, not only of ruthlessly crushing their resistance, but also of breaking ideologically with the entire bourgeois-democratic outlook, with all the philistine phrase-mongering about liberty and equality in general (in reality, this phrase-mongering implies, as Marx demonstrated long ago, the "liberty and equality" of *commodity owners*, the "liberty and equality" of *the capitalist and the worker*).
>
> More, classes can be abolished only by the dictatorship of that oppressed class which has been schooled, united, trained and steeled by decades of the strike and political struggle against capital–of that class alone which has assimilated all the urban, industrial, big-capitalist culture and has the determination and ability to protect it and to preserve and further develop all its achievements, and make them available to all the people, to all the working people–of that class alone which will be able to bear all the hardships, trials, privations and great sacrifices which history inevitably imposes upon those who break with the past and boldly hew a road for themselves to a new future–of that class alone whose finest members are full of hatred and contempt for everything petty-bourgeois and philistine, for the qualities that flourish so profusely among the petty-bourgeoisie, the minor employees and the "intellectuals"–of that class alone which "has been through the hardening school of labour" and is able to inspire respect for its efficiency in every working person and every honest man.[29]

Along with the development of socialism, and establishment of management of large-scale socialist production, the role of other labouring strata grows on faster in completing the transition period. In spite of that, other classes except the proletariat do not have the ability to retain that power, consolidate it and make it invincible for a necessary period. So, for a long time it is unwise to suggest that the proletariat should share the leadership role with other labouring strata. The leadership role should be possessed by the proletariat alone. As Lenin says in this regard:

> The assumption that all "working people" are equally capable of doing this work would be an empty phrase, or the illusion of an antediluvian, pre-Marxist socialist; for this ability does not come of itself, but grows historically, and

29 V. I. Lenin, "Greetings to the Hungarian Workers", *Collected Works*, Eng. ed., Progress Publishers, Moscow, Third Printing, 1977, Vol. 29, pp. 389-90.

> grows *only* out of the material conditions of large-scale capitalist production. This ability, at the beginning of the road from capitalism to socialism, is possessed by the proletariat *alone*. It is capable of fulfilling the gigantic task that confronts it, first, because it is the strongest and most advanced class in civilised societies; secondly, because in the most developed countries it constitutes the majority of the population.

On the duty of the proletariat, Lenin further writes:

> In order to achieve victory, in order to build and consolidate socialism, the proletariat must fulfil a twofold or dual task: first, it must, by its supreme heroism in the revolutionary struggle against capital, win over the entire mass of the working and exploited people; it must win them over, organise them and lead them in the struggle to overthrow the bourgeoisie and utterly suppress their resistance. Secondly, it must lead the whole mass of the working and exploited people, as well as all the petty-bourgeois groups, on to the road of new economic development, towards the creation of a new social bond, a new labour discipline, a new organisation of labour, which will combine the last word in science and capitalist technology with the mass association of class-conscious workers creating large-scale socialist industry.
>
> The second task is more difficult than the first, for it cannot possibly be fulfilled by single acts of heroic fervour; it requires the most prolonged, most persistent and most difficult mass heroism in *plain, everyday* work. But this task is more essential than the first, because, in the last analysis, the deepest source of strength for victories over the bourgeoisie and the sole guarantee of the durability and permanence of these victories can only be a new and higher mode of social production, the substitution of large-scale socialist production for capitalist and petty-bourgeois production.[30]

Our party has said that in the course of building socialism, a "proletarian leadership is not a thing to get or to impose as monopoly, but is a question of earning with revolutionary behaviour and implementing democratically."[31]

This is a question of class analysis. Here, we are talking about the socialist phase, about the transitional period between capitalism and communism. Our party has presented the question of leadership of the proletarian class in a way that it is not "an issue to get and impose" as monopoly is wrong. The presentation has not only brought the idea that another option of leadership should be found, if it does not work "with revolutionary behaviour"; it has also proposed to find that option in the

30 V. I. Lenin, "A Great Beginning", *Collected Works*, Eng. ed., Progress Publishers, Moscow, Third Printing, 1977, Vol. 29, pp. 421-23.

31 Baburam Bhattarai, "Question of Building of a New State Power", *People's Council*, The Organ of the Joint Revolutionary People's Council, Nepal, July 2004, No. 1, p. 12.

class itself too. Some leaders of the proletariat may not be right and if so, the class must change the leader itself. But from the class criteria view, the proletarian class is the most revolutionary class and there can be no option to its class leadership for the completion of the transition. So, the proposal of our party, in the course of the building of socialism, to find an option to the proletarian class leadership through political competition is faulty.

Marxism-Leninism treats the proletarian leadership as a question of undivided leadership. It is not that the proletariat has to impose its leadership on working masses, on the population of non-proletarian and semi-proletarian masses, but it maintains that those working populations accept its leadership voluntarily. Lenin clarifies this regard:

> This new discipline does not drop from the skies, nor is it born from pious wishes; it grows out of the material conditions of large-scale capitalist production, and out of them alone. Without them it is impossible. And the repository, or the vehicle, of these material conditions is a definite historical class, created, organised, united, trained, educated and hardened by large-scale capitalism. This class is the proletariat.
>
> Only a definite class, namely, the urban workers and the factory, industrial workers in general, is able to lead the whole mass of the working and exploited people in the struggle to throw off the yoke of capital, in actually carrying it out, in the struggle to maintain and consolidate the victory, in the work of creating the new, socialist social system and in the entire struggle for the complete abolition of classes.

Further, he writes:

> The dictatorship of the proletariat is *also* a period of class struggle, which is inevitable as long as classes have not been abolished, and which changes in form, being particularly fierce and particularly peculiar in the period immediately following the overthrow of capital. The proletariat does not cease the class struggle after it has captured political power, but continues it until classes are abolished–of course, under different circumstances, in a different form and by different means.[32]

3
State Organisation of the Proletarian State

Our party has raised the question of the form of state organisation under proletarian state power while making an overview of the proletarian state power. After the Great Socialist Revolution in Russia establishing the

32 V. I. Lenin, "A Great Beginning", *Collected Works*, Eng. ed., Progress Publishers, Moscow, Third Printing, 1977, Vol. 29, pp. 420-21.

state organisation to suppress and destroy the capitalistic state machinery and establish a proletarian democracy as a part of the transition to communism emerged as a burning issue. Under the leadership of Lenin, the Russian Communist Party (Bolshevik) accepted the Soviet, with a large majority of workers, soldiers and peasants as the state organisation of the proletarian state power. These are different from the old bourgeois-democratic and parliamentary state organisations. As Stalin says:

> In that the Soviets are the most *all-embracing* mass organisations of the proletariat, for they and they alone embrace all workers without exception.
>
> In that the Soviets are the *only* mass organisations which unite all the oppressed and exploited, workers and peasants, soldiers and sailors, and in which the vanguard of the masses, the proletariat, can, for this reason, most easily and most completely exercise its political leadership of the mass struggle.
>
> In that the Soviets are the *most powerful organs* of the revolutionary struggle of the masses, of the political actions of the masses, of the uprising of the masses–organs capable of breaking the omnipotence of finance capital and its political appendages.
>
> In that the Soviets are the *immediate* organisations of the masses themselves, *i.e.* they are the *most democratic* and therefore the most authoritative organisations of the masses, which facilitate to the utmost their participation in the work of building up the new state and in its administration, and which bring into full play the revolutionary energy, initiative and creative abilities of the masses in the struggle for the destruction of the old order, in the struggle for the new, proletarian order.[33]

On the essence of Soviet state power, Lenin writes:

> Have in fact been debarred by thousands of devices and subterfuges from participation in political life and enjoyment of democratic rights and liberties, that are now drawn into constant and unfailing, moreover, decisive, participation in the democratic administration of the state.[34]

In this regard, Stalin writes:

> So, we can say that "Soviet power is a *new form* of state organisation, different in principle from the old bourgeois-democratic and parliamentary form, a *new type* of state, adapted not to the task of exploiting and oppressing the labouring masses, but to the task of completely emancipating them from all oppression and exploitation, to the tasks facing the dictatorship of the proletariat.

Highlighting its most democratic essence, he further writes:

33 J. V. Stalin, "Foundation of Leninism", *Problems of Leninism*, Eng. ed., Foreign Language Press, Peking, 1976, p. 48.

34 V. I. Lenin, "Proletarian Revolution and Renegade Kautsky", *Collected Works*, Eng. ed., Progress Publishers, Moscow, Third Printing, 1981, Vol. 28, p. 465.

> In that Soviet power is the most all-embracing and most democratic state organisation of all possible state organisations while classes continue to exist; for, being the arena of the bond and collaboration between the workers and the exploited peasants in their struggle against the exploiters, and basing itself in its work on this bond and on this collaboration, Soviet power is thus the power of the majority of the population over the minority, it is the state of the majority, the expression of its dictatorship.
>
> In that Soviet power is the most internationalist of all state organisations in class society; for, by destroying every kind of national oppression and resting on the collaboration of the labouring masses of the various nationalities, it facilitates the uniting of these masses into a single state union.
>
> In that Soviet power, by its very structure, facilitates the task of leading the oppressed and exploited masses by the vanguard of these masses–by the proletariat, as the most united and most politically conscious core of the Soviets.
>
> In that Soviet power, by combining legislative and executive power in a single state organisation and replacing territorial electoral constituencies by industrial units, factories and mills, thereby directly links the workers and the labouring masses in general with the apparatus of state administration, teaches them how to govern the country.
>
> In that Soviet power alone is capable of releasing the army from its subordination to bourgeois command and of converting it from the instrument of oppression of the people which it is under the bourgeois order, into an instrument for the liberation of the people from the yoke of the bourgeoisie, both native and foreign.
>
> In that the Soviet form of state alone, by drawing the mass organisations of the toilers and exploited into constant and unrestricted participation in state administration, is capable of preparing the ground for the withering away of the state, which is one of the basic elements of the future stateless communist society.[35]

Lenin further writes: "Only the Soviet organisation of the state can really effect the immediate break-up and total destruction of the old, *i.e.* bourgeois, bureaucratic and judicial machinery."[36]

In short, the Soviet form of state organisation is, as Lenin and Stalin have said, "not only a higher type of democratic institution ..., but is the only form capable of securing the most painless transition to socialism."[37]

---

35 J. V. Stalin, "Foundation of Leninism", *Problems of Leninism*, Eng. ed., Foreign Language Press, Peking, 1976, pp. 49-51.

36 V. I. Lenin, "First Congress of the Communist International", *Collected Works*, Eng. ed., Progress Publishers, Moscow, Third Printing, 1981, Vol. 28, p. 466.

37 V. I. Lenin, "Theses on the Constituent Assembly", *Collected Works*, Eng. ed., Progress Publishers, Moscow, Third Printing, 1977, Vol. 26, p. 379.

And, "the Republic of Soviets is thus the political form, ... the economic emancipation of the proletariat, the complete victory of socialism."[38]

Certainly, Marxism-Leninism does not subscribe to any particular form of state organisation to complete the transition towards communism. It suggests adopting a concrete form of state organisation according to the concrete condition of the concerned country as clarified from the different forms adopted to complete the transition towards communism in different countries. A different form of state organisation was adopted in China than the Soviet form adopted in Russia. Marxist-Leninists should realise that despite the different forms of state organisation adopted in China, they were not different from the essence of the Soviet form.

Our party has raised the question in relation to the essence of state organisations adopted in the course of transition towards communism in the past. It has emphasised that in order to make a perfectly successful transition, a "new model" should be adopted which is, "free" from the danger of counter-revolution. For example, it says: "In the situation that models exercised in Russia and China badly failed, revolutionaries of our era must take courage to test and develop new models, learning lessons from the past experience."

Here, our party's assertion of "badly failed" "past models of the proletarian dictatorship" adopted in the Soviet Union and in China, is quite wrong. If because of the restoration of capitalism in these countries "models of proletarian dictatorship had badly failed, revolutionaries of our era should learn lessons from experience to develop new models", basing on the same reason, why it could not be said that the 'principle of socialist revolution of Marxism has badly failed and revolutionaries of our era, learning lessons from it, must take courage to amend and change it. The *Development of Democracy in the Twenty-First Century* and Comrade Bhattarai's the *Question of Building of a New Type of State Power* contains several grounds to question whether the analysis of our party in relation to models of proletarian dictatorship is a journey towards that very direction? The restoration of capitalism is the outcome of world imperialism, the strength of international relations of the capitalist class, the existence of bourgeois rights, existence of difference between town and countryside, and physical and mental labour, small-scale production, law of value, commodity production to a certain extent and the subjective weaknesses. We can stop the restoration of capitalism by adopting the essence of the past state organisations under the dictatorship of the proletariat. Doing this, we can move the revolution ahead uninterruptedly. So, our party's contention that instead of past state organisations adopted

38 J. V. Stalin, "Foundation of Leninism", *Problems of Leninism*, Eng. ed., Foreign Language Press, Peking, 1976, p. 51.

under socialism, "new" forms of state organisations should be developed is unreasonable and unacceptable.

By the study of the *Development of Democracy in the Twenty-First Century* and the *Question of Building of a New Type of State Power* on the whole, our party opposes the Leninist concept of undivided leadership of the communist party. Lenin has emphasised that the proletariat should establish its undivided leadership through the communist party over state organisations. Having discarded this principle, our party maintains that leadership of those state organisations should be managed through so-called multi-party competition. In this relation it (our party) mentions that Lenin himself was apathetic to his previous views in his later days. For example, it says: "A general perception emerged that after the experience of the Paris Commune and Russian Soviet the proletariat should implement its leadership through the communist party as its vanguard and the dictatorship through the Soviet or People's Council made on the Paris Commune model."

A statement of Lenin is extracted by Comrade Bhattarai in the *Question of Building of a New Type of State Power*. Our party tries to prove that after the October Revolution Lenin emphasised repeatedly that dictatorship was implemented through the Soviets. It says that in spite of Lenin's thinking in the beginning, in the course of addressing the third Congress of the Communist International in 1921, Lenin said, "the dictatorship of the proletariat would not work except through the communist party. (*LCW*, Vol. 32, p. 199.)

Our party went to the extent that after that as in all socialist state powers, this statement of Lenin was taken "mechanically" and the distinction between the communist party and state power was wiped out. As it says:

> The mistake of wiping out all distinctions between the communist party and state power was established by all socialist states. By taking Lenin's words mechanically, not in any general sense in all socialist countries, a blunder of wiping out the distinction between the communist party and the state power was committed. On the basis of the bitter experience of dissolution of distinction between party and people's representative, organisations, bureaucratic capitalisation of the party and taking the leadership of power as a monopoly, we, revolutionaries of the present era, should take courage to correct them.[39]

Our party says that under the socialist state power of the past whatever form of state organisations was adopted instead of the leading

39 Baburam Bhattarai, "Question of Building of a New Type of State Power", *People's Council*, The Organ of the Joint Revolutionary People's Council, Nepal, July 2004, No. 1, p. 12.

state power into the direction of withering away, led the state power to further strengthening it. The extract below makes it clear:

> Marx's statement that the proletarian state or the dictatorship of the proletariat, "not a political state power", and Engels' saying it "not a state as a literal meaning", means they are not a medium to give permanence to class contradiction, or defend it, but a medium of transformation into a classless society from class society, a thing to end itself along with it.

Further it is stated:

> The way proletarian state powers built in the past, instead of becoming one to serve people and continuously as a medium of revolution, became lords of people and medium of counter-revolution, not being oriented to wither away and got changed into a powerful huge bureaucracy and mechanism of suppression, impels the revolutionaries of our era to take a lesson and to lay the foundation of a new type of state power from the very beginning.
>
> By changing the state power that became the lord of people in the past to the server of people, ultimately we should orient it towards withering away, by way of enhancing vast participation in the state power or institutionalising the process of expanding broad democracy in society.

Further it is said:

> It should be taken as a terrible irony that proletarian state power carrying the essence of dictatorship over limited exploiting class and democracy for the majority working-class is being slandered as a 'dictatorial', whereas the bourgeois democracy for a handful of the exploiting class and dictatorship over the majority of working-class is being prevalent as the ideal model, universal and incessant. Besides the effect of class prejudice of the bourgeoisie and imperialists and huge propaganda, serious weaknesses in the implementation of proletarian state power (for example, practical end of distinction between party and state power, gradual passivity and decline of people's representative institutions, instead of arming people development and extension of professional permanent armed force, gradual deterioration of freedom to electoral system, speech and press, use of state force to solve contradictions among people and within the party, decreasing of participation, supervision and interference of masses in state power and development of bureaucratic and monopolistic attitude), are too significantly responsible. We must take courage to develop proletarian state power of new type in the theoretical light of MLM and Prachanda Path and through the Paris Commune via the Russian Soviet and Cultural Revolution of China including the experience of our revolution in this situation.[40]

40 Baburam Bhattarai, "Question of Building of a New Type of State Power", *People's Council*, The Organ of the Joint Revolutionary People's Council, Nepal, July 2004, No. 1, pp. 12, 15-16.

This is an extremely wrong interpretation and antagonistic analysis of the forms of state organisation adopted under the leadership of Lenin, Stalin and Mao in the socialist state power of the past. World imperialism as well as reactionaries understand the true democratic essence of those forms. The result of this is that they anticipate the danger for their class interest, and do not let this type of state organisations become stable. Our party regards Marxism-Leninism-Maoism as its guiding principle, takes the new democratic revolution as its minimum programme and carried out a protracted people's war for ten years, formed revolutionary base areas and local power, and at a time, reached the stage of counter-offensive, but now it condemns those forms of state organisations adopted under the leadership of Lenin, Stalin and Mao, respectable to all the Marxist-Leninists the world over. Contrary to our party's claim, state organisations in socialist countries, including China, were means of people's interest and revolution too. They were the new type of state organisation, even serving as revolutionary means for their own withering away. The penetration of the capitalist elements into the party and government at the latter phase proved to be the instrumental factor for counter-revolution.

Our party claims that the proletarian state power which carries the essence of democracy of majority of exploited class, is accused of being 'dictatorial' and bourgeois democracy carrying the essence of democracy for a handful of the exploiter class and dictatorship over majority of the working-class is propagated as a sovereign and universal ideal model of democracy. It is again an indirect endorsement of bourgeois democracy. The class view is absent in this analysis. The main question is which class has slandered the proletarian power and which is carrying the essence of democracy for the majority of the exploited class as a 'dictatorial' authority? Its explicit answer is that the proletarian state power is carrying the essence of democracy for the majority of the exploited class, so it is being slandered as a 'dictatorial' by the exploiting class, world imperialism and their domestic agents.

Likewise, which class propagated, the "bourgeois democracy which is carrying the essence of democracy for a handful of exploiting class and dictatorship over the majority of working-class as a sovereign and universal ideal model of democracy"? Here as well, the answer is explicit. This is being propagated by the bourgeoisie, world imperialists and reactionaries of all countries.

On this ground, the Marxist-Leninists should not be defensive, but offensive. By doing so, we can defend and develop proletarian democracy, and then to expose the essence of bourgeois democracy.

4
End of Difference Between Party and State Power

Our party's statement the "gradual passivity and declination of people's representative institutions" was a "serious weakness" in the "implementation of proletarian state power" is a flawed view of history. The proletarian representative institutions were formed consciously first in Russia and then in China during the period of Lenin, Stalin and Mao Tse-tung. In the transition from capitalism to communism, they were mobilised openly and broadly.

In Russia, Trade Unions, Cooperatives, Soviets and Youth League were the mass organisations which established relations among class, masses and the party, whereas the communist party unexceptionably coordinated works of all mass organisations of the working-class. The direction was towards the only goal of the liberation of the working-class. The mechanism of the proletarian state in Russia was like this. Our party's analysis of finding fault in the implementation of proletarian power by not activating people's representative organisation and then blaming the communist parties for their alleged domination over them does not match with the fundamental principle of Marxism-Leninism regarding the concerned questions. Lenin, Stalin and Mao emphasise activating them, and going beyond that expressed the view that passivity in anyone of them or negligence over anyone them would hamper process of completing the period of transition. Lenin's view clarifies the mechanism of the proletarian state:

> Without a number of "transmission belts" running from the vanguard to the mass of the advanced class, and from the latter to the mass of the working people ... the dictatorship of the proletariat cannot be exercised by a mass proletarian organisation. ... The party, shall we say, absorbs the vanguard of the proletariat, and this vanguard exercises the dictatorship of the proletariat. The dictatorship cannot be exercised or the functions of government performed without a foundation such as the trade unions. These functions, however, have to be performed through the medium of special institutions which are also of a new type, namely, the Soviets.[41]

On the system of the dictatorship of the proletariat, Stalin states:

> The party is the main guiding force in the system of the dictatorship of the proletariat. To sum up: the *trade unions*, as the mass organisation of the proletariat, linking the party with the class primarily in the sphere of production; the *Soviets*, as the mass organisation of the working people,

41 V. I. Lenin, "The Trade Unions, the Present Situations and Trotsky's Mistakes", *Collected Works*, Eng. ed., Progress Publishers, Moscow, Fourth Printing, 1977, Vol. 32, pp. 20-21.

> linking the party with the latter primarily in the sphere of state administration; the *cooperatives*, as the mass organisation mainly of the peasantry, linking the party with the peasant masses primarily in the economic sphere, in the sphere of drawing the peasantry into the work of socialist construction; the *Youth League*, as the mass organisation of young workers and peasants, whose mission it is to help the vanguard of the proletariat in the socialist education of the new generation and in training young reserves; and, finally, the *party,* as the main directing force in the system of the dictatorship of the proletariat, whose mission it is to lead all these mass organisations–such, in general, is the picture of the "mechanism" of the dictatorship, the picture of "the system of the dictatorship of the proletariat."[42]

In this regard, further Lenin writes:

> On the whole, we have a formally non-communist, flexible and relatively wide and very powerful proletarian apparatus, by means of which the party is closely linked up with the *class* and the *masses*, and by means of which, under the leadership of the party, the *class dictatorship* is exercised.[43]

The mechanism of the proletarian state was formed in the socialist countries, including China, according to the concrete necessities of them. The forms adopted in Russia need not be the same for every proletarian state as every proletarian state power can form its "transmission belts" according to its need. The difference is in form. From the point of view of essence, *i.e.* goal of liberation to proletariat and other exploited and oppressed sections, they are the same. Question of people's representative institutions in the proletarian state power becoming inactive in later decades to the point of decline is the consequence of the class struggle under socialism.

Our party's statement "gradual declination of the election system and freedom of speech and press" in the course of "implementation of proletarian state power in the past" requires an analysis from a class point of view. It means the "declination of election system and freedom of speech and press" was practised by the proletarian state power in the past in relation to what class and on behalf of which class. Marxism-Leninism does not take the election system and freedom of speech and press indifferently, and it does not allow bourgeois and neo-bourgeois elements be elected and prepare the environment for the dissolution of the proletarian state power. It does not permit an election system that leads the petty capitalist part of working people to be elected and create a challenge to the leadership of the proletarian class. In the proletarian state power, it will make the press as an important vehicle of advancing the socialism,

42 J. V. Stalin, "Concerning Questions of Leninism", *Problems of Leninism*, Eng. ed., Foreign Language Press, Peking, 1976, pp. 182-83.

43 V. I. Lenin, " 'Left-Wing' Communism: An Infantile Disorder", *Collected Works*, Eng. ed., Progress Publishers, Moscow, Third Printing, 1977, Vol. 31, p. 48.

not the mere formal process or right as in the capitalistic system. Lenin says about this:

> The bourgeois republic ensures publicity only formally; in practice, it subordinates the press to capital, entertains the "mob" with sensationalist political trash and conceals what takes place in the workshops, in commercial transactions, contracts, etc., behind a veil of "trade secrets", which protect "the sacred right of property" ... While ruthlessly suppressing the thoroughly mendacious and insolently slanderous bourgeois press, we must set to work systematically to create a press that will not entertain and fool the people with political sensation and trivialities, but which will submit the questions of everyday economic life to the people's judgement and assist in the serious study of these questions.

Lenin says further:

> The press must serve as an instrument of socialist construction, give publicity to the successes achieved by the model communes in all their details, must study the causes of these successes, the methods of management these communes employ, and, on the other hand, must put on the "black list" those communes which persist in the "traditions of capitalism", *i.e.* anarchy, laziness, disorder and profiteering.[44]

Certainly, bourgeois rights like the election system, speech, and press freedom were curtailed in the course of "implementation of proletarian state power in the past". Minorities, who were against socialist system, were deprived of that right. But uninterrupted freedom was made available to the majority of writers and speakers to write and to elect candidates for the building of socialism. This situation was completely turned over by the capitalist and revisionists' penetration into the party and government. They banned the majority people's rights of voting and getting elected as well as the freedom of speakers and writers. After capitalists and revisionists capture the leadership of party and government in the countries with proletarian state powers the rights of the proletarian and working-class, for electing and getting elected and the speaking in favour of socialism, were first curtailed and then came to a close ultimately. Likewise, our party has said that in the course of implementation of proletarian state power in the past, "there was lack of participation, supervision and intervention of masses in state power developing bureaucratic and authoritarian trend". Such an analysis of our party should be seen by linking it with the statements "we must take courage to develop a model of new type of proletarian state power on the basis of ideological light of MLM and Prachanda Path and from the Paris Commune through the Russian Soviet and Proletarian Cultural Revolution of China, including the experience of our own present revolution." Looking at these

44 V. I. Lenin, "The Immediate Task of the Soviet Government", *Collected Works*, Eng. ed., Progress Publishers, Moscow, Third Printing, 1977, Vol. 27, pp. 260-61.

two sayings together, *i.e.* problem and solution suggested for them, our party views the lack of peoples "participation, supervision and intervention in the state power" was due to the defective models of proletarian state in the past, leading to bureaucratic and authoritarian trend. The party thinks that escape from this in future is possible "by developing new type of model of proletarian state power."

Our party has proposed that the problem of the "lack of participation of masses, supervision and intervention" and its outgrowth and the "development of bureaucratic and monopolist attitude" in the course of implementing proletarian power in the past can be solved by rejecting the leading role of the proletariat through its vanguard, the communist party, and then by establishing a multi-party competition procedure. The proposal of our party negates many fundamental principles of Marxism-Leninism. As the *Communist Manifesto* says:

> Of all the classes that stand face to face with the bourgeoisie today, the proletariat alone is a really revolutionary class. The other classes decay and finally disappear in the face of modern industry; the proletariat is its special and essential product. The lower middle class, the small manufacturer, the shopkeeper, the artisan, the peasant, all these fight against the bourgeoisie, to save from the extinction of their existence as fractions of the middle class. They are therefore not revolutionary, but conservative. In fact more, they are reactionary, for they try to roll back the wheel of history.[45]

The proposition of the *Communist Manifesto* is true about the capitalist society and the first phase of communist society, *i.e.* socialist phase. After dethroning the capitalist class in unity with proletariat the petty-bourgeois elements turn against the proletariat. After a revolution as well, the social base for the rise of a new bourgeoisie is possible for long. To control the situation, the leadership of the proletariat through its vanguard should lead the transition and move successfully towards communism. So, the leadership of the proletariat should not be made a subject to be established by the multi-party competition.

Our party's definition of the masses and class as separate categories, does not agree with Marxism-Leninism. Marxism-Leninism says that "masses are divided into classes". For example, Lenin says:

> It is common knowledge that the masses are divided into classes; that the masses can be contrasted with classes only by contrasting the vast majority in general, regardless of division according to status in the social system of production, with categories holding a definite status in the social system of production.

45 Karl Marx and Frederick Engels, "Manifesto of the Communist Party", *Selected Works*, Progress Publishers, Moscow, Fourth Printing, 1977, Vol. 1, pp. 117-18.

Regarding the question that "proletarian leadership is not an issue to get in the sense of monopoly", and "participation of masses, supervision and intervention" should be increased, what can be said that the position of our party is just like a crow lost in fog. The way, our party presents the question whether it is the monopoly of party or class, or monopoly of leader or monopoly of common people in general, it as Lenin says "testifies to most incredibly and hopelessly muddled thinking." Our party, as Lenin has said on German Communists, "In their effort to be clever, make themselves ridiculous."[46]

Our party further says that "direct democracy" that reflects "In the form of direct participation, supervision and intervention of masses in all parts of state organisation and the model of that type of democracy is the Paris Commune." It says in the early years of the Soviet state, Lenin also was in favour of the commune type of proletarian state power, but later he established or imposed party leadership in the form of monopoly. According to it, while building of socialism, that Stalin and Mao carried on, it became the main cause of dismemberment of proletarian state power in the past. Whether the capture of state power by the proletariat and its governance affairs in a comparatively peaceful period of the development of world capitalism, especially in the first stage of the development of world capitalism can be a model in the era of imperialism and proletarian revolution is a serious question. On the basis of the experience of about sixty years (1917-1976) of socialist formation and the experience of the Cultural Revolution and counter-revolution in China, how can the Paris Commune be a model for socialist formation? For this, we have to look at the reasons for the emergence of the Paris Commune and the causes of its dissolution.

In general, the Paris Commune was an extreme form of struggle, going on between capital and labour, between the bourgeoisie and proletariat, and in particular, it was a revolt of the workers of Paris against the national treacherous step of the Thiers and Trochu government handing over Paris to Prussia. The subjective aspect of the Paris revolt was born in the special objectively weak situation from the point of view of scientific socialism. The leadership was not based on the scientific socialist thinking of Marxism, but it was of a Blanquist sectarian who had mistaken ideas on the questions of the role of the masses and state and so on, and a Proudhonist petty-bourgeois socialist tendency.

The Blanquist had the majority in the Paris Commune. They were all powerful in the Central Committee of the National Guard. Proudhonists

46 V. I. Lenin, " 'Left-Wing' Communism: An Infantile Disorder", *Collected Works*, Eng. ed., Progress Publishers, Moscow, Third Printing, 1977, Vol. 31, p. 41.

were in the minority in the Paris Commune. Because of this reason the Paris Commune could not move towards a true proletarian direction. However, the Paris Commune did some important work that became the valuable property to further advance the proletarian state power and international communist movement too. In relation to political and economic areas, and particularly in relation to the administration system, some forms it adopted are viable as a form even today. In fact, in relation to state power, the mobilisation of the Paris Commune was not based on a scientific analysis, but as Engels says, "only by revolutionary, proletarian instinct"[47] This reality helps a lot in understanding the importance and limitation of contribution of the Paris Commune.

Our party has completely neglected this reality of the Paris Commune. As a result, our party has become the right dogmatic in relation to the model of the Paris Commune. The proletarian state and the forms of state organisation adopted by the Paris Commune model are important events in the history of the world socialist movement. However, what is more important for the world socialist movement is the lesson it imparted.

What are the lessons of the Paris Commune?

The Paris Commune's own weaknesses were more responsible than the suppression from the enemy in its quick defeat. Had the Paris Commune saved itself from those weaknesses, it would have triumphed over the bourgeoisie. While discussing the weaknesses of the Paris Commune, Marx and Engels pointed out that failure to apply all round dictatorship over the enemies, and their political parties, and an adoption of liberal policy towards counter-revolutionaries were serious mistakes. For example, the Commune did not attack Versaille immediately to end the conspiracy of Thiers and his 'villagers', not suppressing the 'Party of Aman' and letting them capture many important places by allowing them to organise and carry out their counter-revolutionary plan, for not capturing the Central Bank of France, which Engels said, was a "serious political mistake". About this last mistake, Engels says:

> If there *had been* a little more authority and centralisation in the Paris Commune, it would have triumphed over the bourgeoisie. After the victory we can organise ourselves as we like, but for the struggle it seems to me necessary to collect all our forces into a single band and direct them on the same point of attack. And when people tell me that this cannot be done without authority and centralisation, and that these are two things to be condemned outright, it seems to me that those who talk

47 Karl Marx and Frederick Engels, "The Civil War in France", *Selected Works*, Progress Publishers, Moscow, Fourth Printing, 1977, Vol. 2, p. 186.

> like this either do not know what a revolution is, or are revolutionaries in name only.[48]

The source of these weaknesses is to be found in the thinking that favoured first inactivating and then dissolving the exploitative power without giving serious thought to replace the former after the capture of the power by the Paris Commune. According to this thinking, after the revolution, the majority of people can easily suppress the minority of exploiters, and it will require neither the role of any leadership nor army, police or administration or state machinery. This is an anarchist thinking with no relation to scientific socialism. In the Paris Commune where a majority of Blanquists and presence of Proudhonists held power, such a weakness was quite natural. Eradicating the weaknesses of the Paris Commune and uprooting them, Lenin, Stalin and Mao followed the scientific route for the formation of socialism as directed by Marx and Engels and the lessons provided by the Paris Commune.

5
Allegation Against Lenin, Stalin and Mao

Our party has stated that the development of bureaucracy and bourgeoisification of the whole administration were the result of the wrong line of the then party leadership in the proletarian state powers in the past. This accusation meant Lenin, Stalin and Mao failed to adopt the correct policy and line to eliminate that problems in the course of building socialism. However, the fact is that they all adopted the correct policy and line to eliminate the old bureaucracy and the bureaucratic elements at the source itself in the process of building socialism. They took this question as a question of long-term struggle and attempts. As Lenin says:

> We shall be fighting the evils of bureaucracy for many years to come, and whoever thinks otherwise is playing demagogue and cheating, because overcoming the evils of bureaucracy requires hundreds of measures, wholesale literacy, culture and participation in the activity of the Workers' and Peasants' Inspection.[49]

He further says:

> Abolishing the bureaucracy at once, everywhere and completely, is out of the question. It is a utopia. But to *smash* the old bureaucratic machine at once

48 Engels to Carlo Terzaghi in Turin, "London (after January 6, 1872), Karl Marx and Frederick Engels", *Collected Works*, Progress Publishers, Moscow 1989, Vol. 44, p. 293.

49 V. I. Lenin, "The Second All-Russia Congress of Miners", *Collected Works*, Eng. ed., Progress Publishers, Moscow, Fourth Printing, 1977, Vol. 32, p. 68.

and to begin immediately to construct a new one that will make possible the gradual abolition of all bureaucracy–this is *not* a utopia.

We are not utopians, we do not "dream" of dispensing *at once* with all administration, with all subordination. These anarchist dreams, based upon incomprehension of the tasks of the proletarian dictatorship, are totally alien to Marxism, and, as a matter of fact, serve only to postpone the socialist revolution until people are different. No, we want the socialist revolution with people as they are now, with people who cannot dispense with subordination, control and "foremen and accountants.[50]

Discussing the objective sources that create bureaucracy, Lenin says:

It goes without saying that the element of petty-bourgeois disorganisation (which must *inevitably* be apparent to some extent in *every* proletarian revolution, and which is especially apparent in our revolution, owing to the petty-bourgeois character of our country, its backwardness and the consequences of a reactionary war) cannot but leave its impress upon the Soviets as well. ... There is a petty-bourgeois tendency to transform the members of the Soviets into "parliamentarians", or else into bureaucrats. We must combat this by drawing *all* the members of the Soviets into the practical work of administration.[51]

Throwing light on the long-term struggle against the bureaucracy, Lenin further states:

The struggle against the bureaucracy, however, is certainly not over in our country. The bureaucracy is trying to regain some of its positions and is taking advantage, on the one hand, of the unsatisfactory cultural level of the masses of the people and, on the other, of the tremendous, almost superhuman war efforts of the most developed section of the urban workers. The continuation of the struggle against the bureaucracy, therefore, is absolutely necessary, is imperative, to ensure the success of future socialist development.[52]

Our party's accusation that the proletarian state powers collapsed because of the non-participation of the masses, their negligence and non-intervention in the administration has been fittingly replied by the following extract of Stalin:

If it were only a question of the old bureaucrats, the fight against bureaucracy would be very easy. The trouble is that it is not a matter of the old bureaucrats. It is a matter of the new bureaucrats, bureaucrats

50 V. I. Lenin, "The State and Revolution", *Collected Works*, Eng. ed., Progress Publishers, Moscow, Fourth Printing, 1980, Vol. 25, p. 430.

51 V. I. Lenin, "The Immediate Task of the Soviet Government", *Collected Works*, Eng. ed., Progress Publishers, Moscow, Third Printing, 1977, Vol. 27, pp. 272-73.

52 V. I. Lenin, "Greetings to the Hungarian Workers", *Collected Works*, Eng. ed., Progress Publishers, Moscow, Third Printing, 1977, Vol. 29, p. 109.

> who sympathise with the Soviet Government, and finally, communist bureaucrats. The communist bureaucrat is the most dangerous type of bureaucrat.

Regarding putting an end to bureaucracy in all these organisations, Stalin further writes:

> There is only one sole way of doing this, and that is to organise control from below, to organise criticism of the bureaucracy in our institutions, of their shortcomings and their mistakes, by the vast masses of the working-class. I know that by rousing the fury of the masses of the working people against the bureaucratic distortions in our organisations, we sometimes have to tread on the toes of some of our comrades who have past services to their credit, but who are now suffering from the disease of bureaucracy. But ought this to stop our work of organising control from below? I think that it ought not and must not. For their past services we should take off our hats to them, but for their present blunders and bureaucracy it would be quite in order to give them a good drubbing.
>
> There is talk of criticism from above, criticism by the Workers' and Peasants' Inspection, by the Central Committee of our party and so on. That, of course, is all very good. But it is still far from enough. More, it is by no means the chief thing now. The chief thing now is to start a broad tide of criticism from below against bureaucracy in general, against shortcomings in our work in particular. Only by organising twofold pressure–from above and from below–and only by shifting the principal stress to criticism from below, can we count on waging a successful struggle against bureaucracy and on rooting it out. ... From this follows the immediate task of the party: *to wage a ruthless struggle against bureaucracy, to organise mass criticism from below, and to take this criticism into account when adopting practical decisions for eliminating our shortcomings.*[53]

Despite the higher mass mobilisation against the bureaucracy in proletarian state power by Lenin and Stalin, in latter days bureaucratic trends created a serious problem. Taking a lesson from this, Mao launched mass mobilisation in a multi-dimensional way from the bottom against the bureaucracy. The Great Proletarian Cultural Revolution is an example. So, it is not the "lack of participation of masses, their supervision and intervention" as our party claims, it is the existence of certain socio-economic causes that create trouble hourly and daily, leading to a bureaucratic trend that developed as a serious problem in the past in the proletarian powers. Bourgeois rights, small-scale production, production of commodity, law of value are the grounds that create bureaucratic anomalies under socialism.

---

53 J. V. Stalin, "Organised Mass Criticism from Below", *The Essential Stalin, Major Theoretical Writings*, 1905-52, Edited and with an Introduction by Bruce Franklin, Rahul Foundation, Lucknow, India, pp. 221-23.

6
Military Formation in Socialism

Our party has been criticised for giving emphasis on the "occupational permanent army" "instead of arming people" in the course of "implementation of proletarian state power in the past". This idea is expressed in the *Development of Democracy in the Twenty-First Century*:

> What experiences of revolution and counter-revolution clearly in the twentieth century demonstrated is that the masses can develop invincible people's army capable to defeat the most modern and strong army of the enemy decisively, going ahead almost from zero on the basis of proletarian correct revolutionary ideology, policy and plan, but the same army can become counter-revolutionary after a wrong ideology controls it all round. Experience also proves with reference to the people's army that proved invincible at war front against the enemy through getting united on the ground of sacrifice, devotion and ideological honesty even in a weak and difficult situation before revolution, a physical environment may arise to make it confined to special management in barrack after revolution, waiting with an attitude to get appointed under the bourgeois modern regular army. If procedure and structure could not be developed to guarantee proletarian thinking, supervision, control it will spread into growth and reach a point, where the army will naturally change into a tool for service to counter-revolution. To stop retreat, there should be emphasis to mobilise the people's army with almost importance to the ideological and political aspect of the army from the very beginning and equip the general mass and the whole party rank with the consciousness of revolt against counter-revolution. Along with this, people's army of the twenty-first century is not to become modern through special training and arms by staying in barracks, after capturing state power, but it should guarantee the remaining task of revolution by militarising the general masses. It should be emphasised in army rank with the clear view that only by developing armed people from the ideological and physical point of view, foreign reactionary intervention and counter-revolution can be stopped. The main responsibility of the people's army in the twenty-first century should be to develop conscious armed masses to use the right of revolt.[54]

Likewise, it is said in the *Question of Building of a New Type of State Power*:

> For different reasons, in Russia ... anticipation of Bolsheviks that, in the near future, the Red Army will prepare a base to substitute the regular army with armed masses was not fulfilled, rather with the course of time, the Red Army changed into a vast occupational army and finally, came to be the

54 Prachanda, "Development of Democracy in the Twenty-First Century, *Selected Works*, Janadisha Publications, Nepal, July 2007, Vol. 2, pp. 412-13.

> means of counter-revolution. In the same way, the People's Liberation Army veteran through twenty-two years of tremendous people's war, changing its colour in the form of the permanent army, finally became the carrier of counter-revolution. On the basis of this bitter experience army and state power directed by MLM and in the light of scientific thinking related to state power, we should emphasise formation of the army, defender of new proletarian state power and in the form of medium of uninterrupted revolution, equipped with revolutionary thinking and politics, linked with general masses and capable of organising the revolt of the armed masses.[55]

Our party's view about the army under socialism is based on a lopsided understanding of the steps taken by the Paris Commune and in relation to their response of Marx, Engels and Lenin. Immediately after capturing state power, the Paris Commune dissolved the permanent army and substituted it with armed people, which Marx, Engels, Lenin praised highly. Marx says: "The first decree of the Commune, therefore, was the suppression of the standing army, and the substitution for it of the armed people."[56]

Lenin had the same view until the October Socialist Revolution in Russia. As he says, "The standing army to be replaced by the arming of the entire people."[57]

However, in the course of a solution to external and internal problems, after the revolution, Lenin felt the necessity of a new permanent army. Proletarian permanent armies were formed in accordance with that latter line of Lenin in all socialist countries. Our party takes this latter line as responsible for the dissolution of proletarian state powers, one after another in the past. Actually this is the line adopted by communist, including Stalin and Mao who conducted proletarian power. It has forwarded a view that dissolution of proletarian power in future can be prevented by reverting to the path shown by the Paris Commune in regard to formation of army under socialism. In fact, the forming an army under socialism is a question of establishing a proletarian state in the place of a bourgeois state; it is a matter of formation of new state machinery in the place of the old machinery of state; and the abolition of classes and struggle that goes on among them. It is a question of completing the transition into communism from capitalism successfully too. The most important part of the lesson of the Paris Commune in the history of the communist movement is that: "The working-class cannot simply lay hold of the ready-made state machinery,

55 Baburam Bhattarai, "Question of Building of a New Type of State Power", *People's Council*, The Organ of the Joint Revolutionary People's Council, Nepal, July 2004, No. 1, p. 14.

56 Karl Marx and Frederick Engels, "The Civil War in France", *Selected Works*, Progress Publishers, Moscow, Fourth Printing, 1977, Vol. 2, p. 220.

57 V. I. Lenin, "Task of Proletariat in Our Revolution", *Collected Works*, Eng. ed., Progress Publishers, Moscow, Fourth Printing, 1980, Vol. 24, p. 70.

and wield it for its own purposes."[58] It was this lesson that Marx and Engels "regarded one principal and fundamental lesson of the Paris Commune as being of such enormous importance that they introduced it as an important correction into the *Communist Manifesto*."[59]

Our party is of the view that the Paris Commune had already solved the problem of forming a new type of army (arming of the whole people) after capturing the state power. It says that proletarian state power faced the problem of counter-revolution because of Lenin and Stalin adopting a different line and policy different from the Paris Commune after the socialist revolution in Russia. This is not true. The Paris Commune was the first proletarian state power and solved the question of the army under two contradictory poles of the lack of experience and the lack of scientific socialist understanding, as well as the influence of Blanquist sectarians and Proudhonists petty-bourgeois view. In spite of this, the plan of the Paris Commune related to the army was socialistic fundamentally by revolutionary instinct only. So, the Paris Commune left the responsibility of solving (a complete theory, strategy and tactics) the problem of the military line in a proletarian state power to the future proletarian revolution.

By discarding Marxism-Leninism-Mao Tse-tung Thought, which has enriched the revolutionary experience of sixty years from the new proletarian state machinery established in the place of the ruined old bourgeois state machinery after a proletarian revolution, our party leadership has proposed a return to the Paris Commune. With the experience of sixty years of deep and extensive experience of the world proletariat, in relation to formation of new proletarian state machinery, is it reasonable to take the Paris Commune as a general model or not? A historical materialist analysis will answer the question.

Our party has used the word 'masses' excessively, like other questions, on the military formation under socialism. The proletarian class must involve other organs of the working-class in greater numbers in the new state machinery. However, by doing so, it should not be forgotten that in a class-divided society, masses are also divided into classes. To speak of the masses under socialism means the workers and peasants. To use the term peasant also includes a large part of the petty-capitalist class. Due to a small-scale production, production of commodity, law of value, difference between physical and mental labour and between town and countryside, a number of people who are in favour of socialism at a certain stage, can also go to the opposite side at another stage and join the counter-revolution. In

58 Karl Marx and Frederick Engels, "The Civil War in France", *Selected Works*, Progress Publishers, Moscow, Fourth Printing, 1977, Vol. 2, p. 217.

59 V. I. Lenin, "The State and Revolution", *Collected Works*, Eng. ed., Progress Publishers, Moscow, Fourth Printing, 1980, Vol. 25, p. 419.

that situation, the group equipped with weapons may not become a means to uninterrupted revolution, instead can be a means of counter-revolution.

Neglecting this problem completely, the argument of our party leadership that counter-revolution can be stopped by arming the people is not based on the class analysis and international balance of forces. The Paris Commune had a short life, so it did not have to face this problem. The proletarian class won over the middle and petty-bourgeois class in the Paris revolution. So, in the days of the formation of socialism, the contradiction was bound to sharpen between those middle and petty-bourgeois sections of people and the proletariat. The proletarian history of over hundred years has proved how the counter-revolution was waged by the capitalist roaders from within the people's community, party, government and the military even in the situation of adopting better and mature methods.

Some decades after the Paris revolution capitalism developed into a new and specific stage of capitalism. Over the years, capitalism has spread worldwide along with the development of militarism and bureaucracy. Capitalist machinery generally has been perfected by the imperialists in this stage. Therefore, at the first stage of development of capitalism, the line that the proletariat adopted in relation to the formation of the army cannot be a general line in the era of imperialism and proletarian revolution. It means the plan of forming the army after the proletariat seizure of state power also needs changes according to the new conditions in the era of imperialism and proletarian revolution in the backdrop of the destruction of the old mechanism to replace it with a new state mechanism.

During the period of the Paris revolution, the proletarian revolution was seen as an immediate problem. The first stage of the development of capitalism did not provide materials to understand the question of proletarian revolution as a very complicated and long-term process. The step the proletarian took in relation to the state power after the Paris revolution shows that it ignored how the whole historical period for the transition from capitalism to communism was required. Some steps that the Paris commune took immediately after the revolution were of the nature that could be adopted only in the latter years of socialism, *i.e.* in the latter period of transition from capitalism to communism. The Paris Commune contains many positive lines like the provision of dissolution of the permanent army after the revolution, but it made a mistake by doing forthwith without preparing its new mechanism and taking into consideration the objective conditions.

The proletariat, after having captured state power, has to accept bourgeois rights, small-scale production, commodity production, law of value, differences between city and countryside and physical and mental labour, as the inheritance of the previous social and economic system. Those birth marks of capitalism cannot be removed overnight as they need a long transitional period. The formation of the army under socialism cannot be separated from the objective reality for two main reasons. Firstly, it divides masses into classes. Internal reactionaries and world imperialism can utilise a part of the masses against the proletarian state power. Secondly, in the presence of these types of capitalist birth marks and imperialist encirclement, the destruction of the old army is not the destruction of the concept of a permanent army. Its meaning is liberating the old army (army that is formed under the world bourgeois point of view and is the means of people's suppression) from the slavery to the native and foreign capitalist class and breaking the capitalist chain of command, and then changing into a means for the liberation of people under proletarian leadership. So far as the question of the permanent army is concerned, even after the state power is captured in the present era of imperialism and proletarian revolution, a long period is required to make the transitional period a success. While in a debate with the CRC, CPI (ML), Chairman of the Revolutionary Communist Party of the United States, Comrade Bob Avakian states correctly:

> The most concentrated expression of state power is the armed force of the state *and* the fact that, so long as there is a state–so long, in other words, as society is divided into classes–the armed forces will *represent once class or another.* Such armed forces cannot represent "the whole people" or "the society as a whole" without class distinction. Under the conditions of socialism–which is not only a class society but a society marked by *antagonistic* class divisions–calls for abolishing the standing (full time, professional) army and replacing it by the arming of "the whole people" amount to calling for the abolition of the proletariat's monopoly of armed force, which in turn amounts to calling for the abolition of the dictatorship of the proletariat.
>
> Once more, this is because the fundamental contradictions marking socialist society as a transition from capitalism to communism constitute a material basis for the continuing existence of classes and specifically the continual regeneration of the bourgeoisie, the continual engendering of the new bourgeoisie, both from among the functionaries of the party and state apparatus and from among the ranks of the people generally. In this situation, the abolition of a standing army *under the leadership of the party* of the proletariat (its *single communist vanguard party*) and its replacement by the arming of "the whole people" would result, in reality, in the development of *different* armed forces *representing different classes*, including the bourgeoisie. And this would be the case even if the overthrown ruling classes and their (open) supporters were excluded from the category of "the whole people" that is to be armed in place of the standing army of the proletarian state. The armed forces of the proletariat would be undermined and weakened; and the strength, including the armed strength, of other class forces, including

> bourgeois forces aiming at capitalist restoration, would be built up. In fact, in such a situation it would be impossible for the proletariat to retain state power and continue the advance towards communism. And this can be seen to be all the more the case when it is kept in mind that "domestic" counter-revolutionaries would invariably seek out alliances with foreign imperialist powers and other reactionary states. Thus, the abolition of a full-time, highly trained armed force of the proletarian state would fatally cripple it in the battle against imperialist aggression and against the forces of capitalist restoration within the socialist country itself.[60]

Proletarian class struggles before the October Socialist Revolution in Russia had not developed to the extent of solving the problem of the old state machinery. Although the Paris Commune made basic changes in relation to the old state machinery, it did not give clear ideas about the state machinery to be established after having destroyed the old state machinery, largely because of its certain limitations and weaknesses, mainly the lack of scientific socialist principles. The Paris Commune gave such an important lesson that Lenin and Stalin developed the seed of the Paris Commune after the October Socialist Revolution in Russia, while smashing the old bourgeois state machinery, for forming a new proletarian state machinery. It is how they corrected the weaknesses of the Paris commune, and gave a total solution to the problem of establishing a proletarian state machinery after the revolution. After that the fundamental theory, strategy and tactics related to the proletarian class have been enriched with the latest events, which serve as base materials. The Paris Commune, Soviet Power, people's dictatorship in China and the Great Proletarian Cultural Revolution under the leadership of Mao are the highest stages of the enrichment.

After the success of the great October Socialist Revolution of Russia in 1917, while solving this problem, the proletarian class found a Marxist-Leninist solution under the leadership of Lenin and Stalin. After the revolution, two types of ideas on the question of the formation of the army appeared in Russia. One was to support the guerrilla units, and the other was forming the permanent Red Army. The concept of supporting the remnants of the guerrilla clashed with the concept of forming a permanent army, terming it a "*socialist militarism*." "Left Communists" and some members of the party itself forwarded these types of ideas. Lenin and Stalin criticised the thinking of defeating the imperialist military intervention through guerrilla warfare in civil war in the course of moving to communism. Lenin and Stalin made it clear that the defence and building of socialism was not possible without the formation of a well trained regular army. Stalin stated: "Either we create a real worker and

60 Bob Avakian, "Democracy, More than Ever, We Can and Must Do Better Than That", *A World to Win*, 1992/17, pp. 55-56.

peasant–primarily a peasant–army, strictly disciplined army, and defend the Republic, or we perish."[61]

The Eighth Congress of the Russian Communist Party gave a Marxist-Leninist solution to the issue of military under socialism and it established the line of the formation of a strong proletarian regular Red Army for the defence and building of socialism. In this relation, the statement of Lenin given in the Eighth Party Congress throws much light:

> The organisation of a Red Army was an entirely new question which had never been dealt with before, even theoretically. Marx once said that it is to the credit of the Paris Communards that they carried into effect decisions which were not borrowed from some preconceived theories, but were dictated by actual necessity. Marx said this about the Communards in a somewhat ironical vein because there were two predominant trends in the Commune–the Blanqusists and the Proudhonists–and both were compelled to act contrary to their doctrines. We, however, acted in conformity with the tenets of Marxism. At the same time, the political activities of the Central Committee in each concrete case were determined entirely by what was absolutely indispensable. We were often obliged to feel our way. This will be strongly emphasised by any historian capable of presenting an integrated picture of the activities of the Central Committee of the party and of the Soviet government during the past year. This fact becomes all the more striking when we try to embrace our past experience in a single glance. But this did not deter us in the least even on October 10, 1917, when the question of seizing power was decided. We did not doubt that we should have to experiment, as Comrade Trotsky expressed it. We undertook a task which nobody in the world has ever attempted on so large a scale.
>
> This is also true of the Red Army. When the war drew to a close the army began to break up, and many people thought at the time that this was a purely Russian phenomenon. But we see that the Russian Revolution was in fact the dress rehearsal, or one of the rehearsals, for the world proletarian revolution. When we discussed the Treaty of Brest, when the question of peace arose early in January 1918, we did not yet know when, and in which other countries, armies would begin to disintegrate. We proceeded from experiment to experiment; we endeavoured to create a volunteer army, feeling our way, testing the ground and experimenting to find a solution to the problem in the given situation. And the nature of the problem was clear. Unless we defended the socialist republic by force of arms, we could not exist. A ruling class would never surrender its power to an oppressed class. And the latter would have to prove in practice that it is capable not only of overthrowing the exploiters, but also of organising its self-defence and of staking everything on it. We have always said that there are different kinds of wars. We condemned the *imperialist* war, but we did not reject

61 J. V. Stalin, *History of the Communist Party of the Soviet Union (Bolsheviks)*, Short Course, Kamgar Prakashan, Delhi, October 1985, p. 235.

> *war in general.* Those who accused us of being militarists were hopelessly muddled. And when in the report of the Berne Conference of yellow socialists I read that Kautsky had said that the Bolsheviks had introduced not socialism but militarism, I smiled and shrugged my shoulders. As if there was ever a big revolution in history that was not connected with war! Of course not! We are living not merely in a state, but *in a system of states*, and it is inconceivable for the Soviet Republic to exist alongside the imperialist states for any length of time. One or the other must triumph in the end. And before that end comes there will have to be a series of frightful collisions between the Soviet Republic and the bourgeois states. If the ruling class, the proletariat, wants to hold power, it must, therefore, prove its ability to do so by its military organisation. How was a class which had hitherto served as cannon-fodder for the military commanders of the ruling imperialist class to create its own commanders? How was it to solve the problem of combining the enthusiasm, the new revolutionary creative spirit of the oppressed and the employment of the store of the bourgeois science and technology of militarism in their worst forms without which this class would not be able to master modern technology and modern methods of warfare?
>
> Here we were faced with a problem which a year's experience has now summed up for us. When we included the question of bourgeois specialists in the revolutionary programme of our party, we summed up the party's practical experience in one of the most important questions. As far as I remember the earlier teachers of socialism, who foresaw a great deal of what would take place in the future socialist revolution and discerned many of its features, never expressed an opinion on this question. It did not exist for them, for it arose only when we proceeded to create a Red Army. That meant creating an army filled with enthusiasm out of an oppressed class which had been used as mere cannon-fodder, and it meant compelling that the army to utilise all that was most coercive and abhorrent in what we had inherited from capitalism.[62]

In fact, the source of opposition by our party to forming a strong regular army is the guerrilla mentality, (the 'guerrilla remains') defeated by Lenin and Stalin at the Eighth Congress of the Communist Party of Russia, March-April 1919.

May-December, 2008
Canberra, Australia

62 V. I. Lenin, "Eighth Congress of R.C.P. (B.)", *Collected Works*, Eng. ed., Progress Publishers, Moscow, Third Printing, 1977, Vol. 29, pp. 152-54.

Non-Marxist-Leninist View About the Role of the Communist Party in the Proletarian Revolution

Fourth Letter Sent to the Party Headquarters Regarding the Role of the Communist Party in the Proletarian Revolution

Our party's proposal, the *Development of Democracy in the Twenty-First Century*, is directly related to the role of the party of the proletariat in revolution. Marxism-Leninism believes the historical period of capturing state power and moving towards communism can be completed by the proletariat through the undivided leadership of the communist party. However, in the proposal the *Development of Democracy in the Twenty-First Century*, our party states that the Marxist-Leninist principle regarding the communist party's role in a revolution is wrong. Contrary to Marxism-Leninism, our party claims that revolution can be completed not through undivided leadership of the communist party, but by forming a leadership through multi-party competition. It further says that if defeated in the multi-party competition, the communist party should wait and should leave the place for the winner (either single majority party or the coalition) to take the leadership for the advancement towards communism. Thus, our party has given up the class point of view, and has adopted a bourgeois point of view in relation to the role of the communist party in a revolution as well as the advancement towards communism as revealed from the authentic documents of the party and ideas expressed by the party leaders. For example, the document approved by a full sitting of the Central Committee of the CPN(Maoist) held in May 2003 states:

> A Party, revolutionary in a particular time, and situation, can turn into a counter-revolutionary at another time and circumstances. The thinking that a party after capturing the state power under the democratic or socialist revolution always remains revolutionary, will deny 'free' democratic or socialist competition for the masses politically against the party. On the other, with no political competitor, it may gradually turn into a comfort seeker, mechanised or bureaucratic. Then the state authority under it may also become mechanised and bureaucratic, creating the danger for formal democracy that will victimise the people and spoil their creative and dynamic energy as seen in history.
>
> It is vital to allow political competition within the constitutional boundary of anti-feudal and anti-imperialist democratic state power, which will create a situation to proletarianise and revolutionise the communist party constantly. If the party cannot revolutionise it continuously by institutionalising the right of the masses to raise another revolutionary party, or leadership to state power, counter-revolution cannot be stopped effectively. So, there should be emphasis on competition to serve people under democratic political competition among different anti-feudalist, anti-imperialist political parties, institutions and organisations that accept the constitutional boundary of state authority to cooperate with the communist party not only in a mechanised way, but to give emphasis on the dialectical relation of democratic political competition to serve people.
>
> Once after capturing state authority, the party leadership has to prove the correctness of its vision and the need of getting mixed with the masses. Emphasis should be given to end the trend of the need of proving sacrifice, devotion and loyalty to the masses. Likewise, the right of the self-decision of people should not be curtailed in the name of the centralisation of thinking and leadership in state power.[1]

While answering a question from *The Hindu* correspondent in an interview February 8, 9 and 10, 2006 Chairman Prachanda says:

> Our well worked out position on strategic and theoretical criteria is to go into multi-party system. The decision taken now is not "tactical". This is a serious policy. After the multi-party system is established through interim government, constituent assembly and Loktatrick Ganatantra, we are ready to participate in a peaceful competition with you.[2]

---

1 Prachanda, "Development of Democracy in the Twenty-F'rst Century", *Selected Works*, Janadisha Publications, Nepal, July 2007, Vol. 2, pp. 414-16

2 Prachanda, "Realisation of the Responsibility to Adopt a Peaceful Way (Interview)", *Selected Works*, Janadisha Publications, Nepal, February 2007, Vol. 1, p. 426.

In answer to the question "Do you believe in the multi-party system or does your party prefer a one party system, and would your party like one Party rule in future?", by Charles Heavy Land of the BBC World Service on March 14, 2006, Chairman Prachanda said:

> Let me address the question seriously. Three years ago, in a meeting of the Central Committee, synthesising the experience of communist rule in the twentieth century, we forwarded the new proposal about the development of democracy. State power of the twenty-first century cannot be the same as that of twentieth. Therefore, our Central Committee passed the proposal of the *Development of Democracy in the Twenty-First Century* unanimously. The inner significance of the proposal is its focus on peaceful competition among all political parties that are against feudalism and imperialist power. At present, in the agreement of seven political parties it is mentioned that we accept multi-party competition. From the experience of the twentieth century, we learned and passed a resolution that a new consciousness should be developed on democracy and dictatorship. The opposition perceives us as dogmatic, but they themselves are dogmatic. Opposition parties look at us through the spectacles of the twentieth century. But we have already entered the twenty-first century and are looking at the possibility of state power in the twenty-first century to ensure possible rights of people and manage competition in an organised way. We are thinking about how to ensure such a competition free from oppression and suppression. ... Taking our determination purely as tactical, people understand that we are deceiving others. In reality, we have had the experience of the whole century, and we have discussed and synthesised in our party with the conclusion of shows the need of the development of democracy in the twenty-first century.[3]

Likewise, while answering the question by *Janadesh*, "what is your view about much discussed proposal of the party related to the development of democracy, which has brought forward a concept that there should be multi-party competition in socialist society as well? What is the essence and justifications for it? Is it possible to achieve the goal of communism and withering away of classes, parties and state?" Comrade Prachanda says:

> Proposal of our party in relation to the *Development of Democracy in the Twenty-First Century* is brought forward on the basis of the study of positive and negative experience in relation to the dictatorship and democracy of the twentieth century. As per the proposal, our party is confident that only by organising party competition within anti-feudalism and imperialism constitutional framework, we can strengthen proletarian dictatorship and ensure strong control, supervision, and intervention of masses in state power to prevent counter-revolutionary forces from raising their head. Only by strengthening dictatorship, on the basis of development of democracy, we can prepare a base for eliminating classes, parties and state. In form

3 Prachanda, "We Believe in People's True Democracy (Interview)", *Selected Works*, Janadisha Publications, Nepal, February 2007, Vol. 1, p. 451-52.

> this process enhances political consciousness of masses continuously through multi-party competition, but it will energise socialist competition in its essence as Lenin, the Great, says. The broader and the stronger the socialist competition is organised, the broader and the rapid will be the base for withering away of the state. Saving proletarian democracy from being mechanical and formal, and making it people-oriented is the major essence of the objective of our proposal of the development of democracy.

Responding to another *Janadesh* question, "whether all parties would be allowed to organise the army according to their own idea in case of multi-party competition is accepted in the new democratic republic or in socialism", Chairman Prachanda says:

> The thing to be clear here is the class character of the state. Experience of history and conclusion of Marxism shows to imagine a state indifferent to class means a bourgeois idealist hypocrisy. The new democratic state we imagine is a state with joint-dictatorship of different classes of people against feudalism and imperialism under the leadership of the proletariat. Such a state cannot be established without destroying the state working for the interest of feudalism and imperialism. In this process of destruction, masses should erect army and other state mechanisms working for their own interest under the leadership of the party. When the anti-feudalist and anti-imperialist state is established, there will be no need to make separate armies for political parties that represent people of different classes and ideologies as there will be no hostile contradiction in their interests. Democratic competition is conducted under such democratic dictatorship of people will strengthen the people's state. Formation of the army can arise only in two quite different situations: One, if the party, leading the democratic state itself, changes into the counter-revolutionary one and starts exploitation, oppression and suppression. In that case, using the right of revolt, any political force of people can make and should make the army. The other situation is when any political party competitive in people's name degenerates to the level of lackey to feudalism and imperialism and with their support and enticement indulges itself in armed activities. In that situation, certainly the state imposes dictatorship against it on behalf of the people's state to solve problem. People's democratic and socialist constitutional boundaries should not be forgotten in all circumstances.[4]

In an interview published in the monthly *Sansleshan*, December 22, 2006, Prachanda says:

> The main substance of New Democracy of Mao is anti-feudalism and anti-imperialism, 'bourgeois-democratic revolution' itself. But, as it occurs under the leadership of the proletariat, it is called new democracy. So far as democracy of the twenty-first century we have proposed is concerned,

4 Prachanda, "I Want to Give a New Message of Liberation (Interview)", *Selected Works*, Janadisha Publications, Nepal, February 2007, Vol. 1, pp. 480-81.

> it is a system to organise political competition under the dictatorship of the proletariat, a step ahead to the new democracy. We have defined the democracy of the twenty-first century as democracy with political competition under the dictatorship of the proletariat as well. This is why it is an accreditation developed after Stalin in Russia and the death of Mao in China keeping in mind to represent the changes of the twenty-first century.

In answer to another question, Chairman Prachanda says:

> A political party represents a certain ideology and a certain class. When such a party is weak to mobilise people from the organisational point of view, it should take tactics of ali round exposure. By resorting to ideological-political exposure only, a party representing a class, establishes its political strength. Going ahead, when the party establishes itself as the leadership of all classes and common people, it should take responsibility of moving in unity with all the maximum forces for creation of a new society. What we have done now is on the foundation of the ten-year people's war. ... The new situation ripe through political exposure and people's war, gives us responsibility to polarise all possible forces to unify the whole country and provide leadership.[5]

Comrade Bhattarai states that the models of proletarian dictatorship of the past have failed because of the control of the communist party:

> After the October Revolution, Lenin emphasised repeatedly that the proletarian dictatorship should be applied through the Soviet. But in the course of addressing the Third Congress of the Comintern, he said that "the dictatorship of the proletariat would not work except through the communist party." (*LCW*, Vol. 32, p. 199.) Taking this mechanically, instead of taking the general meaning, led to the weakness in the socialist state powers wiping out difference between the communist party and state authority. So, the revolutionaries today must take courage to correct those mistakes. With the period gap of time difference between the party and people's representative institution continued getting wiped out, bureaucratic capitalisation grew in the party itself and the party went on taking the monopoly of leadership of state authority. We must find the correct and new process of implementing the class dictatorship and proletarian leadership in the state authority on the basis of this bitter experience. Dictatorship is not of party or person and proletarian leadership, not an issue of getting or imposing as monopoly, but an issue to earn by revolutionary practice and implement democratically.

How do we end that situation? He says further:

> For this, firstly, it should be established by practice, that the communist party gets leadership over the state power by its proletarian revolutionary character, not as an absolute right or "monopoly", and that there should be

5 Prachanda, "Revolt is Inevitable if Consensus Breaks (Interview)", *Selected Works*, Janadisha Publications, Nepal, February 2007, Vol. 1, pp. 506-08.

> an institutionalised provision for a class or masses to forsake or discard the party devoid of proletarian character.

What type of provision is the "institutionalised provision" that he has prescribed?

Let's examine his expression further:

> Taking a lesson from the bitter experience of the masses failure for an organised revolt against counter-revolution, we should guarantee the system of opening political parties remaining under certain progressive and revolutionary constitutional limitation with new reference, and they should be allowed to conduct 'competitive' type of activities, and not the only 'cooperative' type with the communist party.

Is there no danger to the proletarian state power from it? Commenting on this, he says:

> After the source of political and economic monopoly of feudal and bourgeoisie, respectively on land, capital and the military monopoly over the hired occupational army are crushed, it is factually illogical to hesitate for a communist party, claiming majority of proletarian and oppressed class representation, to allow political competition within a certain constitutional process.

Is this not pluralism? In answer to the question, Comrade Bhattarai says: "It in no way strengthens the bourgeois pluralism, rather it is a MLM agreeing scientific way to solve the contradictions present among the people so long as class-divided society exists."[6]

This is the "developed" thinking of our party on the role of a communist party in revolution, which, he says, is the "synthesis of the experiences of communist rule of the twentieth century." It has stated that in the twenty-first century, the role of the communist party in a revolution should not have the absolute type of leadership, but it must take part in the multi-party competition for leadership. It says that the communist party should be ready to sit in opposition if it cannot earn leadership in competition, and this view does not agree with the Marxism-Leninism-Mao Tse-tung Thought and experiences and lessons of the world communist movement. Such a view throws the organisational principle and about one hundred and fifty years' experience into the dust bin. In the course of "creative" development of democracy in the twenty-first century and under the name of correcting "mistakes and weaknesses" committed under proletarian state power in the past, our party has forwarded so-called new thinking regarding the role of the communist party. In fact, it is not related only to the question

6 Baburam Bhattarai, "Question of Building of a New Type of State Power", *People's Council*, The Organ of the Joint Revolutionary People's Council, Nepal, July 2004, No. 1, pp. 12-13.

of leadership, but between the two world outlooks too–the bourgeois world outlook and proletarian world outlook–in regard to the class–political party–leader and masses.

Our party's view about the role of a communist party in revolution has provoked debate in a serious way within the world communist movement again. Our party leadership claims such a view as a unique contribution within the world communist movement to be quite new, which is baseless as this is neither basically new nor even their own as claimed. It is the rotten logic of the old and modern revisionists. Even if we do not turn backward, such a view of our party leadership is the liquidationist thinking of the ex-CRC, CPI(ML) Secretary K.Venu. If our party leadership does not correct this thinking in time, undoubtedly it will meet the fate of K. Venu.

1
Proletariat and the Communist Party

What is the proletariat? What is the communist party? What is the relation between them? Before we go to find answers to these questions, it is necessary to discuss this question, 'What is a class?' Here is an analysis by Lenin:

> Classes are large groups of people differing from each other by the place they occupy in a historically determined system of social production, by their relation (in most cases fixed and formulated in law) to the means of production, by their role in the social organisation of labour, and, consequently, by the dimensions of the share of social wealth of which they dispose and the mode of acquiring it. Classes are groups of people one of which can appropriate the labour of another owing to the different places they occupy in a definite system of social economy.[7]

In answer to the question, what is the proletariat? Frederick Engels says:

> The proletariat is that class of society which procures its means of livelihood entirely and solely from the sale of its labour and not from the profit derived from some capital; whose weal and woe, whose life and death, whose whole existence depend on the demand for labour, hence, on the alternations of times of good business and times of bad business, on the fluctuations resulting from unbridled competition. The proletariat, or class of proletarians, is, in a word, the working-class of the nineteenth century.

7 V. I. Lenin, "A Great Beginning", *Collected Works*, Eng. ed., Progress Publishers, Moscow, Third Printing, 1977, Vol. 29, p. 421.

Since the classes and struggle between them came into force, the poor and the working-class are in existence too. It does not mean that other classes and struggle between them, and the existence of the proletariat surfaced simultaneously. All the poor and the labouring masses are not proletarian. They are social products of a particular form of social production. From the point of view of relation with the means of production, and from their role in social organisation, the proletariat is fundamentally different from other poor people and the working-classes. The proletariat is a fundamental element of a certain socio-economic system. A social economic system cannot be sustained only with one fundamental element. It is composed of a unity of opposites. Another fundamental element is the capitalist class. The unity of those two contradictory elements–capitalist class and proletariat–is capitalism. Therefore, it is wrong to think that the proletariat was in existence before the origin of capitalism. Frederick Engels puts the historical materialist view brilliantly:

> The proletariat arose as a result of the industrial revolution which unfolded in England in the latter half of the last century and which has repeated itself since then in all the civilised countries of the world. This industrial revolution was brought about by the invention of the steam-engine, of various spinning machines, of the power-loom, and of a great number of other mechanical devices. These machines which were very expensive and, consequently, could only be purchased by big capitalists altered the entire hitherto existing mode of production and ousted the hitherto existing workers because machines produced cheaper and better commodities than the workers with their imperfect spinning-wheels and hand-looms. Thus, these machines handed over industry entirely to the big capitalists and rendered the workers' scanty property (tools, hand-looms, etc.) worthless, so that the capitalists soon owned everything and nothing was left to the workers. In this way the factory system was introduced in the realm of textile production. The impetus to the introduction of machinery and the factory system once having been given, the latter rapidly invaded all the other branches of industry, notably the textile, and book-printing trades, pottery, and hardware industry. More and more did labour come to be divided among many workers, so that the worker who formerly had made the entire article, now merely produced a part of the article. This division of labour made it possible to supply products more speedily and therefore cheaper. It reduced the labour of each worker to a very simple, constantly repeating mechanical operation, which could be performed by the machine not only equally well, but even a good deal better. In this way, all these branches of industry one after another fell under the dominion of steam-power, machinery, and the factory system, just like the spinning and weaving industries. But thereby all of them fell into the hands of the big capitalists, and here too the workers were deprived of the last shred of independence. Gradually, in addition to actual manufacture, the handicrafts likewise fell increasingly under the dominion of the factory system, because here too big capitalists pushed

small masters more and more aside by erecting large workshops, in which much expense was spared and the labour could also be conveniently divided among the workers. In this way it has come about that in all civilised countries almost all branches of labour are carried on under the factory system, that in almost all these branches handicraft and manufacture have been ousted by large-scale industry. As a result, the former middle classes, especially the smaller master handicraftsmen, have been increasingly driven to ruin, the former position of the workers has completely changed, and two new classes which are gradually absorbing all other classes have come into being, namely:

I. The class of big capitalists who, in all civilised countries, already now almost exclusively own all the means of subsistence and the raw materials and instruments (machinery, factories, etc.), needed for the production of these means of subsistence. This class is the bourgeois class or bourgeoisie. II. The class of those who own absolutely nothing, who are compelled therefore to sell their labour to the bourgeois in order to obtain the necessary means of subsistence in exchange. This class is called the proletarian class or proletariat.[8]

The basic contradiction of this epoch is between the capitalist and proletarian class, a driving force of modern society. The history of the class struggle of the proletariat from its birth up to now shows that the long process of class struggle develops from low to high, immaturity to maturity, non-alignment to organisation, spontaneous to undivided leadership of the vanguard, and enriched with the Marxist-Leninist principle. The proletarian class is the only true revolutionary class, considering the origin of the proletariat and other classes engaged in the struggle against the capitalist class, and the role in the social organisation of labour, the part of social property they own, the quantity and the share they receive, and the relation of property in a certain socio-economic system. In the struggle against the capitalist class and capitalist system, the other classes, despite whatever courage, sacrifice and devotion they may render, they cannot lead this struggle to a decisive conclusion. After a certain point, they find themselves in a situation mood to compromise with the capitalist class or to change themselves into capitalists. Regarding the revolutionary class character of the proletariat, Marx and Engels write in the *Communist Manifesto*:

Of all the classes that stand face to face with the bourgeoisie today, the proletariat alone is a really revolutionary class. The other classes decay and finally disappear in the face of modern industry; the proletariat is its special and essential product.

The lower middle class, the small manufacturer, the shopkeeper, the artisan, the peasant, all these fight against the bourgeoisie, to save from extinction their existence as fractions of the middle class. They are therefore not

8 Frederick Engels, "Principle of Communism", Karl Marx and Frederick Engels, *Selected Works*, Progress Publishers, Moscow, Fourth Printing, 1977, Vol. 1, pp. 81-82.

> revolutionary, but conservative. What is more, they are reactionary, for they try to roll back the wheel of history. If by chance they are revolutionary, they are so only in view of their impending transfer into the proletariat, they thus defend not their present, but their future interests, they desert their own standpoint to place themselves at that of the proletariat.
>
> The "dangerous class, " the social scum, that passively rotting mass thrown off by the lowest layers of old society, may, here and there, be swept into the movement by a proletarian revolution, its conditions of life, however, prepare it far more for the part of a bribed tool of reactionary intrigue.
>
> In the conditions of the proletariat, those of old society at large are already virtually swamped. The proletarian is without property; his relation to his wife and children has no longer anything in common with the bourgeois family-relations; modern industrial labour, modern subjection to capital, the same in England as in France, in America as in Germany, has stripped him of every trace of national character. Law, morality, religion, are to him so many bourgeois prejudices, behind which lurk in ambush just as many bourgeois interests.
>
> All the preceding classes that got the upper hand, sought to fortify their already acquired status by subjecting society at large to their conditions of appropriation. The proletarians cannot become masters of the productive forces of society, except by abolishing their own previous mode of appropriation, and thereby also every other previous mode of appropriation. They have nothing of their own to secure and to fortify; their mission is to destroy all previous securities for, and insurances of, individual property.[9]

The proletariat adhere to the great struggle of ending exploitation of man by man and nation by nation in the struggle against the capitalist class, and they go ahead towards achieving this goal, "to be strong enough to win on the decisive day it must ... form a separate party distinct from all others and opposed to them, a conscious class party."[10]

In this very reference, Marx and Engels write:

> In its struggle against the collective power of the possessing classes the proletariat can act as a class only by constituting itself a distinct political party, opposed to all the old parties formed by the possessing classes. This constitution of the proletariat into a political party is indispensable to ensure the triumph of the social revolution and of its ultimate goal: the abolition of classes.[11]

---

9 Karl Marx and Frederick Engels, "Manifesto of the Communist Party", *Selected Works*, Progress Publishers, Moscow, Fourth Printing, 1977, Vol. 1, pp. 117-18.

10 "Engels to Gersin Tries in Copenhegen, London, December 18, 1889", *Karl Marx and Frederick Engels, Selected Correspondence*, Eng. ed., Progress Publishers, Moscow, Third Revised Edition 1975, p. 386.

11 Karl Marx and Frederick Engels, "The Hague Congress", *Selected Works*, Progress Publishers, Moscow, Fourth Printing, 1977, Vol. 2, p. 291.

Such a party is the communist party, known as the Social-Democratic Party in the past. By the end of the First World War or up to the October Socialist Revolution 1917, the majority of Social-Democratic Parties and their leaders gave up their responsibility to the proletarian class as they sank into the opportunist marsh of lackeys. As they served the world imperialism, the phrase "Socialist-Democracy" did not reflect the aim of the proletariat in a real sense, and the Seventh Extraordinary Congress (March, 1918) established the political party of proletarian as 'Communist Party', instead of using the term 'Social-Democratic' according to a proposal of Lenin. Questions that arise here are:

- Why did it become necessary for workers to create a communist party instead of making their own party?
- Can there be an identity of interests of the proletariat and can their goal be achieved through a communist party?
- Are the interests of the proletarian class and communists similar?

Discussion on the issues from different points of view started right from the beginning of Marxism, which gave satisfactory and scientific answers to them. Marx and Engels discussed this in detail in the *Communist Manifesto* which says:

> The communists do not form a separate party opposed to other working-class parties. They have no interests separate and apart from those of the proletariat as a whole. They do not set up any sectarian principles of their own, by which to shape and mould the proletarian movement.
>
> The communists are distinguished from the other working-class parties by this only: 1. In the national struggles of the proletarians of the different countries, they point out and bring to the front the common interests of the entire proletariat, independently of all nationality. 2. In the various stages of development which the struggle of the working-class against the bourgeoisie has to pass through, they always and everywhere represent the interests of the movement as a whole.
>
> The communists, therefore, are on the one hand, practically, the most advanced and resolute section of the working-class parties of every country, that section which pushes forward all others; on the other hand, theoretically, they have over the great mass of the proletariat the advantage of clearly understanding the line of march, the conditions, and the ultimate general results of the proletarian movement. The immediate aim of the communists is the same as that of all the other proletarian parties: formation of the proletariat into a class, overthrow of the bourgeois supremacy, conquest of political power by the proletariat.[12]

---

12 Karl Marx and Frederick Engels, "Manifesto of the Communist Party", *Selected Works*, Progress Publishers, Moscow, Fourth Printing, 1977, Vol. 1, pp. 119-20.

The relation between the proletarian class and the communist party is built on the foundation of dialectic, so the communists do not form a separate party against the interests of the working-class, as they have no separate interest of their own. They are composed of the highest and most active parts of working-class of every country. A communist party is equipped with theoretical knowledge superior in comparison to the vast masses of proletarian class, with a clear knowledge of situation and the path ahead for the proletarian movement. The question of representing the class interests of proletariat correctly is really crucial for a political party of the proletarian class. Only a true Marxist-Leninist party can represent the class interests of proletarian class in a revolutionary way. In the present era of imperialism and proletarian revolution, *i.e.* in the epoch of overthrowing of imperialism and establishing dictatorship of the proletariat, the communist party should become a vanguard of the working-class from both a theoretical and practical point of view. Only then can it fulfil this role successfully when it is guided by most revolutionary theory and it is the communist party that can fulfil the role of 'vanguard'. As Lenin says: "Without revolutionary theory there can be no revolutionary movement."[13]

In the present era of imperialism and proletarian revolution, to fulfil the role of a vanguard of the proletariat in overthrowing imperialism and establishing dictatorship of the proletariat and moving towards communism, the communist party, as Stalin says, "must be, first of all, the *advanced* detachment of the working-class. The party must absorb all the best elements of the working-class, their experience, their revolutionary spirit, their selfless devotion to the cause of the proletariat."

He further says: "In order that it may really be the advanced detachment, the party must be armed with revolutionary theory, with a knowledge of the laws of the movement, with a knowledge of the laws of revolution. Without this, it will be incapable of directing the struggle of the proletariat, of leading the proletariat."[14]

Stalin on another occasion says: "A party of the working-class cannot perform the role of leader of its class, cannot perform the role of organiser and leader of the proletarian revolution, unless it has mastered the advanced theory of the working-class movement, the Marxist-Leninist theory."[15]

---

13 V. I. Lenin, "What is to be Done?", *Collected Works*, Eng. ed., Progress Publishers, Moscow, Fifth Printing, 1977, Vol. 5, p. 369.

14 J. V. Stalin, "Foundation of Leninism", *Problems of Leninism*, Eng. ed., Foreign Language Press, Peking, 1976, p. 99.

15 J. V. Stalin, *History of the Communist Party of the Soviet Union (Bolsheviks)*, Short Course, Kamgar Prakashan, Delhi, October 1985, p. 355.

Likewise, Mao says:

> If there is to be revolution, there must be a revolutionary party. Without a revolutionary party, without a party built on the Marxist-Leninist revolutionary theory and in the Marxist-Leninist revolutionary style, it is impossible to lead the working-class and the broad masses of the people to defeat imperialism and its running dogs.[16]

Revolutionary theory is vital for the mobilisation and then directing the leadership of the proletarian movement. But the importance of theory should not be taken in a dogmatic sense as the theory (Marxism) is enriched from the general experience of the working-class movement worldwide, *i.e.* revolutionary practice. Stalin says in this regard:

> Theory is the experience of the working-class movement in all countries taken in its general aspect. Of course, theory becomes purposeless if it is not connected with revolutionary practice, just as practice gropes in the dark if its path is not illumined by revolutionary theory. But theory can become a tremendous force in the working-class movement if it is built up in indissoluble connection with revolutionary practice; for theory, and theory alone, can give the movement confidence, the power of orientation, and an understanding of the inner relation of surrounding events; for it, and it alone, can help practise to realise not only how and in which direction classes are moving at the present time, but also how and in which direction they will move in the near future.[17]

This is why the communist party called the vanguard as well as the leader of working-class. If a party does not lead the working-class in accordance with the Marxist-Leninist theory, it has to grope in darkness, *i.e.* it cannot meet the goal. To liberate the proletariat from such a state, the communist party should be equipped with the knowledge related to Marxist-Leninist principles, movement and laws of revolution. This is how the party can eradicate the passivity of the spontaneous movement and political indolence of the working-class and rise above the transient interests of workers and raise the level of awareness of the general people to the height of protecting proletarian interest.

It is inconceivable to think of the party separate from the working-class, considered as the body. It provides leadership to the working-class as an advanced and organised detachment. So, it is inconceivable to think of the party, separating it from the working-class. Its life, its existence is closely intertwined with all the labouring people. Stalin further says:

---

16 Mao Tse-tung, "Revolutionary Forces of the World Unite", *Selected Works*, Eng. ed., Foreign Language Press, Peking, 1965, Vol. 4, p. 284.

17 J. V. Stalin, "Foundation of Leninism", *Problems of Leninism*, Eng. ed., Foreign Language Press, Peking, 1976, p. 20.

> Unless it has wide connections with the masses, unless it constantly strengthens these connections, unless it knows how to hearken to the voice of the masses and understand their urgent needs, unless it is prepared not only to teach the masses, but to learn from the masses, a party of the working-class cannot be a real mass party capable of leading the working-class millions and all the labouring people. ... A party perishes if it shuts itself up in its narrow party shell, if it severs itself from the masses, if it allows itself to be covered with bureaucratic rust.[18]

So, to keep its position of advanced detachment and to keep it in the position of leadership of the struggle of the working-class, it must keep living contact and relation with its class. As explained in the *Communist Manifesto*: "Communists do not form a separate party opposed to other working-class parties" and there are "no interests separate and apart from those of the proletariat as a whole", and "they do not set up any sectarian principles of their own, by which to shape and mould the proletarian movement" on any particular model to give any special shape and standing under this basic character, during the complicated situation of the struggle of the working-class, strategy and tactics, reserve force and tactics, their retreat and in identifying for correct guidance, essential for the party to become an organised detachment of its class. Stalin has said, "If it desires really to direct the struggle of the class it must at the same time be the *organised* detachment of its class."[19]

To fulfil its responsibilities towards the proletarian class and its struggles, the party must be a material force of Marxist-Leninist discipline and organisational principles, it must be an organised detachment of the proletarian class. To work in an organised way and to be able to mobilise the struggle of the working-class, the party must be built and developed on the Leninist organisational principles, *i.e.* on the basis of democratic-centralism. According to Leninism it means:

1. All guidance committees from bottom to top will be elected;
2. Party committees will present a report of their activities to their organisations from time to time;
3. There will be strict discipline and the minority will remain under the majority;
4. All decisions of upper committees must be obeyed by lower committees and by all party members; and,

18 J. V. Stalin, *History of the Communist Party of the Soviet Union (Bolsheviks),* Short Course, Kamgar Prakashan, Delhi, October 1985, p. 362.

19 J. V. Stalin, "Foundation of Leninism", *Problems of Leninism*, Eng. ed., Foreign Language Press, Peking, 1976, p. 102.

5. To be a party member, it will be necessary to take membership of an organisation and participate in the regular activities of that organisation.

According to the Leninist general principle in relation to the party organisations, the communist party is an integral system of organisations from the bottom to top, *i.e.* a methodological unity of them in one unit, not just an aggregate of organisation.

2
Lenin, Stalin and the Role of the Communist Party During the Dictatorship of the Proletariat

The question of the role of the communist party under the proletarian dictatorship is related to the revolutionary transition between the capitalist and communist society. Proletarian dictatorship is the means of this transformation. As Lenin has said, the means of transformation "would not work except through the communist party." Comrade Bhatttarai does not take this remark seriously, and goes to the extent of ignoring it. He argues that Lenin expressed such a view "only in a general sense". His abrupt comment on such a statement of Lenin regarding the party leadership and the fundamental theory of Marxism in regard to that reminds us of the comments of Karl Kautsky on Marx's views on the dictatorship of the proletariat as "a small word used in a letter once in 1875 by Marx". Comrade Bhattarai has made an identical remark in relation to the concept of Lenin about communist party leadership. He quotes Lenin in his article, and says that it should be taken in a general sense. However, he has blamed Stalin and the Comintern for taking it "mechanically", and thinks that it succeeded in wiping out all the differences between the communist party and the state. The text of Lenin's statement is given below:

> Marxism teaches–and this tenet has not only been formally endorsed by the whole of the Communist International in the decisions of the Second (1920) Congress of the Comintern on the role of the political party of the proletariat, but has also been confirmed in practice by our revolution–that only the political party of the working-class, *i.e.* the communist party, is capable of uniting, training and organising a vanguard of the proletariat and of the whole mass of the working people that alone will be capable of withstanding the inevitable petty-bourgeois vacillations of this mass and the inevitable traditions and relapses of narrow craft unionism or craft prejudices among the proletariat, and of guiding all the united activities of the whole of the proletariat, *i.e.* of leading it politically, and through it, the

> whole mass of the working people. Without this the dictatorship of the proletariat is impossible.
>
> The wrong understanding of the role of the communist party in its relation to the non-party proletariat, and in the relation of the first and second factors to the whole mass of working people, is a radical theoretical departure from communism and a deviation towards syndicalism and anarchism, and this deviation permeates all the views of the Workers' Opposition group.[20]

Lenin's view about the leadership role in the communist party for the proletarian revolution is crystal clear. He has thrown light on the role of the communist party concretely and scientifically, repeatedly before the bourgeois-democratic revolution of 1905 and through the whole latter decade after the failure of the above and in the course of the bourgeois-democratic revolution of February 1917 and the October Socialist Revolution of 1917, especially in implementing the dictatorship of the proletariat. Expressions of Lenin in this regard, especially about the (leading) role of the party during the proletarian dictatorship period clarify further. During the debate with Tanner in the Second Congress of the Comintern, Lenin said:

> Tanner says that he stands for the dictatorship of the proletariat, but he does not see the dictatorship of the proletariat quite in the way we do. He says that by the dictatorship of the proletariat we actually mean the dictatorship of the organised and class-conscious minority of the proletariat.
>
> In the era of capitalism, when the masses of the workers are subjected to constant exploitation and cannot develop their human capacities, the most characteristic feature of working-class political parties is that they can involve only a minority of their class. A political party can comprise only a minority of a class, in the same way as the really class-conscious workers in any capitalist society constitute only a minority of all workers. We are therefore obliged to recognise that it is only this class-conscious minority that can direct and lead the broad masses of the workers.[21]

Likewise, on a different occasion Lenin says:

> The dictatorship of the proletariat means a persistent struggle–bloody and bloodless, violent and peaceful, military and economic, educational and administrative–against the forces and traditions of the old society. The force of habit in millions and tens of millions is a most formidable force. Without a party of iron that has been tempered in the struggle, a party enjoying the confidence of all honest people in the class in question, a party capable of

---

20 V. I. Lenin, "Tenth Congress of R.C.P. (B.)", *Collected Works*, Eng. ed., Progress Publishers, Moscow, Fourth Printing, 1977, Vol. 32, p. 246.

21 V. I. Lenin, "The Second Congress of the Comintern", *Collected Works*, Eng. ed., Progress Publishers, Moscow, Third Printing, 1977, Vol. 31, p. 235.

watching and influencing the mood of the masses, such a struggle cannot be waged successfully.[22]

While refuting the wrong thinking of Trotsky and Bukharin on Party leadership, Lenin says that the communist party "exercises the dictatorship of the proletariat":

> The party, shall we say, absorbs the vanguard of the proletariat, and this vanguard exercises the dictatorship of the proletariat.The dictatorship cannot be exercised or the functions of government performed without a foundation such as the trade unions. These functions, however, have to be performed through the medium of special institutions which are also of a new type, namely, the Soviets. What are the practical conclusions to be drawn from this peculiar situation? They are, on the one hand, that the trade unions are a *link* between the vanguard and the masses, and by their daily work bring conviction to the masses, the masses of the class which alone is capable of taking us from capitalism to communism. On the other hand, the trade unions are a "reservoir" of the state power. This is what the trade unions are in the period of transition from capitalism to communism. In general, this transition cannot be achieved without the leadership of that class which is the only class capitalism has trained for large-scale production and which alone is divorced from the interests of the petty proprietor. But the dictatorship of the proletariat cannot be exercised through an organisation embracing the whole of that class, because in all capitalist countries (and not only over here, in one of the most backward) the proletariat is still so divided, so degraded, and so corrupted in parts (by imperialism in some countries) that an organisation taking in the whole proletariat cannot directly exercise proletarian dictatorship. It can be exercised only by a vanguard that has absorbed the revolutionary energy of the class. The whole is like an arrangement of cogwheels. Such is the basic mechanism of the dictatorship of the proletariat, and of the essentials of transition from capitalism to communism. From this alone it is evident that there is something fundamentally wrong in principle when Comrade Trotsky points, in his first thesis, to "ideologically confusion", and speaks of a crisis as existing specifically and particularly in the trade unions. If we are to speak of a crisis, we can do so only after analysing the political situation. It is Trotsky who is in "ideological confusion", because in this key question of the trade unions' role, from the standpoint of transition from capitalism to communism, he has lost sight of the fact that we have here a complex arrangement of cogwheels which cannot be a simple one; for the dictatorship of the proletariat cannot be exercised by a mass proletarian organisation. It cannot work without a number of "transmission belts" running from the vanguard to the mass of the advanced class, and from the latter to the mass of the working people.[23]

On another occasion, Lenin says:

---

22 V. I. Lenin, " 'Left-Wing' Communism: An Infantile Disorder", *Collected Works*, Eng. ed., Progress Publishers, Moscow, Third Printing, 1977, Vol. 31, pp. 44-45.

23 V. I. Lenin, "The Trade Unions, The Present Situation and Trotsky's Mistakes", *Collected Works*, Eng. ed., Progress Publishers, Moscow, Fourth Printing, 1977, Vol. 32, pp. 20-21.

> The dictatorship is exercised by the proletariat organised in the Soviets; the proletariat is guided by the Communist Party of Bolsheviks, ... No important political or organisational question is decided by any state institution in our republic without the guidance of the party's central committee.
>
> Actually, all the directing bodies of the vast majority of the unions, and primarily, of course, of the all-Russia general trade union centre or bureau (the All-Russia Central Council of Trade Unions), are made up of communists and carry out all the directives of the party. Thus, on the whole, we have a formally non-communist, flexible and relatively wide and very powerful proletarian apparatus, by means of which the party is closely linked up with the *class* and the *masses*, and by means of which, under the leadership of the party, the *class dictatorship* is exercised.[24]

The expressions of Lenin related to the role of the communist party during the period of proletarian dictatorship are vital. Firstly to prove that Lenin did not express his thoughts to the Comintern Congress after being "misled" or by mistake, or by giving it little value. He deliberately maintained this question related to acquiring proletarian dictatorship and the problem of the building of socialism. His thinking about the party leadership is an important foundation of Leninism, not just casual thinking. Therefore, the expression for such an important foundation of Leninism, which Comrade Bhattarari dismissed as a complete rejection to "general sense", is a disgrace to Leninism and disregard to the principle of party leadership. This is an illogical, philosophically it is metaphysics, whereas politically it is a bourgeois view.

Secondly, these statements of Lenin quoted above are clear in themselves with no need of explanation. They give a synthesis of Lenin's thinking in relation to the role of the communist party and its position under the proletarian dictatorship. Side by side, they help us also understand from what point of view and what way he reached that decision. They also help us understand his principle and the related concepts, which give a clear answer to such things. By minimising Lenin's principle of the relation between the role of the communist party in the period of proletarian revolution, Comrade Bhattarai has challenged the historical materialism. Some of Lenin's quoted statements, which need explanation and analysis, will be discussed as and when they appear relevant.

Opportunists and immature communists quote Lenin by separating the quotes from their spirit. It is unfortunate that our party, which fought a people's war for ten years, built a strong People's Liberation Army, formed and developed revolutionary base areas and local power and then became a focal point of hope for the world proletariat and oppressed people of the

24 V. I. Lenin, " 'Left-Wing' Communism: An Infantile Disorder", *Collected Works*, Eng. ed., Progress Publishers, Moscow, Third Printing, 1977, Vol. 31, pp. 47-48.

world, has now presented Lenin's views about the role of the communist party in a distorted form by separating it from its spirit and essence, which will be discussed further. Without a thorough understanding of some of the above statements, confusions arise in revolutionaries as well. The imperialists and their agents are successful to penetrate into a communist party to defame Leninism by giving wrong presentations to the expressions of Lenin. The debate in relation to what the party has raised now, what the CRC, CPI(ML) raised two decades ago, has its origin in the period of Lenin himself, and this topic was much debated immediately after his death. This is not a "new" debate. For that, reading of Stalin's defence of Leninism on the question is sufficient. Some statements of extracts quoted above need to be discussed:

1. "The dictatorship of proletariat, we mean, in essence, the dictatorship of its organised and class-conscious minority."

At another place Lenin has said that "after two and a half years of the Soviet power we came out in the Communist International and told the world that the dictatorship of the proletariat would not work except through the communist party."[25]

Lenin said "*in essence*" (Stalin's italics), the proletarian dictatorship is the dictatorship of the communist party. Opponents of the dictatorship of the proletariat have taken Lenin's remark and tried to defame the principle of proletarian dictatorship. Taking the statement of Lenin as a base, some Marxists went ahead with the wrong idea that proletarian dictatorship is a communist party dictatorship. Within the world communist movement itself, this debate has been marked. In his period, Stalin solved this problem by running a theoretical struggle of a very high rank and along with defending Leninism, made a detailed explanation about the things that were necessary to be explained.

In the course of discussing the relation between the communist party leadership and proletarian dictatorship, he asked the party to pay serious attention to the phrase "*in essence*" that Lenin used. "In essence does not mean on the whole." He says:

> Although the party carries out the dictatorship of the proletariat, and in this sense the dictatorship of the proletariat is, *in essence*, the "dictatorship" of its party, this does not mean that the "dictatorship of the party" (its leading role) is *identical* with the dictatorship of the proletariat, that the former is *equal* in scope to the latter. There is no need to prove that the dictatorship of the proletariat is wider and richer in its scope than the leading role of the party. The party carries out the dictatorship of the proletariat, but it carries out the

25 V. I. Lenin, "Tenth Congress of R.C.P. (B.)", *Collected Works*, Eng. ed., Progress Publishers, Moscow, Fourth Printing, 1977, Vol. 32, p. 199.

dictatorship of the *proletariat*, and not any other kind of dictatorship. Whoever identifies the leading role of the party with the dictatorship of the proletariat substitutes "dictatorship" of the party for the dictatorship of the proletariat.

2. "No important political or organisational question is decided by any state institution in our republic without the guidance of the party's central committee."

There has been frequent criticism that Lenin thought the dictatorship of the proletariat and party guidance to be the same. There is no ground to this criticism. This denotes their ignorance in understanding the dictatorship of the proletariat, or their aim of serving imperialism by presenting Leninism wrongly. The answer given by Stalin clarifies this:

> Not a single important decision is arrived at by the mass organisations of the proletariat without guiding directives from the party. That is perfectly true. But does that mean that the dictatorship of the proletariat *consists entirely* of the guiding directives given by the party? Does that mean that, in view of this, the guiding directives of the party can be identified with the dictatorship of the proletariat? Of course not. The dictatorship of the proletariat consists of the guiding directives of the party plus the carrying out of these directives by the mass organisations of the proletariat, plus their fulfilment by the population. Here, as you see, we have to deal with a whole series of transitions and intermediary steps which are by no means unimportant elements of the dictatorship of the proletariat. Hence, between the guiding directives of the party and their fulfilment lie the will and actions of those who are led, the will and actions of the class, its willingness (or unwillingness) to support such directives, its ability (or inability) to carry out these directives, its ability (or inability) to carry them out in strict accordance with the demands of the situation. It scarcely needs proof that the party, having taken the leadership into its hands, cannot but reckon with the will, the condition, the level of political consciousness of those who are led, cannot leave out of account the will, the condition, and level of political consciousness of its class. Therefore, whoever identifies the leading role of the party with the dictatorship of the proletariat substitutes the directives given by the party for the will and actions of the class.

3. "The party, shall we say, absorbs the vanguard of the proletariat, and this vanguard exercises the dictatorship of the proletariat."

There is the criticism of the view falsely ascribed to Lenin that he believed that the proletarian dictatorship and party dictatorship were the same thing.

On account of assuming the leadership of the proletariat, the party being its vanguard, it can be said that in a figurative capacity, it rules the proletarian state power. But that is true only in a figurative sense, not on the whole. It cannot substitute class authority, or they both cannot be the same. For example Stalin says:

> In this sense the party *takes* power, the party *governs the country*. But this must not be understood in the sense that the party exercises the dictatorship of the proletariat separately from the state power, without the state power; that the party governs the country separately from the Soviets, not through the Soviets. This does not mean that the party can be identified with the Soviets, with the state power. The party is the core of this power, but it is not and cannot be identified with the state power.

About those who understand the above sayings of Lenin in this way, Stalin further observes:

> 1. Lenin uses the word *dictatorship* of the party not in the strict sense of the word ("power based on the use of force"), but in the figurative sense, in the sense of its undivided leadership;
>
> 2. Whoever identifies the leadership of the party with the *dictatorship* of the proletariat distorts Lenin, wrongly attributing to the party the function of employing force against the working-class as a whole;
>
> 3. Whoever attributes to the party the function, which it does not possess, of employing force against the working-class as a whole, violates the elementary requirements of correct mutual relations between the vanguard and the class, between the party and the proletariat.[26]

It is said that history is the mirror of the present. So, some aspects of the debate during the period of Lenin and Stalin help us understand the debate raised in our party for a few years in relation to the role of the communist party under the proletarian state power. Our party leadership is distorting Leninism and proletarian revolution by bringing the debate to the surface ahead.

3
Role of the Communist Party in the Proletarian Revolution

From a study of the party document *Development of Democracy in the Twenty-First Century* and the works of leading comrades, it becomes clear that it has divided in two parts the talk and debate related to the role of the communist party in regard to a semi(neo)-colonial and semi-feudal country such as Nepal. The first is the role of the communist party in a new

26 J. V. Stalin, "Concerning Questions of Leninism", *Problems of Leninism*, Eng. ed., Foreign Language Press, Peking, 1976, pp. 185-88, 190.

democratic revolution, and the other is the role of the communist party in a period of the dictatorship of the proletariat.

A. Role of the Communist Party in the New Democratic Revolution

Our party's view that transformation into new democracy and socialism is possible by intervening continuously into the state power through a legal political competition with the Nepali Congress, the CPN(UML), Madhesi-based parties, the RPP and so on, rejects the universal law of revolution with violence of Marxism-Leninism, as well as the principle of party leadership. In the present era of imperialism and proletarian revolution, the capitalist class cannot succeed the bourgeois revolution under its own leadership as it is not as revolutionary as it was in the past. So, in the situation of having adopted a reactionary class character after losing its revolutionary class character, its political representative, *i.e.* the bourgeois party cannot lead revolution. Now the responsibility of completing the bourgeois-democratic revolution has also fallen on the shoulders of the proletarian class. In the capacity as the vanguard of the proletarian class, democratic revolution in this era is possible only under the undivided and continuous leadership of the communist party, and not by changing of leadership after a gap of some years through political competition. In this regard, the Communist Party of China rightly expresses in the great debate between revolutionaries and modern revisionists that "it is necessary that the proletarian party should maintain its ideological, political and organisational independence and insist on the leadership of the revolution."[27]

Democratic revolution is an integral part of world socialist revolution as many elements of socialism are parts of the democratic revolution too. That is saturated with the basic character of the transition into socialism. For the success of the bourgeois-democratic revolution, filled with socialist elements and for its uninterrupted development towards socialism, a driving force is necessary, which can be none but the proletarian class. Being the vanguard of the proletarian class, only the communist party can handle the responsibility of completing the two-stage (bourgeois-democratic and socialist) revolution successfully. That is not plausible by the change of leadership through political competition, just after a gap of a few years. This is the general experience of the movements already in progress at present in all colonial, semi(neo)-colonial, semi-feudal countries against imperialism and feudalism. This is the essence of Mao Tse-tung Thought regarding the democratic revolution.

27 "Apologists of Neo-Colonialism", *The Great Debate*, Mass Line Publications, 1994, p. 154.

The issue of change in leadership through political competition is not an issue simply of a change of leadership of a party. In essence, this is an issue of the change of leadership of a class. The leadership of one party is transferred to another party through the political competition at the first stage of revolution, but the class leadership may not remain the same. In the election, if other political parties other than the proletariat win, they may adopt the strategy of eliminating the proletarian essence of the state power. Therefore, the proposal of our party regarding the leadership to choose through political competition and that the party elected by people should take leadership, rejects the basic principle of Marxism-Leninism in relation to class leadership in revolution. It forwards the thinking that in this era of imperialism and proletarian revolution, any class, whether comprador, bureaucratic capitalist class or national capitalist class, can fulfil democratic revolution, proletarian class leadership is not inevitable. This is a naked amendment of Mao Tse-tung Thought in regard to the leadership of the bourgeois-democratic revolution.

The transformation of a semi(neo)-colonial and semi-feudal Nepalese society into an independent democratic society is the first step of the Nepalese revolution and, the second step is to build a socialist society. This is true not only with reference to our country, but it is equally true in relation to all semi(neo)-colonial, semi-feudal countries. According to the thought of Mao in colonial, semi(neo)-colonial countries at first stage or at first step, the social character of such revolution is still bourgeois-democratic, and its purpose is to open the path of development of capitalism. The old type of bourgeois-democratic revolution is led by the capitalist class with the aim of establishing capitalist society and state under the bourgeois dictatorship. It is a new type of revolution as a first step under the proletarian leadership, which aims at establishing a new democratic society and state under the joint dictatorship of workers, peasants including all revolutionary classes. This revolution opens further a wide path for the socialist transformation. As Mao Tse-tung says:

> Such a revolution attacks imperialism at its very roots, and is therefore not tolerated but opposed by imperialism. However, it is favoured by socialism and supported by the land of socialism and the socialist international proletariat. Therefore, such a revolution inevitably becomes part of the proletarian-socialist world revolution.[28]

Surprisingly our party says that the Nepalese revolution of the new type can be completed through a legal political competition by intervening continuously in the state power with the Nepali Congress, the CPN(UML) Madhesi-based parties, the RPP, and so on. However, the proposal does not

28 Mao Tes-tung, "On New Democracy", *Selected Works*, Eng. ed., Foreign Language Press, Peaking, 1965, Vol. 2, p. 344.

mention what will happen to the class leadership while changing the party leadership. If a political party represents a class, then it is a vanguard part of that class. If it is accepted that a political party represents a class, it should accept a change in the political parties brings change in the class leadership as well. Let us take an example of the capitalist society where more parties than one class exists and the change in government makes no difference. Whichever party comes to power, except some issues, though they may have some different thinking and working policies, basically they act according to the general line of the world capitalist interest. When leadership of the communist party is established through legal political competition, then an earthquake like impact is felt in the position of the class leadership of the capitalist class. The leadership of the communist party established by election cannot lead the revolution ahead because of army, police, court and bureaucracy do not support it and there would be no cooperation between them. National reactionaries and world imperialism will also pose obstacles all the time.

On the basis of our party's line of "party competition", through legal political competition with political parties including the Nepali Congress, CPN(UML), Madhesi-based parties and so on, the democratic state power with the joint dictatorship of the revolutionary class, *i.e.* the first stage of the Nepalese revolution cannot be achieved. Our party's political line is not to impose dictatorship of revolutionaries over traitors and reactionaries; rather it wants to establish the old type of capitalist state power, which is an organ of world imperialism to perpetuate oppression to the common masses. In cooperation with all revolutionary classes and under the undivided leadership of the proletariat, a new type of democratic state system can be created, for which the leadership of the communist party in the capacity of the vanguard of the proletariat is essential. The unprincipledness and bankruptcy of our party to accomplish revolution is revealed when it plans to establish the supremacy of the communist party by putting forward multi-party competition, and inducting the political representatives of feudal, comprador, bureaucratic, reactionaries and traitors. Every political power has its own system of government. What is the meaning of an appropriate government system of a political power? It means the authority to gain the maximum benefit to the class it is related to. Every state authority is a tool for the class oppression. The ruling class organises state authority in favour of its class. Mao says in this regard:

> This is a matter of how political power is organised, the form in which one social class or another chooses to arrange its apparatus of political power to oppose its enemies and protect itself. There is no state which does not have an appropriate apparatus of political power to represent it.

The capitalist class establishes a formal democratic governing system to suppress its enemy, the proletarian class and other working sections, and to defend itself and the old state power. The executive, legislative and judiciary were established as the idols of formal democracy. In relation to our country as well to organise state power after the revolution, to suppress the enemy classes, a suitable governing system should be established as said by Mao based on the democratic-centralism, which can express the will of the large revolutionary people, and wage war with the enemy effectively. It is impossible for revolutionary classes after the revolution to establish a government and suppress their enemies and defend their classes through a multi-party system, without the leadership of the communist party, as our party claims. The multi-party system with competition is suitable for the capitalist class to regain its lost state power, to defend itself and suppress and exploit working-classes, including the proletariat. So, such type of government system cannot be supported for a new democratic power.

Marxism-Leninism-Mao Tse-tung Thought believes that "the politics of new democracy is a concentrated expression of the economy of new democracy", which mean a government system is directly related to organising a new democratic economic system. The transition towards socialism can be led correctly only by organising a new democratic economic system with a democratic-centralised system under the leadership of the communist party, not by multi-party competition. The direction of the new democratic economic system must be oriented towards socialism and again socialism. Regarding the basic character of the new democratic state and its character, Mao says:

> In the new-democratic republic under the leadership of the proletariat, the state enterprises will be of a socialist character and will constitute the leading force in the whole national economy, but the republic will neither confiscate capitalist private property in general. ... The republic will take certain necessary steps to confiscate the land of the landlords and distribute it to those peasants having little or no land.[29]

The historical responsibility put forward by Mao in regard to managing the capital in a new democratic economic system; bringing equality in land ownership and abolishing feudal relations in the countryside cannot be fulfilled without the leadership of the vanguard communist party. Our party's policy about multi-party competition is an ideological bankruptcy as proved by the life-and-death struggle after the success of the New Democratic Revolution in China while building the new economic system. Firstly, the minimum programme of revolution in China was capitalist-democratic and its objective was to open the door for development of capitalism. Many

29 Mao Tes-tung, "On New Democracy", *Selected Works*, Eng. ed., Foreign Language Press, Peaking, 1965, Vol. 2, pp. 352-53.

people joined the communist party and movement at that period, being influenced by its programme. In the struggle against feudal, comprador, bureaucratic capitalism and imperialism, the role of such elements was progressive, and they cooperated with the revolution. Their main interest was to open the door for the development of capitalism in the country. The minimum programme for the communists, naturally, was the maximum for them. However, the proletariat and communist party should not stop after the attainment of the minimum programme of revolution. According to its pre-declared policy and programme, after the attainment of the minimum programme of revolution, instead of stopping mid-way, they move towards their maximum goal, towards socialism and communism. Mao's statement contained in the report presented in the second plenary session of the Communist Party of China's Seventh Central Committee in 1949 that the main contradiction will occur between the capitalist and working-class after the success of the democratic revolution has to be understood in this light.

Our party's belief that by dissolving the leadership role of the communist party, the minimum and maximum programme of revolution can be achieved through multi-party competition is completely wrong. As the new type of democratic revolution that "attacks imperialism at its very roots" and as "a part of proletarian socialist world revolution" cannot be accomplished without the leadership of the proletariat through the communist party. Similarly, the ultimate goal of advance towards socialism and communism cannot be achieved without the leadership of the communist party. Under the leadership of the bourgeois and petty-bourgeois parties, it is not possible to develop the national economy, and give a socialist essence to state industrial institutions, and remain a leading force of the whole national economy. Likewise, it is not possible to encourage the development of capitalist production not to keep control over people's livelihood, but to have the ownership of land and then abolish the present feudal relations in the countryside as well as to manage capital and bring equality in the land ownership. So, the leadership of the communist party is essential.

If leadership of transitional state power (new democratic state power) goes into the hands of capitalist or other democratic parties, they will lead the state power towards the goal of consolidating capitalism, and not as the minimum programme of revolution or as the first step of the maximum programme (socialism and communism) of revolution. Therefore, to seek for alternatives for the leadership of the communist party to lead the transitional stage towards socialism and communism, or for the first step of socialist revolution, is simply suicidal. Regarding this, on the eve of the new democratic revolution and after it, the two-line struggle in the party and government in China is quite educational.

In China, in the immediate aftermath of the revolution, some leaders who had played an important role in the revolution, suggested that the development of capitalism would take a long time and that the party should focus on its strengthening. The capitalist roaders, in the party and government advocated continuously for the consolidation of new democracy in all areas, *i.e.* politics, economy and culture, and opposed the line of socialist transformation in those areas. If the demand of multi-party competition had arisen in China, not as cooperative alone, but also competitive, as our party suggests, it would not have been possible to defeat the capitalists and move towards socialism. There were various democratic parties in China also, and if they had not been kept under the leadership of the communist party, they would not have gone ahead with the maximum political programme of socialism and communism as cooperators.

When a system and activities run cooperatively by accepting the leadership of the communist party, it becomes possible to move towards socialism, with fundamental works such as regulating capital and bringing equality in land ownership, abolishing feudal relations in rural areas, etc., after the new democratic revolution. Elements such as the national capitalist and petty-capitalist class that accepted the programme of the communist party during the period of the new democratic revolution do not remain firm against imperialism till the end. They were compelled to accept the programme of the party under certain situations, so most of them surrendered in front of imperialism ultimately.

In the imperialist era, it is not possible for capital to get continuous existence and extension within a national boundary. Either it should lead itself ahead as an organ of world finance capital or it has to disappear itself. After the revolution, those elements that joined the revolution under the influence of the democratic programme of the communist party do not accept their end and consider themselves as an integral part of the world finance capital. If on the basis of the history of their contribution in the past, they are allowed to conduct activities in competition with the communist party, they will lead the country not towards socialism, but will retreat towards capitalist dictatorship in cooperation with international capital. Likewise, the petty-capitalist or democratic elements can be linked and transformed in transition towards socialism under the leadership of the communist party. If they are allowed competitive activities with the communist party, imperialism will enter the country to wage a counter-revolution comfortably.

From the point of cultural transformation as well, the leading role of the communist party is essential. In every semi(neo)-colonial and semi-feudal country, there are semi(neo)-colonial and semi-feudal politics and economy, as well as neo-colonial and semi-feudal culture too. In politics, economy and culture, made up of a coalition between imperialism and feudalism, imperialism is always dominant. The objective of the new democratic revolution is to fully eradicate imperialism and feudalism in all these areas and to build proletarian politics, economy and culture. It is not possible to build a scientific culture, and develop objective truth in principle and practice, against all feudal and conservative culture through multi-party competition with the shift of political parties to the power after a gap of a few years. For that, the leadership of the communist party as the vanguard of the proletariat is inevitable. A progressive move towards socialism in the areas of politics and economy and building a national scientific culture under the leadership of bourgeois-democratic parties is not possible.

So, our party's view "system should be ascertained to open political parties and they should be allowed to focus on activities not only of the 'cooperative' type" but also of a 'competitive' type with the communist party" is completely non-Marxist-Leninist as it serves world imperialism.

B. Role of the Communist Party During the Proletarian Dictatorship

According to Karl Marx: "Between capitalist and communist society lies the period of the revolutionary transformation of the one into the other. Corresponding to this is also a political transition period in which the state can be nothing but *the revolutionary dictatorship of the proletariat.*"[30]

The role of the party during the period of the revolutionary dictatorship of the proletariat is an inter-related question with how the transformation from capitalism into communism can be carried out successfully. For the transition from these two separate social systems, from bottom to top, and present into future, as Marx says, the main thing is *the revolutionary dictatorship of the proletariat* itself. The communist party's central role can be nothing but the advancement towards communism. The main question should be how this transition period can be completed in a revolutionary mode. To avoid deviation from the Marxism-Leninism-Mao Tse-tung Thought, we should adhere to the concrete bases of the material life of socialist society and the world situation to escape from the political and ideological follies in regard to fulfilling the revolutionary role of the communist party during the transition. The objective conditions of the imperialistic society and the world situation not only make the proletarian dictatorship indispensable, but also make the role of the communist party essential during the transition.

30 Karl Marx and Frederick Engels, "Critique of Gotha Programme", *Selected Works*, Progress Publishers, Moscow, Fourth Printing, 1977, Vol. 3, p. 26.

Classes always rule through their vanguard and our party, which supports the rule of the proletarian class, proposes to establish its vanguard's leadership role only after a political competition, leaving the proletarian class deprived of leadership and finally paralyses it.

Marxism-Leninism-Mao Tse-tung Thought believes that even after the proletariat has established itself to the position of the ruling class after having ended bourgeois rule, a long troublesome and continuous class struggle for the abolition of classes persists. The remains of the old are seen at every step under socialism only concretises Marx's view of bourgeois rights in socialism and Lenin's saying "under communism there remains for a time not only bourgeois law, but even the bourgeois state, without the bourgeoisie."[31] The dictatorship of the proletariat would not work except through the communist party. Revolution cannot be complete without a revolutionary party free of opportunism and uncompromising towards capitulationism, and having a revolutionary attitude towards the capitalist class and its state power. Otherwise, waging a concerted and ideological struggle against the capitalist class born out of the existing bourgeois rights and small-scale production, is not possible for building socialism.

Unlike our party's view in the period of proletarian dictatorship, Stalin says: "To leave the proletariat without such a party means to leave it without revolutionary leadership; and to leave it without revolutionary leadership means to ruin the cause of the proletarian revolution."[32]

By linking the analysis of Marxism-Leninism-Mao Tse-tung Thought that "classes and struggle among them exist in socialism" to the "MLM agreeing with the scientific way to solve contradictions present among the people so long as class-divided society exists", [33] our party justifies the multi-party competition in the period of the dictatorship of the proletariat too.

Such a view of our party towards Marxism-Leninism-Mao Tse-tung Thought in relation to classes in socialism and struggle between them is wrong. To justify its proposal of multi-party competition, it accepts the existence of classes in socialism, but it is silent about the character and nature of the struggle between them. These questions determine the form and nature of class struggle, so keeping silent about their nature and seeking new methods of conduction is sheer opportunism. Lenin has talked in

31 V. I. Lenin, "The State and Revolution", *Collected Works*, Eng. ed., Progress Publishers, Moscow, Fourth Printing, 1980, Vol. 25, p. 476.

32 J. V. Stalin, *History of the Communist Party of the Soviet Union (Bolsheviks)*, Short Course, Kamgar Prakashan, Delhi, October 1985, p. 353.

33 Baburam Bhattarai, "Question of Building of a New Type of State Power", *People's Council*, The Organ of the Joint Revolutionary People's Council, Nepal, July 2004, No. 1, p. 13.

detail about how even immediately after the proletariat capture of state power, the capitalist class remains active in the area of material production of society for long, which cannot be abolished overnight. On the basis of the existence of money, limited mobile property, strong net of relations with people, the capacity of organisation and management, high education, relations with educated people, bureaucracy, strong relations with the security forces such as the army, police and skill in warfare and so on, the defeated class keeps the hope of an inevitable revival. As Lenin says: "The exploiters inevitably cherish the hope of restoration, and this *hope* turns into *attempts* at restoration ... with energy grown tenfold, with furious passion and hatred grown a hundredfold, into the battle for the recovery of the "paradise", of which they were deprived, on behalf of their families."[34] The main international ground for this is imperialism.

Our party's contention that in the historical period of transition from capitalism to communism, society is divided into classes and classes should be allowed to organise into political parties, neglects to solve the issue of the defeated exploiting class, which attempts to reclaim its lost power with ten times more force. Marxism-Leninism considers that the dictatorship of the proletariat is essential to crush the opposition from the dethroned exploiting classes and strengthen the achievements of the proletarian class, and to lead the proletarian revolution to victory. Stalin states:

> The revolution can defeat the bourgeoisie, can overthrow its power, even without the dictatorship of the proletariat. But the revolution will be unable to crush the resistance of the bourgeoisie, to maintain its victory and to push forward to the final victory of socialism unless, at a certain stage in its development, it creates a special organ in the form of the dictatorship of the proletariat as its principal mainstay.[35]

Stalin's remarks is based on the facts from the history of the world proletarian movement. Let us take the Paris Commune: Proletarian power was not established under the leadership of the communist party, and as Lenin says, could not create a "rule based directly upon force and unrestricted by any laws"[36]. So, it could not crush the counter attack of the capitalist class, and sustain its victory in order to move towards the final victory of socialism. As a result, the Paris Commune was defeated within two and a half months.

---

34 V. I. Lenin, "Proletarian Revolution and Renegade Kautsky", *Collected Works*, Eng. ed., Progress Publishers, Moscow, Third Printing, 1981, Vol. 28, p. 254.

35 J. V. Stalin, "Foundation of Leninism", *Problems of Leninism*, Eng. ed., Foreign Language Press, Peking, 1976, pp. 38-39.

36 V. I. Lenin, "Proletarian Revolution and Renegade Kautsky", *Collected Works*, Eng. ed., Progress Publishers, Moscow, Third Printing, 1981, Vol. 28, p. 236.

The view of Stalin above and the essence of overall experience leads to the dictatorship of the proletariat only. Our party's proposal that the communist party has to prove its leadership through political competition, otherwise it should be ready to sit in opposition denies the dictatorship of the proletariat itself. It is puzzling that after the class leadership is accepted, how can the vanguard communist party leadership be an issue of multi-party competition? The origin and development of any class finally organises itself into a political party, which means as said by Lenin "classes are led by political parties"[37]. Our party seems to have hatched a conspiracy to deprive the proletariat of its dictatorship with its dualism of accepting the dictatorship of the proletariat and then bringing down its leadership to the leadership of other classes (petty-bourgeois classes), as evident by their frequent changes during the election.

The non-Marxist-Leninist thinking of our party in relation to classes and class struggle in the transition from capitalist to communist society is reflected well in a statement of Comrade Bhattarai:

> After the source of political and economic monopoly of the feudal and bourgeoisie, respectively on land, capital and the military monopoly over hired occupational army are crushed, there remains no factual or logical argument to hesitate for a communist party that claims majority of proletarian and oppressed class representation to allow political competition within certain constitutional process.

Firstly, what does Comrade Bhattarai mean when he says the communist party claims the representation of the majority of the proletarian and oppressed class? By using such a confusing word like 'claim', does Bhattarai mean the communist party is yet to prove its commitment to the proletariat and oppressed people? Does he mean that history and the contemporary world have still not proved its authenticity? Bhattarai's argument is misleading.

Secondly, Comrade Bhattarai argues that we should not be afraid of being in a minority in a situation where the majority of the proletarian and oppressed classes are in favour of building socialism. However, such a logic does not agree with Marxism-Leninism. The number is not the basic factor of the transition period, because even if the majority of the proletarian and oppressed are in favour of socialism, it still is engrossed with problems like the strength of capital on a world scale and its relation with the domestic capital, the existence of bourgeois rights, the difference between the town and countryside and physical and mental labour, the production of commodities, the law of value, the role of money, and small-scale production rooted in

37 V. I. Lenin, " 'Left-Wing' Communism: An Infantile Disorder", *Collected Works*, Eng. ed., Progress Publishers, Moscow, Third Printing, 1977, Vol. 31, p. 41.

the social production. In spite of the broad approval and cooperation from the majority of proletarian and oppressed people, the socialist state powers were dissolved in the past, a testimony that multi-party competition on the basis of the majority would lead to the march of formal democracy. So, the proposal of our party leadership to solve this concrete problem of the dictatorship of the proletariat is to accept bourgeois thinking and principle in reality.

Thirdly, Comrade Bhattarai suggests that the communist party should not hesitate for political competition in socialism under the limitation of a certain constitutional process, and Comrade Prachanda too has stated that party competition should be organised under socialism as well, within the anti-feudal and pro-imperialist boundaries. Both of them believe that after the proletariat captures power and establishes itself as a ruling class, other competitive parties will pose no obstacle to push socialism towards communism. They have not presented themselves in the same way as the essence of their statements given here, but their view about proletarian dictatorship cannot be anything different than what has been summed up here. It means under such a situation there would be no difference irrespective of which political party gains majority during the transition period.

Our party's analysis regarding how during the transition of proletarian dictatorship framing of the constitution negates the proletariat as a vanguard or how the constitution itself becomes the documented form of a vanguard raises vital issues. Our party treats the constitution neither as a new sphere nor a new form of class struggle. Rather, for the party, it is the "legality", "law and order", "the "general good" "an abstract blessing" of the liberal professors.[38] After an anti-feudalist and anti-imperialist constitution is formed, it believes that we should move ahead by organising political competition in socialist society as well, which is bourgeoise thinking. Under the dictatorship of the proletariat, Marxist-Leninists do not take the mono-party or multi-party absolutely because, theoretically, it can be considered that even though petty-capitalists are allowed to organise in political parties, they can change in favour of socialism and communism, which is possible under the dictatorship of the proletariat, not under any other dictatorship. This means, the proletariat has to take a decision on the basis of how to give continuity to it, how to safeguard it and strengthen it. The decision has to be taken on the basis of the way international capital, the domestic counter-revolutionaries and individual property relations can be finally abolished by the proletarian class through its vanguard.

38 V. I. Lenin, "How the Socialist-Revolutionaries Sum Up the Revolution...", *Collected Works*, Eng. ed., Progress Publishers, Moscow, Third Printing, 1977, Vol. 15, p. 337.

Our party takes over this question, only from a theoretical point of view, and it neglects its practical aspect completely. As a result, it sees no necessity of promoting the leadership role of the proletarian class through its vanguard, *i.e.* the communist party in relation to the implementation of a socialist constitution. After the socialist constitution is formed, the undivided leadership of its vanguard becomes unnecessary for the proletarian class, *i.e.* the constitution can lead or regulate the transition towards communism, vindicating the ideas of our party leadership wrong, theoretically and politically. As Karl Marx states:

> The law must be founded upon society, it must express the common interests and needs of society–as distinct from the caprice of the individuals–which arise from the material mode of production prevailing at the given time... As soon as it ceases to fit the social relations, it becomes simply a bundle of paper. You cannot make the old laws the foundation of the new social development, any more than these old laws created the old social conditions.[39]

What does this view mean? It means that the constitution is based on society; society is not based on the constitution. Finally, a constitution must follow the speed of change that occurs in the production of material things and as that constitution does not follow the development of material things; it is simply equal to a rough piece of paper, and it is wrong to take that as the guiding force for the new social development. On this touchstone of Karl Marx, our party leadership claims that after the formation of a socialist constitution, a historical period of transition from capitalism into communism is guided and regulated by the constitution. Can it be settled by multi-party competition, without the leadership of the vanguard of the proletarian class, and without the communist party?

After capturing the state power and making a socialistic constitution by the proletarian class, the economic base and the superstructure cannot be turned immediately into a socialistic and communistic structure. So, Marxism divides communism into two phases. The first phase, socialist phase, is defined as a long period of transition. For example, in three and a half decades rule in the Soviet Union, and two and a half decades socialist production system and superstructure in China, socialism and capitalism existed in a parallel manner. It was not certain which of them would ultimately be victorious. So, the transition period cannot be over just by introducing the general line of socialism after the proletariat captures state power.

Socialism and the leadership of the vanguard for the proletariat cannot be guaranteed just by taking the general line of socialist

39 Karl Marx and Frederick Engels, "The Trial of the Rhenish District Committee of Democrats", *Collected Works*, Eng. ed., Progress Publishers, Moscow, 1977, Vol. 8, p. 327.

transformation in the constitution. Until the general direction of socialism is settled, it remains something to be ascertained to fix many concrete policies. Without working under the general line strictly and solving concrete problems during the transition on a Marxist-Leninist pattern, *i.e.* without a concrete solution, the goal of the general line cannot be achieved. The general line taken in the course of advancement from capitalism towards communism is the sum total of the specific situations during that period. It is the general direction of the aggregate factors during the transition period. In this regard Mao says, "without individual character there can be no general character. If all individual character were removed, what general character would remain?"[40]

Certainly, a socialist constitution reflects the general direction of revolutionary transformation towards communism. However, it is wrong to conclude that after a constitution is formed, the leadership of the proletariat through the communist party becomes unnecessary. A socialist constitution and general line of transformation is not absolute. They should be developed according to the development level of socialist politics, economic and culture. That is why, a socialist constitution and general line of socialist transformation should be enriched continuously. If it cannot do that a socialist constitution and general line of socialist transformation, which were formulated at a particular development of socialism cannot direct socialism towards communism and it becomes useless. Without the undivided leadership of the communist party, the socialist constitution can be nothing but a rough piece of paper, with no power to fulfil the objective of revolution. As Mao says:

> Once it is approved, the whole nation, one and all, should observe it. State personnel particularly, and in the first place those present here, should take the lead in observing it. To fail to observe the constitution is to violate it. When promulgated, our Draft Constitution will win the unanimous support of the whole people and enhance their enthusiasm. An organisation must have rules, and so must a state. A constitution is a set of general rules, it is the fundamental law. To codify the principles of people's democracy and socialism in the form of a fundamental law, in the form of the constitution, so that there will be a clear course before the people of the whole country and they will feel sure they have a clear, definite and correct path to follow–this will heighten their enthusiasm.[41]

There is every possibility of our party misinterpreting Mao's statement to fulfil its vested interest. Actually, this is a general definition

40 Mao Tse-tung, "On Contradiction", *Selected Works*, Eng. ed., Foreign Language Press, Peking 1965, Vol. 1, p. 330.

41 Mao Tse-tung, "On the Draft Constitution of Peoples' Republic of China", *Selected Works*, Eng. ed., Foreign Language Press, Peking, First ed., 1977, Vol. 5, p. 145.

of Mao regarding the constitution. On the basis of this definition, it will be a blunder to think that after the making of the constitution, victory will be achieved over several complex hurdles and obstacles that may come in the path that leads to communism. A socialist constitution is drafted under the direct leadership of vanguard of the proletarian class, *i.e.* the communist party and supported by the working-class people. The communist party determines the general direction for achieving its minimum and maximum objective, which is included in the constitution too. So, to think that any political party, after having emerged victorious in the multi-party competition, will implement a document of a general direction and rules and law for the formation of socialism ascertained by the communist party is to neglect even the general law of class struggle under socialism. Our party has said that supporters of imperialism and opponent of socialism would not be allowed to join a political party and get elected through multi-party competition in socialism. Such elements are suppressed under proletarian dictatorship and our party fully agrees with this point, at least theoretically.

As vindicated by the history of the world socialist movement, the main base of the restoration of capitalism is not the defeated capitalist class, crushed as a class under proletarian dictatorship, and its property and all privileges ceased, but also as Lenin says, "existence of the bourgeois state without the bourgeoisie, " *i.e.* force of habit, strength of small-scale production, differences between the town and countryside, differences between physical and mental labour, production of commodities, the law of value, the need of money, the social bases of trade that the proletariat cannot end immediately after seizing power. So, they exist as long as social grounds go on breeding capitalist elements. If the general line of socialism is adopted to implement a socialist constitution, and leadership is selected through party competition, as our party says, then new capitalist elements can challenge the communist party in cooperation with international capital, petty-bourgeois elements, under the guise of the political party. When they come to power, it will be a day dream to think that they will work within the limitations of a socialist constitution and enrich it with the latest development of socialist society. How can the political parties representing petty-bourgeois class, in case they gain leadership through party competition, be expected to implement a transitional general line determined by the communist party and the constitution that is the legal tool to root out individual property and exploitation of man by man?

Our party leadership has been oblivious to the special steps needed under the general line of socialist transformation. The building of socialism is not possible only by following the general line. Socialist transformation is like a complete design for the construction of a building, which requires many materials and the help of technology. If there is a lack of bricks or blocks, doors and windows, rod, cement, stones, sand, technician and skilled builders needed for construction, the building cannot be completed. This is true in the case of social design too. After the general line of socialism is decided, special policies and work plans have to be adopted, keeping in mind the specialities and changes, in national and international situations, and in the class relation in the concerned country, productive forces, and production relations.

In Russia, after three and a half decades under the leadership of Lenin and Stalin, the peace treaty of Brest-Litovsk; formation of poor peasant committees and control over Kulaks; the suppression of the revolt of "Left-Wing" Socialist-Revolutionaries; policies that the party adopted in the course of foreign military intervention and civil war; line of transition towards peaceful economic restructuring; new economic policy; cooperative project; line of socialist industrialisation; working direction for communisation of peasantry; abandoning policy to control Kulaks and making a new policy to eliminate it as a class; amendment of constitution; policies adopted during the Second World War were some of the landmarks of far-reaching importance. These specific policies the party adopted were the links of the general line of revolutionary transformation towards communism.

Had the policy of setting the question of leadership through multi-party competition been taken by dissolving the leadership role of the communist party after the revolution and constitution, as stated by our party, would it be possible to take a general line by adopting a specific policy under the special situations born in the course of building of socialism? If the party competition between the Bolshevik Communist Party and "Left-Wing" Socialist-Revolutionaries was allowed, would it be possible to attain a general line in relation to Kulaks? Would it be possible to adopt socialist competition in the industry for socialism-oriented activities? If the mingling of "Left-Wing" revolutionaries and Menshevik was allowed to align as an organisation for party competition soon after the revolution, would it be possible to implement the general line of socialism? Was the formation of a strong regular Red Army possible if the "Military Opposition" group was not defeated at the Eighth Congress of the Communist Party in Russia? Would it have been possible to go ahead to protect the dictatorship of the proletariat from foreign intervention and civil war if the party had not followed the plan of Lenin and Stalin? If the policy of affiliation with political organisations had been loosened, as our party says, during the period of transition towards peaceful work of economic restructure, would not the Trotskyites, the "Workers Opposition", "Left Communists", "Democratic Centrists" and groups like that not organise themselves in political organisations and affect the national policy of transition towards peaceful economic restructure? If the thinking that the general line and constitution regulate all things had been accepted, as our party says, would it have been possible to establish collectivisation and a commune system and suppress the obstruction by the Kulaks during the socialistic industrialisation in the USSR by allowing Trotskyites sectarians, Zinovievites and Bukharinites to enter the multi-party competition with the communist party? Our party says classes exist in socialism, and it is natural to have political parties in multi-party competition, and they should be allowed to compete with the communist party. If this principle was established in Russia, would the Bukharin-Rykov anti-party group not gather and organise their followers and establish capitalism?

The same is true regarding China. The general line in China was fixed after the success of the New Democratic Revolution in 1949. It was divided into two parts. As Mao Tse-tung says on the first one:

> The time between the founding of the People's Republic of China and the basic completion of socialist transformation is a period of transition. The party's general line or general task for the transition period is basically to accomplish the country's industrialisation and the socialist transformation of agriculture, handicrafts and capitalist industry and commerce over a fairly long period of time.[42]

The other one was the general line brought forward under the leadership of Mao in 1962 for the entire historical period of transition towards communism.

To achieve the general line, the Communist Party of China, under the leadership of Mao Tse-tung, adopted specific policies like formation of mutual aid teams for cooperation in agriculture; formation of socialist collective system; socialist industrialisation; socialist transformation of agriculture; socialist transformation of capitalist industry and commerce; the great leap forward; the emphasis on class struggle; the socialist education movement; advancing revolution while emphasising production and the Great Cultural Revolution, etc. These specific policies were separate links of general line itself fixed by the communist party, and adopted during two and a half decades for building socialism by the Communist Party of China. The general line was the sum total of all these links.

If the policy of deciding the question of leadership through multi-party competition was accepted, would Liu Shao-chi and company not go against "the general line of the party for the transition period" and succeed in their counter-revolutionary general line during the transition period, to "firmly establish the new-democratic social order", "move from

42 Mao Tse-tung, "The Party's General Line for the Transition Period", *Selected Works*, Eng. ed., Foreign Language Press, Peking, First ed., 1977, Vol. 5, p. 102.

New Democracy towards socialism" and "sustain private property"? If after the revolution, the undivided leadership of the communist party was not established, would it be possible to lead the general line of the "entire period of transition from socialism to communism" in the Tenth Plenary Session of the Eighth Central Committee, after having completed the socialist transformation of industrialisation of China's agriculture, handicraft and capitalist industry and commerce? If the leadership had taken part in the multi-party competition, would it be possible to follow the socialist working direction such as the socialist collective system and the great leap forward in China? If the party competition had been organised in the socialist society as well, could the proletarian class have accomplished the great Proletarian Cultural Revolution, which represents a new and higher stage of class struggle in the transition towards communism?

These total historical facts prove that the implementation of the general line of the party and state for transition and legal bases (constitution) can only be led by the communist party. The answer given by Lenin on constitution clarifies the confusion of our party in relation to the socialist constitution.

> What is a constitution? A sheet of paper with the people's rights recorded on it. What is the guarantee of these rights being really recognised? It lies in the *strength* of those classes of the people that have become aware of those rights, and have been able to win them... let us not for a moment forget that *strength* is proved *only* by victory in the struggle.[43]

On a different occasion, Lenin stated that a constitution "expresses the actual relation of forces in the class struggle."[44] What do these sayings of Lenin suggest?

Lenin's statement entails two things. The first is that a socialist constitution is a sign of victory of the proletarian class in the class struggle. The second is that the stability of that victory is determined by the victory of the proletariat in the class struggle that exists during the transition from capitalism to communism. He emphasised not to forget for a moment that strength is proved only by victory in the struggle. Our party leadership accepts the first point, but it neglects the second point. By separating the proletarian authority from the leadership of the communist party, our party has shown the possibility of petty-bourgeois parties taking the leadership through a multi-party competition in the backdrop of the socialist constitution. The stability of victory of the proletarian class depends on the class struggle that is to come. Our party seems to have forgotten the above view of Lenin

43 V. I. Lenin, "Between Two Battles", *Collected Works*, Eng. ed., Progress Publishers, Moscow, Fourth Printing, 1977, Vol. 9, p. 461.

44 V. I. Lenin, "How the Socialist-Revolutionaries Sum Up the Revolution ...", *Collected Works*, Eng. ed., Progress Publishers, Moscow, Third Printing, 1977, Vol. 15, p. 336.

that the transition from capitalism to communism is possible only through the communist party, not under the leadership of petty-bourgeois parties. It means our party wants to solve the problem of transition on the basis of simplistic analysis of formal freedom, equality and democracy. It reveals only their "petty-bourgeois, philistine nature and ideologically slavishly follow in the wake of the bourgeoisie."[45]

The socialist constitution is "a new form of the class struggle."[46] It means the proletarian class should be at a new and higher stage of class struggle during that period, and the leadership of the communist party should be made stronger and effective otherwise, the proletarian class cannot complete the long historical period of transition from capitalism to communism. The communist party is the only political party that can lead the proletarian class to complete the transition. On the basis of its knowledge and experience, as Stalin says, "amidst the complex conditions of a revolutionary situation, and sufficiently flexible to steer clear of all submerged rocks in the path to its goal.[47]

Throughout the historical period of transition from capitalism to communism, the proletarian class requires leadership of that type of political party, which is experienced, united, trained, and purified by the decades of strikes and political struggle against capital. During this period, the proletarian class requires a strong political leadership capable of overthrowing the exploiter class and resisting its counter attack, with revolutionary leadership to crush bourgeois democratic thinking for the sake of liberation to bring equality, while waging war against all kinds of empty phrases. Throughout the whole period, the proletarian class requires leadership of the political party that has won the support of all the workers and oppressed people through the determined struggle against capital, for safeguarding of the socialism. As Lenin says:

> It must lead the whole mass of the working and exploited people, as well as all the petty-bourgeois groups, on to the road of new economic development, towards the creation of a new social bond, a new labour discipline, a new organisation of labour, which will combine the last word in science and capitalist technology with the mass association of class-conscious workers creating large-scale socialist industry.[48]

45 V. I. Lenin, "A Great Beginning", *Collected Works*, Eng. ed., Progress Publishers, Moscow, Third Printing, 1977, Vol. 29, p. 422.

46 V. I. Lenin, "How the Socialist-Revolutionaries Sum Up the Revolution...", *Collected Works*, Eng. ed., Progress Publishers, Moscow, Third Printing, 1977, Vol. 15, p. 337

47 J. V. Stalin, "Foundation of Leninism", *Problems of Leninism*, Eng. ed., Foreign Language Press, Peking, 1976, p. 98.

48 V. I. Lenin, "A Great Beginning", *Collected Works*, Eng. ed., Progress Publishers, Moscow, Third Printing, 1977, Vol. 29, p. 423.

In relation to the quality and capacity of the communist party during the dictatorship of the proletariat, Lenin says:

> Under the proletarian dictatorship, millions of peasants and small proprietors, hundreds of thousands of office employees, officials and bourgeois intellectuals, of subordinating them all to the proletarian state and to proletarian leadership, of eradicating their bourgeois habits and traditions, ... as we must–in a protracted struggle waged on the basis of the dictatorship of the proletariat–re-educate the proletarians themselves, who do not abandon their petty-bourgeois prejudices at one stroke, by a miracle, at the behest of the Virgin Mary, at the behest of a slogan, resolution or decree, but only in the course of a long and difficult mass struggle against mass petty-bourgeois influences.[49]

Throwing light on the most complicated nature of this task and its importance during the transition period, Lenin further writes:

> The second task is more difficult than the first, for it cannot possibly be fulfilled by single acts of heroic fervour; it requires the most prolonged, most persistent and most difficult mass heroism in *plain*, *everyday* work. But this task is more essential than the first, because, in the last analysis, the deepest source of strength for victories over the bourgeoisie and the sole guarantee of the durability and permanence of these victories can only be a new and higher mode of social production, the substitution of large-scale socialist production for capitalist and petty-bourgeois production.[50]

These tasks to be carried out during the historic transition period can be accomplished only by a communist party, the vanguard of the proletariat. Our party also accepts that except the communist party, other parties are petty-bourgeois class parties. The Marxist principle that rejects any compromise with any petty-bourgeois political parties regarding the leadership and considers the undivided leadership of the communist party, a vanguard of the proletariat, essential during the historic transition from capitalism to communism. About this, Leninism has availed us sufficient material.

Even after the proletarian class captures power from the capitalist class, their effective presence in social production as a petty-bourgeois class remains intact. Under socialism, there exists a strong net of small-scale production. As Lenin says, "they *cannot be ousted*, or crushed; we *must learn to live* with them."[51] During the revolution, such elements have

49 V. I. Lenin, " 'Left-Wing' Communism: An Infantile Disorder", *Collected Works*, Eng. ed., Progress Publishers, Moscow, Third Printing, 1977, Vol. 31, pp. 115-16.

50 V. I. Lenin, "A Great Beginning", *Collected Works*, Eng. ed., Progress Publishers, Moscow, Third Printing, 1977, Vol. 29, p. 423.

51 V. I. Lenin, " 'Left-Wing' Communism: An Infantile Disorder", *Collected Works*, Eng. ed., Progress Publishers, Moscow, Third Printing, 1977, Vol. 31, p. 44.

worked broadly in favour of revolution with the proletarian class. But after the revolution, as Lenin says, "their tendency to go back to bourgeois "order", under the "wing" of the bourgeoisie, the non-proletarian and semi-proletarian mass of the working population."[52] On the basic tendency of the wide sections of the petty-bourgeois class, in the aftermath of the revolution, Lenin says:

> In the train of the capitalist exploiters follow the wide sections of the petty-bourgeoisie, with regard to whom decades of historical experience of all countries testify that they vacillate and hesitate, one day marching behind the proletariat and the next day taking fright at the difficulties of the revolution; that they become panic-stricken at the first defeat or semi-defeat of the workers, grow nervous, run about aimlessly, snivel, and rush from one camp into the other.[53]

According to Lenin, "economic conditions, the conditions of commodity production, inevitably turn the peasant (not always, but in the vast majority of cases) into a huckster and profiteer."[54] Surprisingly, our party leadership proposes a system for 'competitive' activity, not as 'cooperative' with the communist party in socialism. If this system is established as our party proposes, landlords and the capitalist class thrown out of power will use this system (multi-party competition) to restore their power in cooperation with the international capital and the petty-bourgeois political parties by dissolving proletarian dictatorship in a peaceful way. During the long historical period of transition from capitalism to communism, wide sections of the petty-bourgeois class, which remain unstable due to the economic situation of a small-scale production exist in socialism, cannot transform themselves, as per the principles of socialism.

If the communist party does not establish the undivided leadership of the proletariat, then naturally, the defeated capitalist class, and international capitalism will win them over and benefit from their unstable class character. The proposal of our party for 'competitive' politics, not that of 'cooperative' with the communist party, pushes them under the leadership of the bourgeois party from the communist party. Marxism-Leninism-Mao Tse-tung Thought always emphasises that in socialism, through the communist party, the proletarian class should deepen its power by waging the class struggle against the conservatism, and the uncertainty and deviation of the petty-bourgeoisie. The petty-

52 V. I. Lenin, "A Great Beginning", *Collected Works*, Eng. ed., Progress Publishers, Moscow, Third Printing, 1977, Vol. 29, pp. 422-23.

53 V. I. Lenin, "Proletarian Revolution and Renegade Kautsky", *Collected Works*, Eng. ed., Progress Publishers, Moscow, Third Printing, 1981, Vol. 28, p. 254.

54 V. I. Lenin, "Economic and Politics in the Era of the Dictatorship of the Proletariat", *Collected Works*, Eng. ed., Progress Publishers, Moscow, Third Printing, 1977, Vol. 30, p. 113.

bourgeois class, which hesitates to break relations with the bourgeoisie and remains undecided whether to support proletarian leadership to have a strong relation and unity with the proletariat, will change camps with only a slight pressure. As Lenin has suggested that "they can (and must) be transformed and re-educated only by means of very prolonged, slow, and cautious organisational work."[55]

The petty-bourgeois elements who support communist party leadership but go over to the camp of the defeated oppressor class and international capital in the transition period, firstly, should be dealt with mercilessly and secondly, without hesitation to transform them in favour of socialism. By applying these two methods, petty-bourgeois elements can be converted into socialism. During the long historical period of transition from capitalism to communism, our party wants to orient the petty-bourgeois elements for the sake of organising themselves as parties within socialism, not in a cooperative, but also in a competitive way with an assurance that communist party will sit in opposition and accept the leadership of other parties that is in a majority in the election. It is indispensable to put the wider section of petty-bourgeois parties, which are the outgrowth of the existence of the small-scale production in socialism, under the leadership of a party representing a higher system of production as well as class.

During the long historical period of transition from capitalism to communism, as our party states, petty-bourgeois elements should get the opportunity to compete, not just cooperate, through organising their political parties, and if they win, then the communist party should accept their leadership. Contrary to this, they should be given training that a bright future can be ensured only under the leadership of the proletarian class through the communist party. We have to make them understand that their real liberation is possible only by accepting the rule of the proletarian class through the communist party, and not in being "free" from it. Marxism-Leninism believes that if properly guided through the communist party regarding the importance and necessity of proletarian leadership, the non-proletarian and semi-proletarian masses of people, comprising unstable elements of the petty-bourgeoisie, they would take not as bondage, but a vanguard in transition. Lenin's insight is quite informative:

> Great and inevitable as may be their petty-bourgeois vacillations and their tendency to go back to bourgeois "order", under the "wing" of the bourgeoisie, the non-proletarian and semi-proletarian mass of the working population cannot but recognise the moral and political authority of the

55 V. I. Lenin, " 'Left-Wing Communism: An Infantile Disorder", *Collected Works*, Eng. ed., Progress Publishers, Moscow, Third Printing, 1977, Vol. 31, p. 44.

> proletariat, who are not only overthrowing the exploiters and suppressing their resistance, but are building a new and higher social bond, a social discipline, the discipline of class-conscious and united working people, who know no yoke and no authority except the authority of their own unity, of their own, more class-conscious, bold, solid, revolutionary and steadfast vanguard.[56]

Bafflingly, our party terms it as a bond in the form of one party dictatorship in socialism, whereas even the petty-bourgeois vulnerable elements too consider it nothing than the moral and political authority of the proletariat. By denouncing the leadership role of the communist party in socialism, our party leadership wants to deprive the proletarian class of its historical responsibility of training the petty-bourgeois masses through the communist party in socialism. This is the serious crime against the non-proletarian and semi-proletarian mass of the working population.

Our party leadership's advocacy for the petty-bourgeoisie, who have an economic base of small-scale production, as well as non-proletarian and semi-proletarian masses of working population, to get the opportunity to take part in competitive politics, not cooperation with the communist party, means our party has forgotten that: "The proletariat seeks to transform the world according to its own world outlook, and so does the bourgeoisie." The petty-bourgeois class does not have a third world outlook, separate from these two world views, and naturally, its view is the world outlook of the capitalist class itself. Making it clearer, Mao says: "It is inevitable that the bourgeoisie and petty-bourgeoisie will give expression to their own ideologies. It is inevitable that they will stubbornly assert themselves on political and ideological questions by every possible means. You cannot expect them to do otherwise."[57]

During the transition from capitalism to communism under the leadership of the communist party by the proletariat, if petty-bourgeois parties too are allowed to compete with the communist party, as our party advocates, basing on the principle of formal freedom, then the parties, other than the communist party will change the socialistic economic base and superstructure as per their capitalistic world outlook. Every class seeks to change the economic base and superstructure according to its own world outlook. A particular class can carry only a particular responsibility. One class cannot fulfil the responsibility of the other class. The same is true about a political party too. It works for the interest of the class it represents. This is why if a socialist society is to move according to the proletarian

56 V. I. Lenin, "A Great Beginning", *Collected Works*, Eng. ed., Progress Publishers, Moscow, Third Printing, 1977, Vol. 29, pp. 422-23.

57 Mao Tse-tung, "On the Correct Handling of Contradictions Among the People", *Selected Works*, Eng. ed., Foreign Language Press, Peking, First ed., 1977, Vol. 5, pp. 409, 411.

world outlook, and not the bourgeois class world outlook, the activities of petty-bourgeois parties should be guided under the undivided leadership of the proletariat through the communist party.

In Russia, after the proletarian revolution, there was no provision to allow political activities, especially the ones which played a negative role in the October Socialist Revolution of 1917. No freedom could be allowed to other political parties to continue their counter-revolutionary activities after the revolution. However, the environment in China was different. Certain democratic parties cooperated with the communist party in the new democratic revolution. So, in relation to the question, democratic parties were in existence and Mao Tse-tung evaluated them highly. On this question, in essence, there was similarity between Lenin and Mao Tse-tung. They took such a view as a question of the national characteristic of this or that revolution, and not as the essential characteristic or a compulsory condition of the logical concept of proletarian dictatorship. But Comrade Bhattarai has presented Mao differently. As he says: "In the past, due to different reasons, it could not be implemented, but Mao himself had been thinking in this direction."[58] He has also quoted Mao: "Which is better, to have just one party or several? As we see it now, it's perhaps better to have several parties. This has been true in the past and may be so for the future; it means long-term coexistence and mutual supervision."[59]

Here Comrade Bhattarai has tried to put Mao against Lenin. Not only that, he has tried to project Mao against his own thought. By quoting the above sayings of Mao, Comrade Bhattarai fulfils his own objective with a claim that Mao was in favour of the multi-party competition in socialism, and that he saw it as a basic question. The statement of Mao, just below the quoted statement by Comrade Bhattarai shows he did not take the question as a basic one, but understood it as special one. In the specific situation of China and in relation to the coexistence of other democratic parties, he says:

> The views set out above are based on China's specific historical conditions. Conditions vary in different socialist countries and with different communist parties. Therefore, we do not maintain that they should or must adopt the Chinese way. The slogan "long-term coexistence and mutual supervision" is also a product of China's specific historical conditions".
>
> It is the desire as well as the policy of the communist party to exist side by side with the democratic parties for a long time to come. But whether the democratic parties can long remain in existence depends not merely on the

58 Baburam Bhattarai, "Question of Building of a New Type of State Power", *People's Council*, The Organ of the Joint Revolutionary People's Council, Nepal, July 2004, No. 1, p. 13.

59 Mao Tse-tung, "On the Ten Major Relationship", *Selected Works*, Eng. ed., Foreign Language Press, Peking, First ed., 1977, Vol. 5, p. 296.

desire of the communist party but on how well they acquit themselves and on whether they enjoy the trust of the people.[60]

Taking Mao's "since classes and class struggle still exists in China, there is bound to be opposition in one form or the other" statement as a basis, Comrade Bhattarai puts forward the multi-party system as an "MLM agreeing system to solve contradictions exist among people scientifically, so long as society remains class-divided".[61]

These two statements superficially sound similar, but the statements of Mao and Bhattarai are not similar. Mao's view represents the world outlook of the proletariat and has the stated objective to transform the petty-bourgeoisie to the proletarian world outlook, just as of Lenin. On the other, Comrade Bhattarai's view represents the bourgeois class world outlook, and aims to push the wider sections of the petty-bourgeoisie in socialism into the cooperators of the defeated oppressing class and international capitalism. To solve the contradictions among people in a socialist society, Mao did not even imagine it possible without the leadership role of the communist party.

Mao took the communist party and democratic party as "products of history. What emerges in history disappears in history. Therefore, the communist party will disappear one day, and so will the democratic parties." Our party leadership, basing themselves on this statement, has proposed "disappearing" the leadership role of the communist party in socialism and placing it on an equal footing with other parties. To quote Mao:

> But at present we cannot do without the proletarian party and the dictatorship of the proletariat and, what is more, it is imperative that they should be made still more powerful. Otherwise, we would not be able to suppress the counter-revolutionaries, resist the imperialists and build socialism, or consolidate it when it is built. Lenin's theory on the proletarian party and the dictatorship of the proletariat is by no means "outmoded", as alleged by certain people. The dictatorship of the proletariat cannot but be highly coercive.[62]

It is wrong to take Mao's view of "long-term coexistence and mutual supervision" as a thinking towards dissolution of the leadership role of the communist party under the proletarian dictatorship. It is even clearer in this statement of Mao:

60 Mao Tse-tung, "On the Correct Handling of Contradictions Among the People", *Selected Works*, Eng. ed., Foreign Language Press, Peking, First ed., 1977, Vol. 5, p. 413.

61 Baburam Bhattarai, "Question of Building of a New Type of State Power", *People's Council*, The Organ of the Joint Revolutionary People's Council, Nepal, July 2004, No. 1, p. 13.

62 Mao Tse-tung, "On the Ten Major Relationship", *Selected Works*, Eng. ed., Foreign Language Press, Peking, First ed., 1977, Vol. 5, p. 297.

> We all know that supervision over the communist party is mainly exercised by the working people and the party membership. But it augments the benefit to us to have supervision by the democratic parties too. Of course, the advice and criticism exchanged by the communist party and the democratic parties will play a positive supervisory role only when they conform to the six political criteria.

Mao has not put all these six criteria on the same level. He states the two of them to be the most important. He says: "Of these six criteria, the most important are the two about *the socialist path and the leadership of the party*." (my italics–Yogendra)[63]

May-December, 2008
Canberra, Australia

63 Mao Tse-tung, "On the Correct Handling of Contradictions Among the People", *Selected Works*, Eng. ed., Foreign Language Press, Peking, First ed., 1977, Vol. 5, p. 414.

Capitulationist Steps Regarding National Independence, Sovereignty and Territorial Integrity

Fifth Letter Sent to the Party Headquarters on the Capitulationist Steps Regarding National Independence, Sovereignty and Territorial Integrity

1
National Independence, Sovereignty and Territorial Integrity

The signing of the Nepal-India Bilateral Investment Promotion and Protection Agreement (BIPPA), during the Prime Minister Baburam Bhattarai's visit to India, has negatively affected the national interest of Nepal. Some comrades in the top leadership, together with the United Madhesi Front (UDMF), signed the four-point agreement on August 28, 2011, overlooking the territorial integrity of Nepal as well as its suicidal impact on the national independence and sovereignty in the long run.

a) **Four-Points Agreement Signed with the United Democratic Madhesi Front**, Sub-point (2) of the fourth point of the agreement states:

As per the arrangement in part 20 of the Interim Constitution, 2007 of Nepal, and the eight-point agreement between the Nepal government and the United Democratic Madhesi Front, we are committed to building a democratic structure with national and inclusive character. For this, establishing the Madhesi community based separate unit as an inclusive process will be immediately started with reference to the demand of recruitment of ten thousand soldiers.

As the four-point agreement mentions, the agreements and understandings had already agreed upon, including the Interim Constitution, 2007, so extracting some parts of them will help us understand the subject matter correctly. For example, the Comprehensive Peace Accord (CPA) made between the then Nepal government and the CPN(Maoist) states:

4.7- The Council of Ministers shall control, mobilise and manage the Nepali Army as per the new Military Act. The Interim Council of Ministers shall prepare and implement the detailed action plan of democratisation of the Nepali Army by taking suggestions from the concerned committee of the interim parliament. This shall include tasks such as determining the right number of the Nepali Army, preparing the democratic structure reflecting the national and inclusive character and training them as per the democratic principles and values of the human rights.

Likewise, it is written in The Interim Constitution, 2007:

3) The President, on the recommendation of the Council of Ministers, shall control, mobilise and manage the Nepal Army in accordance with the law. The Council of Ministers shall, with the consent of the political parties and by seeking the advice of the concerned committee of the legislature-parliament, formulate an extensive work plan for the democratisation of the Nepal Army and implement it.

4) In the case of formulating and implementing the action plan pursuant to clause (3), determination of the appropriate number of the Nepal Army, its democratic structure and national and inclusive characters shall be developed, and training shall be imparted to the army in accordance with the norms and values of democracy and human rights.

4 (A) In order to give the Nepal Army a national character and make it inclusive, enlisting of Madhesi, indigenous ethnic groups, Dalits, women, and people from backward regions into the armed forces on the basis of the principles of equality and inclusiveness shall be ensured by law."

Let us examine the last statement added by the fifth amendment to the constitution and compare these statements of the CPA and the Interim

Constitution, 2007 with sub-point (2) of the Four-Point Agreement. Does it grasp the previous statements? Not at all, as it goes like this: "We promise in building a democratic structure and national and inclusive character of the Nepal Army", and the sentence mentioned immediately after it, "for this, establishing the identity of the Madhesi community as a separate unit at present as an inclusive process will be immediately started with reference to the demand of recruitment of ten thousand." The CPA and Interim Constitution, 2007 aims at restructuring the army so far organised under the feudal monarchic system for hundred years to match with the political changes brought about by the people's war and people's movement. We should not take the changes occurring in the country as a simple result of the people's movement that abolished the 239-years-old monarchical system and established the republic. We should understand this change in the light of the dual state power created by the ten-year people's great war, under the leadership of CPN(Maoist).

The CPN(Maoist), forwarded the minimum programme of new democracy in the present imperialist era and chose violent revolution as a universal path to gain it, which in our country is the path of protracted people's war. In a short period of time, one after another revolutionary base area and local power spread all over the nation and the foetus of people's power at the local and regional level came into existence. The king sought the help of the army only when the Nepal Police and Armed Police could not resist the people's war. Confrontation between the People's Liberation Army, (PLA) and the then Royal Nepal Army (RNA) were usual events in the latter years of insurgency. After the PLA attack on some barracks of the RNA, people's war entered the stage of counter-offensive. The reactionary power was squeezed only to the capital and the district headquarters. The government, having accepted the political existence of new power, called for talks, which was the sign of the governments's recognition to the then CPN(Maoist). Had the military strength of CPN(Maoist) not been strong; with the development and expansion of new power nationwide, and had the parliamentary parties like the Nepali Congress and the Communist Party of Nepal(UML) not got support from the CPN(Maoist), and had the people's movement in 2005 not been supported by the mighty military force of CPN(Maoist), there would have been no yielding of power by the king in favour of democracy. The re-establishment of the dissolved parliament, formation of the Interim Constitution of 2007; the complete passivity of the king during the interim period; and the election of the constituent assembly and ending the 239 years of monarchy in favour of a republic could not have been achieved without CPN(Maoist)'s active involvement.

After signing the CPA, and the end of the people's war, the revolutionary base areas and local power were dissolved. However, the dual power continued. The most important base of power is the army. Under the leadership of a particular political party, these pillars (armies) representing old and new power were in existence. Under the supervision of the United Nations (UN), the Nepal army was kept in barracks and the Maoist army in temporary camps–two parallel state powers in the country. It was accepted by the international powers, and internally by the Nepal government, the UCPN(Maoist) {after party unity CPN(Maoist) named UCPN(Maoist)}, and all other political parties. Marxism-Leninism believes that the status of dual power cannot be sustained for long, and earlier or later, one of the two powers has to be eliminated. With reference to Nepal, the internally feudal, comprador and bureaucratic capitalist class and external world imperialism and Indian expansionism wanted to exterminate the new power, and maintain the old power, though with some changes. Class conscious workers, ploughmen, cow herds, labourers, poor and landless peasants and representatives of the people's army wanted to get rid of the old power completely and see a new power established. In relation to the PLA, our party's policy and work plan is to be concentrated to end the old power, and to extend and consolidate the new power. If we cannot insist on the true Marxist-Leninist line; if we cannot free ourselves from utilitarianism and pragmatism, then feudalism, comprador and bureaucratic capitalism, world imperialism, and Indian expansionism will exterminate the new power without using force in a peaceful way and consolidate the old power. No result in between is possible.

I support the concept of building a national army and to make it an inclusive too. But, it is my firm view that the CPA and the Interim Constitution's sense has been interpreted wrongly.

a) For the unified national army, the Nepal army, and the PLA should be integrated by giving them equal status. It is not the swapping of the PLA into the Nepal army, or not the dissolution of the PLA into the Nepal army. I urge others too to take it as the formation of a unified army after integration by giving them equal status.

b) It is to create equal opportunities for the participation of all castes, ethnicity, women, regional communities in the army without any discrimination. But, as a result of the mistaken concept about all castes, races and people's communities in the country as a nation, the use of the term 'national' in the CPA and Interim Constitution, 2007, has been understood in the sense of separate regiments for different castes, races, backward classes and communities in the Nepal army. Such an interpretation is absolutely wrong in itself. Nepal is a mono-national country, comprising different castes, races and people's communities. The CPA and Interim Constitution, 2007 does not mean taking a certain number from all castes, races, communities and regions and for creating different regiments in the Nepal army. The thinking and planning of reservation of separate regiments of numbers from all castes, races and communities in the army cannot develop a national and inclusive army, to safeguard. national independence, sovereignty and territorial integrity. Internal and external reactionaries will utilise the separate regiments of different castes, races and people's communities in the army to realise their interests, if the army's structure remains communally fragmented. Of late, some Madhesi-based parties and leaders and representatives of ethnic communities are taking part in activities detrimental to the territorial integrity and the unity of the people (the latest example is expression of the then Defence Minister Shard Singh Bhandari). So, more serious thought should be given to this question. The national army is the defender of a country. It can fulfil its responsibility only when it is built on a foundation of unity of a high standard, both physically and mentally. A foundation of that type of unity is the nation and nationality, not different castes and races. This is why the national army should not be just a knot of Madhesi, Limbu, Tharu, Newar and so on. It is not a total of persons recruited being of a particular caste, race, community or region. It is the symbol of the unity of patriots who think of themselves as citizens of Nepal, despite whatever caste, race, community or region he or she originates from.

The Four-Point Agreement with the UDMF of the UCPN(Maoist) is an example of the extreme utilitarian view. To form a government under the leadership of Comrade Bhattarai at the time was necessary to get the support of the UDMF for fulfilling their vested interest. Therefore, the party accepted the condition of the UDMF to start the process of recruiting from the Madhesi community to establish a separate regiment in the Nepal army, without any hesitation despite its harmful impact on building a national army. However, on building a national army by integrating the Nepal army and the PLA, the party leadership adopted a suicidal policy. Because of their utilitarian view, if they need support and approval of other castes, races, communities and so on, and if these groups demand a separate regiment in the Nepal army, the party will also gladly accept in future too. The question arises here that if the Madhesi community is given a reservation of a certain number, why not give the same to other communities too?

2
Leading the Peace Process to its Logical Conclusion

The issue of leading the peace process to its conclusion should be made interrelated and integrated to building a national army with an adjustment between the Nepal army and the PLA, and by the democratisation of the former. Building of new national defence policy, a High Level Truth and Reconciliation Commission and Disappeared Investigation Commission by taking back cases against the Maoists during the people's war and adopting the revolutionary land reform to solve the problems of tillers, bonded labour, poor and landless peasants is equally important. The new constitution should establish labourers' right and ensure the welfare of oppressed and backward communities, scheduled castes, women, Madhesis, Muslims, backward regions and the national capitalists. It should guarantee the national independence, sovereignty and territorial integrity and the development of the national economy.

Under the tactical line of the peaceful development of revolution adopted in the context of the ten-year long people's great war and the special political situation emerged in the country, bringing the peace process to a logical end is directly linked to the new democratic revolution. We have not come to the peace process after having been defeated by the enemy or to run away from revolution. Our party followed this line in the developed special political situation of Nepal as an exception of the possibility of peaceful development of revolution in the history of Nepal. Therefore, for us, leading the peace process and fulfilling the historical responsibility of revolution should go together. We must strongly reject peace that strikes a counter blow to the great goal of the ten-year people's great war and consolidates the world imperialism, Indian expansionism, Chinese state capitalism, feudalism, comprador and bureaucratic capitalism in the country. Such a peace is futile for us. Peace is not absolute, it is relative. So, the peace process that is fruitful for world imperialism, Indian expansionism, revisionism including Chinese, feudal, comprador and the bureaucratic capitalist class is worthless for revolutionary communists and the patriotic forces. The conclusion of the peace process that is fruitful for revolutionary communists and patriots is worthless for the world imperialism, Indian expansionism, and revisionists as well as feudal, comprador and bureaucratic capitalists. The main problem of the peace process in Nepal is a struggle of life and death between the above parties. That is the special stage of class struggle and national struggle at present. With reference to the peace process within our party, non-Marxist-Leninist poisonous weeds are growing widely.

The bourgeois pacifist view is going to take control of the party, which is a serious issue.

Within the party, the chairman-prime minister group represents the bourgeois pacifist view on the question of the peace process. As a result, there is a "fruitful-historical" unity between the chairman-prime minister group and the world imperialism, Indian expansionism, Nepali Congress, CPN(UML) and Madhesi-based parties. Its latest proof is the agreement made by the chairman-prime minister with the political parties on November 1, 2011. Imperialists, Indian expansionists, revisionists and feudal, comprador and bureaucratic capitalist elements have termed the Agreement as a dawn of the new era. This Agreement is a big blow to the revolutionary communists and patriots whereas for reactionaries within the country and outside, and their agents, it is the moment to rejoice. Why are the chairman and the prime minister euphoric over the agreement? Question arises.

Prachanda and Bhattarai have adopted the pacifist view, so to expect anything other from them is like expecting plums from a peach tree. Other parties focus only on the peace process, and ignore the building of the national army through the integration of the PLA and the Nepal army, the democratisation of the Nepal army; the formation of a new national defence policy; the forming of a Truth Investigation and Reconciliation Commission, Commission for the Disappeared, and the dismissal of cases filed against the Maoists during the people's war. Likewise, they do not care for adopting the revolutionary land reform to solve the problems of bonded ploughmen, poor peasants and tillers; ensure the welfare and rights of backward races, schedule castes, women, Madhesis, Muslim community, backward regions, the national capitalists, workers and peasants in the new constitution. They are not interested in guaranteeing the sovereignty, national independence and territorial integrity under the general law of the class struggle. Why did the chairman and prime minister follow this path? How did they accept the demands of the other political parties to divide the peace process and constitution into two parts and to take the other part only after the first is completed? In the Agreement of parties signed by the party chairman on November 1, 2011, the question of building a constitution is taken as secondary, describing it as the "issue including peace process"–as a latter issue. The first chapter of the mentioned Agreement says:

> To fulfil the responsibility of peace process and constitution building, national consensus is inevitable. Certainly, after having taken the peace process of Nepal to its fruitful conclusion, the political process of constitution building needs to begin. So, according to CPA, the interim constitution of Nepal, 2007, and agreement has reached among different political parties at different times we have agreed to fulfil the remaining

tasks of the peace process immediately and make the constitution in order to forward the politics of consensus.

In the Agreement between the parties, there are seven topics and seventeen sub-topics. Out of them, four topics and thirteen sub-topics are related to the UCPN(Maoist) alone. That picture of subject means: the obstruction to the peace process is mainly the UCPN(Maoist), while other internal and external forces have not obstructed, nor will they put hurdles in future. The agreement among the parties focused on reaching reconciliation at the earliest with a view to compelling the UCPN(Maoist) to abide by the provisions of it at any cost and to turn the party into just like a lion without nails, teeth and paws so that no revolution could rise in Nepal for decades. There are mainly two topics in the Agreement: one about the adjustment of combatants of the Maoist army, and the other is the implementation of agreements of the past and the creation of an environment of confidence. My main view in regard to the integration of the combatants of the Maoist army has been presented in the course of discussing the sub-point (2) of the four-point of the agreement reached with the UDMF. The fourth point, sub-point (2), in relation to the agreement of parties, is a treachery to the people and a surrender to reactionary elements as it has devalued and insulted the great PLA and martyrs. The signing an agreement to dissolve the PLA through disarming it in exchange for constitution writing and a government of "national consensus", our party has signed on a death warrant.

It is essential to put matters in a correct way to clarify the questions regarding the implementation of the agreements and creating an atmosphere of mutual trust. The Agreement of parties is not in favour of the country and people as its sixth point states: "Implementation of the agreement, of the past and create environment of trust." Out of five sub-points, four are related to the UCPN(Maoist), which is responsible for implementing 80% and other internal and external political forces for 20%. How could the party Chairman Prachanda and Prime Minister Bhattarai accept such an insulting and objectionable agreement?

In relation to the form of Commissions as per the agreements of the past between the parties, it is written:

a) As per the CPA, ordinance related to the Reconciliation Commission and Disappeared Investigation Commission will be passed after the approval of legislative parliament according to the spirit of reconciliation.

b) Cases of conflict-period will be settled with the spirit and sentiment of the CPA and Interim Constitution-2006.

Those statements are not concrete, as they are very abstract and mentioned just in a very normal sense. Likewise, they are not connected to the question of building a national army and a national defence policy.

Before the integration of the Maoist army, Commissions should be formed and activated and all the cases against the Maoists levelled during the people's war should be written off to end the hatred and enmity and for creating an atmosphere of brotherhood.

By taking the bill to the legislative parliament, it should have been passed by a national consensus. The adjustment of the PLA should have been adjusted after all the cases imposed on the Maoists were dismissed or taken back. That would have proved our party's prudence. Only after that, the work of adjustment of the Maoist army should have been taken up. On this issue, we should have presented a condition. Just as with other questions and agreements between parties, here as well, the demands of other parties were fulfilled forthwith, that means, in cash, whereas the demands of the UCPN(Maoist) were put on hold, that means, on credit. It is astounding that the chairman and prime minister agreed to such an unequal principle of cash and credit.

Likewise, in the sub-points of point 6 in relation to implementation and creation of an environment of faith and trust in the Agreement between the parties, it states:

a) Private and public buildings, land captured by UCPN(Maoist) during armed conflict, will be returned to the concerned persons for their possession and use after the organisational decision by UCPN(Maoist) within November 23, 2011. Regarding the income of land for the duration under the capture, adequate compensation will be made available to the concerned persons."

b) According to the spirit of the Comprehensive Peace Agreement, the Interim Constitution of Nepal, 2007 and scientific land reform, right of peasants will be protected."

Here, particular and general, concrete and abstract, cash and credit are mixed up. On the one hand, a particular date is fixed, while to return land and other property captured during the people's war by the poor and landless people, but nothing has been mentioned for alternative arrangement for them, except saying, "The rights of peasants will be protected by adopting scientific land reform." The historical facts speak that solutions to such problems demands a long duration. Land and other property captured by labouring masses during the people's war should not be returned unless another adequate arrangement is made in another place, and till then the landless peasants should not be ousted from the line.

The party chairman (including prime minister) not only agree to oust them from the land without an alternate option by November 23, 2011, but are also committed to compensate the feudal, comprador and bureaucratic capitalist class for the duration of the property capture, which is a shameful surrender to the class enemy. Such a commitment from the leader of people's war in favour of the reactionary class is painful and shameful too. It has exposed their non-Marxist-Leninist thinking towards the revolutionary land reform, and it does not end just with promise, but they are equally firm on its implementation too. They already knew that poor peasants, tillers and other poor people would reject the order, so they have a prepared plan in Agreement with other political parties. For example, it is said in sub-point (e) of point 6: "Agreement to return property will be supervised and if not implemented, the responsibility to get it implemented goes to the local administration. Political parties have to cooperate with them."

If the property of feudal, comprador and bureaucratic capitalists captured under the leadership of party in the people's war was to be returned, it should have been done by the party. Why has it become "the responsibility of local administration?" It should be returned by the party, not under the local administration. The use of force is necessary when the party is under the pressure of reactionaries to return the property without making alternate and adequate arrangements. The provision of the use of force is there in the Agreement because the property is returned without any alternative arrangement.

Once the 'scientific land reform' proposal is implemented, the problems of the base class of revolution, bonded labourers, ploughmen, poor peasants and tillers will be automatically solved. To talk of the rightful owner without implementing scientific land reform is a farce. Actually, the feudalist, comprador and bureaucratic capitalist classes themselves do not want to implement scientific land reform. They want to paralyse it. Contrary to exposing that type of strategy and putting it as the major condition to implement scientific land reform, our party chairman-prime minister group has become a puppet of the feudal, comprador and bureaucratic capitalist classes.

There has been an absolute view of some comrades in the top leadership of our party regarding the constitution, with no spirit of class struggle. Just resembling the Nepali Congress, the CPN(UML) and the Madhesi-based parties, they too say a constitution must be prepared at any cost, and the UCPN(Maoist) should accept even if their principle are rejected by the majority. They have left the class view, as per the demand of other parties over hundreds of issues in the name of respecting the "majority". It is a non-Marxist-Leninist attitude to end the class struggle by a majority.

Marxism-Leninism holds the constitution as a form of class struggle, not the above class, but as a legal expression of a particular social existence. Communists should always see whether the issue is a new constitution building or amendment as a step in the great journey of class struggle. At present, we are not going to frame a constitution in a normal condition, but in the context of the ten-year people's great war, nineteen days great mass movement, line of peaceful development of revolution, end of the 239-year monarchical system, and the establishment of the republican system. So, our strategy should be directed towards our objective too. Certainly, old forces will exert pressure on us to frame the same type of constitution, but we should not kneel to them one after the other, but should opt for revolt, if necessary. Some of the top comrades of our party leadership have chosen the first alternative. By defeating this thinking with the two-line struggle, we should give possible perfection to the spirit of the new democratic revolution. The constitution should be made a document of the expression of the real relation of class forces in Nepalese society, and it should be framed as a collection of fundamental laws, welfare and the right of workers, peasants, schedule castes, women, Madhesis, Muslims, ethnic people, oppressed and backward communities and national capitalists with the guarantee of national independence, sovereignty and territorial integrity.

Our view in relation to the constitution should be according to the line of the peaceful development of revolution. In the changed political context of the country with the class struggle and class-based relations, any attempt moving towards the new democratic revolution peacefully. This is the essence of this line. We should go in that direction, otherwise any constitution that does not subordinate with strategy is not acceptable to us. We should voice our views clearly, and the thinking of some comrades of our party leadership to forsake everything for the constitution is completely wrong and unacceptable.

3

Political Economy of the Nepal-India Bilateral Investment Promotion and Protection Agreement

The Nepal-India Bilateral Investment Promotion and Protection Agreement (BIPPA), postponed for a period for more than a decade, was concluded on October 21, 2011. Discussions are going on for and against, which has come to be a national issue at present. The prime minister, who gave consent to the agreement through a side track without it, any pre-discussion in parliament, among different political parties, in standing committee or the central committee of his own Party, has defended himself. For example, immediately after meeting his Indian counterpart, the Prime Minister Dr. Manmohan Singh, Dr. Bhattarai, in a brief talk with journalists with reference to BIPPA, says:

> Now, nationalism cannot survive without going for economic development and prosperity. In the context of China and India developing so quickly, living in poverty and destitution will not help in preserving our nationalism. Prosperity is not possible without attracting external capital ... BIPPA attracts external capital and it opens a gate for fast development of Nepal. I have dared the risk ... Now, the country cannot develop without daring risk. Gambling as well should be dared-sometime is to say."–*The Kantipur Daily*, October 22, 2011

While answering the question, "how far the provision of compensation incase of any damage or closure of Indian industries will be in favour of Nepal", he states:

> The main thing is that there is no option that promotes foreign investment for economic prosperity of Nepal. Our party has a plan and promise to raise per capital income to three thousand dollar of every Nepali citizen in 10 years. If promise is to be realised, the risk must be taken. Having decided that someone has to take the risk, I have taken the risk. In this very background, we have made agreement. Again, in different countries, payment for damages is guaranteed even for common strikes. But, with us, not for common strikes, payment for damages is managed only for political general strikes. There was no option to invite investment than this provision."–*Nayapatrika Daily*, October 22, 2011

While briefing the parliament on his visit to India, the prime minister explained that BIPPA could create adequate employment, reduce the increasing trade deficit, generate more opportunities for employment, and increase revenue as well. He further illustrated that if the agreement could be implemented, it would radically change the bilateral relation between the two countries, and begin an era of equality based trade between two countries, making India Nepal's market first time.

Except these, he explained that a new era would begin in Nepal-India relations and if this agreement could be implemented, and Nepal being a market of India by now, would be radically changed to India becoming market of Nepal once an agreement was reached on the basis of equality.

A member of the prime minister's team and the Finance Minister Comrade Barshaman Pun in an interview to weekly *Ghatana Ra Bichar* about BIPPA says:

> About this oppositional voices are raised. But it is not that there is loss to Nepal from that. This Agreement brings foreign investment in country. Nepal does not always remain in the present situation. Some time in future, we will reach the position to invest in foreign country on one side and on the other this is a message as well that there is investment-friendly environment in Nepal. If bigger investors come, they increase economic mobility within the country, make the economic sector dynamic. In that

dynamicity, our country achieves self dependency, and economy can be strong. Therefore, in the long-term BIPPA does good to Nepal and the Nepalese people.

"If it is so, is it not correct to say that India alone will take benefit from Nepal by the BIPPA agreement?"

In answer to this question, he says:

> During talks with the Indian Prime Minister, and Finance Minister, Pranav Mukharjee told us by now India completed BIPPA with eighty-nine countries. What he experiences is that there has been no benefit to India. This Agreement is needed more for Nepal than to India. Therefore, we have shown greater interest, and not India. Being an emerging economy, India too requires external investment. In that situation, if investors become more attracted towards Nepal on the basis of this Agreement, India will be at a loss. It will be better to understand this fact in this light.

Likewise, in answer to another question, "Nepal has been passing through a transitional period. Therefore, industries established on Indian investment may claim a substantial amount because of bandhas and strikes. So, how can Nepal bear all these?", he replies:

> Now we should not even imagine conflict and war. Now, the country has embarked on political stability. The peace process will reach a conclusion, the constitution will be made and in 10-15 years' duration, the present Nepal will have entered into a stage of prosperity. If we stay in this very condition, this Agreement will gain nothing. But if we go ahead, we should not hesitate to say that this Agreement is in the interest of the country. It may look fraught with the risk of loss, in the long run it will be in the interest of the country."

In reply to Mohan Baidya Kiran's allegation of committing treachery and the threat of taking action against the prime minister by the party, he says:

> It may have been so because of a type of mentality that any work done in Nepal in cooperation with India is declared treacherous. But, we have not done anything treacherous to the nation and the party policy. In the end, all will realise and cooperate as it has been done with an intention of changing the face of the nation economically.

The arguments forwarded in favour of BIPPA, while defending it, by the Vice-Chairman of UCPN(Maoist) and Prime Minister Bhattarai and a member of the standing committee of the party and Finance Minister Barshaman Pun, prove that their views related to foreign investment are completely wrong. Their views about the economic development of a semi(neo)-colonial country like Nepal in the era of imperialism and proletarian revolution, are a true copy of Teng Hsiao ping's view, making no differences between "a white cat and a black cat." In reality, their view is not only theoretically wrong but also traitorous as it goes against the declared party line. My intention here is not to add some points, or delete some from the BIPPA, but to discuss the Marxist-Leninist principle regarding the foreign investment in the following pages.

The Agreement states:

> The Government of Nepal and India (hereinafter referred to as the "Contracting Parties");
>
> Desiring to create conditions favourable for fostering greater investments by investors of one state in the territory of the other state;
>
> Recognising that the encouragement and reciprocal promotion and protection of such investments are essential to stimulate private sector initiative and will increase prosperity in both states.

The main point in the above statement is the development of the open market itself that emphasises privatisation and rejects the role of the state in the development of the economy. Capitalist scholars and policy makers themselves have different opinions at different times in great variety regarding the market economy. In the history of economic thought, the position of emphasising the role of the state and protection was stronger at one time, whereas in other periods, the emphasis on the role of the private sector and open market was stronger. The countries after having achieved a higher stage of development of capitalism started searching the international market for export of their commodities, service and capital. However, policies on national industry and commerce adopted by the small and backward countries became problematic for them.

Modern history is the struggle between the policy of free export of commodities, service and capital of a few developed countries and the economy of small nations, just on the way to development, regarding the policy of control and protection of the state. The development of monopoly capitalism and the policy of open market displaced the role of the state and the policy of protection in economy. The concentration of production and rise of monopolists, the change in the role of banks, the rise of finance capital composed of bank capital and industrial capital; the partition of the world between capitalist associations and between great powers smoothened the opening of colonial markets. But that situation did not last for long, nor was it possible either. Barely had two decades passed when the previous division met with a serious setback.

Uneven development of capitalism was the instrumental factor in bringing change in their earlier state and strength as exemplified by the First World War and new "understanding" seen in relation to redivision of the world. According to "understanding", the monopolist associations and great powers started exporting their commodities, service and capital in the undeveloped and weaker countries and exploiting raw materials. They pressurised the concerned countries to end the role of state and policy of protection in the economy. The free market economy, which was anarchic in essence could not last for long. By 1930, they were entrapped in a great economic crisis known as the Great Depression in the capitalist world. At that time in the Soviet Union, there was not an open market economy, but socialist planned economy. Monopoly capital, finance capital and monopolist capitalist associations were not in existence there. Naturally, regulation of production, distribution and price determination was controlled by the socialist state, not by a few monopolists. As a result, the great economic depression of 1930s could not adversely impact the Soviet economy.

In this context, even bourgeois economists as well have emphasised the need of revaluation of the free market economy of the past. For instance, J. M. Keynes reached the conclusion that for the crisis in capitalist economy worldwide, emphasis given on the role of the private sector in greater quantity and weakening the role of the state were the main reasons. He argued that it was not the free market economy, but to a great extent, state-controlled economy which could stop the cyclic economic crisis. About a decade after the great depression, the world fell into the trap of the Second World War, and many developed countries followed Keynes' suggestion. That continued to be effective for three decades. He gave those suggestions to lead the world capitalist system ahead smoothly to free it from the cyclic crisis.

A contradiction exists between the leading role of the state in economy and finance capital, financial oligarchy and monopolist capitalist associations. Keynes' suggestion was followed by the imperialist states in the background of the great depression of 1930, and the ruin caused by the Second World War, seeing no other possibility.

A contradiction between the leading role of the state in economy and finance capital and financial oligarchy as well as monopolist capitalist associations reached an extreme point. By the 1970s, some of these countries, with big state controlled companies, started privatisation. By the end of the 1990s in the capitalist economy, free market economy made its position stronger. After the dissolving of the so-called socialist rule in 1990 in the Soviet Union and East European countries, the world imperialism and its pillars, World Bank, International Monetary Fund, GATT (later World Trade Organisation), Asian Development Bank and other international organisations initiated the policy of liberalisation. At present, the worldwide open market economy is a natural outcome of that. In the present era of monopoly capitalism, the open market economy means not only free transportation of commodities but also free transportation of service and finance capital. In comparison to the commodity transportation, owners have been gaining greater profits from the service and capital exports.

From the open market economy, a few countries of the world have accumulated capital unexpectedly while backward countries are facing a crisis of existence and are likely to be entrapped in the net of neo-colonialism. India has opened its market economy and China has transformed into an integral part of the world capitalist economy from a socialist economy. Naturally, Nepal has been oriented towards an open market economy. Specially, after taking membership of the World Trade Organisation, in Nepal, foreign capital investment and trade has increased very fast. If the UCPN(Maoist) had not started the people's war in February 13, 1996, and had not adopted revolutionary policies, there would have been unimaginable foreign capital investment in the country. Because of the policy of discouraging foreign investment during the people's war period, foreign monopolist investment could not enter Nepal in the desired quantity. During that period, they kept exerting pressure over the Nepal government to create a favourable environment for investment promotion.

After Colgate-Palmolive and Dabur companies, the Indian investment, faced hurdles, India pressed the then government for agreement to protect the Indian investment. After the end of the people's war, and the frequent obstruction in the India invested upper Karnali Hydo-project by the Maoist supporting workers, India pressurised to finalise the agreement immediately. The present Agreement is a result of the same, which is an irony that the obstacle was created by the Maoist workers to industries run and under construction on Indian investment, and the solution was proposed and emphasised by the Indian government, but not concluded for a decade, has now been accomplished in the period of the Maoist-Led government.

When the monopoly capitalists and monopolist firms develop from accumulation of capital, they export capital where there is higher profit, cheaper labour, sufficient raw materials, and where there is security of investment. India has still not become a developed capitalist country, but a handful of people and some firms have accumulated a huge amount of capital. In this context, they need an international market for capital investment to earn a higher profit. They have taken hydroelectricity, education, health, communication and herbs as sectors of profit for long, so they want to capture these sectors in Nepal strategically. As a result, they are exerting pressure on their government for such an arrangement. They have invested capital for profit in the hydro sector in Bhutan, whereas they are still vying for it in Nepal. India was pressurising Nepal for an agreement on investment security for some time–a decade should be seen in that very prospect.

For some years, on the one hand, Indian monopolist capitalists are found withdrawing from investment with the fear of insecurity of investment, and on the other, Chinese investment is increasing. The ruling class of India has a strategy to make Nepal a monopoly market of Indian capital by reaching an agreement with Nepal with the guarantee of security of capital investment in Nepal. If it could not be so, they have understood there would be "danger" of escape of the Nepalese market of capital investment from their hands. Vice-Chairman of UCPN(Maoist) and Prime Minister Bhattarai has taken steps to implement this plan (plan to establish capital investment over the Nepalese market). For that, the Indian ruling class and big houses will be obliged to him.

India has never treated Nepal as an independent sovereign country and considers Nepal as a protectorate state (politically, economically, diplomatically and so on). In relation to the open market as well, the same is true. By establishing monopoly over capital investment, commodity and service export, it wants to make Nepal a protectorate state more than before. By obstructing in different ways the import of capital from the third countries, and export of Nepali goods and services to other countries, India wants to stifle the national economy of Nepal, without making a direct military intervention, by exploiting the vulnerability of our country's politicians and government officials ready to sell themselves for power and money.

Issues like payment of damages to the Koshi sufferers, removal of dam construction at the border site in a one-sided manner in contravention of international law, providing land in Koilabas for the land taken for the construction of Sharada Dam, return of encroached land, and solution to the border problem, held under consideration for decades have come under the shade with the prime minister's decision to give the BIPPA a final touch. It is a betrayal of the national interest.

The overwhelming support to the BIPPA agreement, concluded hastily to fulfil the interest of India, is a testimony of how strong is the net of the intellectuals, agents, comprador capitalism and their political parties as well as social organisations in Nepal. In the country, dozens of industries and dozens of governmental, semi-governmental industries and organisations are either bankrupt, or on the verge of closure. The government, incapable of supporting such sick industries to reopen, or stop from bankruptcy, has formalised the BIPPA with India. Industrialists and business people who profess to be nationalists and advocates of national industries have also campaigned for the support to the agreement instead of offering grants and loans to rescue them. Treaties and agreements like BIPPA are an integral part of the strategy of establishing superiority over countries such as ours through privatisation, liberal or open market by the imperialists. In the era of monopoly capitalism, capital investment or giving loans are not directed to develop the national economy, rather they make the fragile condition of countries further dependent on them with their access to cheaper labour and raw materials intact. With these treaties, agreements and understandings, imperialism compel weak and undeveloped countries to pull into the net of imperialist globalisation. If this situation is not corrected forthwith, the future of countries like Nepal will be even bleaker.

Defending the BIPPA, the prime minister and finance minister have given various arguments in support of their deal with India, which can be summed up in one sentence: "Foreign capital investment is indispensable for the economic development of Nepal." This is not the idea of the bourgeois economists, or bourgeois policy makers, the leaders of the Nepali Congress, the CPN(UML) or Madhesi-based parties and groups, or comprador capitalist class in reference to our country, but by the leaders of the UCPN(Maoist), who concede Lenin's principles regarding monopoly capitalism, financial oligarchy, division and redivision of the world by monopoly organisations, and between the great powers, as the guidelines, and then fought the ten-year people's war for new democracy, socialism and communism; for which thousands of people sacrificed their lives. Whatever opinions and arguments they have presented in relation to foreign investment, particularly the BIPPA, in relation to capital export, finance capital, monopoly capital, they have deserted the Marxist-Leninist principle to join the camp of bourgeois economists and policy makers.

The Prime Minister Bhattarai is of the view that without economic development and prosperity, and getting rid of poverty and destitution, national existence cannot be safeguarded. He says that attracting external capital is to strengthen nationalism, and he sees no other option. Likewise, Finance Minister Barshaman Pun too more nakedly than the prime minister, has said, "After bigger investors come, they increase economic mobility within the country, make the economic sector dynamic. Within that dynamism, our country can achieve a self-dependency and economy will be strong". Such opinions and arguments further impel debate on the model of development and their views on capital. For the world communist movement, disputes and discussions on these questions are not new. After the death of Stalin, the great leader and teacher of the world communist movement, discussions in the Soviet Union regarding above issue took a serious turn in the communist movement. The Communist Party of China under the leadership of Mao Tse-tung led the revolutionary communists and proletarian class around the world against the revisionist views forwarded by the new Soviet leadership. In the era of imperialism and proletarian revolution, the two views on how to achieve the goal of economic development and prosperity are the capitalist view and the proletarian view.

The UCPN(Maoist) believes in the proletarian view regarding economic development, prosperity and finance capital. In ten years of the people's great war, it exercised remarkable economic development and prosperity in the revolutionary base areas accordingly. Now practising the line of peaceful development of revolution means the continuation of the same proletarian line for the economic development and prosperity of the country, not the realisation and consolidation of capitalism. While emphasising the need for the economic development and prosperity, Prime Minister Bhattarai and Finance Minister Barshaman Pun have taken the base of the present economic condition and the state of poverty, which is true. According to historical materialism, after taking on an issue and understanding it, one should find out the causes behind it. The historical materialism has its one way of solving the problem. We should first know the existing problem and the causes behind it and seek the solution by bringing required changes.

Having neglected this Marxist method, Prime Minister Bhattarai and Finance Minister Barshaman Pun have taken a short cut; first by portraying the bad economic condition and poverty of the country, and then trying to "find a solution" without exploring historical causes. For economic prosperity of Nepal, they see "no option to the enhancement of foreign investment", which, they think, "will make our country self-dependent and economically strong", and reach the conclusion that "without economic development and prosperity, nationality cannot be saved". It shows how committed they are to invite imperialist capital to Nepal.

It will be wrong to think that they have made such mistakes unintentionally as they are comrades as well as policy makers of our party. About the causes of economic destitution and poverty of the country, our party has a clear view, policy and programme. It understands the semi(neo)-colonial and semi-feudal condition for about two hundred years is responsible for that, and side by side, it has clarified that an economically developed and prosperous Nepal can be built by bringing change in the present semi(neo)-colonial and semi-feudal condition. This view is in harmony with Marxism-Leninism-Mao Tse-tung Thought. The Vice-Chairman and Prime Minister Bhattarai and standing committee member and Finance Minister Barshaman Pun have been changing the party line knowingly, in a planned way. Their views, policy and programme regarding the ways for saving nationality, foreign capital investment just made public as the road map for the country's economic development and prosperity, should be understood in this light.

Revolutionary Communists of Nepal and the world, the proletarian class and the people of all oppressed nations had hoped that by rooting out the state power of imperialism, Indian expansionism, feudalism, comprador and bureaucratic capitalism to make an independent and sovereign Nepal under the leadership of the party that fought ten-year people's great war. It was expected the top leaders would invite people of the country for developing national industries and commerce to build an independent economy. Contrary to that, following the bourgeois economists and policy makers, they have declared that there "is no option other than enhancement of foreign investment", "after foreign capital has entered, the country will get self-dependence, and the economy will be strong", "not going towards economic development and prosperity nationality can be saved." Bourgeois economists and policy makers should find themselves jobless as the Nepalese Maoist leaders themselves are doing their job with such announcements in an excellent way.

After the Sugauli Treaty of 1816, Nepal had become a semi-colony of British-India. So long as British-rule existed in India, Nepal remained a semi-colony of British-India. After the end of British colonial rule in India, India inherited their legacy. Indian leaders, who suffered the direct brutal oppression of the British colony, should have abandoned colonial policy in the neighbouring countries and also should have liberated nations within India too by including this in their declaration of independence. Contrary to it, perpetuating semi-colonialism and colonialism of neighbouring countries is shameful and hateful. The reason for the worst economic condition and poverty that Prime Minister Bhattariai and Finance Minister Barshaman Pun have mentioned is imperialism and Indian monopoly capitalism. It is because of the oppressive semi-colonialism of India and neo-colonial exploitation of world imperialism that the national economy of Nepal could not develop. So far as the factors that cause such economic conditions of Nepal are not abolished from the root, the economic development, self-dependence and building of a strong national economy and protection of national independence, sovereignty and territorial integrity is not possible. Prime Minster Bhattarai and Finance Minister Barshaman Pun, have asked for charity of finance capital from imperialists and expansionists for the country's overall development, but we should fight for national liberation on our own.

Their argument that foreign capital investment will bring economic prosperity and secure national independence is fundamentally wrong as well as a deviation from the Marxist-Leninist line. Contrary to their claims, Lenin states:

> As long as capitalism remains what it is, surplus capital will be utilised not for the purpose of raising the standard of living of the masses in a given country, for this would mean a decline in profits for the capitalists, but for the purpose of increasing profits by exporting capital abroad to the backward countries. In these backward countries profits are usually high, for capital is scarce, the price of land is relatively low, wages are low, raw materials are cheap.

Such a view helps us understand many things related to foreign capital. For example, he says: "Typical of the old capitalism, when free competition held undivided sway, was the export of *goods*. Typical of the latest stage of capitalism, when monopolies rule, is the export of *capital*."

In the era of finance capital, export takes place mainly in two ways: one is loan capital that is invested on government loan; the other is industrial capital that is invested in different industries. Lenin has not just discussed the issue of capital export, he has discussed also the issue how capital beyond limit is accumulated by some and certain countries for which owners go through a cut throat competition to find an international market.

Having reached the threshold of the twentieth century, we see monopoly is established in two ways: One is that in most developed countries with monopoly associations of big capitalists, and the other one is the excessively rich countries in monopoly conditions, which have accumulated capital takes in vast form. In developed countries this "surplus capital" is seen in excessive quantity.

What is the meaning of surplus capital? Is there no sector in such a country for capital investment as life standard has developed enough in all the sectors and the capital becomes surplus? In answer to this, Lenin says:

> It goes without saying that if capitalism could develop agriculture, which today is everywhere lagging terribly behind industry, if it could raise the living standards of the masses, who in spite of the amazing technical progress are everywhere still half-starved and poverty-stricken, there could be no question of a surplus of capital. This "argument" is very often advanced by the petty-bourgeois critics of capitalism. But if capitalism did these things it would not be capitalism; for both uneven development and a semi-starvation level of existence of the masses are fundamental and inevitable conditions and constitute premises of this mode of production.

On the peculiarity of the epoch of finance capital and character inherited in it, Lenin writes: "The capital-exporting countries are nearly always able to obtain certain "advantages", the character of which throws light on the peculiarity of the epoch of finance capital and monopoly."

To make that further clear, he extracts a part of *Die Bank* magazine of 1913 and mentions it in his book.

> 'A comedy worthy of the pen of Aristophanes is lately being played on the international capital market. Numerous foreign countries, from Spain to Balkan states, from Russia to Argentina, Brazil and China are openly or secretly coming into the big money market with demands, sometimes very persistent, for loans. The money markets are not very bright at the moment and political outlook is not promising. But not a single money market dares to refuse a loan for fear that its neighbour may forestall it, consent to grant a loan and so secure some reciprocal service. In these international transactions the creditor nearly always manages to secure some extra benefit: a favourable clause in commercial treaty, a coaling station, a contract to construct a harbour, a fact concession, or an order for guns.

Further Lenin comments on how capital exporting countries impose monopolist methods.

> Finance capital has created the epoch of monopolies, and monopolies introduce everywhere monopolist principles: the utilisation of "connections" for profitable transactions takes the place of competition on the open market. The most usual thing is to stipulate that part of the loan granted shall be spent on purchases in the creditor country, particularly on orders for war materials, or for ships, etc., In the course of the last two decades (1890-1910), France has very often resorted to this method. The export of capital thus becomes a means encouraging the export of commodities. In this connection, transactions between particularly big firms assume a form which as Schilder "mildly" puts it, 'borders on corruption.'... Thus finance capital, literally, one might say, spreads its net over all countries of the world.

Lenin says the present era is "a peculiar epoch of world colonial policy." For the present context, naming this peculiar epoch is not anything else but the neo-colonial stage. This is more dangerous than the colonialism of the past as its soul is mere finance capital. Contrary to the claims of the Prime Minister Bhattarai and Finance Minister Barshaman Pun that by investment of foreign capital there will be "economic prosperity of our country, and from that our country will achieve self-dependence, economy becomes strong" and "nationality can be saved", the reality is that it further propels the country into the chain of neo-colonialism, and grows countless transitional forms of dependence in the country. Throwing light on these very questions, Lenin writes:

> The interests pursued in exporting capital also give an impetus to the conquest of colonies, for in the colonial market it is easier to employ monopoly methods (and sometimes they are the only methods that can be employed) to eliminate competition, to ensure supplies, to secure the necessary "connections", etc. ... The non-economic superstructure which grows up on the basis of finance capital, its politics and its ideology, stimulates the striving for colonial conquest.

Monopoly capitalism adopts new ways of financial and diplomatic dependence on countries exporting capital, not by military intervention, but it does not mean that it never adopts military intervention. They (Bhattarai and Pun) have never mentioned even more dangerous forms of dependence than the direct military intervention of neo-colonialism in countries importing capital, which is the reason behind that advocacy of foreign investment for national development and prosperity. By doing so, they have served the monopoly capitalism. In the era of monopoly capitalism how forms of dependence grow behind politically "independent" capital importing countries is explained by Lenin:

> Finance capital and its foreign policy, which is the struggle of the great powers for the economic and political division of the world, give rise to a number of *transitional* forms of state dependence. Not only are the two main groups of countries, those owing colonies, and the colonies themselves, but also the diverse forms of dependent countries which, politically, are formally independent, but in fact, are enmeshed in the net of financial and diplomatic dependence.

If the view of Prime Minister Bhattarai and Finance Minister Barshaman Pun about how foreign investment is executed, the nation will be trapped into a further complicated financial and diplomatic net of dependency. Firstly, it will be a dumping pit of world imperialism and Indian monopolist; secondly, an outlet of capital investment; thirdly, it will be a centre of raw materials and exploitation; fourthly, an assembly shop for multinational companies; and, fifthly, in terms of politics, a neo-colony of world imperialism and Indian expansionism. Certainly, as Lenin says: "The export of capital influences and greatly accelerates the development of capitalism in those countries to which it is exported." (Lenin, *Imperialism, The Highest Stage of Capitalism*, Various Pages).

Lenin's statement explains that foreign capital investment will not make the country "economically prosperous" and "self-dependent", and "nationality secure". Here, the question arises as to what type of development of foreign capital investment influences and what type of development takes place in the imperialist era. Does it create a positive impact on national capitalism? Does it help grow national capitalism fast? In the present era of imperialism and proletarian revolution, communist revolutionaries do not take the development of capitalism in the ordinary or old sense. They understand it with two meanings: One is the transitional phase on the way to socialism and communism, and other is a component of world imperialism as an integral part of world finance capital.

The new democratic state power is in the first category, whereas the establishment of comprador capitalist state power belongs to the second category. From the import of monopoly capital, a new type of capitalist-democratic development is not possible at all. Of course, which "affects development of capitalism" as Lenin has said, and makes the "development of capitalism quite fast", but this development is the development of comprador capitalism in the present era. Such development of capitalism does not promote national economy to achieve self-dependence, and to safeguard national independence, rather the country will be trapped into the financial and diplomatic net. From the investment of foreign capital and the resulting development of comprador capitalism, countries like Nepal will get pulled into the wheels of international capitalism for building a solid and strong ground for imperialist exploitation and oppression. The view of Prime Minister Bhattarai and Finance Minister Barshaman Pun has helped in spreading a veil over the special characteristics of monopoly capitalism in the present era, and it will strengthen comprador capitalist state power in Nepal. By doing so, they have proved themselves as qualified advocates for the monopoly capitalism.

Imperialism utilises capital export as the major tool to perpetuate the colonial system in a new form in countries such as Nepal to secure its commodity markets, source of raw materials, cheap labour, capital investment market, and military strategic goal. Contrary to this, Prime Minister Bhattarai and Barshaman Pun take the finance capital as a magic rod that will create a prosperous, self-dependent Nepal and save the national sovereignty overnight.

The main purpose of the foreign investment is to reproduce monopoly capital with extended quantity. If the finance capital enters our country, it comes with a particular purpose, that is to exploit cheap labour and raw materials as much as possible, and to establish monopoly for export commodity, service and capital. However, Finance Minister Barshaman Pun is not prepared to agree to it. Rejecting this characteristic of monopoly capital, he advocates that even without its own interest, monopoly capital is ready to invest for other countries' economic prosperity, and to make the concerned country self-dependent. He has presented the BIPPA as a living example of this, which proves his extract given above "This agreement is not essential to India, rather this has been necessary to Nepal. So, we have shown interest in it, not India." Whatever smearing and veiling he uses, no fundamental change will come in the basic character of monopoly capitalism. Either loan or investment, forms of capital export should be taken as an interest of the capital reproduction in the accumulation of fathomless owners of capital, and a type of fear. As in the Berlin review, *Die Bank*, for October 1913 had said, "Not a single money market dares to refuse a loan for fear that its neighbour may forestall it, consent to grant a loan and so secure some reciprocal service."

Regarding investment, Barshaman Pun has said: "Nepal will not always remain in the present condition. We shall also reach the condition to invest in a foreign country." Now the question arises, was the ten-year people's great war and the martyrdom of thousands of people for exporting capital, for oppression and exploitation in foreign countries in the future? Is the objective of the new democratic revolution for the capital investment in foreign countries in the future?

The view of Prime Minister Bhattarai and Finance Minister Barshaman Pun reveal that they either do not know even the ABC of the Marxist political economy, or they are abandoning the struggle against the imperialism and neo-colonialism deliberately.

At present, we are living in the era of finance capital. Lenin said that finance capital "spreads its net all over countries." It has been proved more than ever; that our country has been pulled into the worldwide capitalist wheel cycle of world imperialism and its agents in the past have imprisoned the country within the worldwide capitalist cogwheels. It is our responsibility to free our country from such a wheel cycle of international capitalism. We cannot allow Nepal to be an integral part of the web of finance capital. First of all, we have to build the national economy.

In the era of imperialism and proletarian revolution, the national economy should either be a part of the world socialism, or a part of the world imperialism. Our national economy will be a transitional economy which will move towards socialist economy. We don't adopt the type of policy and programmes which hinders the move towards socialism and communism. That type of national economy can be established under the leadership of the proletariat. In this transitional stage, we do not confiscate capitalist private property in general, but it will not be the leading force in the whole national economy. State enterprises of socialist character will be the leading force in our national economy. Regulation of capital, certain steps to confiscate the land of the landlords and distribute among landless, not giving permission for the foreign capital to exploit the country, and the end of neo-colonial exploitation, will be some essential elements of our proposed national economy.

Our economy is still very backward and locked in a web of finance capital, trapped in the wheels of international capitalism, which cannot be freed overnight and changed into an independent national economy. So, we have to move by making immediate and long-term policies and programmes. No Marxist-Leninist can and should deny this while building a national economy. To fulfil the purpose of abolition of those remains, for the time being, we have to accept foreign investment in a regulated form. Certainly, it is not possible to cancel by a decree the relation with the

World Bank, International Monetary Fund, World Trade organisation, Asian Development Bank, and other imperialist organisations. The character of political leadership is vital in this regards. If political leadership of the country is revolutionary and truly patriotic (if they are committed to develop socialist economy), a favourable situation can be created for handling these organisations to a certain extent. Contrary to this, if the political leadership lies in the hands of imperialism, then their plans and programmes will not free the economy out of the web of the wheel cycle of international capitalism, rather it will strengthen those relations.

After the end of monarchy and election of the constituent assembly, state power has remained in the hands of feudal, comprador and bureaucratic capitalist classes–the enemies of revolution. Our party has led second time the government with the support from the world imperialism, Indian ruling class and the feudal, comprador and bureaucratic capitalist classes. By accepting their demands without objection, the party is continuing in the government, which cannot liberate the country from the web of finance capital, rather, it will strengthen the authority of finance capital infinitely. The policy and programme of the present government concerning the foreign capital investment is not a tactics, but a strategic one.

Finance Minister Barshaman Pun has said that we should not even imagine conflict and war as the country has embarked on political stability. The peace process will reach its conclusion, the constitution will be made. Such a statement is deplorable. Marxism-Leninism does not reject conflict and war absolutely, so his remark abandons the Marxist-Leninist view on war and peace. The communist never includes conflict and war in agenda. Conflict is always initiated by the reactionaries. War is always started and imposed by the reactionaries. People oppose counter-revolutionary war with a revolutionary war and foil national counter-revolutionary war with national revolutionary war. Finance Minister Barshaman Pun's view on war and peace is nothing else, but the revisionist theory that assumes peaceful coexistence, peaceful competition, peaceful cooperation, and then imperialism will come to its natural end.

November 2011
Canberra, Australia

On the Opportunity for the Peaceful Development of Revolution

Sixth Letter Sent to the Party Headquarters Regarding the Anti-Leninist View On the Opportunity for the Peaceful Development of Revolution

Marxism-Leninism believes in the possibility for the development of revolution at certain historical conditions in a peaceful way too, and this view has existed ever since the inception of the communist movement. In certain specific historical conditions, Marx and Lenin did raise the possibility that a revolution may develop peacefully. However, as Lenin pointed out, the peaceful development of revolution is "a possibility very seldom to be met with in the history of revolutions."[1] Lenin had said in another place, "In Russia, this revolution can, by way of *exception* (my Italics–Yogendra), be a peaceful one."[2] However, after the development of capitalism into

1 V. I. Lenin, "The Tasks of the Revolution", *Collected Works*, Progress Publishers, Moscow, Third Printing 1977, Vol. 26, p. 67.

2 V. I. Lenin, "First All-Russia Congress of Soviet of Workers' and Soldiers' Deputies (June 16 - July 7, 1917)", *Collected Works*, Progress Publishers, Moscow, Fourth Printing 1980, Vol. 25, p. 23.

imperialism between true revolutionaries and revisionists and opportunists have fundamentally opposing understanding in regard to Marxist-Leninist teaching on peaceful development of revolution.

Communists would always prefer to complete the revolution in a peaceful way. In the present imperialist era, countries are integrated into the web of world finance capital, with highly centralised and powerful state mechanisms such as the army, judiciary, bureaucracy, etc. In such a condition, can revolution be completed in a peaceful way? Obviously not. The ruling class never gives up its power voluntarily; it must be dethroned by force, so the violent revolution is a universal law of proletarian revolution.

Contrary to this objectivity, by neglecting the fundamental contradictions of imperialism and going along the historical idealist road, opportunists reject the universal law of violent revolution and forward the idea that revolution can be completed through a peaceful development. The revisionists of the Second International forwarded the idea that moving into socialism is possible through a parliamentary road, and violent revolution is not necessary. Lenin exposed the bourgeois essence of such thinking. After the completion of the socialist revolution in October 1917, he verified practicality of the universal law of Marxism. In the aftermath the demise of Stalin, modern revisionists of the USSR reestablished the view of revisionists of the Second International in relation to revolution in a new dress. Mao Tse-tung led the Marxist-Leninists of the whole world in a struggle against the bourgeois road of modern revisionism. Regarding this, the Great Debate initiated by the Communist Party of China against the Soviet revisionists is important. The Communist Party of China comments in the open letter issued by the Communist Party of the Soviet Union on March 31, 1964:

> Events since World War II have demonstrated yet again that the chief component of. the bourgeois state machine is armed force and not parliament. Parliament is only an ornament and a screen for bourgeois rule. To adopt or discard the parliamentary system, to grant parliament greater or less power, to adopt one kind of electoral law or another–the choice between these alternatives is always dictated by the needs and interests of bourgeois rule. So long as the bourgeoisie controls the military-bureaucratic apparatus, either the acquisition of a "stable majority in parliament" by the proletariat through elections is impossible, or this "stable majority" is undependable. To realise socialism through the "parliamentary road" is utterly impossible and is mere deceptive talk.[3]

The struggle launched against the old and new revisionism under the leadership of Lenin, Stalin and Mao Tse-tung at different periods has proved

3 Communist Party of China, "The Proletarian Revolution and Khrushchev's Revisionism", *The Great Debate*, Mass Line Publications, Kerala, India 1994, p. 292.

the unprincipledness and bankruptcy of the parliamentary road. So, the struggle against the "parliamentary road", instead of being a struggle within the communist movement is out of the question. It has been proved time and again that only the party that has adopted a bourgeois character after degenerating from the proletarian class character treats the "parliamentary road" as the universal road to reach new democracy and socialism. So, there is no confusion within the world communist movement about it, which is easily recognised, and can be struggled against too.

Let us consider the universal law of revolution. Unlike advancing through the violent road for decades, the road of peaceful development of revolution is very seldom to be met with success, so it cannot at all be a universal law of revolution. In spite of this, as Lenin said and Marxist-Leninists of the whole world strongly believe, in the history of revolution, sometimes, a moment of possibility of the peaceful development may arise as an opportunity. If such an opportunity appears, communists must not make the mistake of missing it and continue with the violent road. In such a case, communists will follow the line to fulfil the remaining tasks of revolution through a peaceful development. The 'peaceful development of revolution' is a line to be adopted at a special condition of revolution; it is not as straight and explicit as that of the "parliamentary road". This is a complicated and dangerous road. For a certain period, instead of being an issue of outside struggle of the party, it becomes an inter-party issue. In certain situations, this line can be a double-edged sword. In the long and difficult journey of revolution, a sector of the party leadership gets tired, or bourgeoisified and may be in search of "safe landing" (*i.e.* to liquidate revolution). Such elements are always in the search of some pretexts to liquidate revolution, and other comrades cannot identify their real aim of "safe landing" (*i.e.* to liquidate revolution) easily. They adopt the strategy to use the possibility of peaceful development. As the really honest elements of the revolution also use such an opportunity, the line comes to be the line for the whole party. One side of the blade of this sword of peaceful development of revolution cuts the throat of revolution, whereas the other side of the blade adopts a strategy to complete the remaining tasks of revolution.

Two examples of the utilisation of the opportunity of the peaceful development of revolution are in the history of the world communist movement. Once in Russia from the end of February 1917 up to the first week of July, under the leadership of Lenin, and the second time in China in 1945 under the leadership of Mao Tse-tung. Lenin and Mao tried their best to complete the remaining tasks of revolution peacefully in that particular condition. However, domestic and external reactionaries did not allow this, and they used all strategies to destroy the revolution. So, Lenin and Mao completed the revolution by resorting to the violent road of revolution again, which is an applied form of the universal and the particular road to revolution.

In the history of the new democratic revolution in our country, in the period after the ten-year people's war under the leadership of the CPN(Maoist), the possibility of fulfilling the remaining tasks of revolution through the road of peaceful development emerged. With that very prospect, the party adopted this road. Glancing back over the six years of the party after having adopted and taken this road, one can conclude that instead of completing the remaining tasks of revolution, the main leadership of the UCPN(Maoist), used this opportunity to liquidate revolution. The main leadership of our party has become engrossed with an incurable "parliamentary cretinism" and the party is trapped in a never ending parliamentary marsh and will ruin the revolutionary goals and achievements of the ten-year long people's war.

After having entered the road of peaceful development, the main leadership of the party has completely neglected the issue of capturing state power and adopted the strategy of completing the remaining tasks of revolution by holding a simple majority, or two third seats in the parliament, or constituent assembly. That can be marked explicitly in the slogan of Loktantrik Ganatantra, which is purely a parliamentary road. Such a line first negates the need of establishing a new state power by destroying the old state power, just by forming the government with majority in the parliament, or constituent assembly. Second, it re-establishes the redundant revisionist principle of continuing the mechanisms of the old state power like the army, police, bureaucracy and judiciary, which can be made loyal to the party through reforms alone. Third, it limits the class struggle within parliament. This demands the conformity to all other forms of struggle to the parliamentary struggle regarded as the highest and conclusive. Fourth, it converts the glorious CPN(Maoist), drenched with the blood of thousands of martyrs, into an electoral parliamentary party, or into an appendage and tool of the world imperialism and Indian expansionism.

The history of the parliamentary struggle of communists, shows that "The proletarian party must never base its thinking and policies for revolution and its entire work on the assumption that the imperialist and reactionaries will accept a peaceful transformation". In the light of the general principle of Marxism-Leninism, for the maximum application of the peaceful development of revolution, whenever it seems possible, there must also be the full preparation of non-peaceful development for revolution to fulfil the remaining tasks of revolution, otherwise the world imperialism, Indian expansionism and domestic reactionaries will defeat our attempt of capturing the state power. We cannot complete the revolution without tit for tat, and we must learn the lesson of preparation of the non-peaceful development. Had Lenin not made that type of preparation, in October, when the conditions for revolution were mature enough for the socialist revolution, capturing state power would not have been possible at all. Based on a Marxist-Leninist principle and with this line in relation to the preparation of the October Revolution, the Communist Party of China under the leadership of Mao Tse-tung states:

> The proletarian party must prepare itself for two eventualities–while preparing for a peaceful development of the revolution, it must also fully prepare for a non-peaceful development. It should concentrate on the painstaking work of accumulating revolutionary strength, so that it will be ready to seize victory when the conditions for revolutions are ripe or to strike powerful blows at the imperialists and the reactionaries when they launch surprise attacks and armed assaults.
>
> If it fails to make such preparations, the proletarian party will paralyse the revolutionary will of the proletariat, disarm itself ideologically and sink into a totally passive state of unpreparedness both politically and organisationally, and the result will be to bury the proletarian revolutionary cause".[4]

Has the UCPN(Maoist) grasped this fundamental lesson of the historical experience while preparing the peaceful development of revolution?

The answer appears in the negative. The party's preparation for non-peaceful development of revolution is a far cry. Instead of the painstaking work of accumulating revolutionary strength, the leadership of the UCPN(Maoist) has dissolved the whole foundation for revolution established during the people's great war of ten years. The decisions of the leadership of the party to dissolve the revolutionary base areas, local power, and merging the People's Liberation Army into the Nepal Army are especially mentionable. As a consequence, we have reached such a situation that if there is an attack and army intervention from domestic and external reactionaries, or if a favourable situation for capturing state power appears, we will be helpless to do anything in favour of revolution. The elimination of the foundations of revolution prepared by the people's war of ten years, and the absence of any new preparations for a non-peaceful development of revolution has paralysed the revolutionary objectives of peaceful development of revolution.

The fundamental mistakes of the leadership of the UCPN(Maoist) over the question of power is linked directly to the preparation for seizure

4 Communist Party of China, "A Proposal Concerning the General Line of the International Communist Movement", *The Great Debate*, Mass Line Publications, Kerala, India 1994, pp. 14-15.

of power. Lenin says in this regards: "The fundamental issue of revolution is the issue of power"[5] In reality, the main goal of Marxism-Leninism is to capture political power, as Marx and Engels said: "The first step in the revolution by the working-class, is to raise the proletariat to the position of the ruling class"[6]

Whether it is preparation for the peaceful development of revolution, or for non-peaceful preparation, the communist party must work to capture state power–this is the central point. We must take lessons from the slogan given by Lenin after the bourgeois revolution of February 1917, in Russia, about marching (from February 27 up to July 4) towards the socialist revolution during the peaceful development. However, the UCPN(Maoist) leadership, having neglected this question completely, has centralised itself in the game of making and breaking governments.

There is a fundamental difference between the slogan of power and that of making and breaking of governments. The slogan of power is related to the capturing state power earlier or later, and it strives to take power into its hands. Doing this, the party can raise its own class to the position of the ruling class. To raise the working-class to the position of ruling class is far from forming a government on the basis of a strong presence in parliament, or constituent assembly. Firstly, the meaning of forming a government under the leadership of the UCPN(Maoist) means the presence of other parties in the present composition of the constituent assembly. Such a government cannot take any decision against the basic interest of the old power in relation to our country the feudal, comprador, and the bureaucratic capitalist class. If it goes to the extent of affecting the basic interests of the class and their political representative involved in the government they will oppose, and if necessary, will topple it too. Due to the pressure from the other parties, standing in opposition and participating in the government, the party will have to drop revolutionary claims one after the other, or keep the claims to the extent of facing the fall of the government.

Secondly, in Nepal, the state mechanism, *i.e.* army, police, bureaucracy and judiciary fundamentally represent the interests of imperialism, Indian expansionism, feudalism, comprador and bureaucratic capitalism. If by having been voted to power, the UCPN(Maoist) wants to bring change in the favour of workers, tillers, cow boys, plough men, bonded workers, poor and landless peasants and in the favour of national independence, territorial integrity, and an independent and self-dependent economy, then the old state machinery, *i.e.* bureaucracy, judiciary, and if necessary even

5 V. I. Lenin, "On Slogan", *Collected Works*, Progress Publishers, Moscow, Fourth Printing 1980, Vol. 25, p. 189.

6 Karl Marx and Frederick Engels, "Manifesto of the Communist Party", *Selected Works*, in three volumes, Vol. 1, p. 126.

army will foil it with the support of imperialism, and Indian expansionism. So, either the party has to maintain the leadership of the government by taking full support of world imperialism, Indian expansionism and the old state machinery with promises to work in their favour, or be prepared to get toppled any moment.

We cannot move to our objective of a revolution by discarding the preparation of non-peaceful development as proven by history and our own experience. It means the proletariat cannot apply revolutionary policy and programme only by sending their representatives to parliament, or constituent assembly, when the state power is not in their hands. The central point of the present political line of the peaceful development of revolution, as the UCPN(Maoist) leadership claims, is not to capture the majority of seats in the parliament, and concurrently in government, but it should be based on the principle of capturing state power and establish new state machinery by destroying of the old one, and implement policies and programmes through them. Because of the liquidationist policy and programme of the leadership, we are moving away every hour, every day and every month from achieving these objectives. The major cause of this is the non-Marxist-Leninist view of the party leadership on the state power while following the present line of the peaceful development of revolution.

Certainly, state power cannot be captured overnight during the period of peaceful development of revolution. However, we need to determine the form of future power, and accordingly, we should fix the tactical slogan of power as a part of preparation for capturing the central state power. The central point of the total work must be focused onto transferring power into the hands of a proposed state organisation. For example, the worker, peasant and army representatives of Soviet Power were created in the early years of the February bourgeois revolution of 1917 in Russia. Under the leadership of the Bolshevik Communist Party, they raised the slogan of transfer of power into the hands of Soviets for a peaceful period (from February 27 to July 4) of revolution. The Bolshevik Communist Party struggled for the transfer of power into the hands of the Soviets, instead of engaging itself into the game of forming a government with the constitutional democrats, October sectarians, representatives of the capitalist class, the Socialist-Revolutionaries, and Mensheviks under the capitalist state power and then taking the leadership of such a government.

The slogan raised by the Bolshevik Communist Party was tactical as well as strategic. Tactically, the slogan rightly captured the contradiction and the balance of forces in the Russian society and the specific traits of that historical period with an objective investigation. The slogan of the transfer of power into the hands of the Soviets was correct in the light of the special situation at that time in two ways. Firstly, between February 27 to July 4, no important political forces either could oppose or stop the transfer of power into the hands of the Soviets. Secondly, "peaceful development would then have been possible, even in the sense that the struggle of classes and parties *within* the Soviets could have assumed a most peaceful and painless form, provided full state power had passed to the Soviets in good time."[7]

In reality, as Stalin said, the Soviet "was an organ of the alliance of workers and peasants against the tsarist regime, and at the same time it was an organ of their power, an organ of the dictatorship of the working-class and the peasantry."[8]

From the point of view of their class composition, Soviets could deal with important strategic works of separating petty-capitalists scattered in Russian society at that time by bringing them close to the workers. For example, Lenin says:

> Had they possessed full state power, the main shortcoming of the petty-bourgeois groups, their chief sin, that of trusting the capitalists, really would have been overcome, would have been criticised by the experience of their own measures. The change of classes and parties in power could have proceeded peacefully within the Soviets, provided the latter wielded exclusive and undivided power. The contact between all the Soviet parties and the people could have remained stable and unimpaired. One must not forget for a single moment that only such a close contact between the Soviet parties and the people, freely growing in extent and depth, could have helped peacefully to get rid of the illusion of petty-bourgeois compromise with the bourgeoisie. The transfer of power to the Soviets would not, and could not, in itself have changed the correlation of classes; it would in no way have changed the petty-bourgeois nature of the peasants. But it would have taken a big and timely step towards separating the peasants from the bourgeoisie, towards bringing them closer to, and then uniting them with, the workers.[9]

The slogan of "all power to the Soviets" that Lenin forwarded during the peaceful development of revolution is an appropriate example of the dialectical relation between strategy and tactics. Stalin states:

> Tactical leadership is a part of strategic leadership, subordinated to the tasks and the requirements of the latter. The task of tactical leadership is to master all forms of struggle and organisation of the proletariat and to ensure that

7 V. I. Lenin, "On Slogan", *Collected Works*, Progress Publishers, Moscow, Fourth Printing 1980, Vol. 25, p. 186.

8 J. V. Stalin, *History of the Communist Party of the Soviet Union (Bolsheviks)*, Kamgar Prakashan 1985, p. 178.

9 V. I. Lenin, "On Slogan", *Collected Works*, Progress Publishers, Moscow, Fourth Printing 1980, Vol. 25, pp. 186-87.

> they are used properly so as to achieve, with the given relation of forces, the maximum results necessary to prepare for strategic success.[10]

The Communist Party of China, under the leadership of Mao Tse-tung too followed the same exercise and raised the slogan of the Coalition Government in China in 1945. In the specific situation at that time, when the Japanese invaders were not completely defeated, it was only possible to defeat them by forging a national unity at a high level by unifying the anti-Japan forces, and mobilising them fast. But the Kuomintang was the main hindrance to fulfil the historical task. Mao Tse-tung gave the slogan for a coalition government and set a special programme on the basis of the general programme of revolution. The coalition government was directed not against the Japanese invaders and one party dictatorial of Kuomintang alone, but it was coming together of all democratic and national forces, and also the prelude of proposed new democratic dictatorship. The democratic coalition government was not only an institution for the unity of all democrats and those loyal to the nation in creating a national unity against the single party dictatorship of the Kuomintang and against the Japanese invaders, it was also the pre-form of the new democratic dictatorship.

The UCPN(Maoist) adopted the line of the peaceful development of revolution at the prospect of a special political condition developing in the country. Contrary to giving a sound tactical slogan of power subordinating to the minimum programme of revolution in Nepal, it forwarded the bourgeois slogan of Loktantrik Ganatantra. Tactics should have been treated and understood as the process of the party's development, and then it (tactics) should have been pushed forward simultaneously, which it failed to do so. In the beginning, the slogan of Loktantrik Ganatantra helped in galvanising bourgeois parties in the fight against the monarchy, so after the establishment of the republic the tactics of Loktantrik Ganatantra should have been adjusted to enrich the minimum programme of the party, which did not happen.

The UCPN(Maoist) does not have any vision for power, nor a programme different from other parliamentary parties in the transitional phase. Its leadership is confused and ambiguous and its policy and programme resemble the programmes of parliamentary parties because of the illusion that once it adopts them, they will be automatically revolutionary. Because of this, instead of succeeding in moving towards handing over power into the hands of people, feudal, comprador and bureaucratic capitalist state power have become more powerful as they have consolidated their grip and strengthened the old machinery of the present state such as the army, police,

10 J. V. Stalin, "The Foundation of Leninism", *Problems of Leninism*, Foreign Language Press, Peking, 1976, p. 89.

bureaucracy and judiciary. Such factors are bound to reverse the path of revolution.

The party, which exercised people's power in various parts of the country, in the latter part of the people's war could have given the slogan for power and made some formal changes to meet the new situation developed in the country. However, contrary to presenting the concrete slogan for central power, the party leadership dissolved the revolutionary base areas and local power, clearing the path to the feudal, comprador, and bureaucratic capitalist state power. The party leadership agreed to be a partner of feudal, comprador, and bureaucratic capitalist class. In Russia, in spite of the slogan given by the Bolshevik Communist Party and struggle for that the power was not handed over and it went into the hands of the bourgeois class. But in our country, in the history of the peaceful development of revolution for six years, the people's power built during the period of the people's war was dissolved, and feudal, comprador and bureaucratic capitalist forces consolidated their power.

In Russia, the Bolshevik Communist Party gave the slogan of "All Power to the Soviets" and tried its best to implement that demand. However, some leaders within the Soviets and a great part of the Soviets handed over power to the capitalists voluntarily. The Socialist-Revolutionaries and Menshevik leaders compromised to form a new Russian government without any information to Bolsheviks to avoid protest. In spite of the opposition from the Bolsheviks after the labourers and Soviets came to know about it, the majority approved the decision and new state power arose in Russia, consisting, as Lenin said, of representatives of the "bourgeoisie and landlord who had become bourgeois." However, the situation in our country is quite different. The slogan of Loktantrik Ganatantra given by our party is just a mask for feudal, comprador and bureaucratic power, and the UCPN(Maoist) main leadership has handed over power to them.

Even though Socialist-Revolutionaries and Mensheviks handed over power to the representatives of the "bourgeoisie and landlords who had become bourgeois" in Russia, the active presence of Soviets of workers peasants and the army's support for the ideological-political line of the Bolshevik Communist Party brought a dual power situation. As Stalin says, "the result was a peculiar interlocking of two powers, of two dictatorships: the dictatorship of the bourgeoisie, represented by the Provisional Government, and the dictatorship of the proletariat and peasantry, represented by the Soviet of Workers' and Soldiers' Deputies."

However, in our country, the UCPN(Maoist) itself has given the slogan of bourgeois power, so no question arises which forces handed over power and which political forces opposed it. Certainly, the army is the main organ of power and the UCPN(Maoist) has an internationally recognised army (PLA) with weapons. Thus, along with the presence of feudal, comprador and bureaucratic power, there is the existence of the power of workers, peasants and those loyal to the nation. The army is a major organ of power, but not everything. In relation to the general and specific question of state power, the basic factor is to have correct ideological and political line and state organisation, which directs the power and state machinery, including the army.

After having entered the peace process, our party dissolved the people's power built during the people's war, considered to be the preliminary forms of future state organisation. The PLA still exists, but without a revolutionary ideology and political line and state organisation. As a result, the PLA is confined under the supervision of imperialist and domestic reactionaries, ending the possibility of handing over power into the hands of the people, so it is the miscarriage of people's war of ten years. The prospect of the dissolution of the people's power and the PLA has reached its final stage leading to the rapid decline. So, it has become impossible to take power away from feudal, comprador and bureaucratic capitalists now.

In Russia, in the beginning it was the majority of Mensheviks and Socialist-Revolutionaries, which handed over power voluntarily into the hands of the capitalist class. The analysis of Lenin and Stalin using historical materialism helps us understand our present situation. Stalin puts forward the ideas of Lenin:

> How is it to be explained that the majority in the Soviets at first consisted of Mensheviks and Socialist-Revolutionaries? How is it to be explained that the victorious workers and peasants *voluntarily* surrendered the power to the representatives of the bourgeoisie?
>
> Lenin explained it by pointing out that millions of people, inexperienced in politics, had awakened and pressed forward to political activity. These were for the most part small owners, peasants, workers who had recently been peasants, people who stood midway between the bourgeoisie and the proletariat. Russia was at that time the most petty-bourgeois of all the big European countries. And in this country, "a gigantic petty-bourgeois wave has swept over everything and overwhelmed the class-conscious proletariat, not only by force of numbers but also ideologically; that is, it has infected and imbued very wide circles of workers with the petty-bourgeois political outlook. (Lenin, *Selected Works*, Eng. ed., Vol. VI, p. 49.) It was this elemental petty-bourgeois wave that swept the petty-bourgeois Menshevik and Socialist-Revolutionary parties to the fore.
>
> Lenin pointed out that another reason was the change in the composition of the proletariat that had taken place during the war and the inadequate class-consciousness and organisation of the proletariat at the beginning

> of the revolution. During the war major changes had taken place in the proletariat itself. About 40 per cent of the regular workers had been drafted into the army. Many small owners, artisans and shopkeepers, to whom the proletarian psychology was alien, had gone to the factories in order to evade mobilisation. It was these petty-bourgeois sections of the workers that formed the soil which nourished the petty-bourgeois politicians–the Mensheviks and Socialist-Revolutionaries.
>
> That is why large numbers of the people, inexperienced in politics, swept into the elemental petty-bourgeois vortex, and intoxicated with the first successes of the revolution, found themselves in its early months under the sway of the compromising parties and consented to surrender the state power to the bourgeoisie in the naive belief that a bourgeois power would not hinder the Soviets in their work.[11]

What Lenin and Stalin have said in relation to the then situation of Russia, is also true in relation to the events developed in our country since the CPN(Maoist) entered the peace process. Whether Russia at that time, or other communist parties around the world, a part of the leadership itself changes into capitalists, basing upon the socio-economic ground, including a petty-bourgeois, *i.e.* the owners of small property, peasants, and the people between the capitalist and proletarian class. Compared to Russia, such a socio-economic ground is a hundred times stronger in our country. This very petty-capitalist wave as explained by Lenin, has infected a large part of the UCPN(Maoist) leadership and the majority of the whole party, and the class-conscious people qualitatively and ideologically too. It has polluted the political line, main leadership and the majority of the party, spoiling the people's power created by the people's war of ten years. It is ready to dissolve all the gains of the people's war for the constituent assembly, just for a constitution and absolute peace.

It is the result of the strong petty-capitalist ebb and tide that large part of the UCPN(Maoist) leadership is intent to return the property captured during the people's war period and dissolve the PLA at once. If revolutionary leaders and cadres within the party, from top to bottom, do not perceive it sincerely, the whole party will change into a bourgeois party and will fail to materialise the dream of the thousands of martyrs who died while fighting for a new democratic Nepal.

December, 2011
Canberra, Australia

11 J. V. Stalin, *History of the Communist Party of the Soviet Union (Bolsheviks)*, pp. 178-79.

Appendix

Comrade K.B. Mahara
Chief, Foreign Department, UCPN(Maoist)
Central Office, Perish Danda
Kathmandu, Nepal

Dear Comrade,

I would like to place on record my dissent regarding the 3-point agreement between the UCPN(Maoist) and the Nepal government concluded on January 14, 2011. I strongly believe that by signing on the paper of agreement, our party has actually signed its own death-warrant. With this agreement, our party has betrayed the ten-year people's war and the PLA, the martyrs of the people's war, the proletarian class, the RIM, and the Marxism-Leninism-Mao Tse-tung Thought/Maoism.

Comradely,
Yogendra Dhakal

Emailed on January 16, 2011
Canberra, Australia

Comrade Prachanda
Chairman
UCPN(Maoist)
Central Office, Perish Danda
Kathmandu, Nepal

Subject: Dissent and Resignation

Dear Comrade,

I assume you are aware of my view on the 3-point agreement with the Nepal government, signed by you on January 14, 2011. The next day I mailed my strong dissent to the party's foreign department chief, Comrade K.B. Mahara.

One after another our party has been deviating from the basic principles of Marxism-Leninism, specifically the class character of democracy, the replacement of the New Democratic Revolution (NDR) by the Loktantrik Ganatantra, the anti-Leninist view on the Right of Self-determination of Nations, the leading role of the Communist Party in the NDR, and the dictatorship of the proletariat (DOP). Furthermore, our party has put in jeopardy the achievements of the people's war, mainly, by dissolving of the revolutionary base areas and local state power, and recently handing over the chain-of-command of the UCPN(Maoist)'s People's Liberation Army (PLA) to the Army Integration Sub-Committee (AISC) (actually to the old state power). It is my strong view that the transferring of the PLA command from the party to the AISC is a betrayal of the ten-year people's war, and to the martyrs of the people's war, the PLA, the RIM, other fraternal communist parties, and the proletariat of the world. This is the first betrayal in the twenty-first century by a communist leadership to the proletarian class.

A serious conspiracy has been hatched for long to trap the UCPN(Maoist) by internal and external reactionaries to foil the need of establishing NDR in Nepal. By dissolving the revolutionary base areas and local power, and severing the link between the PLA and UCPN(Maoist), our party leadership, knowingly or unknowingly, has become an accomplice of that grand design.

Handing over the PLA to the AISC is totally wrong. Both the Nepal army and the PLA should be handed over to the new state power, *i.e.* to a New Democratic State Power of Nepal to realise a Marxist-Leninist solution.

Dear Chairman,

While the national flag was hoisted by the Prime Minister Madhav Kumar Nepal, you were pulling down the flag of the PLA, created through the blood of thousands of martyrs under your leadership. The handing over of PLA and the training for mass insurrection is nonsensical talk and behaviour. As an envoy of Nepal, it is my duty to plead the policy and programme of the government to the international community here. World imperialism and blood suckers of oppressed people and nations are applauding the actions of the government of Nepal and our party leadership on the PLA issue. As a sincere friend of the proletarian class, I cannot be part of the Nepal government's policy and programme, mainly the liquidationist policy and programme under the name of the peace process of our party. I am passing through a conflict of interest. Either I should accept this situation and should discharge duty loyally, or leave the Ambassadorial responsibilities voluntarily.

Dear Chairman,

Voluntarily I choose the second one. I always want to be a sincere friend of the proletarian class. I always want to be a sincere pupil of Marx, Engels, Lenin, Stalin, and Mao Tse-tung. That is why I cannot carry on the responsibilities at the cost of my conscience. Treating this as a resignation letter, please free me from the Ambassador's responsibility.

Looking forward to the earliest reply from you.

Comradely,
Yogendra Dhakal

Emailed on January 23, 2011
Canberra, Australia

Comrade Suresh Aale Magar
Member, Foreign Department
UCPN(Maoist)
Perish Danda, Kathmandu, Nepal

Dear Comrade,

I want to state my strong position concerning the PLA's integration and handover of their arms to the Army Integration Sub-Committee. It is my firm belief that accepting other parties' conditions, mainly the conditions put by the Nepali Congress to dissolve the PLA with their arms would be another suicidal act for our party. It is a path of liquidationism, and not of revolution. If by not fulfilling the conditions, other parties are not ready to extend the date of the constituent assembly, it is all right. Let them do what they want. We will do what we want. It is not against revolution. If other parties want to go for fresh election, it is not bad; we should be ready. If they want to introduce military rule with Indian backing, we will charter the nationalist movement by forming a broader united front. In both cases, we will be the winner. Please convey my view to our leadership.

Revolutionary Greetings
Yogendra Dhakal

Emailed on May 26, 2011
Canberra, Australia

Comrade Suresh Ale Magar
Member, Foreign Department
UCPN(Maoist)
Perish Danda, Kathmandu, Nepal

Dear Comrade,

Thank you so much for your reply. I appreciate your position on the PLA integration. The question of dual-security of our leaders is a burning issue of the day. Our office bearer has already decided to end this situation. In my opinion, this decision is a blunder. We cannot separate this question with the Leninist line of peaceful development of revolution. This question is based on the Comprehensive Peace Accord (CPA) and the Interim Constitution, 2007. Reactionaries are not committed to go through those documents, so why are we in a hurry to surrender our leaders' security from our own army? Corruption, foreign manipulation, penetration within the state security mechanism are crystal clear. This security could not give security to the general public, and this security could not save the former Royal family, how can we believe them that they provide a high level of security for our leaders? So, I urge our leadership to take a correct policy on the subject, and not to surrender our own security system. We must flatly reject any proposal that asks us to surrender our security system.

Revolutionary Greetings
Yogendra Dhakal

Emailed on June 4, 2011
Canberra, Australia

K. B. Mahara
Chief, Foreign Department, UCPN(Maoist)
UCPN(Maoist)
Perish Danda, Kathmandu, Nepal

Dear Comrade,

I am extremely worried about the present political development taking place in our country. In this regard–

1) The formation of a government under the leadership of our party:

The circumstance understanding the UDMF to accept the leadership of government was fundamentally wrong. Most of the UDMF-elements are pro-Indian, and for long they obstructed attempts to form the government under our Chairman's leadership. The Four-Point agreement signed between the UCPN(Maoist) and UDMF is basically wrong. In this regard, I strongly object to the point of the Agreement that mentions initiating process of recruiting 10, 000 Madhesi youths in Nepal army with a separate unit. It opens the door to our southern neighbour to fulfil her interests. To accept this condition is nothing other than accepting the condition of national betrayal in the long-run. Therefore, the above agreement should be scrapped immediately.

2) Prime Minister Bhattarai has issued a decree to return the property of the feudalists seized during the people's war. To make his decree successful, he has instructed the CDOs to implement his order. As well, after taking the support of Chairman Prachanda, he has handed over the keys to AISC. And he is in a big hurry to kick-start the regrouping process of PLA. Why is the PM in such a hurry to do all these things? Whom does he want to serve? Time will answer these questions correctly.

It is very serious–why does the PM want to do these things ahead of his visit to New York to attend the 66th General Assembly of the UN? Does he want to please the imperialist and expansionist bosses? The result will provide an answer to these questions.

Comradely,
Yogendra Dhakal

Emailed on September 18, 2011
Canberra, Australia

About the Author

Yogendra Dhakal, known by his pen name Ajay Sharma, and born on August 5, 1957 in Nepal, is a prolific writer, political analyst, and an intellectual dedicated to the cause of revolution through his writings as well as active involvement in the communist movement of Nepal for the last three and a half decades. He was jailed twice for political reasons, once in India in 1986, and then again in Nepal in 1990 during the People's Movement. His political career began in the Communist Party of Nepal (Mashal), where he actively worked for over twenty-five years. He regards the veteran communist leader Comrade Mohan Bikram Singh his political mentor. Later, in 2006 Dhakal joined the Communist Party of Nepal (Maoist). After the recent split in 2012, he supported the Mohan Baidya led faction, and now he is a Central Committee member of the same party. He has been firm and consistent in his revolutionary conviction in his writing and actions. During the two-line struggle in the party, he was always on the side of revolutionary. He has served also as the Nepalese Ambassador to Australia, New Zealand, and the Fiji Islands from February 2008-December 2011. He has authored several books and articles, mostly on theoretical aspects of Marxism-Leninism to arouse mass awareness, and then to expose the revisionist culpable of distorting the Marxism-Leninism-Mao Tse-tung Thought to serve the interest of the exploiting class and countries.